Doggin' The Mid-Atlantic

400 Tail-Friendly Parks To Hike With Your Dog In New Jersey, Pennsylvania, Delaware, Maryland, and Northern Virginia

W9-AZG-887

DOUG GELBERT

illustrations by

ANDREW CHESWORTH

Cruden Bay Books

There is always a new trail to look forward to...

DOGGIN' THE MID-ATLANTIC: 400 TAIL-FRIENDLY
PARKS TO HIKE WITH YOUR DOG IN NEW JERSEY,
PENNSYLVANIA, DELAWARE, MARYLAND AND
NORTHERN VIRGINIA

Cruden Bay Books
PO Box 467
Montchanin, DE 19710
www.hikewithyourdog.com

International Standard Book Number 978-0-9795577-8-1

Manufactured in the United States of America

*"Dogs are our link to paradise...to sit with a dog on a hillside
on a glorious afternoon is to be back in Eden,
where doing nothing was not boring - it was peace."*
- Milan Kundera

Ahead On The Trail

Introduction

The Middle Atlantic states are a great place to hike with your dog. Within a short drive in the region you can hike on sand trails, climb mountains that leave your dog panting, walk on some of the most historic grounds in America, explore the estates of America's wealthiest families or circle lakes for miles and never lose sight of the water.

This book describes and rates 400 Middle Atlantic parks that welcome dogs. What makes a great place to take your dog hiking? Well, how about a paw-friendly surface to trot? Grass and sandy dirt are alot more appealing than asphalt and rocks. A variety of hikes is always good - long ones for athletic dogs and short ones for the less adventurous canine. Dogs always enjoy a refreshing place to swim as well. Each park has been asssigned a rating of between 1 and 4 paws as follows:

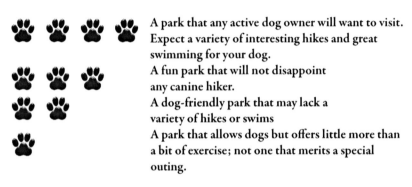

A park that any active dog owner will want to visit. Expect a variety of interesting hikes and great swimming for your dog.

A fun park that will not disappoint any canine hiker.

A dog-friendly park that may lack a variety of hikes or swims

A park that allows dogs but offers little more than a bit of exercise; not one that merits a special outing.

Did I miss your favorite? Let us know at *www.hikewithyourdog.com*.

For dog owners it is important to realize that not all parks are open to our best trail companions (see page 14 for a list of parks that do not allow dogs). It is sometimes hard to believe but not everyone loves dogs. We are, in fact, in the minority when compared with our non-dog owning neighbors.

So when visiting a park always keep your dog under control and clean up any messes and we can all expect our great parks to remain open to our dogs. And maybe some others will see the light as well. Remember, every time you go out with your dog you are an ambassador for all dog owners.

Now, grab that leash and hit the trail!
DBG

Hiking With Your Dog

So you want to start hiking with your dog. Hiking with your dog can be a fascinating way to explore the Mid-Atlantic region from a canine perspective. Some things to consider:

Dog's Health

Hiking can be a wonderful preventative for any number of physical and behavioral disorders. One in every three dogs is overweight and running up trails and leaping through streams is great exercise to help keep pounds off. Hiking can also relieve boredom in a dog's routine and calm dogs prone to destructive habits. And hiking with your dog strengthens the overall owner/dog bond.

Breed of Dog

All dogs enjoy the new scents and sights of a trail. But some dogs are better suited to hiking than others. If you don't as yet have a hiking companion, select a breed that matches your interests. Do you look forward to an entire afternoon's hiking? You'll need a dog bred to keep up with such a pace, such as a retriever or a spaniel. Is a half-hour enough walking for you? It may not be for an energetic dog like a border collie. If you already have a hiking friend, tailor your plans to his abilities.

Conditioning

Just like humans, dogs need to be acclimated to the task at hand. An inactive dog cannot be expected to bounce from the easy chair in the den to complete a 3-hour hike. You must also be physically able to restrain your dog if confronted with distractions on the trail (like a scampering squirrel or a pack of joggers). Have your dog checked by a veterinarian before significantly increasing his activity level.

Weather

Hot humid summers do not do dogs any favors. With no sweat glands and only panting available to disperse body heat, dogs are much more susceptible to heat stroke than we are. Unusually rapid panting and/or a bright red tongue are signs of heat exhaustion in your pet. Always carry enough water for your hike. Even days that don't seem too warm can cause discomfort in dark-coated dogs if the sun is shining brightly. In cold weather, short-coated breeds may require additional attention.

Trail Hazards

Dogs won't get poison ivy but they can transfer it to you. Stinging nettle is a nuisance plant that lurks on the side of many trails and the slightest brush will deliver troublesome needles into a dog's coat. Some trails are littered with small pieces of broken glass that can slice a dog's paws. Nasty thorns can also blanket trails that we in shoes may never notice.

Ticks

You won't be able to visit any of the region's parks without encountering ticks. All are nasty but the deer tick - no bigger than a pin head - carries with it the spectre of Lyme disease. Lyme disease attacks a dog's joints and makes walking painful. The tick needs to be embedded in the skin to transmit Lyme disease. It takes 4-6 hours for a tick to become embedded and another 24-48 hours to transmit Lyme disease bacteria.

When hiking, walk in the middle of trails away from tall grass and bushes. And when the summer sun fades away don't stop thinking about ticks - they remain active any time the temperature is above 30 degrees. By checking your dog - and yourself - thoroughly after each walk you can help avoid Lyme disease. Ticks tend to congregate on your dog's ears, between the toes and around the neck and head.

Water

Surface water, including fast-flowing streams, is likely to be infested with a microscopic protozoa called *Giardia*, waiting to wreak havoc on a dog's intestinal system. The most common symptom is crippling diarrhea. Algae, pollutants and contaminants can all be in streams, ponds and puddles. If possible, carry fresh water for your dog on the trail - your dog can even learn to drink happily from a squirt bottle.

Black Bears

Are you likely to see a bear while out hiking with your dog? No, it's not likely. it is, however, quite a thrill if you are fortunate enough to spot a black bear on the trail - from a distance.

Black bear attacks are incredibly rare. In the year 2000 a hiker was killed by a black bear in Great Smoky National Park and it was the first deadly bear attack in the 66-year history of America's most popular national park. It was the first EVER in the southeastern United States. In all of North America only 43 black bear mauling deaths have ever been recorded (through 1999).

Most problems with black bears occur near a campground (like the above incident) where bears have learned to forage for unprotected food. On the trail bears will typically see you and leave the area. What should you do if you encounter a black bear? Experts agree on three important things:

1) Never run. A bear will outrun you, outclimb you, outswim you. Don't look like prey.

2) Never get between a female bear and a cub who may be nearby feeding.

3) Leave a bear an escape route.

If the bear is at least 15 feet away and notices you make sure you keep your dog close and calm. If a bear stands on its hind legs or comes closer it may just be trying to get a better view or smell to evaluate the situation. Wave your arms and make noise to scare the bear away. Most bears will quickly leave the area.

If you encounter a black bear at close range, stand upright and make yourself appear as large a foe as possible. Avoid direct eye contact and speak in a calm, assertive and assuring voice as you back up slowly and out of danger.

Rattlesnakes

Rattlesnakes are not particularly aggressive animals but you should treat any venomous snake with respect and keep your distance. A rattler's colors may vary but they are recognized by the namesake rattle on the tail and a diamond-shaped head. Unless cornered or teased by humans or dogs, a rattlesnake will crawl away and avoid striking. Avoid placing your hand in unexamined rocky areas and crevasses and try and keep your dog from doing so as well. If you hear a nearby rattle, stop immediately and hold your dog back. Identify where the snake is and slowly back away.

If you or your dog is bitten, do not panic but get to a hospital or veterinarian with as little physical movement as possible. Wrap between the bite and the heart. Rattlesnakes might give "dry bites" where no poison is injected, but you should always check with a doctor after a bite even if you feel fine.

Porcupines

Porcupines are easy for a curious dog to catch and that makes them among the most dangerous animals you may meet because an embedded quill is not only painful but can cause infection if not properly removed.

Outfitting Your Dog For A Hike

These are the basics for taking your dog on a hike:

- **Collar.**
  It should not be so loose as to come off but you should be able to slide your flat hand under the collar.

- **Identification Tags.**
  Get one with your veterinarian's phone number as well.

- **Bandanna.**
  Can help distinguish him from game in hunting season.

- **Leash.**
  Leather lasts forever but if there's water in your dog"s future, consider quick-drying nylon.

- **Water.**
  Carry 8 ounces for every hour of hiking.

I want my dog to help carry water, snacks and other supplies on the trail. Where do I start?
To select an appropriate dog pack measure your dog's girth around the rib cage. A dog pack should fit securely without hindering the dog's ability to walk normally.

Will my dog wear a pack?
Wearing a dog pack is no more obtrusive than wearing a collar, although some dogs will take to a pack easier than others. Introduce the pack by draping a towel over your dog's back in the house and then having your dog wear an empty pack on short walks. Progressively add some crumpled newspaper and then bits of clothing. Fill the pack with treats and reward your dog from the stash. Soon your dog will associate the dog pack with an outdoor adventure and will eagerly look forward to wearing it.

How much weight can I put into a dog pack?
Many dog packs are sold by weight recommendations. A healthy, well-conditioned dog can comfortably carry 25% to 33% of its body weight. Breeds prone to back problems or hip dysplasia should not wear dog packs. Consult your veterinarian before stuffing the pouches with gear.

How does a dog wear a pack?
The pack, typically with cargo pouches on either side, should ride as close to the shoulders as possible without limiting movement. The straps that hold the dog pack in place should be situated where they will not cause chafing.

How does a dog wear a pack?

The pack, typically with cargo pouches on either side, should ride as close to the shoulders as possible without limiting movement. The straps that hold the dog pack in place should be situated where they will not cause chafing.

Are dog booties a good idea?

Dog booties can be an asset, especially for the occasional canine hiker whose paw pads have not become toughened. Some trails around New Jersey involve rocky terrain. In some places, there may be broken glass. Hiking boots for dogs are designed to prevent pads from cracking while trotting across rough surfaces. Used in winter, dog booties provide warmth and keep ice balls from forming between toe pads when hiking through snow.

What are good things to put in a dog pack?

Low density items such as food and poop bags are good choices. Ice cold bottles of water can cool your dog down on hot days. Don't put anything in a dog pack that can break. Dogs will bang the pack on rocks and trees as they wiggle through tight spots in the trail. Dogs also like to lie down in creeks and other wet spots so seal items in plastic bags. A good use for dog packs when on day hikes around is trail maintenance - your dog can pack out trash left by inconsiderate visitors before you.

What should a doggie first aid kit include?

Even when taking short hikes it is a good idea to have some basics available for emergencies:

- 4" square gauze pads
- cling type bandaging tapes
- topical wound disinfectant cream
- tweezers
- insect repellent - no reason to leave your dog unprotected against mosquitoes and blackflies
- veterinarian's phone number

Low Impact Hiking
With Your Dog

Every time you hike with your dog on the trail you are an ambassador for all dog owners. Some people you meet won't believe in your right to take a dog on the trail. Be friendly to all and make the best impression you can by practicing low impact hiking with your dog:

- Pack out everything you pack in.

- Do not leave dog scat on the trail; if you haven't brought plastic bags for poop removal bury it away from the trail and topical water sources.

- Hike only where dogs are allowed.

- Stay on the trail.

- Do not allow your dog to chase wildlife.

- Step off the trail and wait with your dog while horses and other hikers pass.

- Do not allow your dog to bark - people are enjoying the trail for serenity.

- *Have as much fun on your hike as your dog does.*

The Other End Of The Leash

Leash laws are like speed limits - everyone seems to have a private interpretation of their validity. Some dog owners never go outside with an unleashed dog; others treat the laws as suggestions or disregard them completely. It is not the purpose of this book to tell dog owners where to go to evade the leash laws or reveal the parks where rangers will look the other way at an unleashed dog. Nor is it the business of this book to preach vigilant adherence to the leash laws. Nothing written in a book is going to change people's behavior with regard to leash laws. So this will be the last time leash laws are mentioned, save occasionally when we point out the parks where dogs are welcomed off leash.

How To Pet A Dog
Tickling tummies slowly and gently works wonders.
Never use a rubbing motion; this makes dogs bad-tempered.
A gentle tickle with the tips of the fingers is all that is necessary
to induce calm in a dog. I hate strangers who go up to dogs with their
hands held to the dog's nose, usually palm towards themselves.
How does the dog know that the hand doesn't hold something horrid?
The palm should always be shown to the dog and go straight
down to between the dog's front legs and tickle gently with
a soothing voice to acompany the action.
Very often the dog raises its back leg in a scratching movement,
it gets so much pleasure from this.
-Barbara Woodhouse

No Dogs

Before we get started on the best places to take your dog, let's get out of the way some of the trails that do not allow dogs:

Allegany County
Dan's Mountain State Park

Anne Arundel County
Jug Bay Wetlands Sanctuary
Sandy Point State Park

Baltimore County
Hart-Miller Island State Park
(dogs are allowed on Pleasure Island, accessible only by boat)
Patapsco State Park - Avalon Area, Hollofield Area,
McKeldin Area, Orange Grove Area

Calvert County
Breezy Point Beach
Calvert Cliffs State Park

Caroline County
Martinak State Park

Charles County
Myrtle Grove Wildlife Management Area
Smallwood State Park

Dorchester County
Blackwater National Wildlife Refuge

Frederick County
Cunningham Falls State Park

Garrett County
Deep Creek Lake State Park
Herrington Manor State Park
New Germany State Park
Martinak State Park

Montgomery County
Seneca Creek State Park - Clopper Day Use Area

Queen Anne's County
Chesapeake Bay Environmental Center

Washington County
Fort Frederick State Park
Greenbrier State Park
Hagerstown City Park
Washington Monument State Park

Worcester County
Assateague State Park
Pocomoke River State Park - Shad Landing

Bergen County
Flat Rock Brook Nature Center
Monument Park
Tenafly Nature Center

Burlington County
Rancocas Nature Center

Camden County
Palmyra Cove Nature Park

Cape May County
Cape May County Park
Cape May Migratory Bird Refuge
Cape May State Park - trails

Gloucester County
Ceres Park
Greenwich Lake Park
Red Bank Battlefield Park
Scotland Run Park
Washington Lake Park

Middlesex County
Plainsboro Preserve

Monmouth County
Deep Cut Arboretum

Morris County
Bamboo Brook Education Center
Great Swamp National Wildlife Refuge
Willowwood Arboretum
Martinak State Park

Ocean County
Forsythe NWR - Holgate

Passaic County
Weis Ecology Center

Somerset County
Lord Stirling Park

Sussex County
Wallkill River National Wildlife Refuge

Warren County
Johnsonburg Swamp
Pequest Wildlife Management Area

PENNSYLVANIA

Berks County
Hawk Mountain Sanctuary

Bucks County
Bowman's Hill Wildflower Preserve
Churchville Nature Center
Five Mile Woods Forest Preserve
Honey Hollow Environmental Education Center
Peace Valley Nature Center

Chester County
Battle of the Clouds Park
Binky Lee Preserve*
Crow's Nest Preserve*
East Whiteland Township Preserve
Great Valley Nature Center
Jenkins Arboretum
Kardon Park
Kerr Park
Sharp's/Canterbury Woods*
Stroud Preserve*
Valley Creek Park

Delaware County
Hildacy Farm*
Saw Mill Park
The Willows Park
Tyler Arboretum
Wawa Preserve*

Lackawanna County
Lake Scranton

Monroe County
Mountain View Park

Montgomery County
Alverthorpe Park
Briar Bush Nature Center
Gwynned Wildlife Preserve*
Lorimer County Park
Mill Grove/Audubon Wildlife Sanctuary
Morris Arboretum
Saunders Woods*
Stone Hills Wildlife Preserve
Upper Schuylkill Valley Park

Pike County
Childs Recreation Area
Dingmans Ferry
Raymondskill Falls

Wayne County
Dorflinger-Suydam Wildlife Sanctuary

York County
Nixon Parks (on trails)

indicates a park where dogs are allowed but not encouraged to visit

Fairfax County
Fraser Preserve
Winkler Botanical Preserve

Fauquier County
Wildcat Mountain Natural Area
Sandy Point State Park

Prince William County
Bull Run Mountain State Natural Area
Occoquan Bay National Wildlife Refuge

DELAWARE

Abbott's Mill Nature Center

Phone - (302) 422.0847
Website - http://www.delawarenaturesociety.org/abbotts/index.html
Admission Fee - Yes, to use the trails
Directions - *Milford, Sussex County; southwest on Route 113. Take Route 36 west to Road 620 and turn right, following signs.*

The Park
In 1795 local carpenter Nathan Willey bought the land on this site. By 1802 he had finished a large grist mill and asked authorities to build a road to it. Willey died in 1812. Over the next century the property passed through many hands, with the mill remaining viable. Ainsworth Abbott took possession of the mill in 1919 and remained here until 1962. The state of Delaware bought the property in 1963 and today is operated as the downstate center for the Delaware Nature Society.

The Walks
There are two short hiking trails open for dogs at Abbott's Mill, both leaving and returning to the parking lot from the same trailhead. *The Tulip Woods Trail* travels for just under a mile on natural surface paths. Delaware was once under an ancient ocean and the flat, sandy trails here are a souvenir of the area's prehistoric past. The *Millstream Trail* is a ten-minute exploration, mostly on boardwalk, beside Johnson's Branch. Both of these walking paths are completely in the forest and your dog will hike in shaded comfort on even the hottest days.

> **Where The Paw Meets The Earth:** Natural dirt through woods
> **Workout For Your Dog** - Easy canine hiking
> **Swimming** - A 23-acre pond has access from a boat launch across the road from the main building is a nice cap to a hike with your dog
> **Restrictions On Dogs** - None

Something Extra
On your exploration of the nature center you will see the state tree of Virginia (the dogwood), the state tree of Maryland (the white oak) and the state tree of Delaware (the American holly). The colorful holly tree has been a symbol of the winter holiday season since ancient times. Found in abundance in Delaware forests, a major export industry was developed in the early 1900s. By the 1930s, Delaware was the leasding producer of holly wreaths in America. So important was the tree to Delaware's economy during the Depression that the American holly was designated the state tree.

Alapocas Woods Natural Area

Phone - (302) 577.7020
Website - http://www.destateparks.com/wilmsp/wilmsp.htm
Admission Fee - None
Directions - *Wilmington, New Castle County; behind the DuPont Experimental Station, off Route 141 on Alapocas Drive. The trailhead is in the woods at the back of the parking lot. You can also access the trails from Alapocas Drive.*

The Park
The original 123 acres of the 145-acre park were deeded to Wilmington in 1910 by William Poole Bancroft, founder of the city's park system. Today, Alapocas is a part of Wilmington State Parks, although the gate on the bridge connecting the park to Rockford Park is locked more often than not.

The Walks
The main *Alapocas Woods Trail* tumbles up and down wooded hillsides for 1.8 miles. After a narrow start (a new trail segment), the path is wide, the trees are mature with little understory to block your views and the canine hiking is splendid. Most of the way, including side loops like the *Paw-Paw Trail* (that is the tree, not a dogs-only trail), the footpaths are covered in paw-friendly dirt. If, however, you venture off the main track and hike down to the Brandywine River you will do so on a steep, rocky track that is hard on foot and paw. Your reward for this exploration is a descent into the industrial heritage of the river. As you walk along the water you will be in the shadow of the Bancroft Mills complex, once the largest cotton finishing works in the world.

> **Where The Paw Meets The Earth:** Natural and macadam down by the Brandywine
> **Workout For Your Dog** - Plenty of rolls around the park
> **Swimming** - Yes, the namesake creek is superb
> **Restrictions On Dogs** - None

Something Extra
Squeezed between the Piedmont and coastal plain zones, Alapocas offers some of the most dramatic geology in Delaware. The granite cliffs here are high enough to claim the state's only natural waterfall and plentiful enough for the Brandywine Granite Company to have once quarried over 600,000 tons of Wilmington "Blue Rocks" from this site between 1883 and 1888.

Ashland Nature Center

Phone - (302) 239.2334
Website - http://www.delawarenaturesociety.org/ashland/index.html
Admission Fee - Yes, to use the trails
Directions - *Hockessin, New Castle County; off Route 41 on Barley Mill Road, between Creek Road (Route 82) and Brackenville Road.*

The Park

A mill operated here as early as 1715. Since 1964, when the Delaware Nature Society was founded, 130 acres at Ashland Nature Center have been preserved for the conservation and study of natural resources.

The Walks

There are four self-guiding nature trails here, each a loop between .8 and 1.3 miles. *Sugarbush* and *Treetop* trails explore the wooded hillside beyond the Ashland Covered Bridge, built in the days before the Civil War; the adjoining *Succession* and *Flood Plain* trails visit meadow, marsh, pond and forest. There is a good deal of hillwalking at Ashland, save for the benign *Flood Plain Trail.*

> **Where The Paw Meets The Earth:** Natural dirt and grass
> **Workout For Your Dog** - The park is set in rolling hills
> **Swimming** - Birch Run and the Red Clay Creek flow through the property; neither is deep enough to dog paddle in
> **Restrictions On Dogs** - None on the trails

Something Extra

The Ashland Covered Bridge across the Red Clay Creek, built in the days before the Civil War, is one of Delaware's only two remaining historic covered bridges.

Banning Park

Phone - None
Website - None
Admission Fee - None
Directions - *Wilmington, New Castle County; the entrance is off Maryland Avenue (Route 4) at the intersection with Boxwood Road.*

The Park
Banning Park is Wilmington's premier recreation park. This heavily-used urban park features a central road loop through ballfields and picnic areas. The park also offers a wooded area squeezed between the Amtrak railroad lines and busy Maryland Avenue.

The Walks
There is a certain wonderment to wandering among tall trees as you are serenaded by the bustle of passing cars and the rumble of heavy locomotives. The terrain in the woods is flat; the well-worn dirt paths are wide and dog-owner friendly. The stroll around the main road is pleasant in early morning before the park surges to life.

> **Where The Paw Meets The Earth:** Natural and paved surfaces
> **Workout For Your Dog** - Flat trails
> **Swimming** - There is ample opportunity for your dog to go swimming in Lewis Pond and the often vegetation-choked Follies Pond
> **Restrictions On Dogs** - None

Something Extra
Doggie Social Hour! The dogs gather each Sunday morning to wag tails and exchange tales of their harrowing week gone by.

Battery Park

Phone - None
Website - None
Admission Fee - None
Directions - *New Castle, New Castle County; located in New Castle at the end of Delaware Street, off Route 9. Convenient parking lots are located along 3rd Street.*

The Park

New Castle, originally named Fort Casimir, was founded in 1651 by Peter Stuyvesant, who was sent to provide the Dutch with command of all river traffic. Its strategic location led to constant bickering among colonizing European nations until the English established permanent control. William Penn stepped ashore a few yards from Battery Park in 1682 to take possession of his extensive land holdings that would become Pennsylvania and Delaware. The Trustees of New Castle Common, a body of 13 Trustees, oversee a nonprofit charitable organization founded by Penn, which was incorporated in 1764 and reincorporated by assembly in 1792. The Trustees bought and developed Battery Park, established the river walkway and rehabilitated the adjacent wetlands.

The Walks

The paved walking path out of Battery Park reaches 2.5 miles along the Delaware River. In addition to unobstructed vistas across the Delaware, there are some interesting marsh views on the opposite side of the trail as well. The walking is flat and easy. When you arrive back in Battery Park, reverse your course and take your dog on the brick sidewalks through historic New Castle.

> **Where The Paw Meets The Earth:** Macadam path
> **Workout For Your Dog** - Easy canine hiking
> **Swimming** - The Delaware River laps gently to shore here and there are several points of access for your dog to enjoy a great swim - a concrete boat ramp, small sand beaches and a rocky beach at the end of the trail
> **Restrictions On Dogs** - None

Something Extra

The ticket office of the New Castle and Frenchtown Railroad in Battery Park dates to 1832 and is the oldest ticket office in the United States. Battery Park was the terminus for the pioneering railroad.

Bellevue State Park

Phone - (302) 761.6963
Website - http://www.destateparks.com/bvsp/bvsp.htm
Admission Fee - Yes, May to October
Directions - *Wilmington, New Castle County; north of the city off Exit 9 of I-95. The main entrance is on Carr Road, between Marsh Road and Silverside Road.*

The Park

Bellevue is the former estate of William du Pont, Jr., one of Delaware's greatest sportsmen. Here he stabled his Foxcatcher Farms horses and five Kentucky Derby horses worked on the training track now used by cyclists and joggers. He brought pari-mutuel racing to Delaware and designed Delaware Park. As president of the Wilmington Country Club he donated the golf course's original holes to the city of Wilmington for the Porky Oliver Golf Course. The tennis courts at Bellevue were one of the greatest private tennis complexes ever when du Pont hosted international stars at his famous "tennis Sundays." He married one of America's greatest court stars, Margaret Osbourne, in 1947. Bellevue became a 328-acre state park in 1976, ten years after William du Pont's death.

The Walks

The main attraction for hikers at Bellevue is the 9-furlong (1 1/8 miles) training track. It is wide, flat and exceedingly pleasant to walk. Unfortunately for canine hikers, in recent years the dirt track has been covered in crushed stone and dogs have been banned. Your dog can still trot on the grass shoulder, however. You can also cobble together a canine hike around the perimeter of the park by following paved bike paths and unpaved horse trails. These lead to community gardens, a small nature preserve, the historic paddocks and estate buildings.

> **Where The Paw Meets The Earth:** Dirt and grass and pavement
> **Workout For Your Dog** - Easy strolling around the estate
> **Swimming** - No, the park pond is for fishing not dog paddling
> **Restrictions On Dogs** - No dogs on the training track

Something Extra

When William du Pont took over the property he transformed a Gothic Revival castle into a graceful replica of President James Madison's home, Montpelier. It is now the centerpiece of the park.

Blackbird State Forest

Phone - (302) 653.6505
Website - http://state.de.us/deptagri/forestry/forest.shtml
Admission Fee - None
Directions - *Smyrna, New Castle County; office is located in the Tybout Tract, about 4 miles northwest of Smyrna. Take Route 15 South and make a left on Oliver Guessford Road. Follow to the end. Make a right on Blackbird Forest Road and the entrance to the office is 1/3 mile down on the left. From Route 13, turn left on Blackbird Forest Road (County Road 471). Continue for 1.5 miles to the office.*

The Park

The Blackbird State Forest manages about 3,400 acres on 10 non-connecting tracts. Here you can see such New Castle County arboreal regulars as yellow poplar, white oak, maple, gum and bayberry mingling with an occasional regal loblolly pine just north of is natural range.

The Walks

An informal tangle of fire road, deer paths and primitive trails extend for over 40 miles in the forest. The best canine hiking is in the Tybout Tract where the paths are generally wide and well-trod. Most of the trails in the other tracts are rustic enough in many places to be termed "overgrown" at certain times during the year.

> **Where The Paw Meets The Earth:** Dirt and pine straw
> **Workout For Your Dog** - Flat, flat, flat
> **Swimming** - Not much water fun in narrow streams of the forest
> **Restrictions On Dogs** - None

Something Extra

Of immediate interest in the Blackbird Forest are the Delmarva Bays or "whale wallows." These series of shallow depressions, filled with water in rainy times, are found only in the Blackbird State Forest and the Millington Wildlife Management Area in nearby Kent County, Maryland. Their origins are a mystery - local lore maintains that they are the result of struggling whales, stranded after a biblical flood receded. Other theories suggest glacial scraping or even meteorites. Whatever their origins, when wet, these "living museums" support rare plants and wildlife. Seven of the Delmarva Bays have been dedicated as nature preserves in the Blackbird State Forest. A prominent "whale wallow" near the office in the Tybout Tract is opposite the southernmost picnic area. Although there are no trails leading to this Delmarva Bay, you can claw your way through the woods to reach it.

Bombay Hook National Wildlife Refuge

Phone - (302) 653.9341
Website - http://www.fws.gov/northeast/bombayhook/
Admission Fee - Yes
Directions - *Smyrna, Kent County; off Scenic Route 9, north of Leipsic. From Delaware 1 take the Smyrna South Exit, following signs to Route 6 East.*

The Park

European settlement of this area began in 1679 when the Indian Machacksett, Chief Sachem of Kahansink, sold Dutch settlers some marshland called "Boompies Hoock" - roughly translated as a thicket of trees in German. The cost was "one gun, fower hands of powder, three Mats coats, one anckor of Liquors and one Kittle." Many of the trees that gave Bombay Hook its name were destroyed in the Great Storm of 1878. Bombay Hook joined the National Wildlife Refuge System, a legacy of Theodore Roosevelt, in 1937. Since then the refuge's 15,978 acres have been managed to provide a diversity of habitats: freshwater, brackish and salt marsh, bay, grassland, crop-land and forest to encourage plant and animal diversity.

The Walks

At Bombay Hook there are several short nature trails but your best canine hiking bet may be around the refuge on the hard-packed dirt auto road. Vehicle traffic is sparse and moving turtle-slow when it comes.

> **Where The Paw Meets The Earth:** Dirt roads and board walks
> **Workout For Your Dog** - Flat, open walking
> **Swimming** - Over 13,000 of the refuge's acres are tidal marshes intersected by winding rivers and creeks but none of it is for doggie aquatics
> **Restrictions On Dogs** - None

Something Extra

Much of the energies at Bombay Hook are devoted to supporting mi-grating geese and ducks. There are even crops of winter wheat and clover grown for the wildlife. As a result the refuge lists 278 species of birds that can be seen along the western shore of the Delaware Bay. If you want to see waterfowl, visit during March and November. If you are interested in shorebirds and songbirds come during May, August and September.

Brandywine Creek State Park

Phone - (302) 577.3534
Website - http://www.destateparks.com/bcsp/bcsp.asp
Admission Fee - Yes, May to October
Directions - *Talleyville, New Castle County; the main entrance is on Adams Dam Road, between Thompson's Bridge Road (Route 92) and Rockland Road. Other parking areas are at Thompson's Bridge and off Rockland Road, opposite Rockland Mills.*

The Park
Once a du Pont family dairy farm, this spectacular swath of land became a State Park in 1965. Delaware's first two nature preserves are located here: Tulip Tree Woods and Freshwater Marsh, at the edge of Brandywine Creek. The stone walls that criss-cross the 850-acre park are the legacy of skilled Italian masons who crafted the barriers from locally quarried Brandywine granite - the original "Wilmington Blue Rocks."

The Walks
There are eight blazed trails totalling 14 miles on both sides of the Brandywine Creek. All are short, all are woodsy and if you can't reach out and touch the water you are moving up or down a hill. The *Hidden Pond Trail* and the *Indian Springs Trail* each travel along the water and visit 200-year old tuplip polars. The star walk at Thompson's Bridge is the rugged, 1.9-mile *Rocky Run Trail*, winding around the closest thing to a mountain stream in Delaware. Nearby, the *Multi-Use Trail* tags the stream for the better part of two miles.

> **Where The Paw Meets The Earth:** Dirt and grass
> **Workout For Your Dog** - Some good - but not lethal - climbs
> **Swimming** - Yes, the namesake creek is superb
> **Restrictions On Dogs** - None

Something Extra
In the winter of 1802 a rudderless French immigrant living in New Jersey named Eleuthere Irenee du Pont was invited to the Brandywine Valley to hunt game. It was not a successful trip. The damp weather fouled his gunpowder so that his musket continually misfired. It was so bad du Pont decided to re-enter the industry he had turned his back on in France as a youth: black powder. When it came time to launch his new business he remembered what you see today in thepark: the hardwood forests that would burn to charcoal, one of the ingredients he would need for powder; the abundant granite in the hills to build his mills; and the swift-flowing river to power the mills. And so he returned to Delaware to found a dynasty. Incidentally, the favorite breed of dog for the du Pont family when they lived here: the greyhound.

Brandywine Park

Phone - (302) 577.7020
Website - http://www.destateparks.com/wilmsp/wilmsp.htm
Admission Fee - None
Directions - *Wilmington, New Castle County; the main parking lot for Brandywine Park is on the north banks of the river at the foot of Monkey Hill, off of 18th and Van Buren streets.*

The Park

Brandywine Park, Delaware's first park, created in 1885 and partially designed by Frederick Law Olmsted, can stand beside any of America's downtown riverwalks for person and dog. The 178-acre park of wooded trails, formal gardens, and sculptures was added to the National Historic Register in 1976.

The Walks

The 1.8-mile *Brandywine Nature Trail* connects Brandywine Village and Rockford Park. Through Brandywine Park it traces the north shore of the Brandywine River for about a mile. Once across the Swinging Bridge, the trail veers away from the water towards Rockford Park via Kentmere Parkway. Along the way you'll enjoy native and ornamental plantings in the Rose Garden, the Waterwalk Garden, the Four Seasons Garden, the historic Josephine Gardens and elsewhere.

> **Where The Paw Meets The Earth:** Concrete sidewalk and macadam
> **Workout For Your Dog** - Plenty of rolls around the park
> **Swimming** - Dogs can enjoy a dip in the Brandywine River and in the mill race cut on the south side; in 1954, the Brandywine Canoe Slalom, America's first ever slalom race for kayaks, ran in these waters south of the Washington Street bridge
> **Restrictions On Dogs** - None

Something Extra

A canine hike through Brandywine Park provides a quick lesson in the history of bridge architecture. The classical arch form is represented in grand style with the magnificent stone viaduct across the river and numerous reinforced concrete spans. There is even a small iron arch bridge over the mill race. A prototypical 19th century pier and girder iron bridge transports trains over the Brandywine River. And the pedestrian footbridge across the water, the Swinging Bridge, is a little suspension bridge employing the same engineering principles as the legendary Brooklyn Bridge.

Brandywine Springs Park

Phone - None
Website - None
Admission Fee - None
Directions - *Mill Creek, New Castle County; at the corner of Newport Gap Pike (Route 41) and Faulkland Road (Route 34).
The entrance is on Faulkland Road.*

The Park

One of the first resort hotels and spas in America was built here in 1827. The recreational heritage of the area was revived with the advent of a popular amusement park decades later featuring, among other attractions, a boardwalk and a roller coaster. The Friends of Brandywine Springs Park have erected stations housing turn-of-the-20th century photographs to help recreate its heyday as a pioneering amusement park in the United States.

The Walks

The historic Brandywine Springs Park is an ideal spot for a quick walk of a half-hour or so. Many people walk dogs around the picnic areas in the ballfields in the upper section of the park. The lower, wooded section - where the amusement park was located - features wide trails that fishhook along Hyde Run and Red Clay Creek. Both the upper and lower sections are flat walks; the connecting trails between the two areas require short hikes up and down the interceding steep grade. The gentlest of these is the trail at the Council Oak, the remains of a 330-year old tree that stands at the woods' edge opposite the park entrance. It is said that George Washington met with his war council beneath the oak on September 8, 1777 and made the decision to fall back to the Brandywine River and defend Philadelphia against the marching British Army instead of engaging the invaders behind the Red Clay Creek. Washington would ultimately be routed in Chadds Ford, in part because his knowledge of that countryside was vastly inferior to the British.

> **Where The Paw Meets The Earth:** Dirt and grass trails
> **Workout For Your Dog** - If she's looking for a steep hill she can find it
> **Swimming** - The Red Clay Creek is deep enough for a dog to jump in and the fast-moving Hyde Run is fun to romp in
> **Restrictions On Dogs** - None

Something Extra

When the historic Wilmington & Western tourist railroad is operating (the stretch of tracks in the park has been washed away by floods twice in recent years), you may chance to see the old-fashioned train rumble across the open wooden trestle spanning Red Clay Creek.

Brecknock Park

Phone - None
Website - None
Admission Fee - None
Directions - *Camden, Kent County; from Route 113 veer right onto Old Camden Road and the park is immediately on the right.*

The Park
Alexander Humphreys received a warrant of 600 acres here in 1680 and is believed to have called it "Brecknock" after a shire in Wales. The first mill along the banks of the Isaac Branch of the St. Jones River was constructed in 1740, beginning almost two centuries of grain production. By 1812 a state-of-the-art, three-story Oliver Evans mill had replaced it. Evans, a Delawarean born in Newport, built the nation's first automatic mill on the Red Clay Creek. In 1928 a hurricane washed away the mill's dam and the mill itself was demolished during a World War II scrap metal drive. The land was acquired for a Kent County park in 1993 and the boardwalk for the Isaac Branch Nature Trail was a construction project of a team of Americorps volunteers. The mansion on the property dates to the mid-1700s and is listed on the National Register of Historic Places.

The Walks
Your canine hiking day at Brecknock begins with an easy walk around an open field studded with plantings of Virginia Pine, River Birch, Scarlet Oak and Red Cedar. A completely different park awaits you as drop down to the *Isaac Branch Nature Trail* at the back of Brecknock. The remainder of your canine hike will be along and over the slow-moving wetlands. This is an out-and-back trail of about one mile, much of it on boardwalk. Back in the recreational section of the park there is an exhibit on the history of milling and plenty of greenspace for a lively game of fetch.

> **Where The Paw Meets The Earth:** Boardwalks and natural surfaces
> **Workout For Your Dog** - Mostly easy-going travel
> **Swimming** - Isaac Branch is not a canine swimming hole
> **Restrictions On Dogs** - None

Something Extra
Take time to visit the Native Butterfly Garden created at Brecknock Park. Different species of butterflies have different preferences of nectar, in both colors and tastes so a wide variety of food plants give the greatest diversity of visitors. In a butterfly garden you'll see groups of the same plants that are easier for butterflies to see than singly planted flowers. Wild and cultivated plants are staggered, as well as blooming times of the day and year.

Bringhurst Woods/Rockwood Mansion

Phone - (302) 761.4340 (museum)
Website - http://www.rockwood.org/home/webpage1.asp
Admission Fee - None, for the grounds
Directions - *Wilmington, New Castle County; use Exit 9 off I-95
for Carr Road. The parking lot for Bringhurst Woods is between
Marsh Road and the Washington Street Extension.*

The Park
Bringhurst Woods is part of the Northern Delaware Greenway that
links northern New Castle County from Fox Point State Park on the
Delaware River to the Maryland border in White Clay Creek State
Park. The southern terminus of the short hike is the splendid man-
sion of Rockwood and trails through the 72-acre estate.

The Walks
The main path of the Greenway is paved as it cuts through mature
hardwoods along Shellpot Creek. You always seem to be walking up
and down in Bringhurst Woods, but never laboriously. There are also
natural trails on the opposite side of Shellpot Creek but these are
neither maintained - a hodgepodge of sand, dirt, grass, rocks and
discarded bricks - nor enjoyable. Once you reach Rockwood, you
are free to explore the elegant gardens and sculpted grounds of the
estate with your dog. The English-style garden is home to several
Delaware state champion tress. The paths are lighted and open until
10:00 p.m. Rockwood is also worth a hike during a winter's night
when the grounds are elaborately decorated. Be aware that this hike
will force you to potentially walk your dog across two heavily-traveled roads. .

> **Where The Paw Meets The Earth: -** Macadam
> **Workout For Your Dog** - Little humps and rolls
> **Swimming** - Shellpot Creek boasts more rocks than water
> but there is an occasional pool to splash about in for dogs
> **Restrictions On Dogs** - None

Something Extra
A canine hike through Rockwood affords a chance to study up-close
a rare country home designed in the rural Gothic style. The Garden-
esque landscaping, unique to Delaware estates, blends the Brandywine granite of the mansion to the boulders on the grounds. The
mansion was built as a retirement home from 1851 to 1857 by the
merchant banker Joseph Shipley, descendant of the founding family
of Wilmington, with apologies to Thomas Willing.

Cape Henlopen State Park

Phone - (302) 645.8983
Website - http://www.destateparks.com/chsp/chsp.htm
Admission Fee - Yes, May to October
Directions - *Lewes, Sussex County; one mile east of town at the end of Route 9, off of Route 1.*

The Park
Cape Henlopen has the distinction of being one of the first parks in America: in 1682 William Penn decreed that Cape Henlopen would be for "the usage of the citizens of Lewes and Sussex County." The area had been Delaware's first permanent settlement 50 years earlier by ill-fated Dutch colonists who were massacred by local Indians. Cape Henlopen's strategic location at the mouth of the Delaware Bay led the United States Army to establish Fort Miles among the dunes in 1941. In 1964, the Department of Defense declared 543 acres on the cape as surplus property and the State of Delaware established Cape Henlopen State Park. Today the park boasts more than 5,000 acres, including four miles of pristine beaches where the Delaware Bay meets the Atlantic Ocean. It is Delaware's largest state park.

The Walks
More than 10 miles of trails, including 6 miles along the Atlantic Ocean. The 3.1-mile paved *Dune Overlook Trail* is a must - and don't skip the spur to the 80-foot Great Dune.

> **Where The Paw Meets The Earth:** Everything from sand to macadam
>
> **Workout For Your Dog** - Good when trotting on soft sand; otherwise easy
>
> **Swimming** - Yes! Atlantic Ocean and Delaware Bay
>
> **Restrictions On Dogs** - Dogs are not permitted around the Seaside Nature Center or on the *Pinelands Nature Trail*, dogs are prohibited from all swimming and sunbathing beaches from May 1 to September 30, dogs are allowed in the campground.

Something Extra
Remnants of Cape Henlopen's military past remain nestled among the massive sand dunes. Bunkers and gun emplace-ments were camouflaged deep in the sand and concrete observation towers were built along the shoreline to bolster America's coastal defenses during World War II. Lookouts scanned the Atlantic Ocean for German U-boats during World War II and although the fort's huge guns were never fired in battle, a German submarine did surrender here after the war.

Carousel Park

Phone - None
Website - None
Admission Fee - None
Directions - *Mill Creek, New Castle County; halfway between Newark and Wilmington, is on Limestone Road (Route 7) between Milltown Road and New Linden Hill Road. Smaller parking lots are at the end of Old Linden Hill Road, off Limestone Road, and on Skyline Drive, off New Linden Hill Road.*

The Park
Carousel Park is another legacy to recreation in Delaware from the du Pont family, being a former family estate. Long the home of public riding stables, New Castle County has worked to make the park a mecca for hiking as well.

The Walks
Carousel is a suburban park given over to walking - no playgrounds or ballfields here. The main trail (*The Carousel Loop*) is a three-mile walk around the circumference of the park. Many short connecting trails dissect the park as well. All told their are 14 trails in the park winding through open fields, horse pastures, ponds, hardwoods (*Land of the Giants*) and pine trees (*Sherwood Forest*). Carousel Park is set in rolling hills; a healthy climb is required to reach *Strawberry Field* in the back of the park. The Carousel Loop is covered with paw-pleasing wood chips the entire way.

> **Where The Paw Meets The Earth:** Some gravel roads but mostly dirt and wood chips
> **Workout For Your Dog** - Rolling terrain
> **Swimming** - Enchanted Lake is an ideal spot for canine aquatics
> **Restrictions On Dogs** - None

Something Extra
An off-leash Bark Park at Carousel Park has been established in an open field above Enchanted Lake. With the easy access to the lake this is the best dog park in the Mid-Atlantic. Yes, it is.

Chapel's Branch Nature Area

Phone - None
Website - None
Admission Fee - None
Directions - *West Seaford, Sussex; from Route 20, make a left onto Sussex Avenue and continue until the end at a stop light in front of the DuPont nylon plant. Make a right on Harrington Street and look for the parking lot 1/2 mile on your right.*

The Park
In the 1930s a DuPont Company research team led by Dr. Wallace Carothers developed nylon - the world's first true synthetic fiber. In 1939 the company began commercial production in Seaford, selecting the 609-acre site on the Nanticoke River for its proximity to raw material supplies and major markets. The town greeted the company with an impromptu parade. The six-story plant was soon operating 24 hours a day, producing enough yarn in its first year of operation to weave 64 million pairs of nylon stockings. The first nylon yarn produced at the Seaford plant is now on display in the Smith-sonian Institution. The DuPont Company conveyed 190 acres across the street from its plant and the Seaford Golf and Country Club for the Chapel Branch Nature Area, named for a small frame church built in the 1700s.

The Walks
The primary loop in Chapel Hill is about 2.5 miles with a short cut, some spur trails and an access road for prolonged canine hiking in this delightful mixed upland forest. Sunlight filters to the ground throughout this completely shaded ramble. The track starts out wide as it drops gently to the wetlands around Chapel Branch, providing a bit of elevation change. The path narrows in the later stages but remains comfortably roomy with a dog in tow.

>**Where The Paw Meets The Earth:** Uniformly paw-friendly soft dirt and pine straw
>**Workout For Your Dog** - Mostly easy trotting
>**Swimming** - Minimal access and minimal depth in Chapel Branch
>**Restrictions On Dogs** - None

Something Extra
On the other side of the nylon plant, in the downtown area, you can take your dog to the Seaford River Walk at the foot of Pine Street off High Street. The concrete path is two blocks long but there is a grass area to the right with access to the Nanticoke River.

Chesapeake & Delaware Canal Wildlife Area

Phone - None
Website - None
Admission Fee - None
Directions - *St. Georges, New Castle County; accessible from many spots: the town of St. Georges, the Grass Dale Center of Fort DuPont State Park and Summit Road on the north side; the C&D Canal Museum in Chesapeake City, Ratledge Road, and Dutch Neck Road on the south, among others.*

The Park

The land between the Delaware River and the Chesapeake Bay was first surveyed for a canal as early as the 1760s but construction on a great ditch did not begin until 1822. With 2,600 men digging and hauling dirt, the waterway finally opened for business in 1829, slicing 300 miles and eliminating the ocean route between Philadelphia and Baltimore. The federal government took complete control over the canal in 1919 and deepened and widened the channel to eliminate the need for locks. Today the 14-mile long, 450-foot wide Chesapeake and Delaware Canal is one of only two vitally commercial sea-level canals in the United States. Dredged to a depth of 35 feet, the "C&D" is deep enough to handle ocean-going ships. Over 20,000 vessels of all shapes and sizes float down the waterway, making it one of the busiest canals in the world. The lands on either side are managed by the U.S. Army Corps of Engineers and their mandate is to keep the maritime traffic flowing, not to create a recreational paradise for you and your dog.

The Walks

Old, unpaved service roads on either side of the canal provide wide, flat, easy-walking paths. There are also informal trails along the length of the canal. A canine hike is best designed with a two-car shuttle to eliminate the need for back-tracking but otherwise you will just amble along until you decide to turn back. The scenery doesn't change mile after mile and there is no shade for your dog on a hot day so make sure you pack drinking water on any hike in the C&D Canal area.

> **Where The Paw Meets The Earth:** Dirt roads and paths
> **Workout For Your Dog** - Easy going
> **Swimming** - There is no access to the boulder-lined canal
> **Restrictions On Dogs** - None

Something Extra

The dredging of the canal in the 1800s unearthed pockets of fossils from the Cretaceous Period (144 to 65 million years ago). Today, the C&D Canal is Delaware's best place to hunt fossils, mostly "steinkerns."

Delaware Seashore State Park

Phone - (302) 227-2800
Website - http://www.destateparks.com/dssp/dssp.asp
Admission Fee - Yes, May to October
Directions - *Indian River, Sussex County; located between the Atlantic Ocean and Rehoboth Bay on DE Route 1, south of Rehoboth Beach and north of Bethany Beach.*

The Park
Delaware has about two dozen miles of ocean shore- land and about half of those are part of the state park system. And about half of those are in the Delaware Seashore State Park, the First State's most popular park. Now streching across 2,825 acres, the park was created in 1965.

The Walks
There are no formal trails through the park, just plenty of beach to hike on. There is more to see at Delaware Seashore State Park than sea and sand. World War II observation towers still stand as reminders of coastal Delaware's military history. Just to the south, at low tide, stumps of a ghost forest, trees overwhelmed by tide and sand, can still be seen. And if you find your dog acting peculiar it may be the presence of the ghost of a young woman, clad in an old-fashioned bathing suit, who has been seen roaming the dunes. When there is access, a 1.5-mile loop trail explores Burton's Island, one of the inland bay's largest islands. Much of the way the trail is sand-surfaced with a boardwalk covering the saltwater marsh.

>**Where The Paw Meets The Earth:** Natural dirt and sand
>**Workout For Your Dog** - Long trots in the sand
>**Swimming** - If your dog finds the pounding surf of the Atlantic Ocean intimidating, you can turn around and go a few hundred yards to the gentle (usually) water of the inland bays
>**Restrictions On Dogs** - Dogs are allowed on the beach from October 1 to May 1; also Tower Road during the summer

Something Extra
About a mile north of Indian River Inlet is the Indian River Life-Saving Station, built in 1876. It was constructed about 400 feet closer to the waves but almost immediately became engulfed in a dune and was moved to its present location a year later. The station was occupied by six surfmen and a keeper from September to May to aid mariners in navigating the dangerous waters offshore. After the Coast Guard formed they took over operations that continued until the 1960s. The station, with its distinctive diamond-shaped trim, has been restored to its 1905 appearance. It is one of America's oldest life-saving stations still standing.

Delcastle Recreation Area

Phone - None
Website - None
Admission Fee - None
Directions - *Mill Creek, New Castle County; on McKennans Church Road between Limestone Road (Route 7) and Newport Gap Pike (Route 41).*

The Park

Long the gold standard of New Castle County recreation parks, Delcastle offers a paved, multi-use 1 3/4-mile loop. Always busy, this is not the place for your dog if you are looking to commune with nature and not people. The complete loop takes 30-40 minutes and there is no water for your dog to drink along the way that doesn't come out of a fountain. If you are walking the dog and pushing a baby stroller, this is the best place to do it.

The Walks

This is a single-trail park; the circumference canine hike is an open walk in the park.

Where The Paw Meets The Earth: Macadam
Workout For Your Dog - Slight rises at each end of the park
Swimming - None
Restrictions On Dogs - None

Something Extra

You can stop and actually read one of those roadside signs you normally zoom by in your car. Here, near "an emminence at McKennan's Church," a force of American patriots took up a defensive position to act as a decoy prior to the Battle of the Brandywine in the American Revolution.

Fort DuPont State Park

Phone - (302) 834.7941
Website - http://www.destateparks.com/fdsp/fdpp.htm
Admission Fee - Yes, May to October
Directions - *Delaware City, New Castle County; the main parking lot is in the back of the Governor Bacon Health Center. The entrance is off   Route 9 on the south side of the Delaware City Branch Canal. The trailhead is directly behind the small parking lot.*

The Park
On the shore opposite Fort Delaware, Fort DuPont was actively garrisoned during the Civil War and the Spanish-American War; used as a training base in World War I; and detained German prisoners in World War II. It is named for Samuel Francis du Pont who, during the Civil War commanded a fleet of 77 vessels and 12,000 men to a critical Union victory in the Battle of Port Royal Sound. It was the largest United States naval expeditionary force ever assembled up to that time.

The Walks
The 1-mile *River View Trail* loop begins a gently sloping canine hike in the marshland along the Delaware River and finishes in shaded woodlands. If you walk it backwards you have longer sustained views of the river and Fort Delaware on Pea Patch Island. The grass trail takes you past several ruins of the military installation, camoflauged to river traffic.

>**Where The Paw Meets The Earth:** Paw-friendly grass
>**Workout For Your Dog** - Easy canine hike in the old military base
>**Swimming** - There is a small section of the park where a really water-starved dog can reach the Delaware River but it is not a beach.
>**Restrictions On Dogs** - None

Something Extra
The heronry on Pea Patch Island (the story goes that in colonial times a boat hauling peas ran aground on this 178-acre mud flat spilling its cargo and planting a pea patch) is the largest Atlantic Coast nesting ground north of Florida for wading birds. There is ample opportunity to watch ibis, egrets and herons - who live in pairs - go about their lives in the Delaware River.

Holts Landing State Park

Phone - (302) 539.9060
Website - http://www.destateparks.com/holts/hlsp.htm
Admission Fee - Yes, May to October
Directions - *Millville, Sussex County; from Route 1 take Route 26 West to County Road 346 or 347 north to the park entrance.*

The Park

Nanticoke Indians harvested seafood and hunted in the surrounding marshes and forests along the shores of Delaware's inland bays. Later, this property was farmed by the Holt family until 1957 when the farm was sold to the state highway department. In 1965 the first parcel of what would become the 203-acre Holts Landing State Park was transferred to the State Park Commission.

The Walks

The star hiking trail here is the 1.7-mile *Sea Hawk Trail* that takes in three different ecosystems: beach, marsh and forest. You'll start (assuming high tide has left the trail passable) with a walk down the beach and expansive views of Indian River Bay. As you turn away from the water the route utilizes old access roads in a once-cultivated field that is morphing back into woodlands. In this open part of the hike scan the skies and treetops of tall pines for evidence of the ospreys - or sea hawks - that give the trail its name. Ospreys can grow to 23 inches long with a wingspan of more than five feet. They fish by swooping down and snaring fish as big as 4 pounds in their talons.

> **Where The Paw Meets The Earth:** Plenty of paw-friendly sand paths
> **Workout For Your Dog** - Level going all around
> **Swimming** - The shallow waters of Indian River Bay are ideal for splashing and freshwater dog paddling can be had in several borrow pits created by the highway department's road-building crews that have filled with water
> **Restrictions On Dogs** - None

Something Extra

You can enjoy the activities that have gone on for centuries on the bayshore - fishing, clamming or crabbing. The park sports a new crabbing pier and a convenient boat ramp to pursue flounder, trout and bluefish.

Iron Hill Park

Phone - None
Website - None
Admission Fee - None
Directions - *Newark, New Castle County; the entrance for Iron Hill Park is off Whitaker Road, between Old Baltimore Pike and Welsh Tract Road. Any of the four parking areas will provide access to the trails.*

The Park

Welsh settlers began extracting iron from this hill, known to the Lenni Lenape Indians as Marettico - "the hill of hard stone" - as early as 1701. Ore was hauled to North East, Maryland where it was smelted. In September of 1777, the Big Three of the Continental Army - George Washington, Nathaniel Greene and the Marquis de Lafayette - surveyed the progress of the approaching British Army from this hill. The ensuing skirmish just past the base of the hill at Cooch's Bridge on September 3 was the only exchange of gunfire on Delaware soil during the American Revolution.

The Walks

A *Yellow Trail* and a *Red Trail* covers the park's 300 acres. *The Mason-Dixon Trail*, blazed in light blue, cuts through Iron Hill Park and deadends against I-95 before skipping across on Welsh Tract Road and continuing its journey westward. While there are some hardy climbs on Iron Hill, the main dirt trails work around the hill rather than up and down the slopes.

> **Where The Paw Meets The Earth:** Wooded dirt trails
> **Workout For Your Dog** - Moderate on small hills
> **Swimming** - There is no flowing water in the park but some of the played-out ore pits - the mines were abandoned in 1891 - are filled with water.
> **Restrictions On Dogs** - None

Something Extra

A terminus for the Mason-Dixon Trail is the Iron Hill Museum, a converted one-room schoolhouse that illuminates the natural and industrial history of the area. A short, interesting *Iron Mine Trail* snakes through the woods here.

James Farm Ecological Park

Phone - (302) 645.7325
Website - http://www.inlandbays.org/cib_pm/education.php
Admission Fee - None
Directions - *Ocean View, Sussex County; traveling south on Delaware 1, make your first right after crossing Indian River Inlet onto Road 360. Continue to the end and make a right on Cedar Neck Road. The parking lot is on the left, just past the tennis club. Approaching on Route 26, make a left on Cedar Neck.*

The Park

James Farm was created as an ecological preserve through a gift of 150 acres to Sussex County in 1992 from Mary Lighthipe in memory of her son Harold. Beginning in 1998, the Center for the Inland Bays has managed the property for the benefit of the public.

The Walks

A patchwork of color-coded trails explores this thumb of land that pokes into the Indian River Bay. You move your dog through an old horse pasture that has been reforested with a planting of 4000 young trees and then push into a maritime forest on the way to a small sandy beach on Pasture Point Cove. Dogs will love the silky soft sands and gentle waters of the bay. For an open field trot, don't forget the *Purple Trail* across Cedar Neck Road. There is no better place to take your dog for a walk at the beach than James Farm.

> **Where The Paw Meets The Earth:** Wide, paw-friendly trails
> **Workout For Your Dog** - Level throughout
> **Swimming** - No place better than Indian River Bay where the water is knee-deep for a quarter-mile out
> **Restrictions On Dogs** - None

Something Extra

Beginning in 2003, James Farm has been one of 14 locations in Delaware's inland bays used for oyster gardening. More than one million oysters have been deployed to build reefs that will stabilize the bay floor and filter the waters for a more energized aquatic environment. It is estimated that a single oyster can filter 50 gallons of water and more than 100,000 oysters were introduced to the reef at Pasture Point Cove. The oysters attach themselves to a solid substrate - often another oyster - and begin building a reef habitat. Natural oysters have been gone from Delaware's inland bays for over 30 years but someday the efforts of this oyster gardening may yield harvests once again.

Killens Pond State Park

Phone - (302) 284.4526
Website - http://www.destateparks.com/kpsp/kpsp.htm
Admission Fee - Yes, May to October
Directions - *Felton, Kent County; take Killens Pond Road east of Route 13 to the park entrance past Lake Forest High School.*

The Park
Native tribes traditionally gathered for centuries in this area around the waterway that would come to be called "Murderkill" after a Dutch trading party was slaughtered at the mouth of the river by local tribes in 1648. In the late 1700s the river was dammed and the 66-acre millpond created. In 1965, Killens Pond became Kent County's only state park.

The Walks
The first thing your dog will notice while trotting on the trails at Killens Pond is that it is unusually hilly for central Delaware. Just enough to give the 2.75-mile *Pondside Trail* a nice, sporty feel. Your dog will also approve of the wide, roomy paths and the packed sand and pine straw under paw. The trail circles the entire pond, keeping sight of the water most of the way. Chances are you will just be getting warmed up with this pleasing ramble and luckily Killens Pond serves up a few more choices. The *Ice Storm Trail* is a loop that shows the forest regenerating from a 1994 storm that left trees snapping and buckling under the weight of a cocoon of ice. If it is not in use you and your dog can sample the best cross-country course in downstate Delaware on the western edge of the pond.

> **Where The Paw Meets The Earth:** Very paw-friendly sandy dirt
> **Workout For Your Dog** - Nothing a fun-loving dog can't handle
> **Swimming** - The best place to access the pond is at the boat ramp
> **Restrictions On Dogs** - Dogs are allowed in the campground but not the cabins

Something Extra
Killens Pond offers the opportunity to hike through a uniquely diverse forest area as southern species mingle at the northern edge of their range with northern species reaching their southern boundary. Seven seperate species of oak trees share the sandy soil with majestic loblolly pines; American holly jostles with Virginia pine and so on.

Lums Pond State Park

Phone - (302) 368.6989
Website - http://www.destateparks.com/lpsp/lpsp.asp
Admission Fee - Yes, May to October
Directions - *Kirkwood, New Castle County; main entrance on Howell School Road between Red Lion Road (Route 71) and Route 896. The dog park is east of the Main Entrance on Buck Jersey Road.* .

The Park
In the early 1800s the Army Corps of Engineers dammed the St. Georges Creek, once home to Lenni Lenape Indian hunting camps, to hold water for the original Chesapeake and Delaware Canal. The result is Delaware's largest freshwater pond, a 200-acre water playground for boaters, fishermen, swimmers - and dogs.

The Walks
The *Swamp Forest Trail* at Lums Pond circumnavigates the water and covers over seven miles. Along the way you will hike through woods and fields and cross 26 wooden bridges. Look for the toothwork of the active colony of beavers at Lums Pond along the way. If three or four hours of trekking with your dog isn't on your menu, however, don't attempt this trip - unless you flag down a boat you will have to do the whole shebang. The hike around Lums Pond is a little too long and not varied enough to rank higher. Beware that after heavy rains this water-level dirt trail gets very muddy. There are also another ten miles of multi-use trails on the park's 1,757 acres but no short- or medium-length hiking-only trails. You can also take your dog on a unique 200-yard "sensory trail" at Lums Pond that encourages the exploration of nature with other senses beside sight.

>**Where The Paw Meets The Earth:** Mostly dirt but roots and wet spots
>**Workout For Your Dog** - No elevation gain at Lums Pond
>**Swimming** - Access all around the pond
>**Restrictions On Dogs** - Dogs are not allowed in the swimming area in season

Something Extra
Lums Pond features one of the 7 tournament-ready, 18-hole disc golf courses in Delaware (all in state parks).The course is noted for its many holes threaded through the park's trees. You can take your dog along for a casual round or watch the pros each May when the Professional Disc Golf Association visits Lums Pond for tournament play.

Middle Run Natural Area

Phone - None
Website - None
Admission Fee - None
Directions - *Newark, New Castle County; going northeast on Kirkwood Highway (Route 2)turn onto Possum Park Road. After 1.7 miles turn right on Possum Hollow Road. Take a left at the entrance to the park after about 1/2 mile.*

The Park
The White Clay Creek drains some 70,000 acres and 100 square miles in Pennsylvania and Delaware. In Delaware, where Middle Run is one of its three main tributaries, it seems that much of that watershed is choked by sub- urban sprawl. Beginning in 1975, local civic and environmental groups began piece-meal acquisition of pristine woodlands that has resulted in an 850-acre oasis in the center of housing subdivisions, shopping centers and busy roadways.

The Walks
Middle Run features splendid canine hiking on five well-maintained loop trails that cover 14 miles and an additional five short spurs that lead to surrounding communites. All offer interesting - and sometimes challenging - switches in terrain. The purple-blazed *Lenape Trail* visits most of the property in its run of almost 7 miles, one of the longest loop trails in Delaware. The best choice for dog walkers only wanting to sample Middle Run's sylvan charms is the pedestrian-only 2.15-mile *Possum Hollow Trail*. Another good ramble is the *Earth Day Trail* that drops out of the parking lot into a steep valley around Muddy Run.

> **Where The Paw Meets The Earth:** Natural dirt trails
> **Workout For Your Dog** - Absolutely; try the *Snow Geese Trail* to really get your dog's tongue to hanging
> **Swimming** - The streams are only good for splashing - or this would be a solid four-paw destination
> **Restrictions On Dogs** - None

Something Extra
The patches of long-abandoned farmland are good places to spot hawks. Hawks can appear at Middle Run at any time of the year but in fall and spring the skies overflow with migrating hawks making long-distance trips between their breeding grounds and winter residences. Fall migration usually begins in mid-August and continues through late November. Spring migration takes place between March and May.

Nanticoke Wildlife Area

Phone - (302) 875-9997
Website - None
Admission Fee - None
Directions - *Bethel, Sussex County;west to Maryland border; From Route 13, take Route 24 west to Airport Road (Road 494) and turn right. As you reach the wildlife area an office and map-boards will appear on the right.*

The Park
The Nanticoke River springs to life in southern Delaware and flows southwest to the Chesapeake Bay. It is considered one of the Chesapeake's healthiest rivers. Scientists believe the area's unique habitat stems from 10,000 years ago when the land was more exposed and prevailing winds deposited large amounts of sand across the flat terrain. Most of the roads cut through the 3,177-acre wilderness were constructed during the Roosevelt Administration by the Civilian Conservation Corps.

The Walks
Of the managed wildlife areas by the State of Delaware where you get out and explore on old fire roads, Nanticoke is the best to hike with your dog. The packed sand roads are flat, easy to walk and easy on the paw. There are more than 12 miles of these well-maintained access roads; some are closed to all vehicles and others receive sporadic traffic. Keep your eyes peeled for small side trails that can lead to secluded ponds in the forests of black oaks and Virginia pine. The Nanticoke Wildlife Area is divided into a North Area and South Area, severed by Broad Creek. There are more natural surface trails in the North Area and access to the Nanticoke River.

> **Where The Paw Meets The Earth:** Dirt trails and sand roads
> **Workout For Your Dog** - Level terrain throughout
> **Swimming** - Broad Creek and the Nanticoke River are slow-moving and ideal for water-loving dogs
> **Restrictions On Dogs** - None

Something Extra
The chance to see bald eagles - the Nanticoke watershed sports the highest concentration of bald eagles in the northeastern United States. The great birds favor massive nests in the treetops on the edges of the water.

Norman Wilder Wildlife Area

Phone - None
Website - None
Admission Fee - None
Directions - *Dover, Kent County; southwest of the capital. Turn right off Route 13 at Canterbury onto Road 32. Go through the village of Viola and continue straight on Road 108. At a T-instersection, turn right. Parking is in designated areas along the roads, the first at a maintenance area about a half-mile on the right.*

The Park
The former Petersburg Wildlife Area was re-named for Norman G. Wilder, who embarked on a 56-year conservation career after a four-year stint in the Army in the South Pacific in World War II. A graduate of the University of Connecticut, Wilder was named director of the Delaware Game and Fish Commission in 1948.

The Walks
Your canine hiking adventure in Norman G. Wilder Wildlife Area will take place along some 16 miles of fire roads through dense forest and swampland. These roads range from mossy grass to gravelly dirt but all are level and exceedingly easy for your dog to trot. Although you won't notice it, there is enough elevation change here to divide the watersheds of the Chesapeake and Delaware bays.

> **Where The Paw Meets The Earth:** Wooded dirt trails
> **Workout For Your Dog** - Easy hiking all around
> **Swimming** - Barely, in the occasional ditch
> **Restrictions On Dogs** - None

Something Extra
When the leaves are off the trees you can scan the high branches of the towering oaks in the Wilder Wildlife Area for glimpses of American mistletoe. Identified nearly 2000 years ago, Anglo Saxons named the plant "mistle-tan" meaning "dung twig" after bird droppings on a branch. It was thought the plant's existence was entwined with birds but it is actually a parasitic plant that is also known as the Vampire Plant. The mistletoe sends out a root-like structure into the bark of hardwood trees and extracts all its nutrients from its host. The mistletoe's mooching won't kill the oak - if the host dies, it dies. You can recognize mistletoe by its clumps of 2-inch greenish-yellow leaves and clusters of white berries. The tradition of kissing under a sprig of mistletoe dates back hundreds of years. The proper procedure is to pick one berry off the plant for every kiss received. When the berries are gone, so are the kisses. Make sure you dispose of the berries after you're through bussing - they are toxic to dogs and people.

Port Penn Wetlands Trail

Phone - (302) 834.7941
Website - http://www.destateparks.com/wilmsp/wilmsp.htm
Admission Fee - None
Directions - *Port Penn, New Castle County; on Route 9 at the corner of Liberty and Market streets. You can also park in the Augustine Wildlife Area, up Congress Street, at the middle of the Wetlands Trail.*

The Park
Port Penn was named after William Penn when he stopped for a drink of water in either 1682 or 1699. Now, that's star power! For the watermen who toiled along the coast here life pulsed to a regular rhythm: hunting waterfowl in the fall, trapping muskrat in the winter, harvesting the shad runs in spring and fishing for sturgeon in the summer. The *Wetlands Trail* takes you into the heart of this maritime heritage.

The Walks
The *Wetlands Trail* covers 1.5 miles from the trailhead at the Port Penn Interpretive Center. The vistas of the Thousand Island Marsh and the Delaware River are stunning but too many stretches of the trail usher you into green tunnels of close-growing trees and exuberant marsh grasses where you can't see anything. Spurs to observation decks are worth the trip. Under paw the trail is mostly grass but at the end, follow the road back to the Interpretive Center and do not follow the trail across the marsh to the footbridge - the mowers have left the stalks of the reeds that are waiting to impale your dog's paws.

> **Where The Paw Meets The Earth:** Grass and gravel road
> **Workout For Your Dog** - More of a stroll
> **Swimming** - The shorelines here are not for swimming
> **Restrictions On Dogs** - None

Something Extra
There is also the chance to take a half-mile *Village Walk* through Port Penn where several structures date to pre-Revolution times. The Interpretive Center itself began life as a schoolhouse and then served time as a bait shop.

Prime Hook National Wildlife Refuge

Phone - (302) 684.8419
Website - http://www.fws.gov/northeast/primehook/
Admission Fee - None
Directions - *Milton, Sussex County; located 12 miles southeast of Milford and 10 miles northwest of Lewes. Take Route 16 off Delaware 1 for one mile. Turn left into the refuge on Turkle Pond Road.*

The Park
When Dutch settlers first pushed onto these shores nearly 400 years ago they discovered an abundance of purple beach plums and named that area *Priume Hoek*, meaning "Plum Point." In 1963, the United States Fish & Wildlife Service created the refuge to protect more than 10,000 acres of fresh and saltwater wetlands from Slaughter Beach to the Broadkill River.

The Walks
Prime Hook features four walking trails that visit fields, forest and marshlands. All four, located off the main road, can be completed comfortably in an afternoon's visit. The *Pine Grove Trail* follows a serpentine path between Turkle and Fleetwood ponds. The trail is just under one mile long. Up the road is the *Black Farm Trail* that skirts wooded uplands and marshes as it travels around former farm fields. A trail extension leads to a photography blind. This is flat, easy canine hiking. At the park office are two adjoining walks that explore a freshwater marsh. The *Dike Trail* travels atop the spoil from the digging of the Headquarters Ditch straight out for a half-mile and the *Boardwalk Trail* slips across the water after passing by the Morris family cemetery, where eight family members are buried.

> **Where The Paw Meets The Earth:** Soft pine straw-and-leaf surface beneath mature loblolly pines is extremely easy on the paw.
> **Workout For Your Dog** - Easy going throughout
> **Swimming** - Broadkill Beach at Prime Hook is a fantastic place to take your dog for a swim
> **Restrictions On Dogs** - None

Something Extra
The mixed pine-hardwood forest at the edges of the Prime Hook marshes is ideal habitat for the Delmarva Peninsula fox squirrel, an endangered species of mammal since 1967. The largest of the 10 varieties of local tree squirrels, the reclusive creature is hard to spot even though it grows to over two feet long. Look for a flash of white belly and large bushy tail with black edge stripes in tree cavities or scampering along the ground of the open forest - unlike its more agile cousins it doesn't jump from tree to tree.

Redden State Forest

Phone - (302) 856.2893
Website - http://state.de.us/deptagri/forestry/forest.shtml
Admission Fee - None
Directions - *Georgetown, Sussex County; three miles north on East Redden Road, 1/2 mile off of Route 113.*

The Park

The Redden State Forest is Delaware's largest, embracing 9,500 acres in 14 separate tracts of land across central Sussex County in the heart of the state's loblolly pine country. Redden also protects large swaths of wooded wetlands characterized by thriving stands of bottomland hardwoods, including red maple, sweetgum, and mixed oaks. State forest lands are open to hunting during the fall and winter hunting seasons so check ahead for restrictions.

The Walks

While there are 44 miles of trails - mostly unpaved access roads - in the 14 tracts of Redden State Forest, the only destination for canine hikers is the Headquarters Tract. Here you can sample the forest on an interpretive *Educational Trail*, a nature loop that kicks off opposite the park office, housed in an historic carriage house. This flat, sandy footpath can hold water after heavy rains. Hardy canine hikers can set off on an easy-to-walk, 5-mile *Headquarters Loop Trail*, mostly on access roads.

> **Where The Paw Meets The Earth:** Dirt roads and trails
> **Workout For Your Dog** - Some good climbs; mostly across the creek
> **Swimming** - There are ditches and an occasional pond, good for cooling off but your dog can leave his swimming trunks home when coming here
> **Restrictions On Dogs** - None

Something Extra

The centerpiece of the Redden State Forest is the historic Redden Lodge, built in the early 1900s by the Pennsylvania Railroad as a hunting retreat for company executives. The graceful wood-shake building was placed on the National Register of Historic Places in 1980 and was completely renovated in 1995.

Rittenhouse Park

Phone - None
Website - None
Admission Fee - None
Directions - *Newark, New Castle County; adjacent to Route 4 across from the Chrysler plant. The entrance is on West Chestnut Hill off of Route 896.*

The Park

Rittenhouse Park is a small 45-acre nature area administered by the city of Newark. It would be of little interest to canine hikes beyond being a pleasant picnic park save for the segment of the *Mason-Dixon Trail* that runs through the property. The 190-mile long *Mason-Dixon Trail* starts at Whiskey Springs, on the *Appalachian Trail*, in Cumberland County, PA and dips into Delaware before continuing to its eastern terminus at Chadds Ford on the banks of the Brandywine River.

The Walks

Wooded Rittenhouse Park has its own small trail system that works up a hillside but these unmaintained paths are rocky under paw and not rewarding. Instead, stick to the *Mason-Dixon Trail* that hugs the shoreline of the Christina Creek. The ramble through the park is scenic and pleasant but soon deteriorates - both visually and aromatically - as you reach industrial areas, railroad tracks and busy roadways. A satisfying turn-around point on this linear trail is the residential road about a mile into the hike. The adventure begins beyond this bridge. The trail bounds up and down, becomes deep sand in stretches, crosses over water on makeshift bridges and, if the water isn't high, under overpasses. Don't be surprised if your dog sniffs out a feral cat or two. This part of the *Mason-Dixon Trail* ends at Elkton Road.

> **Where The Paw Meets The Earth:** Dirt paths
> **Workout For Your Dog** - A long but not strenuous hike for your dog
> **Swimming** - The entire hike is along the Christina Creek that sometimes pools deep enough for a doggie dip
> **Restrictions On Dogs** - None

Something Extra

The Christina Creek is one of six designated New Castle County trout streams - if you want to bring your dog along on a fishing expedition.

Rockford Park

Phone - (302) 577.7020
Website - http://www.destateparks.com/wilmsp/wilmsp.htm
Admission Fee - None
Directions - *Wilmington, New Castle County; the entrances to the park are at 19th Street and Tower Road and Riverview Avenue and Red Oak Road.*

The Park

Rockford Park dates to 1889, when there were still fears of visitors being harmed by explosions in the DuPont Company black powder yards down the street. William Poole Bancroft began his life-long efforts to preserve open space in the Brandywine Valley here, with a gift of 59 acres. Today the park comprises 104 acres.

The Walks

The main walk at Rockford Park is along the circular road through the property but there are narrow, informal trails in the woods that run in parallel terraces around the steep hill, including one on an old rail bed. You can sculpt a canine hike by circling the road up top and introduce a hill by descending "Sledding Hill." You can also hike through the woods down to the Brandywine River. Other options include the connecting path to Brandywine Park or across the river to Alapocas Woods, providing the gate is open.

> **Where The Paw Meets The Earth:** Paved roads and dirt wood paths
> **Workout For Your Dog** - Absolutely if you head for the river
> **Swimming** - There is no water in the park unless you make your way down to the Brandywine River at the bottom of the hill
> **Restrictions On Dogs** - None

Something Extra

Rockford Park is home to one of the city's most cherished and recognized landmarks - the 115-foot Rockford Tower. The Italian Renaissance Revival style tower, designed by Theodore Leisen, engineer for the Wilmington Board of Park Commissioners, was built on what was called Mt. Salem Hill, the highest point in the city at 330 feet above sea level and completed in 1902. The beautiful natural field stone tower encloses a steel water tank holding 500,000 gallons of water. The Observatory at the top was once a popular tourist destination but closed during repairs in 1972. For the tower's centennial in 2002 the Observatory re-opened and visitors can once again climb the 132 steps to the top weekends from May to October.

St. Jones Reserve

Phone - (302) 739.3436
Website - None
Admission Fee - None
Directions - *Dover, Kent County; located on Kitts Hummock Road off US 113 or Route 9, south of Dover, 1/2 mile past the John Dickinson Plantation.*

The Park

This land was purchased in 1740 when Samuel Dickinson, a wealthy Quaker tobacco planter and merchant in Maryland moved his family to the Jones Neck in the home they called Poplar Hall. His son John was eight years old and would live here until he was 18 before going on to fame as a philosopher in the cause for liberty. Although opposed to open warfare with England, Dickinson donned a uniform in his mid-forties and fought on the side of the Revolutionaries. John Dickinson would come to own six plantations along the St. Jones River before his death in 1808. Part of that land in now the St. Jones Reserve, part of the Delaware National Estuarine Research Reserve, one of only 25 in the United States.

The Walks

There is a one-mile trail that leads from the reserve to Kingston Upon-Hull, a five-bay rectangular wood-and-brick home that dates to 1730. The trail begins with a boardwalk passage through lush marsh grasses that even poke through the slots of wood. The grass pathway then skirts the saltwater marsh before entering a small woodland and finishing through cultivated fields on an old farm road. Estuary Expedition Backpacks are available during Visitor Center hours. These include trail guides, field guides, binoculars, and bird checklists to enhance your canine hike through the wetlands.

> **Where The Paw Meets The Earth:** Dirt paths and boardwalk
> **Workout For Your Dog** - Easy canine hiking all over
> **Swimming** - A dry day for your dog
> **Restrictions On Dogs** - None

Something Extra

This walk is on the edge of the Dover Air Force Base and you are likely to get close-up looks of some of the world's largest aircraft sharing the skies with bald eagles, peregrine falcons, ospreys and Northern harriers.

Silver Lake Recreation Area

Phone - (302) 736.7050
Website - None
Admission Fee - None
Directions - *Dover, in center of the city, Kent County. From Delaware 1, use Exit 98, North Little Creek Road (Route 8). The road becomes Division Street as it crosses Route 13. Cross the water and make a right on State Street. Turn right on Washington Street and continue to the Silver Lake parking area.*

The Park
The St. Jones River meanders through Dover's legislative center and is the focal point for the park. In the 1880s, the St. Jones was famous for its lotus lillies, found only in the Nile River and one other location in the world. Legend has it that a dredging crew in the river in 1887 unearthed a ship of Egyptian design, explaining the presence of the lillies and stirring images of ancient civilizations in Delaware long before Columbus in 1492. Sadly, when the St. Jones was straightened to improve navigation after World War I, the increased salinity in the river killed the flowers. The St. Jones was dammed here and bulges out to form Silver Lake. Lumber and grist mills thrived here as far back as the 1780s and when William M. Shakespeare milled here his oak lumber was a leading material for shipbuilding during the Civil War. The last flour mills closed during the Depression and were torn down in 1944.

The Walks
Paved pathways traverse the 182 acres of open space and hardwood/holly woods along through Silver Lake Park. These trails snake back and forth across the water and extend deeper into the city if you choose to cross the roadways.
> **Where The Paw Meets The Earth:** Paved paths
> **Workout For Your Dog** - Easily traversed paths
> **Swimming** - If the park is not busy, this can be a wonderful place for doggie aquatics.
> **Restrictions On Dogs** - None

Something Extra
A fish ladder has been constructed at the dam that enables visitors to watch close-up as fish pass around the barrier by swimming and leaping up a series of relatively low steps. The fish ladder at Silver Lake is an Alaska Steeppass, based on an original design developed in 1909 by a Belgian scientist, G. Denil, but it has been adjusted and adapted in many ways since then. This type of modular prefabricated fishway was used extensively in remote areas of Alaska.

Taber State Forest

Phone - (302) 698.4500
Website - http://state.de.us/deptagri/forestry/forest.shtml
Admission Fee - None
Directions - *Harrington, Kent County; 12 miles to the southwest. Take Route 14 West into Maryland and make the first left on Burrsville Road that will bring you back into Delaware and down to the park office on the right at 1953 Burrsville Road.*

The Park

Taber State Forest is the smallest of Delaware's three state forests, a bit more than 1,200 acres. It is the only one of the trio contained completely on a single tract of land. Taber State Forest is managed for recreation, wildlife conservation and timber production. The primary tree types found here are loblolly pines and mixed upland hardwood forest.

The Walks

Although a state forest, much of the canine hiking here is in wide open fields. Even the fire roads you are walking on are wide enough to give the hikes an airy feel. The terrain is flat throughout and easy going for any dog.

> **Where The Paw Meets The Earth:** Dirt farm roads and trails
> **Workout For Your Dog** - Easy, level going
> **Swimming** - There are creeks flowing through the property but more for splashing than swimming
> **Restrictions On Dogs** - None

Something Extra

Solitude. This is probably the most remote public hiking location in Delaware.

Ted Harvey Conservation Area

Phone - (302) 739.5297
Website - None
Admission Fee - None
Directions - *Dover, Kent County; southwest on Kitts Hummock Road. From Route 1/Route 113, make a left onto Kitts Hummock Road. Go two miles and turn into the refuge at the sign.*

The Park
This land was the site of Kent County's first European settlement, a 1670 land-grant known as "Kingston Upon-Hull." Owners included the family of Caesar Rodney's mother and John Dickinson, "the Penman of the Revolution." The agricultural lands bordered by the St. Jones River and Delaware Bay were once regarded among the richest in all of the original 13 colonies. The 2,016 acres of woodlots, wetlands and fields are today preserved in the Ted Harvey Conservation Area.

The Walks
The canine hiking here is along gravel and dirt access roads, impoundment dykes and sandy bayshore. There are some nine miles of these trails in essentially one large loop with a short cut across the middle. So any canine hiking adventure in Ted Harvey Conservation Area will last at least an hour. Setting out from the parking area you'll hike along some shady lanes but as you reach the wetlands your dog will be exposed to the full brunt of the sun on hot days for a large part of this walk - bring plenty of drinking water.

> **Where The Paw Meets The Earth:** Dirt roads and sandy beach
> **Workout For Your Dog** - Easy canine hiking all over
> **Swimming** - The trail takes in a big chunk of Delaware Bay shoreline and the waters are gentle enough to entice any dog in for a swim.
> **Restrictions On Dogs** - None

Something Extra
The wild turkey is among the wiliest of game birds, so revered for its wits by Benjamin Franklin that he advocated it for the nation's symbol above the bald eagle. Delaware's estimated population of wild turkey is only 3,000 - fewer than any other state other than Nevada. One place to spot a wild turkey is in the Ted Harvey Conservation Area; an observation/photography blind is located at the north end of the bayshore portion of the trail.

Tidbury Creek Park

Phone - None
Website - None
Admission Fee - None
Directions - *Camden, Kent County; east of town, go south of Route 10, on US113A/Delaware 10A. The park is on the left, a short distance after the intersection with Lebanon Road.*

The Park
Tidbury Creek in the St. Jones watershed has long been a hub of commerce in central Delaware. The waterway supported a shipping industry and a bustling cannery, said to be the nation's largest, packed peaches and tomatoes from the area in the late 1800s. Today, Tidbury Creek Park is part of the Kent County park system.

The Walks
This is the kind of slightly scruffy park with unmaintained trails that is a magnet for dog owners. As a rule of thumb, the less manicured the park, the more welcoming it is to dogs. But in the case of Tidbury Creek Park, it retains a scenic appeal while tredding the ungroomed paths. There is enough elevation change in the park to once require a stairway of 20 steps to move from a lower trail to an upper trail. These hard dirt trails circle a central picnic pavilion through a mixed pine and hardwood forest. Watch for glass that can cut a paw pad as you move atop the ridges. The trails drop down to an open field that ideal for a romp with your dog.
> **Where The Paw Meets The Earth:** Wooded dirt trails and grass
> **Workout For Your Dog** - Easy with some tiny slopes
> **Swimming** - Some of the best around when fishermen aren't here
> **Restrictions On Dogs** - None

Something Extra
Tidbury Creek Park has two warm season fresh-water fishing ponds, stocked with trout in March. If there are no fishermen pursuing their daily limit of six, this is one of the best canine swimming holes in Delaware.

Trap Pond State Park

Phone - (302) 875-5153
Website - http://www.destateparks.com/tpsp/tpsp.htm
Admission Fee - Yes, May to October
Directions - *Laurel, Sussex County; 5 miles east, off Route 24 between Route 13 and Route 113. The park is one mile south on Trap Pond Road (Road 449).*

The Park

Trap Pond is a small portion of the Great Cypress Swamp and features one of the northernmost natural stands of baldcypress trees in North America. In the late 1700s a millpond was constructed to power a sawmill to harvest the valuable lumber. During the Depression in the 1930s, the Civilian Conservation Corps of the federal government put men to work building diverse recreation facilities. In 1951, 14 years after the Delaware legislature authorized the development of the state park system, Trap Pond became the first state park to welcome visitors.

The Walks

The 5-mile long *Boundary Trail* completely circles both the 90-acre millpond and the baldcypress swamp. There is a mixture of natural and paved surfaces and the flat trail is very easy to walk. Note that to complete the loop requires a short walk on Little Hill Road. For canine hikers not interested in a complete circumnavigation of Trap Pond there are short one-mile trails on opposite shores. The *Island Trail* on the western shore visits the shoreline and actually onto one of the namesake islands in the pond before leading back into the forest. On the opposite shore the *Cypress Point Trail* meanders along the edge of the swamp.

> **Where The Paw Meets The Earth:** Natural trails and dirt roads
> **Workout For Your Dog** - Minimal elevation changes
> **Swimming** - The best access is from a wooden dock on the south shore
> **Restrictions On Dogs** - None

Something Extra

Hiking through Trap Pond State Park is an experience like no other in Delaware - your walk in the atmospheric swamp could easily be in the Louisiana bayou. Marvel in the quiet beauty of the baldcypress - one of the few trees capable of living in the water. Each tree sends out small stumps known as "knees" in every direction to help keep from drowning. The boardwalks on the *Cypress Point Trail* enable you and your dog to get close up views.

Valley Garden Park

Phone - None
Website - None
Admission Fee - None
Directions - *Greenville, New Castle County; on Campbell Road (Route 82) between Kennett Pike (Route 52) and Hoopes Reservoir.*

The Park
Valley Garden park was a gift to the people of Delaware from Emily du Pont. It is a little gem, hidden away in the chateau country of northern Delaware. A stream winds its way down a valley to Hoopes Reservoir, and along this stream, verged with rocks of many colors, are planted trees and plants that each in their turn fill all the seasons with color and sweet smell.

The Walks
The main walking trail is a simple 10-minute loop around the tumbling brook. You can also explore the upper regions of the park with its peaceful fields and small stands of woods.
>**Where The Paw Meets The Earth:** Macadam and dirt/grass
>**Workout For Your Dog** - Easy climbs on the park slopes
>**Swimming** - None
>**Restrictions On Dogs** - None

Something Extra
If you are looking for a place to picnic with your dog, this is it.

White Clay Creek State Park

Phone - (302) 368.6900
Website - http://www.destateparks.com/wccsp/index.asp
Admission Fee - Yes, May to October
Directions - *Newark, New Castle County; the main parking lot is in the Walter Carpenter, Jr. Recreation Area on New London Road (Route 896), three miles northwest of Newark. Parking is also available on Hopkins Road at the Chambers House Nature Center, on Chamber Rock Road and the end of Thompson Station Road at the Park Office. Possum Hill is located off Paper Mill Road (Route 72) between Polly Drummond Road and Possum Park Road. The Judge Morris Estate is on Polly Drummond Road.*

The Park

William Penn bought most of this land in 1683 from Lenni Lenape Chief Kekelappen, who was believed to have lived here in Opasis-kunk, the most important of the region's "Indian Towns." In 1968 White Clay Creek began life as a state park with 24 state-purchased acres of land. In 1984 the DuPont Company donated the land that would be the foundation for today's park of 3,384 acres with another 1,253 adjoining acres across the state line in Pennsylvania.

The Walks

Take your pick from almost 40 miles of pristine trails. The *Penndel Trail* that connects the Pennsylvania and Delaware parks would win Best in Show for linear trails and the loops here are the best in the state. The 3-mile hardwood forest ramble in the Judge Morris Estate, the *Long Loop* at Possum Hill and the scenic 5-mile *Twin Valley Loop* at Carpenter Recreation area are all standouts.

> **Where The Paw Meets The Earth:** Paw-friendly dirt and grass
> **Workout For Your Dog** - Anytime you leave the White Clay Creek you'll get your share of hills
> **Swimming** - Yes, the Millstone Pond is as good as it gets and of course White Clay Creek
> **Restrictions On Dogs** - None

Something Extra

The *Twin Valley Trail* swings past the Arc Corner Monument marking one end of the 12-mile arc that forms the Pennsylvania-Delaware state line, unique in American political boundary making. The circular divide dates to William Penn's directive of August 28, 1701. A half-mile to the west there is a monument marking the tri-state junction of Delaware, Pennsylvania and Maryland. In Possum Hill you find a marker for the basepoint of the Mason-Dixon Line, the most famous surveying project in American history.

Woodlawn Trustees Property

Phone - None
Website - None
Admission Fee - None
Directions - *Talleyville, New Castle County; there are no highway signs to direct you here and the parking lots are not marked. The main parking lot is opposite Peters Rock along the Brandywine on Creek Road. Other gravel lots can be found on Ramsey Road, Beaver Valley Road and opposite Woodlawn Road on Thompson's Bridge Road (Route 92). Parking also in Brandywine Commons on Route 202.*

The Park
From 1850 until 1910, feldspar, used in porcelain dishes and false teeth, was mined here in the Woodlawn Quarry. You can still see the remains of these spar pits, with their scatterings of mica and other minerals. In 1910, as his campaign to preserve the Brandywine Valley intensified, William Poole Bancroft bought hundreds of pristine acres in the lush floodplain and rolling woodlands where the Brandywine Creek makes three wide, gentle turns. Bancroft formed the Woodlawn Company to manage these lands, harboring some of the oldest trees in Delaware. Today, more than 2,000 acres are open to the public for recreational use - one of the greatest private gifts to canine hikers to be found anywhere.

The Walks
Many miles and many hours of canine hiking through an enticing mix of open fields and mature forests. Can also continue into Pennsylvania through active farms and long-gone homesteads. Watch for horses and bikes. No maps or navigational aids so come with a mind to explore.
> **Where The Paw Meets The Earth:** Mostly dirt; some old farm roads
> **Workout For Your Dog** - Hilly terrain
> **Swimming** - The Brandywine Creek is wonderful
> **Restrictions On Dogs** - None

Something Extra
Breaking out of the woods at several points on the hilltops you are greeted with splendid views of Granogue, one of the American castles dotting the Brandywine Valley's chateau lands.

MARYLAND

Agricultural History Farm Park

Phone - (301) 495-2503
Website - http://www.mc-mncppc.org/parks/facilities/ag_farm.shtm
Admission Fee - None
Directions - *Derwood, Montgomery County; from Muncaster Mill Road (MD 115) take Muncaster Road north to the park entrance on the left.*

The Park
The Agriculture History Farm exists to remind Marylanders of their agricultural heritage and to depict present-day farm life. Seventy acres of the 410-acre park have been set aside as a rural history museum and other parts of the park have been created as demonstration gardens and fields.

The Walks
This is a sprawling countryside trail system that kicks off in big hills at the back of the park. Up the hill to the right will lead to the *Belgian Loop* around crop fields - don't spend time looking for a traditional band of trail as your dog will be bounding across open grass fields like a real farm dog. In the other direction is the more traditional *Percheron Trail* that skips through the Pope Farm Nursery where trees, shrubs and ornamental plants are propigated for use across Montgomery County's 30,000 acres of parkland. The 1.4-mile natural surface path crosses Rock Creek and its tributaries several times before dead-ending in a neighborhood. A diverting 1.2-mile option is the wooded *Mule Skinner Loop* off the Percheron hike.

> **Where The Paw Meets The Earth:** Mostly paw-friendly grass
> **Workout For Your Dog** - Big rolling hills
> **Swimming** - This is not a dog-paddler's park
> **Restrictions On Dogs** - None

Something Extra
Montgomery County played an important role in the Underground Railroad with many safe houses established for escaping slaves traveling north to freedom. Later Quaker communities helped establish free black farms such as the cluster that existed here, known as Newmantown. You can study the site that contained three houses on 35 acres.

American Chestnut Land Trust

Phone - None
Website - http://www.acltweb.org/index.cfm
Admission Fee - None
Directions - *Prince Frederick, Calvert County; For **Gravatt Tract**: Go 4 miles south on MD 2/4 from the intersection of MD 231 in town; left on Parkers Creek Road, cross MD 765 and then turn right onto Scientists' Cliffs Road; drive .8 miles to the ACLT parking lot on the left. For **Double Oak Farm**: Go two miles east on Dares Beach Road from the light on MD 2/4 in Prince Frederick. Turn right onto Double Oak Road and drive one mile. Turn left onto the lane across from open field, past house to designated parking.*

The Park
In 1986 local landowners banded together to protect their community from approaching development. Largely by digging deep into their own pockets, they put together $500,000 to help purchase two threatened tracts of land totaling 441 acres. Subsequent acquisitions have pushed the trust holdings to 810 acres. The mandate for the organization has expanded to the protection of open space around Parkers Creek - the last undeveloped creek on the western shore of the Chesapeake Bay - and they manage another 1,770 acres.

The Walks
These natural, hiker-only trails are sure to set any dog's tail to wagging. If you only have time for a visit to one of the two hiking tracts serious canine hikers and water-loving dogs will favor the steep hills and trails along Parkers Creek of the Double Oak Farm Tract. The trail of choice for most will be the three-mile *Parkers Creek Loop* but the adventurous may want to test the out-and-back Goldstein Bay Farm Trail. Expect patches of unsure footing under paw and steep hills on this three-mile round trip. The Gravatt Tract features three distinct loops. The Ridge Loop and sections of the *Stream Loop* (it no longer loops thanks to an active beaver community) visit wetlands and old homesteads. The *Laurel Loop* is an early-summer delight with a rich mountain laurel understory and the *East Loop* is a chance to experience a mature oak-hickory forest, decades in development ahead of its neighbors regenerating after centuries in cultivation. Each of the loops can be completed in under an hour.

> **Where The Paw Meets The Earth:** Natural surface
> **Workout For Your Dog** - Mostly easy going
> **Swimming** - Parkers Creek is available for dedicated dog paddlers
> **Restrictions On Dogs** - None

Something Extra
The trust's namesake chestnut tree, once the largest remaining in Maryland, has recently fallen but can still be seen.

Antietam National Battlefield

Phone - (301) 432-5124
Website - http://www.nps.gov/anti/
Admission Fee - Yes, good for 7 days
Directions - *Sharpsburg, Washington County; from I-70 exit onto MD 65 South (Exit 29/29A). Go ten miles to the Visitor Center.*

The Park

On September 17, 1862, Robert E. Lee's first attempt to invade the North came to a climax. After his smashing victory at the First Battle of Bull Run in August, Lee marched his army of 41,000 Southerners against George McClellan's 87,000-man Army of the Potomac. When silence fell again across the field, it had become "The Bloodiest Day of the Civil War." Federal losses were 12,410, Confederate losses 10,700. The fighting was indecisive, but Lee's initial foray into the North was over. Great Britain now hesitated to recognize the new Confederate government and President Abraham Lincoln had the opportunity he needed to issue the Emancipation Proclamation, freeing all slaves in the states in rebellion.

The Walks

The 8.5-mile interpretive driving tour of the battlefield is one-way so it is really too far to do on foot with your dog but there are plenty of places to park and get out to explore, including the solemn "Bloody Lane" - an old sunken road separating area farms where the dead and wounded piled two to five feet deep in the dirt. One place that demands to be explored on foot is the Burnside Bridge, southeast of Sharpsburg where a Rebel force of 450 held off an approaching army of 12,500. At the Burnside Bridge you can access the *Snavely Ford Trail*, a 2.5-mile footpath that traces the creek around open fields. In addition to being a pleasant canine hiking loop, the trail conveys the agrarian feel of the area when two armies clashed here.

> **Where The Paw Meets The Earth:** Dirt and pavement on the park roads
> **Workout For Your Dog** - Some small hills
> **Swimming** - There is some relief for dogs in Antietam Creek on a hot day
> **Restrictions On Dogs** - None

Something Extra

The battle is commemorated during the Sharpsburg Heritage Festival on the September weekend closest to the Antietam anniversary. In December 23,110 candles in bags are set out along the driving route of the battlefield to honor the soldiers who fell here.

Appalachian Trail

Phone - None
Website - http://www.dnr.state.md.us/publiclands/at.html
Admission Fee - None
Directions - *Middletown, Frederick County; access from Route 40 parking lot east of Greenbrier State Park or in various parks: Gathland State Park or Harpers Ferry National Historic Park.*

The Park
Visionaries began talking about a footpath that would follow the crest of the Appalachian Mountains nearly the length of the East Coast back in the early 1900s. Based on proposals from Massachusetts regional planner Benton MacKaye the dream began to become a reality in 1921. Over the next two decades the *Appalachian Trail* was constructed and marked by volunteer hiking clubs.

The Walks
Maryland contains 40 miles of the *Appalachian Trail*, all but two of which travel along the crest of South Mountain. You could complete the state crossing in an energetic weekend with your dog, although most canine hikers opt for day hikes, either out-and-back jaunts or via car shuttle. Elevations range from 250 feet at the Potomac River to a less-than lofty 1,900 feet at High Rock. With a series of parks and the parking lot on Route 40 taking the *Appalachian Trail* in chunks is an easy thing to do. Popular destinations include Annapolis Rocks, about one hour north of Route 40 and Washington Monument about 90 minutes to the south. Both provide long views across the surrounding valleys with only a modest purchase.

> **Where The Paw Meets The Earth:** Rocky pathes and old roads
> **Workout For Your Dog** - Yes, this is the *Appalachian Trail*
> **Swimming** - None
> **Restrictions On Dogs** - None

Something Extra
While you bound across South Mountain today it is easy to forget that the tough quartzite ridge was once a formidable wall for early Americans, boxing settlers in until 1755 when a young surveyor named George Washington helped push a road through a mountain pass. A century later Robert E. Lee used the natural barrier as a screen in his first invasion of the North during the Civil War. On September 14, 1862 his troops defended the South Mountain passes against George McClellan's pursuing Army of the Potomac setting up the climactic Battle of Antietam three days later.

Assateague National Seashore

Phone - (301) 874-2024
Website - http://www.nps.gov/asis
Admission Fee - Yes, good for 7 days
Directions - *Berlin, Worcester County; north entrance is at the end of MD 611, eight miles south of Ocean City. When coming on to the island turn right and avoid going straight into the state park. No dogs allowed there.*

The Park

The first European settlers - a band of four men - came to Assateague in 1688. At times more than 200 people survived on the shifting sands, fishing or clamming or growing what crops they could. In 1833 the first lighthouse was built but ships still ran aground, including the Dispatch, the official yacht of five American presidents. The cruiser was ruined beyond repair when it reached the shore unscheduled on October 10, 1891. Assateague was connected to the mainland until 1933 when an August hurricane tore open an inlet to the Sinepuxent Bay that now separates Assateague from Ocean City. A bridge to the mainland opened in 1962 and in 1965 Assateague Island became a national seashore.

The Walks

Dogs are not allowed on the three short channel-side nature trails and can not go on lifeguarded beaches but that leaves miles of wide, sandy beaches to hike on with your dog any time of the year. Drive to the furthest parking lot from the entrance gate and head up the boardwalk across the dunes. Make a right and ahead of you will stretch hours of unspoiled canine hiking in the surf and sand. Although the national seashore is within a few hours' drive of tens of million of Americans don't be surprised if you have most of this beach to yourself and your dog - especially in the off-season.

> **Where The Paw Meets The Earth:** Sand
> **Workout For Your Dog** - Yes, hiking in sand is tough
> **Swimming** - Absolutely - but pack your own sticks for the dog; not much driftwood stays on the beach
> **Restrictions On Dogs** - Yes in campground but no on the nature trails

Something Extra

Assateague Island is the famous home of the free-roaming "Chincoteague Ponies," a present-day reminder of Assateague Island's past. Although no one is certain when or how the ponies first arrived on the island, a popular legend tells of ponies that escaped a shipwrecked Spanish galleon and swam ashore. However, most historians believe that settlers used the island for grazing livestock (including ponies and other farm animals) in the 17th Century to avoid fencing regulations and taxation. The ponies rule the island and you can see them on the roads or even meet them in the surf.

Baltimore & Annapolis Trail

Phone - (410) 222-6244
Website - http://www.dnr.state.md.us/greenways/b&a_trail.html
Admission Fee - None
Directions - *Glen Burnie to Annapolis, Anne Arundel County; park headquarters are located at the 7.0 mile marker where the trail crosses Earleigh Heights Road.*

The Park
When the first steam train chugged out of Annapolis on the original Annapolis & Baltimore Short Line railroad in 1887 the track traversed woodlands and farm fields. The railroad quickly spawned towns along its route and at its peak 1.75 million people climbed aboard its passenger trains each year. When service was discontinued in 1968 the pattern of development was firmly entrenched. Today, one of every three dogs in Anne Arundel County lives within one mile of the Baltimore & Annapolis Trail Park. Since opening in 1985, the *Baltimore & Annapolis Trail* has been a model in the rails-to-trails movement, hosting an estimated one million users per year. The B&A is the 7th most heavily used rail-trail of more than 1000 such hikes across America.

The Walks
The old rails have been converted into an asphalt ribbon ten feet wide, often with a grassy shoulder to step away from traffic. Dog walkers will be dodging joggers, cyclists, rollerbladers, strollers, equestrians and anything else man can dream of to put on wheels. Despite its heavy use, the *Baltimore & Annapolis Trail* is meticulously maintained by over 400 volunteer caretakers. More than 70 flowerbeds are strung like jewels along the route, which never exceeds a 1% grade.

> **Where The Paw Meets The Earth:** Asphalt
> **Workout For Your Dog** - Easy going anywhere you jump on
> **Swimming** - None
> **Restrictions On Dogs** - None

Something Extra
Near the 10-mile mark the *Baltimore & Annapolis Trail* crosses over Marley Creek where once stood a 140-foot railroad bridge that was washed away during Hurricane Agnes in 1972. Trail planners unearthed an historic highway bridge in Missouri to breech the creek but as it was being lifted into place on the trail in 1989, it crumbled. The present bridge is a hastily-built replacement.

BWI Trail

Phone - (410) 222-6244
Website - http://www.dnr.state.md.us/greenways/bwi_trail.html
Admission Fee - None
Directions - *Linthicum, Anne Arundel County; trail access and parking can be found on Andover Road on the north side of the trail and Dorsey Road (MD 176) on the south.*

The Park
The BWI Airport is the only commercial airport in the United States to offer visitors a recreational hiker/biker trail. Portions of the trail, most of which sit on airport property, have been opening since 1994. The 12.5-mile trail encircles the airport and is patrolled by Anne Arundel County.

The Walks
This is quite likely the noisiest dog walk you will ever take - airplanes, car traffic, trains. But after awhile it all fades into white noise and becomes part of the experience of this unique trail. That said, there are pastoral refuges along the route including woodlands, pine groves and even a horse farm.For canine hikers the *BWI Trail* has several advantages over its rail-to-trail neighbors. Since it isn't constrained by a right-of-way, there is more grassy room on the shoulders for relief from the pounding of paw on asphalt (the trail is paved the entire way save for wooden boardwalks through wetlands); the trail was designed in a pleasing serpentine fashion; and there is a nice sprinkling of hills along the way. And, although few canine hikers are likely to care, the trail is a complete loop rather than an out-and back. No matter how you plan to use the *BWI Trail*, take along drinking water for your dog as it is scarce along the path.

> **Where The Paw Meets The Earth:** Macadam
> **Workout For Your Dog** - A few quick climbs along the way
> **Swimming** - None
> **Restrictions On Dogs** - None

Something Extra
The planes of course. The Thomas A.Dixon Jr. Aircraft Observation Area provides an ideal spot to watch the planes land directly in front of you. You won't be able to see the rubber hit the ground here but you can see it from other spots along the trail. To get the feel of a big jet soaring directly over your head, walk down a half-mile to the east (you'll see stop signs) and stand here. It won't be only jets using the airport either - you can spot an occasional propeller plane as well.

Benjamin Banneker Historical Park

Phone - (410) 887-1081
Website - None
Admission Fee - None
Directions - *Ellicott City, Baltimore County; the entrance is on Oella Avenue off Frederick Road (MD 144). Parking for the Trolley Trail is plentiful in a lot on Oella Aveue and at the western terminus of Edmundsen Avenue.*

The Park
Molly Welsh, an English indentured servant, gained her freedom and began growing tobacco on this prop-erty around 1690. She soon bought two African slaves, freeing the one called "Banneky" and marrying him. Benjamin Banneker was the grandson of that union. He had gained a local reputation for mechanical and mathematical prowess when three Quaker brothers from Pennsylvania arrived in the 1770s to build a flour mill on the Patapsco River. The Ellicott brothers befriended Banneker and lent him books to fuel his isolated studies. In 1791 he left his one-room homestead for the only time in his life to help Andrew Ellicott survey the boundaries for the new capital city of Washington. Upon returning he published an annual almanac of his astronomical observations from 1792 to 1797. Thomas Jefferson lauded the self-taught farmer who is remembered as a pioneering African-American scientist. Baltimore County purchased Banneker's former property in 1985 to establish a museum and 142-acre park.

The Walks
Grand canine hiking lies behind an unpromising little mulched trail that leads into the woods behind the picnic area at the back of the musuem. The wood chip trail is a short loop through a forest thick with a spicebush understory. A wide trail then shoots off the back of the loop and rolls downhill into a stream valley that eventually leaves the park to join the *#9 Trolley Historic Trail.* Turn right and the paved path curves uphill towards a residential area thinly veiled by border woods. To the left the trail slides downhill, following the Coopers Branch until reaching an overlook of Ellicott City.

> **Where The Paw Meets The Earth:** Wood chips, leafy dirt and macadam
> **Workout For Your Dog** - Hilly in the park; flat on the trolley line
> **Swimming** - Coopers Branch is good for a cool splash in rocky pools but not sustained canine aquatics
> **Restrictions On Dogs** - None

Something Extra
Near the Ellicott City terminus of the *#9 Trolley Line* is a railroad cut through solid rock that enables the train to reach town. A wooden boardwalk traverses this shady canyon; above cars rattle across a rickety iron bridge.

Big Run State Park

Phone - (301) 895-5453
Website - http://www.dnr.state.md.us/publiclands/western/big-run.html
Admission Fee - None
Directions - *Grantsville, Garrett County; from I-68 take Exit 22 and follow Chestnut Ridge Road south. Turn left onto Germany Road; park office is two miles on right and the trailhead is further down the road near campsite #3.*

The Park

With 300 acres in Garrett County, Big Run State Park offers rustic camping opportunities with 30 unimproved campsites.

The Walks

The Savage River Reservoir is the star at Big Run State Park but while most park visitors are heading for the boat launch canine hikers can enjoy the scenic *Monroe Run Trail*. Formerly a connection road built in the 1930s by the Civilian Conservation Corps, this 6.4-mile linear trail drops about 500 feet through an untouched stream valley. One thing you'll remember from this ramble are the frequent, unbridged stream crossings - you dog will need her toes on all four paws to count them all.

>**Where The Paw Meets The Earth:** Rocky dirt
>**Workout For Your Dog** - Straight up and straight down
>**Swimming** - Plenty of splashing on the trail and great swimming in the reservoir
>**Restrictions On Dogs** - None

Something Extra

If the campground is full, slide around down the road to the right and look for an open area on the left for a place to pitch a tent.

Black Hill Regional Park

Phone - (301) 972-3476
Website - http://www.mc-mncppc.org/parks/facilities/regional_parks/blackhill/index.shtm
Admission Fee - None
Directions - *Clarksburg, Montgomery County; from I-270 take Exit 18 onto Clarksburg Road (MD 121) south. Turn left on West Old Baltimore Road to park entrance on the right. For the Ten Mile Creek Road area trails, turn right on Old Baltimore Road.*

The Park
Open pit gold mining was conducted in this area for nearly a century between the 1850s and the 1950s. There was never enough precious metal discovered to trigger any gold rushes and when George Chadwick purchased land here for a summer retreat he converted the mine into a Cold War bomb shelter. About a generation ago local water authorities looked over the privately owned farms and woods in this area and saw an emergency water-upply reservoir. Little Seneca Creek was dammed and the metro area's largest lake created. Black Hill Regional Park, a recreation park with 1,854 acres of rolling woodlands, picnic shelters, and water activities, opened in 1987.

The Walks
The bulk of the canine hiking at Black Hill is around Lake Ridge Drive near the park office. The feature trail is the mostly-paved *Black Hill Trail* that loops a peninsula formed by two of the three major fingers of the Little Seneca Lake. There are plenty of access points to the trail here and if you are looking for a short day with your dog this is where you will need to park; trailhead parking for natural surface trails is limited to a lot at *Cabin Branch Trail* that will set you off on a long exploration of Cabin Branch and Little Seneca creeks. Canine hikers may want to leave the main park to the picnickers and fishermen and head for the western area of the park across Clarksburg Road. Here you'll find a trio of hiking loops leading away from Ten Mile Creek Road, an area of pretty streams and quiet woods. Off the old road trail the paths get hilly and your dog will earn his views of Little Seneca Lake.

> **Where The Paw Meets The Earth:** Paved paths and natural ones
> **Workout For Your Dog** - Some hills to set tongues to panting
> **Swimming** - Little Seneca Lake attracts all canine swimmers
> **Restrictions On Dogs** - None

Something Extra
There is an L-shaped dog exercise area just off the *Black Hill Trail*. The fenced doggie playground is shaded but there is no grass.

Blockhouse Point Conservation Park

Phone - None
Website - http://www.mc-mncppc.org/parks/park_maps/map_
pages/blockhousepointcp/blockhousepointcp.shtm
Admission Fee - None
Directions - *Potomac, Montgomery County; on River Road,
MD 190, west of town. Parking is on the south side of the road at
14750 River Road.*

The Park

At the time of the Civil War, this spot was owned by William and
Sarah Reading. Blockhouse Point remained in the Reading family until
sold to Randell and Roselyn Patten in 1947. It was acquired by the
Maryland-National Capitol Park and Planning Commission in 1970.
Montgomery County began acquiring land from private area horse
farms and has pieced together a 630-acre conservation area. There
are no recreational amenities in the park.

The Walks

It doesn't seem like it when you pull into the parking lot but there is
plenty of good climbing ahead for your dog here. Three more or less
parallel trails dead-end at overlooks of the Chesapeake & Ohio Canal.
The easiest way to forge a circuit hike out of the trio is to park at the
smaller, unmarked western lot, but stop at the larger eastern lot to
study the excellent trail map at the information board. All the canine
hiking here is under the canopy of a rich upland forest. Sprinkled in
the understory are high-bush blueberry, spicebush, dogwood and
even an active patch of paw-paw but most of the paths remain wide
and clear. Keep your dog close as you reach the point and pick your
way down along the rocks for outstanding views of the Potomac River
and the C&O Canal. You can access the canal towpath from the main
parking lot for extended trail time with your dog.

> **Where The Paw Meets The Earth:** Wide, dirt paths
> **Workout For Your Dog** - Some short climbs are not
> without merit
> **Swimming** - Streams in the ravine are for splashing
> not swimming
> **Restrictions On Dogs** - None

Something Extra

Known as the Camp at Muddy Branch (18MO542), the fortification
at Blockhouse Point was discovered deserted on July 11, 1864 when
Confederate Colonel John Singleton Mosby of the 1st Virginia Parti-
san Rangers, which included a number of recruits from Montgomery
County, crossed the Potomac River. The Confederates burned the
Blockhouse Point camp but it is the only example of such a Civil War
campsite left undisturbed in the entire Washington Metropolitan area.
Still visible on the site are the ground works of the blockhouses, tent
structures and hearths.

Cabin John Regional Park

Phone - (301) 299-4555
Website - http://www.mc-mncppc.org/parks/facilities/regional_parks/cabinjohn/index.shtm
Admission Fee - None
Directions - *Rockville, Montgomery County; south to between Tuckerman Road to the north and Democracy Boulevard to the south.*

The Park

Cabin John Creek flows from Rockville down to the Potomac River. For much of its length it is now accompanied by a natural surface trail, partly maintained by the Potomac Appalachian Trail Club. Since the trail is in an urban area, dog owners must navigate across many busy roads in the course of its 8.8-miles.

The Walks

The best way for canine hikers to experience the short, steep hills and wooded stream valley is in Cabin John Regional Park. Although the blue-blazed, out-and-back *Cabin John Trail* is the star of the park there are several side trips you can take with your dog to produce small loops and detours. Bikes can use the trails but not horses.

> **Where The Paw Meets The Earth:** Dirt lanes
> **Workout For Your Dog** - You bet; plenty of hill-climbing
> **Swimming** - Cabin John Creek can sometimes pool deep enough for a little dog paddling
> **Restrictions On Dogs** - None

Something Extra

During the summer months, evening concerts are offered to the public free of charge. Bring your dog.

Catoctin Mountain Park

Phone - (301) 663-9388
Website - http://www.nps.gov/cato
Admission Fee - No
Directions - *Thurmont, Frederick County; the Visitor Center, where you can pick up many of the park trails, is on MD 77, west of US Route 15.*

The Park
It took an offer of 200 acres of land rent free for three years and a penny an acre thereafter by Lord Baltimore to lure settlers into this remote region. When they finally came so much wood was cut for charcoal, tanning and lumber that eventually people left the mountains. This time there was no effort to populate the region and in 1935 over 10,000 acres were acquired by the Federal Government and developed as the Catoctin Recreational Demonstration Area. The land regenerated into an eastern hardwood climax forest looking again as it did before the original European settlement. Everyone has heard of Camp David but where exactly it is? Surprisingly it is located right here in Catoctin Mountain Park. When you take your dog there, you will never see Camp David or any evidence that the presidential compound is hidden among the trees but the trails you can hike on are of Presidential quality nonetheless.

The Walks
You could fill up a day of canine hiking at Catoctin Mountain Park just by checking off the many easy self-guiding interpretive trails as you learn about mountain culture and forest ecology. There is plenty of more challenging fare in the park as well. Three of the best vistas - Wolf Rock, Chimney Rock and Cat Rock - are connected by a rollercoaster trail on the eastern edge of the mountain. There is little understory in the woods and views are long.

> **Where The Paw Meets The Earth:** Rocky dirt paths on slopes
> **Workout For Your Dog** - Absolutely
> **Swimming** - Small streams percolate through the mountains but there are no great swimming holes.
> **Restrictions On Dogs** - Dogs are allowed in the campground and on all trails but not across the road in the popular Cunningham Falls State Park.

Something Extra
The forests deep in the rugged Catoctin Mountains provided ideal cover for a whiskey still, made illegal by the onset of Prohibition in 1919. On a steaming July day in 1929 Federal agents raided the Blue Blazes Whiskey Still and confiscated more than 25,000 gallons of mash. Today the airy, wooded *Blue Blazes Whiskey Trail* along Distillery Run leads to a recreated working still and interprets the history of whiskey making in the backwoods of Appalachia.

Cedarville State Forest

Phone - (301) 888-1410
Website - http://www.dnr.state.md.us/publiclands/southern/cedarville.html
Admission Fee - Yes
Directions - *Brandywine, Charles County; From US 301 South travel to Cedarville Road. As you leave Prince George's County take a left on Cedarville Road. Make a right on Bee Oak Road, which is the main entrance to the forest.*

The Park
The Piscataway Indians came to this area in southern Maryland for winter camps. Later settlers attempted - with varying degrees of success - to drain the swamp for cropland. The Maryland Department of Natural Resources came in 1930 to buy thousands of acres of land for a forest demonstration area. Twenty years later, as the trees grew up, many were harvested to provide charcoal to heat other state properties across Maryland. Today's park encompasses 3,510 acres.

The Walks
The *Holly Trail* is Cedarville's longest at five miles and your dog will get a squishy feel for the marshy areas of the forest as you follow orange blazes. For elevation changes clock in on the 3.5-mile *Heritage Trail*. Here you'll see one of the kilns that churned out as much as 3,600 pounds of charcoal a week. Two shorter trails can be explored in less than an hour: the *Plantation Trail* takes in a loblolly pine plantation and the *Swamp Trail* loops through the headwaters of Zekiah Swamp. The forest can keep your dog busy with over 19 miles of marked trails.

> **Where The Paw Meets The Earth:** Packed dirt with sand and pine straw
> **Workout For Your Dog** - Small elevation changes
> **Swimming** - Numerous streams and springs keep the forest well-lubricated and there is a 4-acre pond at the *Plantation Trail* trailhead
> **Restrictions On Dogs** - None; dogs allowed in the campground

Something Extra
Cedarville is home to the headwaters of Zekiah Swamp, Maryland's largest freshwater bog. Plants that live here have to make do with nutrient-poor soils and two have adapted by living off the juices of insects: the northern pitcher plant and the roundleaf sundew. The pitcher plant lures victims with the promise of cool drink that turns deadly when they can't climb back out the ewer-shaped flower because the tiny hairs are facing in the wrong direction. The low-growing sundew traps its prey in sticky tentacles.

Centennial Park

Phone - None
Website - None
Admission Fee - None
Directions - *Columbia, Howard County; north of the city on Clarksville Pike (MD 108).*

The Park
Within two years of opening in 1987 Centennial Park received the Merit Award for Innovative Design from the American Society of Landscape Architects. The centerpiece lake was created as a flood control measure in 1965 and now occupies 50 of the park's surrounding 325 acres.

The Walks
The park features over four miles of asphalt multi-use paths, most of which are featured on the 2.4-mile *Centennial Lake Trail* around the water. This is a rolling, contoured exploration that keeps the lake in sight almost the entire way. The trail is mostly open on the south side and mostly shaded on the north where you will find the Howard County Arboreta, one of the best places to hike with the dog for an arboreal education. Many of the trees along the trail are marked for identification and most of Centennial Park's 60 or so species can be spotted from the path.

> **Where The Paw Meets The Earth:** Macadam
> **Workout For Your Dog** - Easy, rolling loop
> **Swimming** - On the north side of the lake there are a couple of places for the dog to slip into the water but that is all
> **Restrictions On Dogs** - No dogs in the picnic area or on the ballfields

Something Extra
Columbia sprung into existence in the 1960s from the mind of James Rouse, an Eastern Shore shopping mall developer, as America's first planned city. Central to the plans were 80 miles of bikepaths connecting nine diverse villages, including three other man-made lakes near Centennial Park. Wilde Lake, where Columbia's first residents arrived in 1967, is a 1.5-mile circumnavigation. If it feels as if you are walking the dog through someone's backyard at times, you are. Public access is reserved at some private lakeside properties. Trails also run alongside slender Lake Kittamaqundi at the edge of Columbia Town Center and two miles of paths surround 37-acre Lake Elkhorn.

Charlotte's Quest Nature Center

Phone - (410) 374-3395
Website - http://www.charlottesquestnaturecenter.com/
Admission Fee - None
Directions - *Manchester, Carroll County; from Main Street (MD 30) make a right onto York Street and turn left on Wilhem Lane after 1/2 mile to the park.*

The Park

The Pine Valley Nature Center was created in 1995 as an outdoor study area through a unique partnership between Manchester Elementary School and the town council. The school children voted to name their outdoor classroom Charlotte's Quest for the Outside World in honor of Charlotte Collett, a teacher and Council member who shepherded the project to reality.

The Walks

The 4 1/2 miles of trails at Pine Valley Nature Center are the most paw-friendly in the Baltimore area. You may want to shed your shoes and join your dog in hiking the soft grass trails barefooted. Even the dirt trails in the woods are often blanketed in spruce needles. The trail system consists of nine short paths and visits an appealing mix of riparian meadows and woodlands. Trails lead to such attractions as Turk's Spring, the Stream of Life and Avian Cove. A *Nature Trail* winds around a wooded hillside. Like the trail surface, all the climbs at Pine Valley are gentle. For a great game of fetch there is a large grassy field next to the Nature Center.

> **Where The Paw Meets The Earth:** Some of the most paw-friendly trails in Maryland
> **Workout For Your Dog** - Easy hills
> **Swimming** - Walnut Pond is a quiet fishing hole that is an ideal spot for a doggie dip
> **Restrictions On Dogs** - None

Something Extra

Take a moment to stop by the nature center's butterfly garden, a combination of annuals, perennials, trees, and woody shrubs that provide the proper environment for all stages of the butterfly's life cycle. You'll be bound to see some of nature's 28,000 species but don't expect them to be flying without warm sunshine - a butterfly can't take wing until its body temperature is 86 degrees.

Chesapeake & Ohio Canal -Monocacy Aqueduct

Phone - None
Website - http://www.nps.gov/choh/
Admission Fee - None
Directions - *Dickerson, Frederick County; west on Route 28.*

The Park
The Chesapeake & Ohio Canal, dubbed the "Great National Project" when launched by President John Quincy Adams in 1828, ended here, nearly 300 miles short of its goal of Pittsburgh, Pennsylvania. The canine hiking on the towpath at the western terminus in Cumberland provides glimpses into a history of American transportation that includes canals, railroads and the National Road. You will be atop the highest elevation on the C&O Canal at 605 feet but, like any stretch on the canal, this is easy going for your dog.

The Walks
Near the halfway point of the canal towpath is the Monocacy Aqueduct, tucked away in a wooded enclave. This quiet spot doesn't get too much traffic and is an ideal place to begin your explorations of the canal with your dog.

> **Where The Paw Meets The Earth:** Wide, packed dirt trail
> **Workout For Your Dog** - Level canine hiking
> **Swimming** - Absolutely; the banks to the Monocacy River provide easy access to deep water
> **Restrictions On Dogs** - None

Something Extra
Aqueducts, like this one over the Monocacy River, were used to carry the canal across water. The Monocacy Aqueduct was so wonderfully constructed that two attempts by Confederate saboteurs and tons of flood debris over the years have failed to bring it down.

Cosca Regional Park

Phone - (301) 868-1397
Website - http://www.pgparks.com/places/parks/cosca.html
Admission Fee - None
Directions - *Clinton, Prince George's County; from the Capital Beltway (I-495), take Exit 7A South (Branch Avenue/MD 5) and turn right onto Woodward Road and left onto Brandywine Road. Make a right onto Thrift Road to the park and nature center on the right.*

The Park
Around midnight on April 14, 1865 John Wilkes Booth stopped at the Surratt Tavern just north of here on Brandywine Road. He was retrieving rifles, field glasses and other supplies he had stored there before going to Ford's Theatre to assassinate President Lincoln two hours earlier. The tavern owner, Mary E. Surratt would later be convicted for her role in the plot against Lincoln and be the first woman executed by the federal government. Booth continued his escape through this area - although his exact route is uncertain - and would spend six days in southern Maryland before crossing the Potomac where he was captured and killed in Virginia six days later. The 700-acre Louise F. Cosca Regional Park would open a century later in 1967.

The Walks
The canine hiking in Cosca Regional Park centers around the Clearwater Nature Center, tucked into a vibrant forest. Three loop trails set out from the nature center parking lot that can be traveled in their entirety or combined for a canine hiking loop of over two miles. The highlight is a trip around the 11-acre Cosca Lake, whose banks are brush-free for most of the loop. The paths are wide, the hill climbs are gradual and the tall trees are shady - what's not to love for your dog. Off the *Lake Trail* you can also pick up the green-blazed *Perimeter Trail* that leads to the campground and around the developed areas of the park. This route will take more than an hour to complete.

> **Where The Paw Meets The Earth:** Wooded dirt paths
> **Workout For Your Dog** - Plenty of hills to climb, but not arduously so
> **Swimming** - There is plenty of access to Cosca Lake
> **Restrictions On Dogs** - None

Something Extra
Off the *Graybark Trail* you can find the Prince George's Butterfly Garden, featuring both host and nectar plants. The garden is especially rich in host plants and includes pussytoes, several milkweed species, asters, thistle, senna, violets, and herbs. Monarchs raised on the milkweed are tagged by the nature center. The garden often hosts some unusual butterflies of nature's 28,000 species.

Cromwell Valley Park

Phone - (410) 887-2503
Website - http://www.bcpl.net/~cvpark/
Admission Fee - Yes
Directions - *Baltimore, Baltimore County; on Cromwell Bridge Road (MD 567), north of Exit 29 of the Baltimore Beltway (I-695).*

The Park

Cromwell Valley Park is the result of the melding of three former farm properties by Baltimore County in 1994. The land has been cultivated for nearly 300 years and a Christmas tree farm still operates here. Four iron mines once produced ore near the headwaters of Minebank Run and the valley evolved into a major producer of agricultural lime. The remains of kilns used to cook Cockeysville marble into lime powder are still visible in a hillside along the stream.

The Walks

Still a young park, Cromwell Valley has already become a favorite with Baltimore area dog walkers. The park's 367 acres begin in a mile-wide riparian stream valley and taper across open fields and pastures until reaching upland forests. Six short marked trails, totalling about four miles, visit all corners of Cromwell Valley. Most of the walking is on wide former farm roads. For a flat, easy stroll walk the length of the out-and-back *Minebank Run Trail* for 1.2 miles. Although you are only yards from the stream the water is seldom seen but the shrubs and small trees that shelter the banks are a haven for songbirds. The *Willow Grove Trail* climbs steadily to the top of a ridge for a loop through woods filled with tall, straight yellow poplar trees.

> **Where The Paw Meets The Earth:** Dirt and grass farm roads
> **Workout For Your Dog** - Some good climbs on tap
> **Swimming** - Minebank Run is a gurgling little flow of water that is good for cooling off on a hot day but little more
> **Restrictions On Dogs** - None

Something Extra

The sport of orienteering began as a military training exercise in Scandinavian forests in the last decades of the 19th century. It came to America in 1967 at Valley Forge, Pennsylvania. The term "orienteering" comes from the military practice of orientation, finding ones way through unfamiliar ground with a "chart and compass." Cromwell Valley has developed a permanent self-guided course for the practioners of the art. Pick up a topographical map in the office at Sherwood Farm and challenge your dog's nose in a wayfinding contest.

Cylburn Arboretum

Phone - (410) 396-0180
Website - http://www.cylburnassociation.org/index.htm
Admission Fee - None
Directions - *Baltimore, Baltimore City; in northwest part of the city at 4915 Greenspring Lane.*

The Park
Jesse Tyson, heir to a family chrome fortune, began developing Cylburn estate in 1863 by starting construction on a gray stone Second Empire mansion. His home was not ready to live in until 1888 and Tyson, a lifelong bachelor then in his 60s, celebrated by taking a 19-year old wife, Edyth Johns. "I have the fairest wife, the fastest horses and the finest house in Maryland," boasted Tyson. When he died 16 years later his wife carried on the family matrimonial tradition by marrying a younger man. When she died in 1942, husband Bruce Cotton sold the property to the city of Baltimore for a pittance so that the land would be used as a park. After housing neglected children for several years, the Cylburn Arboretum opened to the public in 1958.

The Walks
The 176 acres of Cylburn Arboretum's grounds are visited by five loop trails. These passageways are wide and paw-friendly soft dirt or cedar mulch but you will still want to stray off the paths to read the labels of the many ornamental trees. Most of the walking is easy going along the top of a wooded ridge although the *Woodland Trail* does plunge down a hillside. Beware of the *Witch-Hazel Trail* which is rocky under paw as it lopes down the same hill. There are also several garden areas to explore off the trails. The feature trail at Cylburn, the *Circle Trail*, is enveloped by the relentless pounding of traffic on I-83 but it eventually fades into white noise.

> **Where The Paw Meets The Earth:** Natural surface paths with cedar mulch
> **Workout For Your Dog** - Easy going around the tree museum
> **Swimming** - None
> **Restrictions On Dogs** - None

Something Extra
The collection at Cylburn Arboretum features several Maryland Big Tree Champions including an Italian maple and a paperback maple. Two easy champions to see are on the lawn in the right front of the mansion: a *castor aralia* with large glossy leaves and an *Amur maackia*. Both trees are native to Asia and are resilient to pests. The maackia is a member of the pea family discovered by 19th century explorer Karlovich Maack along the Amur River between Siberia and China.

Double Rock Park

Phone - None
Website - None
Admission Fee - None
Directions - *Parkville, Baltimore County; from I-695 take Exit 31 South (Harford Road) to Parkville. After 1/4 mile cross Putty Hill Avenue at the top of a hill and go downhill for 1/2 mile to Texas Avenue. Turn left and go one mile to the end at Glen Road. Cross road into park entrance.*

The Park

The land that now contains the 102-acre Double Rock Park was part of a 3,000-acre tract first surveyed in 1735 for English overseers William Chetwynd and John Whitwick. It is believed the new owners were interested in exploiting the virgin forests that blanketed the hills they called Grindon. Served only by a very narrow gravel toll road known as the Baltimore and Harford Turnpike, settlement came slowly to the area. In 1874, city surveyor Simon Jonas Martinet purchased 35 acres of land about one mile west of present-day Double Rock Park which he named Parkville. On the heels of the suburban migration following World War II, the park was dedicated in 1947.

The Walks

A popular ball-playing and picnic park on the top of a hill, the active dog owner can find enchanting trails down below. The wide dirt paths are completely wooded with plenty of elevation changes throughout the trail system. The *Yellow Trail*, picked up to the right of the parking lot, works around the perimeter of the property and is joined at several junctions by the *Red Trail* which meanders down and around Stemmer's Run. The stream was restored in 1997 and has a number of interesting nooks and crannies as it flows through the park. The blue-blazed *Falls Trail* starts down the stairs from the parking lot and follows a macadam path two-tenths of a mile to a small waterfall.

> **Where The Paw Meets The Earth:** Wooded dirt paths
> **Workout For Your Dog** - Rolling hills
> **Swimming** - Stemmer's Run is not deep enough for anything other than a refreshing splash
> **Restrictions On Dogs** - None

Something Extra

The namesake rocks for Double Rock Park mark the entrance and are not worth a special trip; more intriguing are the rock perches on the hillside above the stream that make ideal rest stops for a tired dog.

Downs Memorial Park

Phone - (410) 222-6230
Website - http://www.aacounty.org/RecParks/parks/downs_park/index.cfm
Admission Fee - Yes, closed Tuesdays
Directions - *Pasadena, Anne Arundel County; take Pinehurst Road off Mountain Road (MD 177).*

The Park
In the early days of English settlement Bodkin Neck was the property of land speculators. It came under cultivation in 1828 when Henry Dunbar purchased most of the peninsula. The land that would become Downs Park was lumbered until the mid-1800s and eventually cultivated to grow vegetables on Deer Park Farm. In 1913 the property was purchased by H.R. Mayo Thom who converted his now Rocky Beach Farm - named for the red sandstone thrusting out of the sandy beach - into a gentleman's summer estate.

The Walks
A paved perimeter trail loops 3.6 miles around the Downs Park property. Most of the twisting route is easy hiking through woodlands of oak and maple and holly and gum. There are another three miles of unpaved trails through the Natural Area, including an eco-trail with interpretive sites. Many of these natural paths are old farm roads - wide and soft under paw.

> **Where The Paw Meets The Earth:** Macadam and sandy dirt
>
> **Workout For Your Dog** - Level going throughout
>
> **Swimming** - Behind the North Overlook is an isolated, scruffy 40-yard stretch of sand known as Dog Beach just for canine aquatics; there is excellent wave action from the Chesapeake Bay and enough sand for digging.
>
> **Restrictions On Dogs** - Downs Park is one of the most dog-friendly parks in Maryland; a dog drinking bowl is chained to a water fountain and there is a "pet parking" stall outside the Information Center - dogs are not allowed to walk through the formal Mother's Garden

Something Extra
At the South Overlook is an osprey nesting platform to observe the activities of the fish-hunting hawk. Although preferring a flat-topped tree, ospreys will happily choose man-made structures such as these for homes. Out on the water, an osprey will hover above the surface looking for a fish before striking with talons extended. An adult bird will succeed one time in four with this maneuver. There is also an aviary and raptor pen for up-close viewing of these striking carniverous birds.

Druid Hill Park

Phone - None
Website - http://www.ci.baltimore.md.us/government/recnparks/
popups/parks/druid_hill_park.htm
Admission Fee - None
Directions - *Baltimore City; the main entrance for the park is on Madison Avenue. Take Exit 7 west off I-83 onto Druid Park Lake to the entrance on the right past the lake.*

The Park
The city of Baltimore paid $475,000 for the Rogers family estate in 1860 to create the jewel of its park system. Colonel Nicholas Rogers designed his property to resemble a pastoral English park and the city continued the theme with picnic pavilions, grassy promenades, statues and fountains. A massive Tuscan Doric entranceway was built of Nova Scotia sandstone in 1868 at the cost of $24,000 and Druid Lake was formed in 1871 behind the largest earthen dam in America to provide drinking water. Today the historic park covers 600 acres.

The Walks
There are no formal hikes in Baltimore's old dowager - just plenty of room to ramble on rolling hills. The grassy paths have been paved over and some can still be found, including a brick walkway near the tennis courts that once marked the delineation of Druid Park's "separate but equal" facilities for blacks and whites. In 1948 a crowd of 500 onlookers watched as black tennis players were carried off the "whites-only" tennis courts by police in one of America's earliest demonstrations in the civil rights movement. The walk around Druid Lake covers about 1. 5 miles.

> **Where The Paw Meets The Earth:** Macadam and grass
> **Workout For Your Dog** - This is a hilly park
> **Swimming** - Give your dog a day off from the water when coming here
> **Restrictions On Dogs** - None

Something Extra
The Baltimore Zoo opened in Druid Hill Park in 1876 as America's third zoo and it is possible for your dog to glimpse - and certainly smell - a few unfamiliar animals as she trots about the park.

Eastern Neck National Wildlife Refuge

Phone - (410) 639-7056
Website - http://www.fws.gov/northeast/easternneck/
Admission Fee - None
Directions - *Rock Hall, Kent County; from Route 301 take Route 213 North towards Chestertown. In Chestertown, turn onto MD 291 (also marked "to Rt. 20"). At the T-intersection, turn right onto MD 20 South towards Rock Hall. After 12 miles, at the blinking red light in Rock Hall, turn left onto MD 445 and continue six miles to the refuge entrance bridge.*

The Park

European settlers arrived in the mid-1600s when Colonel Joseph Wickes and his partner, Thomas Hynson, were granted tracts until they owned all of Eastern Neck Island. The Hynson heirs gradually sold all their holdings to the Wickes descendents by 1902. In 1950 land here was sold to a developer who began planning a housing subdivision. Alarmed citizens appealed to the federal government and the U.S. Fish and Wildlife Service acquired the entire island between 1962 and 1967 to preserve its valuable wildlife habitat. The present refuge office is the only house ever built in the "Cape Chester" subdivision.

The Walks

There are several miles of quiet park roads that lead to different points on the island but you will want to concentrate on the short footpaths through the refuge. The shortest - but maybe not the quickest if you dally to admire the views - is the *Bayview-Butterfly Trail* that takes in expansive vistas on the Chesapeake Bay, a wooded pond and a restored grassland in less than one-half mile. The *Duck Inn Trail* and *Boxes Point Trail* are out-and-back affairs that cover over a mile round-trip. The going is easy for your dog on wide, natural surfaces alternating between open fields and open forests. The trails lead to the wide Chester River with secluded sandy beaches and frisky waves that will excite any water-loving dog.

> **Where The Paw Meets The Earth:** Dirt, sand, boardwalk
> **Workout For Your Dog** - Level going throughout
> **Swimming** - The open waters of the Chester River are accessed from the trails or at the boatramp at Bogles Wharf Landing
> **Restrictions On Dogs** - None

Something Extra

The 1.2-mile *Wildlife Loop* is devoted to the habitat of the rare Delmarva fox squirrel, found only on the peninsula. The largest of the handful of local tree squirrels, the reclusive creature is hard to spot even though it grows over two feet long. Look for a flash of white belly and large bushy tail with black edge stripes in tree cavities or scampering along the ground.

Eden Mill Nature Center

Phone - (410) 836-3050
Website - http://www.edenmill.org/
Admission Fee - None
Directions - *Pylesville, Harford County; seven miles west. The park is on Eden Mill Road off Fawn Grove Road between Route 136 (Harkins Road) and Route 165 (Federal Hill Road).*

The Park
The first mill here was built in the early 1800s and named for Father Eden, a local priest. Save for a decade after World War I when the mill was converted into a power plant, flour, cornmeal and buckwheat were ground along Deer Creek almost continuously until 1964. At that point Harford County acquired the mill and surrounding 57 acres to settle the final owner's estate. The Eden Mill Nature Center was created in 1991 to preserve the mill and create the trail system through the property.

The Walks
There are 5 miles of trails at Eden Mill, including an elevated board-walk, that stretch across 10 interconnecting paths. These trails are very easy on the paws - grass and soft dirt with only some rocky stretches on the incline of the *High Meadow Trail*. The *Bluebird Trail* is a special dog favorite with its grassy lanes through eye-high brush lending it the flavor of an English maze garden. The terrain at Eden Mill ranges from flat floodplain walking to hillside hiking that demand switchbacks to tackle the steep grades.

>**Where The Paw Meets The Earth:** Grass and soft dirt
>**Workout For Your Dog** - Few climbs needed
>**Swimming** - There is good access to Deer Creek, which generally flows lazily along at canal speed
>**Restrictions On Dogs** - None

Something Extra
On the *Beaver Run Trail*, along Deer Creek, a bench is built directly into the bank that is ideal for dangling your tired paws in the water as it moseys by.

Elk Neck State Park

Phone - (410) 287-5333
Website - http://www.dnr.state.md.us/publiclands/central/elk-neck.html
Admission Fee - None
Directions - *Northeast, Cecil County; from I-95 exit onto Route 272 (North East Road)and go south 2.4 miles to Route 7 (East Cecil Avenue). Cross State Route 7, stay on Route 272 and go 11 miles to the end of the road and the park.*

The Park
At Turkey Point the Northeast and Elk rivers have pinched a finger of land in the Upper Chesapeake Bay so violently that it swells to more than 100 feet above the water. The result is Elk Neck State Park, a vibrant mix of sandy beaches, marshlands and hardwood forests.

The Walks
There are five main trails at Elk Neck State Park. None is longer than two miles and all can be covered in a leisurely afternoon of canine hiking. The *White Trail* through the Thackery Swamp is a self-guiding nature trail. The *Black Trail* skirts the shoreline of the Elk River and the waters of the Chesapeake Bay can be reached from the *Blue Trail* at Turkey Point. You start your explorations on an old access road high above the waters that soon turns towards the Old Turkey Point Lighthouse. The various footpaths radiate off the main trail across the peninsula.

> **Where The Paw Meets The Earth:** Dirt roads and woods paths
> **Workout For Your Dog** - Gradual climbs to Turkey Point
> **Swimming** - Spirited dog swimming on small sandy beaches on the Chesapeake Bay
> **Restrictions On Dogs** - No dogs on the North East Beach

Something Extra
A lighthouse was authorized by Congress in 1831 and two years later a tower and keeper's quarters was situated on a 100-foot bluff where the North East and Elk Rivers converge. Originally, the 35-foot tower had a panel of red glass to warn ships they were approaching the shallows. The beacon was visible for 13 miles and was the highest of 74 lighthouses on the Chesapeake Bay. The keeper's quarters are gone but the tower and spectacular views remain atop the grassy bluffs.

Fair Hill NRMA

Phone - (410) 398-1246
Website - http://www.dnr.state.md.us/publiclands/central/fairhill.html
Admission Fee - Yes, parking fee
Directions - *Rising Sun, Cecil County; take Exit 100 off I-95 on MD 272 North. Turn right on MD 273 and follow to the intersection of MD 273 and MD 213. Turn right to the office.*

The Park

William du Pont Jr., great grand-son of the founder of the chemical giant, built a sporting empire in Delaware that spilled over the state line into Fair Hill. He operated Foxcather Farms, stabling five Kentucky Derby starters over the years. His horse farm at Fair Hill covered more than 5,000 acres and was one of the largest private land holdings in the East. Fair Hill was purchased by the State of Maryland in 1975 and the equestrian trappings of the farm have survived intact, including an active steeplechase course and stable that was home to 2006 Kentucky Derby champion Barbaro.

The Walks

This is the Godzilla of area hiking. Traversing its 5,613 acres are over 75 miles of natural, multi-use trails. Many go through rolling hayfields as befits its stature as a leading equine training center. Most of the trails in Maryland are heavily forested and if you like the feel of sunshine on your face and long hikes across open fields Fair Hill is the place to bring your dog. The trails through the fields are typically doubletrack (old dirt vehicle roads). Singletrack trails dominate in the forested areas. The stiffest climbs are in the vicinity of the Big Elk Creek but most of the trails are like walking a steeplechase course. Fair Hill is also a good place to spot house ruins along the trail.

> **Where The Paw Meets The Earth:** Old dirt farm roads mostly
> **Workout For Your Dog** - Long hikes on rolling terrain
> **Swimming** - If your dog loves a good swim pick a trail near the Big Elk Creek
> **Restrictions On Dogs** - None

Something Extra

The Big Elk Creek surges through the property and is spanned by many trail bridges, including one of Maryland's five remaining covered bridges. The Big Elk Creek Covered Bridge was built in 1860 at a cost of $1,165.00. When it was reconstructed in 1992 after sustaining extensive damage from heavy trucks, the tab was $152,000.

Flag Ponds Nature Park

Phone - (410) 586-1477
Website - http://www.calvertparks.org/flagpond.htm
Admission Fee - Yes, per vehicle
Directions - *Lusby, Calvert County; ten miles south of Prince Frederick on MD 4, turn left at sign.*

The Park

Flag Ponds Nature Park is one of three public beaches on the Chesapeake Bay in Calvert County. Visitors frequently find ancient fossils deposited from the Calvert Cliffs. The park maintains season hours and doesn't open until 9:00 a.m. in season.

The Walks

Most visitors to this small Chesapeake Bay park will jump on the main half-mile trail to the sandy beach but canine hikers know better. The *North Ridge Trail* will lead to two freshwater woodland ponds in the course of a mile or so. The North Loop provides another half-mile of quiet canine hiking. As you go keep an eye out for the abundant Blue Flag Iris wildflower that gives the park its name.

> **Where The Paw Meets The Earth:** Wooded dirt trails
>
> **Workout For Your Dog** - Yes, working the elevation drop down to the bay
>
> **Swimming** - Just try keeping your water-loving pooch out of the Chesapeake Bay
>
> **Restrictions On Dogs** - None

Something Extra

When you finally decide to head down to the beach with your dog you will pass the relics of a major "pound net" fishery that operated here until 1955. One shanty that housed fishermen in season has survived to house an interpretive exhibit of the Bay's historic fishing industry.

Fort Howard Park

Phone - (410) 887-7529
Website - None
Admission Fee - None
Directions - *Baltimore City; follow North Point Road through Fort Howard to its end at the VA Hospital and make a left into the park.*

The Park
The British selected North Point, now part of Fort Howard Park and the southernmost point in Baltimore County, as the landing site for a 6-ship invasion force on September 12, 1814. In the pre-dawn hours 4700 British marines disembarked here to begin a 17-mile march on Baltimore. Later that day the Americans engaged the force in the Battle of North Point, slowing the invaders and triggering a demoralizing chain of events for the British that hastened the end of the War of 1812. The army returned to North Point in 1899 to build Fort Howard as the headquarters for the coastal defense of Baltimore. The fort was named for John Edgar Howard of the Maryland Continental Army who received one of only 14 medals awarded during the American Revolution for his heroism at the Battle of Cowpens. In subsequent years the fort was an infantry training center (under General Douglas MacArthur for a time) through the Vietnam War, when a mock Vietnamese village was constructed here. The base was turned over to Baltimore County for use as a park in 1973.

The Walks
The *Endicott Trail* is a paved walk through the "Bulldog at Baltimore's Gate" that enables your dog to ramble through the gun batteries and ammunition magazines and to clamber on top of the earth-covered parapets that are camoflauged from the open water. Although a dummy grenade was found in the picnic area in 1988 it is unlikely your dog will sniff out any old ordnance here. A nature trail - bushwhacking may be required - leads to the marshy extremities of the shady 61-acre park. Another trail follows under a Ropes Course 20 feet up in the trees. Keep four feet on the ground here.

> **Where The Paw Meets The Earth:** Dirt and concrete
> **Workout For Your Dog** - Not unless you go around a few times
> **Swimming** - The shoreline is mostly broken seawall but there is access to the open water at a small stone beach - beware of broken glass and shells on paws
> **Restrictions On Dogs** - None

Something Extra
Where else can your dog climb into an actual battery and scan the Patapsco River just like gunnery officers who once aimed guns over the water capable of accurately firing 1,000-pound projectiles eight miles?

Fort McHenry National Monument

Phone - (410) 962-4290
Website - http://www.nps.gov/fomc/
Admission Fee - Yes, for the town
Directions - *Baltimore City; from I-95 take Exit 55 (Key Highway)
to Lawrence Street. Turn left and left again on Fort Avenue to end.*

The Park
Francis Scott Key was a 35-year old lawyer selected as an envoy to
secure the release of American doctor William Beanes during the
War of 1812. Sailing under a flag of truce, Key boarded the British
flagship Tonnant. His mission was a success but Key was detained
as the British bombardment of Fort McHenry, a star-shaped defender
of Baltimore Harbor built in the late 1700s, began on the morning
of September 13, 1814. After nearly two days of launching 1500
bombshells, the British abandoned their invasion. Properly inspired,
amateur poet Key scribbled out the lines to "The Defence of Fort
McHenry" on the back of an envelope. It became the "Star-Spangled
Banner" when performed by a Baltimore actor a month later and
was adopted as America's national anthem on March 3, 1931. Two
years later, Fort Mc Henry came under the direction of the National
Park Service and today is the only area designated both a national
moument and historic shrine.

The Walks
Fort McHenry rests on a 43-acre appendage of land in the mouth of
Baltimore Harbor. There are large grassy open fields around the brick
fort with plenty of room for romping for the dog. Cool breezes from the
water and a grove of syacmore trees on the south side provide relief
from the sun if needed. A concrete trail runs along all three sides of
the seawall to create a loop of the park with plenty of opportunity to
soak up historical monuments and shrines. A restored tidal wetland
area keeps feeding and migratory birds arriving.

> **Where The Paw Meets The Earth:** Grass and concrete
> **Workout For Your Dog** - Only after a hard game of fetch
> **Swimming** - None
> **Restrictions On Dogs** - No dogs inside the fort

Something Extra
Fort McHenry sits in the heart of the Port of Baltimore where ships
laden with iron ore, sugar, bananas and other commodities pay call
from all over the world. Looking to the right autos unload on the Patapsco River and directly in front of you bulk container ships disgorge
their cargo. Meanwhile on the water tugboats constantly orchestrate
this merchant ship ballet that unfolds before you as the dog chases
a tennis ball.

Fort Washington National Park

Phone - None
Website - http://www.nps.gov/fowa/
Admission Fee - Yes
Directions - *Fort Washington, Prince Georges County; end of Fort Washington Road off MD210.*

The Park
The first Fort Washington was completed here in 1809 and was the only defense of the nation's capital until the Civil War. Occupying high ground overlooking the Potomac River, the fort was a formidable obstacle to any enemy contemplating a water assault on Washington. When it became obsolete and a defensive installation the post was used as an infantry training facility.

The Walks
Now a 341-acre recreational park, you can take your dog for a hike through the assorted military structures (not allowed in the masonry fort itself - one of the few seacoast American forts still in its original form) and on trails that lead to views of the capital and the Virginia shore, as well as down to the Potomac itself.

> **Where The Paw Meets The Earth:** Some natural footpaths and some concrete paths
> **Workout For Your Dog** - A little scrambling up hills, especially if you drop down to the river level
> **Swimming** - You have to work for it but it is possible
> **Restrictions On Dogs** - Dogs are not allowed inside the fort

Something Extra
The Fort Washington lighthouse is located near the Potomac River on park property.

Frederick Municipal Forest

Phone - None
Website - None
Admission Fee - None
Directions - *Frederick, Frederick County; northwest of the city at the end of Gambrill State Park Road or at the end of Mountaindale Road off US 15.*

The Park
This public forest was once known as the Frederick City Watershed because all the water that falls in the mountains drains into the city's reservoir.

The Walks
Do you favor your hikes with your dog on groomed trails with a detailed map in your hand? If so, do not bother with Frederick Municipal Forest. There are no maps, no markings and no trail maintenance here (although you may catch the blue-blazed *Catoctin Trail* that is running 26 miles across the ridge). Bring your dog with a mind to explore for hours in the solitude of a mountain forest. You will be traveling mostly on fire roads and expect to push your way across many blowdowns of big trees.

> **Where The Paw Meets The Earth:** Some foot paths but mostly rough forest access roads
> **Workout For Your Dog** - Yes
> **Swimming** - Ponds are not destinations of the trails
> **Restrictions On Dogs** - None

Something Extra
You will stumble across many small ponds - these ponds gained national notoriety as a target in the national anthrax scare a few years back, but that isn't any reason to keep your dog from a good swim.

Furnacetown

Phone - (410) 632-2032
Website - http://www.furnacetown.com/
Admission Fee - Not for the state forest
Directions - *Snow Hill, Worcester County; take US 50 East to Salisbury and pick up MD12 south. Make a right on Old Furnace Road to the complex on the left.*

The Park
The brick stack of the Nassawango Furnace was constructed in 1832 to process bog ore, which wsa collected from the swampy soil along the Nassawango Creek. Maryland's only bog ore smelter flourished for two decades, supporting a bustling community of over 300 people. But as high grade iron ore deposits were discovered when Americans settled the Great Lakes region the need for this low-quality iron evaporated. The 19th century furnace and industrial village interpret this unique chapter in Maryland life.

The Walks
Dogs are not allowed in Furnacetown or on its nature trail but the parking lot can be a jumping off point for explorations in the surrounding Pocomoke State Forest. You'll find some wide access roads and informal footpaths that support miles of flat, easy canine hiking.

> **Where The Paw Meets The Earth:** Wide natural surface road trails
> **Workout For Your Dog** - Flat, flat, flat
> **Swimming** - Not a predominant feature of this canine hike
> **Restrictions On Dogs** - No dogs across the street from the parking lot

Something Extra
Stop by Furnacetown for a traditional 19th century Christmas each year.

Gambrill State Park

Phone - (301) 271-7574
Website - http://www.dnr.state.md.us/publiclands/western/gambrill.html
Admission Fee - None
Directions - *Frederick, Frederick County; the park entrance is on Gambrill Park Road off US 40, west of the city and the I-70 interchange.*

The Park
Private individuals with an interest in conservation ushered Gambrill State Park into existence. The land was presented to the City of Frederick on September 7, 1934 to be preserved as a public park on Catoctin Mountain. The City in turn gave the land to the State of Maryland who created the 1,137-acre park. It was named for James H. Gambrill, a Frederick miller and brewer and conservationist who had died in 1932. Most of the recreational facilities, including three native stone overlooks, were built in the 1930s by workers in the Civilian Conservation Corps.

The Walks
Gambrill State Park offers a nicely designed trail system to accommodate any type of hiking outing you are looking for with your dog. All trails begin at the same lot (one mile into the park on the east side of the road) and loop back to your car. Beginners can enjoy the heavily forested mountain top on the *Lost Chestnut* and *Red Maple* trails, each about a mile and, save for one steep descent on the red trail, easy to hike. For most canine hikers the first option will be the 3.3-mile *Black Locust Trail*. You may not think so as you drop off the mountain on a paw-pounding rocky path and then start back up again but your dog's tail will be wagging again after the trail splits from the 26.5-mile blue-blazed *Catoctin Trail* that is running the length of the mountain. This trail is especially tasty after you cross the road when you burrow through tunnels of mountain laurel. If you are hankering for a full afternoon of canine hiking on Catoctin Mountain take off on the *Yellow Poplar Trail* that keeps to the ridge crest for the most part.

> **Where The Paw Meets The Earth:** Rocky, rocky paths
> **Workout For Your Dog** - Some long mountain ascents
> **Swimming** - Not on Catoctin Mountain
> **Restrictions On Dogs** - Not allowed in the picnic areas

Something Extra
A real treat for your dog - at a strategic point in your outing on the *Black Locust Trail* - is the Bootjack Spring. There is no other water source on the trail and it is a happy discovery indeed on a hot day to find the cold water flowing.

Garrett State Forest

Phone - (301) 334-2038
Website - http://www.dnr.state.md.us/publiclands/western/garrett.html
Admission Fee - None
Directions - *Oakland, Garrett County; five miles northwest, off US Route 219.*

The Park
In 1906 Robert and John Garrett, descendents of Baltimore & Ohio railroad baron John Work Garrett, donated 1,917 acres for what became Maryland's first state forest. Today the forest covers more than 7,000 acres of wooded slopes and valleys. Mountain streams drip into swamps and bogs.

The Walks
The state forest includes two state parks, one of which - Herrington Manor - doesn't allow dogs so canine hiking here is limited to old logging roads and the gravelly Snaggy Mountain Road. This is not difficult hiking for your dog with long, steady ascents and your dog can go off leash in Garrett State Forest.

> **Where The Paw Meets The Earth:** Rough-surfaced old logging roads
> **Workout For Your Dog** - As hard as he wants to go up the ascents
> **Swimming** - Mountain streams await you more than ponds
> **Restrictions On Dogs** - Dogs are allowed in all areas of the forest, including the campgrounds

Something Extra
You can keep your leash in your hand.

Gilbert Run Park

Phone - (301) 932-1083
Website - None
Admission Fee - Yes
Directions - *La Plata, Charles County; eight miles east on MD Route 6.*

The Park
Wheatley Lake is the centerpiece of this 180-acre park.

The Walks
Surrounding the lake is a 2.5-mile trail, mostly swallowed by mature woodlands. Your dog will get a good workout on the hills at the back of the lake from the parking lot and long stretches of relaxed trotting as well.

> **Where The Paw Meets The Earth:** Natural surface footpaths
>
> **Workout For Your Dog** - Yes, it's a little rollercoaster of a canine hike
>
> **Swimming** - Away from th eday-use are on the trail are good spots for a doggie swim
>
> **Restrictions On Dogs** - None

Something Extra
The St. Charles Humane Society stages its annual dog walk here.

Gillis Falls Reservoir Site

Phone - None
Website · None
Admission Fee - None
Directions - *Mt. Airy, Carroll County; from I-70 take Woodbine Road (MD 94) north off Exit 73. Make a left in about 1 mile on Newport Road, following signs to Carroll County Equestrian Center on Grimville Road.*

The Park
Carroll County owns 1200 acres of land around the Middle Run and Gillis Falls where they are waiting approval to create a reservoir. In the meantime an equestrian trail system has been developed through the watershed by volunteers. These trails are closed Mondays, Wednesdays, Fridays and Saturdays from September 1 through February 28 and for two weeks beginning the Saturday after Thanksgiving due to a controlled hunting program.

The Walks
The Gillis Falls equestrian trails cover about 3.5 miles of wooded access roads. The terrain drops sharply in and out of the Gillis Falls stream valley on paths that feature many rocky stretches under paw. The elevation changes and varying moisture content of the soil conspire to allow differing forest types to dominate on different points of the hike. The trails are laid out in varying loops of short duration. Hiking at Gillis Falls will necessitate at least two stream crossings and several more depending on your route. Only one bridge spans the sparkling clear stream waters. This is not a problem except at the confluence of Gillis Falls and Middle Branch which can be forded only by horse, dog or wet shoe.

> **Where The Paw Meets The Earth:** Rock-studded dirt paths
> **Workout For Your Dog** - Long treks with spirited climbs
> **Swimming** - Stream waters are seldom deep enough for canine aquatics beyond splashing
> **Restrictions On Dogs** - None

Something Extra
Civilization once took hold in the Gillis Falls valley and nature is slowly reclaiming building foundations, collapsed ruins and lampposts along the trail. One such cinderblock structure, now riddled with bullet holes, looks like a former hideout for Bonnie and Clyde.

Great Falls Tavern

Phone - (301) 767-3714
Website - http://www.nps.gov/choh/planyourvisit/greatfallstav-ernvisitorcenter.htm
Admission Fee - Yes, a 3-day pass
Directions - *Potomac, Montgomery; The park entrance is at the junction of Falls Road (Route 189) and MacArthur Boulevard. Take Exit 39 off I-495 and continue on River Road (Route 190) West before turning left on Falls Road.*

The Park
A canal that could connect the Potomac River to the Ohio River in Pittsburgh would provide a continuous water link from New Orleans to the Cheasapeake Bay. The canal, dubbed the "Great National Project" by President John Quincy Adams, was finally started on July 4, 1828. It would take 22 years to complete - actually construction just stopped since the canal route never made it out of Maryland with only 184.5 of the planned 460 miles dug - and was obsolete before it opened. Battling the young and ever-improving railroads, the Chesapeake & Ohio Canal lasted for 75 years floating cargo from Cumberland, Maryland to Georgetown. The ditch survived filling in through the efforts of Supreme Court Justice William O. Douglas who championed the canal as "a long stretch of quiet and piece."

The Walks
The packed sand and paw-friendly towpath is one of the most scenic of its ilk. Away from the Potomac a trail system penetrates the wooded hills above the river. These wide dirt trails make for easy dog walking through an airy, mature forest. The key route is the *Gold Mine Loop* that pushes out from behind the Visitor Center. Various short spur trails, some marked and some not, radiate off the 3.2-mile loop.

> **Where The Paw Meets The Earth:** sand and dirt trails
> **Workout For Your Dog** - Some sporty canine hiking
> **Swimming** - Along the *River Trail* there are a few spots where it is not too wild and wooly for a cautious dip
> **Restrictions On Dogs** - Dogs are not allowed on the *Billy Goat Trail*

Something Extra
During the Civil War, a Union private camped at Great Falls discovered gold-bearing quartz while tending to his chores. After the war he returned to Great Falls and began mining operations that triggered a mini-gold rush to the area. Although the Maryland Mine was active from 1867 until 1939, it yielded less than $200,000 of precious metal. The *Falls Road Spur* takes you to the ruins of the mine and mine diggings can be seen at several places on the trails.

Green Ridge State Forest

Phone - (301) 478-3124
Website - http://www.dnr.state.md.us/publiclands/western/greenridge.html
Admission Fee - None
Directions - *Flintstone, Allegany County; eight miles east off I-68 at Exit 64.*

The Park

Today Green Ridge State Forest is Maryland's second largest with over 40,000 tree-covered acres. A century ago your dog would have hiked long and far to find a tree here. Iron mining and sawmills depleted the forest and what trees were still surviving in the early 1900s were burned or cut by the Merten family who converted the forest into "the largest apple orchard in the universe." The orchard failed in 1918 and in 1931 the State of Maryland acquired the first acreage here and began the forest's renaissance.

The Walks

Canine hiking in the state forest is concentrated along the *Green Ridge Hiking Trail*, a 24-mile linear trail that can be chopped into a handful of day hikes. Or launch a multi-day backpacking expedition - you can even tie in with the Chesapeake & Ohio Canal towpath for a circuit hike of almost 50 miles. If your dog loves water, he might be up for it - mountain streams and swimming holes abound along this trail.

> **Where The Paw Meets The Earth:** Dirt trails with some rocks and multi-use paths suitable for all-terrain vehicles
> **Workout For Your Dog** - Definitely
> **Swimming** - Sample the Potomac River, White Sulphur and Orchard ponds, Town Creek, 15-Mile Creek and Sideling Hill Creek
> **Restrictions On Dogs** - None

Something Extra

The Old Town Road on the east side of the forest was built during the 1750s as a military road connecting Fort Frederick with Fort Cumberland by order of Maryland Governor Sharpe. The Old Town Road was surveyed by one of Maryland's greatest frontiersmen Colonel Thomas Cresap. Follow the road to Old Town, the oldest settlement in Allegany County, settled by Colonel Cresap in 1740. "Point Lookout," off of Old Town Road, is a site overlooking the Potomac River Valley east. From this perch, Union soldiers tried to detect Confederate movements in the valley during the Civil War.

Greenbelt Park

Phone - (301) 344-4250
Website - http://www.nps.gov/gree/
Admission Fee - None
Directions - *Greenbelt Park, Prince Georges County; from I-95, take Exit 23, Kenilworth Avenue South to (Route 201) Greenbelt Road (Route 193). Make a left; the park is a quarter mile on the right.*

The Park
The story of Greenbelt Park is the tale of many a public park in Maryland - except this time the steward is the federal government. This land was once covered with vibrant forests as far as the eye could see, all of which fell before the broadaxes of European colonists. For a century afterwards the ground poured forth sustenance for tobacco and corn until it could give no more. The land was abandoned and left barren. As the land began to recover developers in the 1930s sketched plans to transform it into one of the many "model towns" slated to be developed around Washington D.C. As it happened, Greenbelt Park was acquired in 1950 along with the land to build the Baltmore-Washington Parkway and the recovering forest survived as an 1,100-acre oasis of passive greenspace.

The Walks
The first thing to know about canine hiking at Greenbelt Park is that parking is limited and visitors are encouraged to take advantage of public transportation so come early when you bring your dog. Once on the trails you will find well-groomed, wide paths - there are garbage cans out in the middle of the woods and the many tree blowdowns are attended to quickly. Casual canine hikers can take advantage of the three nature loops, all around one mile in length. The *Azalea Trail* trips through streamlands to link the park's three picnic areas and the centrally-located *Dogwood Trail* highlights the regenerative forest with pioneering Virginia pines still able to steal a bit of light from the surrounding oaks and maples. For a good long canine hike jump on the six-mile *Perimeter Trail*. If the droning traffic noise begins to intrude on your outing there are plenty of connector trails and roads to cut things short.

> **Where The Paw Meets The Earth:** Mostly soft dirt and pine straw
>
> **Workout For Your Dog** - Mostly flat and easy
>
> **Swimming** - Small creeks are not great swimming holes
>
> **Restrictions On Dogs** - None

Something Extra
Where can you visit Washington, D.C. and spend the night inside the Beltway with your dog for $14? Greenbelt Park. The park campground has 174 sites available on a first-come, first-served basis and is open all year round and dogs are allowed.

Greenwell State Park

Phone - (301) 373-9775
Website - http://www.dnr.state.md.us/publiclands/southern/greenwell.html
Admission Fee - None
Directions - *Hollywood, St. Mary's County; take Route 235 towards town and turn on to MD 245 East (Sotterley Gate Road) and travel 2.5 miles. Make a right on to Steerhorn Neck Road. The park entrance is the second drive on the left.*

The Park

During his childhood John Phillip Greenwell's mother died, leaving his disabled father to raise the family's six children. Greenwell grew up to become a successful Washington-area commercial real estate investor and in 1941 purchased Rosedale Farm. Greenwell accurately refurbished the farm to its Revolutionary War-era beginnings. The focal point of the property was the Rosedale Manor with its Victorian rose garden that sits majestically above the Patuxent River. In 1971 he deeded the 167-acre farm to the State of Maryland for use as a public park, with one important stipulation - it was to be used especially by those with disabilities. The State purchased the adjoining Bond farm and has agressively pursued Greenwell's vision for a park accessible to all. The therapeutic riding program is widely praised, there are camps for the disabled and on-going plans to make all activities in the park fully accessible.

The Walks

Take your pick of canine hikes on these old farm roads. There are ten miles of multi-use trails on nine named routes from multiple parking lots. Where the trails leave the farm roads for footpaths some of the going can get a bit tricky but for the most part your dog will enjoy easy going at Greenwell. You'll be hiking with your dog through cultivated soybean fields and along forest edges. If your dog tires of the sunny croplands, duck onto an inviting forest trail. Several routes meander down to the wide Patuxent River. About half of the trail system is open to hunting but these routes are easily passed over if the season is active.

> **Where The Paw Meets The Earth:** Old dirt farm roads
> **Workout For Your Dog** - Easy going across the old farm
> **Swimming** - There is a small beach area and canoe launch with access to the Patuxent River
> **Restrictions On Dogs** - None

Something Extra

The chance to examine Maryland tobacco farm history with three original tobacco farms, including the oldest hand-hewn log barn still standing in St. Mary's County.

Gunpowder Falls State Park-Belair Road

Phone - (410) 592-2897
Website - http://www.dnr.state.md.us/publiclands/central/gun-powder.html
Admission Fee - None
Directions - *Kingsville, Baltimore County; the parking area and trailheads are on the northbound side of US 1 (Belair Road) after it crosses the Big Gunpowder Falls, about 5.4 miles north of the I-695 Beltway). Polar parking lots on the ends of the park are on the south side of the river on Harford Road (MD 147) and on Jones Road off the Pulaski Highway (US 40).*

The Park
The fall line between the Piedmont and coastal plains occurs in this section of the park, just west of Route 40. Sloops could come up the Big Gunpowder Falls as far as this point to load shipments from the many mills operating upstream. A popular ferry once operated at Long Calm, the stretch of river west of today's I-95. The Marquis de Lafayette camped here famously during the American Revolution. Today the park's trails run for 8 miles along the Big Gunpowder Falls water chutes.

The Walks
The highlight for canine hikers here is the Sweathouse Branch Wildlands Area that provides some of the best loop trails in the Gunpowder park system. The outside loop links the *Wildlands Trail* (pink), the *Stocksdale Trail* (blue) and the *Sweathouse Trail* (yellow) and covers 5.1 miles. The healthy hill climbs and wide trails give a big feel to this walk as it meanders through differing forest types. The *Lost Pond Trail* runs in a 3.1-mile long lasso on its way to an abandoned mill pond. The yellow-blazed *Sawmill Trail* visits the ruins of the 1833 Carroll family sawmill. These trails require several stream crossings and are often muddy. For all-day hikers the *Big Gunpowder Trail* picks its way through the woods along the entire length of the river on the south bank, eventually reaching the last rapids of the Gunpowder.

> **Where The Paw Meets The Earth:** Dirt trails with some rocky patches
> **Workout For Your Dog** - Long trails with a few climbs
> **Swimming** - The dam-controlled Big Gunpowder Falls is often only deep enough only for splashing
> **Restrictions On Dogs** - None

Something Extra
In the center of the Big Gunpowder Falls, about 1.2 miles east of the parking lot, are the Pot Rocks. Best accessed from the *Big Gunpowder Trail*, you and the dog can walk out and examine the conical depressions created in the bed rock by swirling waters armed with millions of years worth of grinding cobbles. These unique potholes can be a foot or more deep.

Gunpowder Falls State Park-Hereford

Phone - (410) 592-2897
Website - http://www.dnr.state.md.us/publiclands/hereford.html
Admission Fee - None
Directions - *Pasadena, Baltimore County; take Exit 27 off I-83 onto Mt. Carmel Road. The main lot is at the end of Bunker Hill Road off York Road. Other trailheads are on Mt. Carmel, York, Masemore, Falls and Big Falls roads.*

The Park

Gunpowder Falls State Park embraces more than 17,000 acres of property in distinct tracts from the Maryland-Pennsylvania state line to the Chesapeake Bay. The Hereford Area on the Big Gunpowder River preserves 3,620 acres of pristine Maryland woodlands. Located where rivers tumble down the fall line of the Piedmont Plateau to the flat Coastal Plain, there was plenty of water power here to drive the industry of a young America. Ruins of these mills, including a gunpowder mill which exploded on the Panther Branch on July 7, 1874, can still be seen in the park.

The Walks

At Hereford the canine hiker can find any length or type of hike to set tails wagging. The marquee trail among 20 miles of hiking is the 7.1-mile *Gunpowder South Trail* that includes bites of trail more reminiscent of West Virginia than Baltimore, especially the western segment from Falls Road to Prettyboy Dam. While most of the narrow dirt trails at Hereford are easy on the paw, this waterside path is rocky and requires a fair amount of rock scrambling. Your reward is stunning views of the rugged gorge. Walking along the *South Trail*, and its companion *North Trail* on the opposite bank, is generally level as it follows the meanderings of the stream. For hearty climbers, look to the many side trails which can be wedded to the *South Trail* to form several loops of between one and two miles of length.

> **Where The Paw Meets The Earth:** Rock-studded dirt
> **Workout For Your Dog** - Moderate stretches mingled with climbs
> **Swimming** - Plenty of great pools in the stream
> **Restrictions On Dogs** - Dogs are not allowed in the campground

Something Extra

The *Gunpowder South Trail* continues past the park boundaries to the base of the Prettyboy Dam where you can watch water releases from the reservoir. This water blasts out from the bottom of the lake providing a steady supply of chilled water favored by trout and the Big Gunpowder Falls is a nationally recognized trout stream.

Gunpowder Falls State Park-Jerusalem Mill

Phone - (410) 557-7994
Website - http://www.dnr.state.md.us/publiclands/central/gunpowder.html
Admission Fee - None
Directions - *Kingsville, Baltimore County; the park office is in Kingsville on Jerusalem Mill Road off US 1.*

The Park

Established as a grain mill in 1772, Jerusalem Mill operated until 1961. Restoration began in 1985 and has expanded to include the entire Village of Jerusalem with tenant houses, smith shops, and a general store. Since 1995, the Jerusalem Mill has housed the administrative headquarters for all of sprawling Gunpowder Falls State Park.

The Walks

There are many miles of hiking along the Little Gunpowder Falls on both sides of park headquarters here. Upstream from Jerusalem Mill the white-blazed *Little Gunpowder Trail* is a bouncing ramble through the woods. The return trip on the linear trail can loop into the hillsides on blue-blazed side trails like the *Quarry Trail*. Downstream (cross the bridge by the Mill to pick up the trail) the route takes in more open fields as it leads to a loop around the Kingsville Athletic Fields. For a quick loop, stop at the Jericho Covered Bridge and return on the yellow-blazed horse trail.

> **Where The Paw Meets The Earth:** Dirt trails
> **Workout For Your Dog** - Long, easy-going trails
> **Swimming** - The trails stay true to the whims of the Little Gunpowder Falls with many access points to the water
> **Restrictions On Dogs** - None

Something Extra

Downstream from Jerusalem Mill about 1/2 mile is Jericho Covered Bridge, one of only six remaining covered bridges in Maryland and the only one of its kind in Baltimore and Harford counties. Old folk wisdom held that these bridges were built to resemble a barn to entice a wary horse across water but the bridges are covered simply to protect the expensive wooden decks. The ford at this point across the Little Gunpowder Falls dates to Colonial times; the bridge was constructed in 1865. Builder Thomas F. Forsyth used three truss types in its construction: the simple Multiple King Post; the horizontal Queen Post extension; and the Burr Arch, patented in 1804 by Theodore Burr, for stability. Renovated in 1981, the Jericho Covered Bridge still carries traffic.

Gunpowder Falls State Park-Pleasantville

Phone - (410) 557-7994
Website - http://www.dnr.state.md.us/publiclands/central/gun-powder.html
Admission Fee - None
Directions - *Belair, Baltimore County; from Harford Road (MD 147), take Fork Road west and make a right on either Bottom Road or, quickly following, Pleasantville Road. Parking is along the street and more plentiful at Bottom Road than Pleasantville.*

The Park

This isolated trail system on the Little Gunpowder Falls comes to canine hikers courtesy of the Maryland and Pennsylvania Railroad, known affectionately as the Ma & Pa. To create the railbed nineteenth century railroad engineers clawed their way up the steep river valley here levelling hillsides and filling ravines. That railbed of the abandoned line now makes up the bulk of the hiking at Pleasantville.

The Walks

There are three hikes at Pleasantville, including a candidate for the "Least-Traveled Path" in the Baltimore area - the *Pleasantville Loop*. This 1.5-mile trek begins with one of the steepest climbs in the Gunpowder Falls State Park system to reach the start of the loop. Virtually indiscernible as a trail in most parts, let the dog lead the way and keep an eye out for white blazes. The loop follows a creative series of 270-degree turns through the thick forest with only occasional glimpses of the river below before returning to that steep stem trail. The main hiking is across Pleasantville Road (a tricky crossing with a dog). Linear trails run along the river on both sides for two miles between Pleasant- ville and Bottom roads that can be combined for a loop across narrow bridges. The hike on the Baltimore County (white blazes) side is more topsy-turvy, tumbling in and out and around ravines; the Harford side (yellow blazes) uses more of the Ma & Pa trailbed, which crossed the river near the center of these trails, and is a bit tamer. It also adheres more closely to the flow of the river.

> **Where The Paw Meets The Earth:** Wooded dirt paths
> **Workout For Your Dog** - One steep climb
> **Swimming** - Good, but there is not as much access to the river as might be expected due to high banks and vegetation
> **Restrictions On Dogs** - None

Something Extra

The Baltimore region offers many chances to hike along the right-of-ways of historic railroads, but perhaps none so exotic as here. It is easy to picture the slow-moving steam trains chugging through this lush valley as you amble along.

Gunpowder Falls State Park-Sweet Water

Phone - (410) 557-7994
Website - http://www.dnr.state.md.us/publiclands/central/gun-powder.html
Admission Fee - None
Directions - *Jacksonville, Baltimore County; from Sweet Air Road (MD 145) turn onto Greene Road and make a left on Moores Road to park entrance.*

The Park
Unlike other sections of Gunpowder Falls State Park, the water is not the star at Sweet Air. Only a short segment of the trail system follows the Little Gunpowder Falls, which flows thinly near its headwaters at this point. The attraction at Sweet Air is a patchwork of open fields (still under cultivation) and wooded landscapes on either side of the river.

The Walks
Sweet Air offers more than twelve miles of well-marked rambles on four main trails and several connector branches. The feature hike is the white-blazed *Little Gunpowder Trail*, serving up a buffet of Sweet Air splendor in the course of its 3.8 miles: fern-encrusted hillsides, upland farm fields and ultra-green forests. Short loops off this trail visit a quiet woodland pond and a small white pine plantation. Look for a cornucopia of trail surfaces - soft dirt, hard pack, wood chip and mown grass. A total exploration of Sweet Air will include the blue-blazed *Boundary Trail* which means wading through the Little Gunpowder to walk into Baltimore County. If this proves enjoyable, consider some of the rogue trails at Sweet Air near the water.

> **Where The Paw Meets The Earth:** Natural surface trails throughout
> **Workout For Your Dog** - Moderate canine hiking
> **Swimming** - Gunpowder Falls is generally deep enough only for sustained splashing but the farm ponds on the property make for good dog paddling
> **Restrictions On Dogs** - None

Something Extra
Rest stops have been set up along the trails that give Sweet Air the feel of an English manor park, a good place to come and forget about time. One of the best is at a pretty stretch of riverwalk where a sycamore tree has grown horizontally inches above the water and its branches are growing vertically like a grove of slender trees.

Hampton National Historic Site

Phone - None
Website - http://www.nps.gov/hamp/
Admission Fee - None
Directions - *Towson, Baltimore County; from I-695, take Exit 27-B north (Dulaney Valley Road) and make an immediate right on Hampton Lane to the entrance on the right.*

The Park

When Captain Charles Ridgely, heir to an iron and shipping fortune, began construction on Hampton mansion in 1783 this now highly suburbanized part of Baltimore County was so remote that wolves howled at night and locals ridiculed the project in the wilderness as "Ridgely's Folly." In 1948, after housing six generations of Ridgelys, the Georgian mansion became the first site in the National Park Service to be recognized for its architectural merit and not its historical significance. Once a sprawling, self-sufficient empire of 25,000 acres, all that remains of the original Hampton estate is 63 acres.

The Walks

The elegant stuccoed mansion is off limits to your dog but that is no reason he can't strut around the grounds like royalty. He can trot down the Great Terrace behind the house, once used for bowling on the green, and into the formal English boxwood garden. Where once a 700-tree orchard stood is an open field ideal for a game of fetch. Scattered among the 200 historic specimen trees are original outbuildings - stables that once housed Maryland's fastest horses, a citrus-growing orangery and slave quarters. On the front lawn is a grass-covered brick dome enclosing a 33-foot deep pit that was used as an ice house.

> **Where The Paw Meets The Earth:** Grass and brick and cobble
> **Workout For Your Dog** - No
> **Swimming** - None
> **Restrictions On Dogs** - No dogs in the mansion

Something Extra

One wonders what Charles Ridgely would think of his final resting place were he able to see it today. When placed inside the family's Greek Revival vault after his death, his land holdings included enough land to make up half of present-day Baltimore. Yet the Ridgely family cemetery now squeezes against an interstate highway with a view of a neighbor's backyard play set. Still, the brick-walled family cemetery is a unique historical destination open to your dog.

Harpers Ferry National Historic Park

Phone - (304) 535-6029
Website - http://www.nps.gov/hafe/
Admission Fee - Yes, for the town
Directions - *Harpers Ferry, Washington County; to reach Mary-land Heights, take the last left off of Route 340 before crossing the Potomac River. Turn right on Sandy Hook Road and continue to the parking area across from Harpers Ferry along the C & O Canal.*

The Park
Few places pack as much scenic wonder and historical importance into such a small area as Harpers Ferry National Historic Park where the Shenandoah and Potomac rivers join forces. George Washington surveyed here as a young man. Thomas Jefferson hailed the confluence as "one of the most stupendous scenes in Nature" and declared it worth a trip across the Atlantic Ocean just to see. Meriwether Lewis prepared for the Corps of Discovery in 1804 by gathering supplies of arms and military stores at Harpers Ferry. A United States Marine Colonel named Robert E. Lee captured abolitionist John Brown at Harpers Ferry when he attempted to raid the United States Arsenal and arm a slave insurrection. General Thomas "Stonewall" Jackson scored one of his greatest military victories here during the Civil War. Congress appropriated funds for a national monument in Harpers Ferry in 1944 and 2,300 acres of Maryland, Virginia and West Virginia were interwoven into the National Historic Park in 1963.

The Walks
Dogs are welcome in Harpers Ferry National Historic Park and hikes are available for every taste and fitness level. On the Maryland side of the Potomac River is the towpath for the Chesapeake & Ohio Canal; the trail is wide, flat and mostly dirt. Beside the canal, the Maryland Heights rise dramatically 1,448 feet above the rivers. The *Stone Fort Trail* up the Heights is the park's most strenuous hike and one of the most historic.

> **Where The Paw Meets The Earth:** packed dirt to rocky slopes
> **Workout For Your Dog** - Absolutely if he wants it
> **Swimming** - There is some access to the Shenandoah River
> **Restrictions On Dogs** - Dogs cannot take the shuttle bus into Lower Town so you will have to hike to the historic river junction

Something Extra
You walk your dog across the Potomac River bridge - there is open grating that can intimidate skittish dogs - to Lower Town in Harpers Ferry. Climbing up the steep grade out of Lower Town is a short trail to Jefferson Rock, where Thomas Jefferson recorded his impressions in 1783.

Hashawha Trails

Phone - (410) 848-2517
Website - http://ccgovernment.carr.org/ccg/hashawha/default.asp
Admission Fee - None
Directions - *Westminster, Carroll County; go north on Route 97 and turn right on John Owings Road. Go 1.5 miles and make a left on Hashawha Road. The Nature Center is up the hill on the right.*

The Park
Carroll County maintains nearly 8 acres of open space for every 100 residents and nearly 1900 of those acres are at the Union Mills Resorvoir Site. In 1972 the county purchased the land to establish the Bear Branch Nature Center and the surrounding Hashawha (an Indian term meaning "old fields") Environmental Center trails.

The Walks
There is something for every canine hiking taste at the well-designed Hashawha trails. Out for a simple trot? The blue blazed *Vista Trail* is a 1.2-mile circuit on mostly level ground that takes in fields, woods and ponds. Toss in the *Stream Trail* (green blazes) and you add a restored log cabin, grassy meadows, the gurgling Bear Branch Creek and a boardwalk crossing over part of Lake Hashawha. This blue-green circuit totals a bit less than 3 miles. For longer hikes take to the wooded hills of the *Wilderness Trail* (yellow blazes) where four loops pile upon one another until reaching Big Pipe Creek. The complete outer loop brings 2.2 miles of rolling and sometimes rocky trails into your hiking day. Looking for an all-day hiking adventure? There are eight more miles of marked trails laid out by the Carroll County Equestrian Council, including the *Kowomu Trail*, beyond the Hashawha trails. These can also be accessed from their own parking lots. Don't overlook the short interpretive *Bear Path Trail* behind the Nature Center that helps explain our everyday environment.

> **Where The Paw Meets The Earth:** Natural surface; sometimes rocky
> **Workout For Your Dog** - Mostly flat and easy with an occasional hill
> **Swimming** - The streams at Hashawha provide a welcome splash on a hot day but aren't deep enough for extended dog paddling
> **Restrictions On Dogs** - None

Something Extra
Here is the chance for your curious dog to look a bald eagle in the eye. The Nature Center maintains a M.A.S.H. unit for raptors who have been injured too badly to be returned to the wild. The cages for eagles, kestrels, hawks, owls, turkey vultures and other recovering birds of prey are on the Vista Trail.

Herring Run Park

Phone - None
Website - None
Admission Fee - None
Directions - *Baltimore City; linear park is accessed by parking on bordering neighborhood streets. Crossroads include Harford Road (MD 147) and Belair Road (US 1).*

The Park

Before being annexed by Baltimore City in the early 1900s the land around Herring Run was a rural quiltwork of farms and estates. A village named Georgetown thrived in the area and near the present-day Sinclair Lane Elementary School a horse farm rented mounts for local residents to ride along the stream. Herring Run suffered considerable abuse as the city filled in around it but in recent years the park, which claims 324 acres of land along Herring Run, has regained it place of importance in the surrounding neighborhoods.

The Walks

A paved serpentine path traces the winding course of Herring Run for four miles on the southern edge of the stream. Along the way are wide grassy fields and secluded alcoves of mature woodlands. To complete the entire route does involve crossing busy streets so use caution. Herring Run Park is a magnet for dog owners in the surrounding neighborhoods and it is not unusual to happen upon a doggie play group by the waterside.

>**Where The Paw Meets The Earth:** Macadam
>
>**Workout For Your Dog** - Little dips and rolls
>
>**Swimming** - Herring Run is ideal for doggie splashing and occasionally there are pockets deep enough for dog paddling
>
>**Restrictions On Dogs** - None

Something Extra

In 1881 engineers began a reservoir system for providing Baltimoreans water by damming Tiffany's Run on the city's then northern edge. The resulting Lake Montebello was filled by a series of brick water tunnels but only served as a reservoir for four years. Instead its water cleaned filter beds in the Montebello Filtration Plant. Today, in the northwest section of Herring Run Park, Lake Montebello looks much as it always has. The hike around the lake is 1 1/2 miles and there are separate lanes for walkers, runners, cyclists and vehicular traffic.

Kinder Farm Park

Phone - (410) 222-6115
Website - http://www.kinderfarmpark.org/
Admission Fee - None
Directions - *Millersville, Anne Arundel County; just west of Governor Ritchie Highway (MD 2) on Jumpers Hole Road.*

The Park

In 1898 German immigrant A. Gustavus Kinder purchased 41 acres of farmland north of the Severn River and began growing fruits and vegetables for sale in Baltimore. The Kinders gradually expanded their agricultural operation until over 1,000 acres were under cultivation. After World War II, the Kinders moved from truck farming to cattle production and began selling off land for residential development. In 1979 they sold 288 acres of pastureland to Anne Arundel County for development as Kinder Farm Park.

The Walks

A 2.4-mile asphalt trail snakes around the Kinder Farm property visiting fields and meadows and dipping into reforestation areas. This is easy walking and connects to the *East-West Boulevard Trail* for even longer excursions with your dog. More interesting to the canine hiker are the unimproved farm roads that run through the park. These sand/dirt paths duck into woodlands and across old fields. For the dog who has never been to a farm, a trail leads past the farmhouse/park office (circa 1926) and a close-up view of four concrete silos.

> **Where The Paw Meets The Earth:** Sandy dirt farm roads and grass fields in addition to the asphalt
>
> **Workout For Your Dog** - Easy rolling routes
>
> **Swimming** - There are four small ponds at Kinder Farm but because of aquatic vegetation or limited access these are not prime doggie swimming holes
>
> **Restrictions On Dogs** - None

Something Extra

Back beside the secluded Bunk's Pond is a forest of bamboo, planted as an ornamental grass. Although mostly associated with southeast Asia, native bamboo is estimated to have once covered 5 million acres of the southeastern United States. Many of the 1200 species of this hardy grass grow eagerly in temperate regions like these timber bamboo plants that have sprouted to over 25 feet tall. They are wonderful at absorbing sound and make this pondside walk a quiet, special place. Beware under paw, however, as the trail has been cut through the stalks.

Lake Waterford Park

Phone - (410) 222-6248
Website - http://www.aacounty.org/RecParks/parks/lakewaterfordpark/index.cfm
Admission Fee - None
Directions - *Pasadena, Anne Arundel County; at the corner of Pasadena Road and Waterford Road (MD 648).*

The Park
This land was part of two land grants by Lord Baltimore, Gambriells Purchase and Howard's Pasture. An estate was carved from the property and a mill built to grind grain. After the mill was torn down in 1900 the area became known as a hiding place for hoboes. Subsequently, Waterford Mill, named for the 18th century Elizabeth Water, was farmed, used to raise commercial goldfish and even tried as a resort. Today Lake Waterford Park consists of 108 acres around the centerpiece 12-acre lake stocked with trout, carp, crappie, bass, pickerel and bluegill.

The Walks
Don't dismiss Lake Waterford as another multi-use recreational trail upon seeing the paved paths at the trailheads. Beyond the picnic pavilions are a cornucopia of short, interconnecting nature trails. These are paw-friendly paths of sandy dirt and pine straw and the hiking is easy - wooden bridges and steps have been built to smooth out the rough spots. The *Blue Trail* offers the most scenic diversion of the seven colored trails as it traces the lakeshore. There are many unmarked side trails as well, several of which are narrow fisherman's paths leading to the water. The trails are all wooded.

> **Where The Paw Meets The Earth:** Paw-friendly sandy dirt
>
> **Workout For Your Dog** - A good stroll
>
> **Swimming** - There are many access points along the trails for the dog to slip into Lake Waterford
>
> **Restrictions On Dogs** - None

Something Extra
Lake Waterford sponsors an Adopt A Duck program to help support its population of domestic ducks and geese which are much in evidence as you walk on the paved section of trail by Lake Waterford.

Leakin Park/Gwynn Falls Park

Phone - (410) 557-7994
Website - None
Admission Fee - None
Directions - *Baltimore City; the entrance to Leakin Park is on Windsor Mill Road; a centralized parking location for both parks and the Gwynns Falls Trail is at the Winans Meadow Trailhead on Franklintown Road.*

The Park

In 1922 J. Wilson Leakin, an attorney of means, died and gave Baltimore money from his rental properties to buy a large city park. Planners settled on the Gwynns Falls valley in western Baltimore, once the boundary of the Iroquoian and Algonquian speaking tribes. Much of the original land for the park when it opened in 1948 came from the estate of Thomas Winens which overlooked the Dead Run valley. Today Leakin Park and the adjoining Gwynns Falls Park, at 686 acres the largest public park in Baltimore, comprise over 1000 acres of recreational opportunity.

The Walks

Gwynns Falls is largely undeveloped so most of your hiking will be in Leakin Park. The trails are surprisingly lush for an urban park, with a thick understory thriving beneath towering trees. The primeval feeling of the park is so pervasive it was chosen as a filming site for the horror film *Book of Shadows: Blair Witch 2*. Remnants of the Winans estate are sprinkled throughout the park: the family home, an 1850s stone Victorian mansion called Crimea; a wedding chapel; a waterwheel; and ruins of a mock fort that may have been built during the Civil War. The first 4.5 miles of a planned 14-mile trail to the Inner Harbor, *Gwynns Falls Trail*, has been completed to Leon Day Park.

> **Where The Paw Meets The Earth:** Rocky surfaces under paw
> **Workout For Your Dog** - You bet, hearty hill climbs
> **Swimming** - Dead Run is an aptly named trickle of a stream and access to the swift-flowing Gwynns Falls is limited
> **Restrictions On Dogs** - None

Something Extra

Thomas Winans made his fortune building the Russian transcontinental railroad for Czar Nicholas I. He learned railroading from his father Ross who invented the swivel wheel truck that enabled trains to negotiate curves. Their railroad heritage is preserved at Leakin Park by the Chesapeake & Allegheny Live Steamers who maintain 3 miles of track for miniature steam train that carry passengers (sorry, no dogs) free of charge the second Sunday of every month.

Liberty Reservoir

Phone - None
Website - None
Admission Fee - None
Directions - *Oakland, Baltimore County; accessed primarily be three east-west roads that dissect the property: from north to south they are Westminster Road (MD 140), Deer Park Road, and Liberty Road (MD 26).*

The Park
When Liberty Dam walled off the North Branch Patapsco River in 1953 a reservoir greater in size than Loch Raven and Prettyboy combined gurgled into being. Its 9200 slender acres contain 82 miles of shoreline. There are many miles of attractive, isolated hiking on fire roads in the Liberty watershed but access along busy roads can be problematic for dog owners. Also, skitterish dogs would do well to avoid Liberty Dam Road where you'll find the closest thing to a park on the reservoir. The police shooting range and a local gun club are located here.

The Walks
The land in this valley before the plugging of the river was mostly pasture and cropland. Thus the wooded buffers around the reservoir are still filling in, giving these walks an airier feel than their water-holding cousins. But like Loch Raven and Prettyboy there is plenty of up-and-down hiking and the fire roads tend to make for long and straight routes. There are several small creeks coursing through the watershed and trail crossings at these sites will be a wet shoe affair. Although not wide, officials have removed rocks from the stream bed to aide emergency vehicles in getting across. Good for trucks and dogs but not for hikers in cold weather.

> **Where The Paw Meets The Earth:** Scruffy dirt roads and natural paths
> **Workout For Your Dog** - Long trails bounding up hills
> **Swimming** - Not really
> **Restrictions On Dogs** - None

Something Extra
Pack your fishing rod with your hiking gear when you come to Liberty Reservoir, which has emerged as the home of Maryland's largest land-locked rockfish. Only a few years back the state record fish weighed 36 pounds but stripers of 40 pounds and more are being pulled regularly from the 3,100-acre lake. Liberty's unique water density and a high oil content that surrounds the egg sac of Chesapeake Bay strain rockfish allow for what biologists once thought impossible - the actual reproduction of rockfish in a small reservoir.

Little Bennett Regional Park

Phone - (301) 972-6581
Website - http://www.mc-mncppc.org/Parks/enterprise/park_facilities/little_bennett/bennett_trails.shtm
Admission Fee - None
Directions - *Clarksburg, Montgomery County; from I-270 take Exit 18 and head north on Clarksburg Road, MD 121. Turn left on MD 355 and then right into the Campground Entrance. There is also trailhead parking on Clarksburg Road across MD 355.*

The Park

Grist mills opened along the Little Bennett Creek and in 1798 Jesse Hyatt built a sort of "super" mill that gound corn for local farmers and wheat for export. By 1804 the mill supported the town of Hyattstown with six houses.Growth spurted in the Little Bennett Valley and by 1860 it was a thriving rural community. It was important enough to skirmish over a couple of times in the Civil War. The Baltimore & Ohio railroad was siphoning much of the freight traffic off the Great Road but it wasn't until the 1950s and the building of I-270 that the nutrient-poor rocky slopes finally quit supporting this rural community. In 1975 the valley became Little Bennett Regional Park, Montgomery County's largest expanse of unbroken woodland at 3,700 acres.

The Walks

There is a full menu of canine hiking at Little Bennett Regional Park - 23 miles worth. Most dog owners will want to concentrate on the south side of Hyattsville Road where horses and bikes are banned. A dozen short, twisting trails explore the hollows and ridges around Little Bennett Creek and its tributaries. You can easily get a couple hours of trail time on these mown meadowand forested trails. When you reach the *Mound Builder Trail*, look down and not up for the mounds - they are the work of harmless Allegheny ants. Don't give up on the multi-use trails just to keep your dog out of the path of the occasional bike or horse. The roads are rockier, the hills are steeper, the paths can be muddier but you will miss an eclectic mix of natural and historic delights.

> **Where The Paw Meets The Earth:** Dirt paths, gravel roads
>
> **Workout For Your Dog** - Big walks and some big hills too
>
> **Swimming** - The water in the park is mostly for splashing
>
> **Restrictions On Dogs** - None; dogs are permitted in the campground too

Something Extra

Little Bennett Regional Park contains the richest assembly of historic structures and sites of any county park in Maryland. Along the trails and park roads you can see a chapel dating to 1871, mills and mill houses, log buildings, the site of a popular rye whiskey distillery and a one-room schoolhouse that remains in its original state.

Loch Raven Reservoir

Phone - (410) 795-6151
Website - None
Admission Fee - None
Directions - *Sunnybrook, Baltimore County; accessed from Exit 27 of the Baltimore Beltway (I-695) on Dulaney Valley Road (MD 146). Some of the more popular parking areas can be found on Seminary Road, Providence Road, Morgan Mill Road at Loch Raven Road, the Dulaney Valley Road bridge, Warren Road and at the end of Pot Springs Road.*

The Park
Robert Gilmor, son of a successful Baltimore merchant, bought 2,000 acres in the Gunpowder River valley with dreams of building a castle resembling those of his ancestral Scotland. His mansion Glen Ellen never quite accomplished his vision and the estate was sold to the city just before he died in 1883. A dam and water tunnel to funnel water into Baltimore were built in 1881 and enough property was acquired by the 1920s to raise the height of the dam and create the 10-mile long Loch Raven Reservoir - the name being a tip of the hat to Robert Gilmor's beloved Scottish lochs.

The Walks
There is enough hiking on wide fire roads at Loch Raven to require days to complete. Throw in the ubiquitous side trails and it could take a dog's life to see the entire watershed. All the trails through the buffer zone around the "loch" are heavily wooded with mature trees that help protect the reservoir's water quality. Many of the trails track along high ridges with commanding views of the water, especially when the trees are not in leaf. A day of hiking Loch Raven with your dog will involve many hill climbs, some that will leave both human and dog panting. There are stream crossings and rough stretches of trail, especially through ravines.

> **Where The Paw Meets The Earth:** Dirt paths
> **Workout For Your Dog** - Plenty of hills and long trails
> **Swimming** - Swimming and wading are not permitted in Loch Raven
> **Restrictions On Dogs** - None

Something Extra
Simply having the opportunity to hike these scenic trails is the biggest bonus at Loch Raven. Most municipalities do not allow access to its reservoirs and in fact recreational use here is an on-going experiment. If any activity is judged to adversely affect the water supply (like dogwalking) for Loch Raven's 1.8 million users, the privilege will be withdrawn.

Ma and Pa Heritage Trail

Phone - (410) 638-3535
Website - None
Admission Fee - None
Directions - *Belair, Harford County; parking for Phase I is available at Tollgate Road opposite the Equestrian Center and on Mast Street, one block west of Route 924. To access Phase II, use Blake's Venture Park on Melrose Lane or Friends Park on Jarrettsville Road in Forest Hill.*

The Park

The married couple in question are the states of Maryland and Pennsylvania which were wedded by a short-line railroad carrying freight and passengers between Baltimore and York. It took the peripatetic line 77.2 twisting miles of track to cover the 49-mile distance as the crow flies. The much beloved Ma and Pa operated from 1901 until 1956, hauling enough milk from area dairy farms to be known as the "Milky Way." The Foundation for the Pres-ervation of the Ma and Pa Railroad set out in the mid-1990s to create a hiker/biker trail on seven miles of the old railroad bed in the Bel Air/Forest Hill area.

The Walks

The *Ma and Pa Trail* is a stone dust path that differs from its other "rail-to-trail" brethren by its abundance of dips and swirls in the trail, a legacy of the local line's 476 curves. Much of the route is wooded although there is never a feeling of "getting away from it all" along the route. The tunnel under MD 24 was built especially for equestrians from a less congested age. There is also hiking available in 421-acre Heavenly Waters Park, although dogs are confined to a macadam trail aound the duck pond.

> **Where The Paw Meets The Earth:** Smooth crushed stone
> **Workout For Your Dog** - Small rolling undulations in the path
> **Swimming** - No real dog dipping opportunities on the route
> **Restrictions On Dogs** - None

Something Extra

Standing on a hillside overlooking the *Ma and Pa Trail* is Liriodendron, an elegant mansion built as a summer home by Baltimore surgeon Howard Kelly to assuage the homesickness of his Prussian bride in 1897. Dr. Kelly, who pioneered the use of radium in cancer therapy and helped found Johns Hopkins Medical College, named his new escape after the tulip poplar tree, Liriodendron. The couple was married for 53 years before both passed away in 1943 six hours apart, neither knowing the other was dying. A woodland trail winds around the back of the property and leads up to the grounds. It can be reached via a parking lot near the Mast Street parking lot.

Matapeake Park

Phone - None
Website - None
Admission Fee - None
Directions - *Stevensville, Queen Anne's County; from US 50/301 exit to South MD 8 and turn right on Marine Academy Drive to park on the right.*

The Park
This is a small Queen Anne's County Park on the Chesapeake Bay used mostly by fishermen to get out onto the water.

The Walks
The canine hiking highlight here is a pleasant one-mile wood-chip trail through a pine forest but the reason to come here is a stretch of sandy beach where your dog is welcome off-leash. The beach is a bit too industrial for sunbathers which makes it the perfect place for dogs to romp. Matapeake Park is just south of the Bay Bridge with splendid views of the bay and bridge.

> **Where The Paw Meets The Earth:** Wood chips and soft dirt
> **Workout For Your Dog** - Only tired from swimming
> **Swimming** - One of the best places you can take your dog in Maryland
> **Restrictions On Dogs** - No dogs in the fishing pier area of the park

Something Extra
The views of the Bay Bridge are among the best going.

Middle Patuxent Environmental Area

Phone - (410) 313-4726
Website - None
Admission Fee - None
Directions - *Clarksburg, Howard County; north of town; the entrance is on Trotter Road, east of Clarksville Road (MD 108).*

The Park

In the 1960s the Rouse Company deeded this property to Howard County when it was acquiring land to build nearby Columbia. Middle Patuxent Valley Association was organized in 1996 to protect 928 acres of diverse wildlife and vegetation in the Middle Patuxent Environmental Area, now managed by Howard County Parks and Recreation.

The Walks

Although the going can get confusing at times, there are two basic hikes   at Middle Patuxent. The main loop leading from the parking lot uses farm roads to reach the river and then circles back up to the crest of a ridge. Once you go down this trail you sign on for the entire loop which can take up to an hour. Often unmaintained, the hike can turn into a doggie steeplechase over fallen trees as the vegetation shifts from airy woodland to vibrant forest. Much of the trail is soft dirt but many areas are traversed on grass, a legacy of the Rouse days when the land was planted with ornamental olive trees and fescue grasses best suited for golf courses and lawns. The *Southwind Trail* has been created off the main loop and also leads to the river where majestic sycamore trees overhang the banks. The route travels up through Clegg's Meadow, decorated with warm-weather native grasses that have been reintroduced to the park.

> **Where The Paw Meets The Earth:** Grass and dirt
> **Workout For Your Dog** - Small hills
> **Swimming** - The banks of the Middle Patuxent River are
> often high but there is ample opportunity for a good swim
> **Restrictions On Dogs** - None

Something Extra

The mottled brown American Woodcock is a long-time favorite of birdwatchers who cherish its unique courtship display. In springtime, at dusk, males arrive at "singing grounds" and begin flying in upward spiraling circles before swooping back to earth where they herald their flights in song. Woodcocks require four habitats in close proximity: feeding cover, nesting cover, roosting areas and open ground for courtship. At Middle Patuxent seven acres have been set aside for woodcock habitat management.

Millington Wildlife Management Area

Phone - None
Website - None
Admission Fee - None
Directions - *Massey, Kent County; from US 301 take MD 330 East to the park office on left.*

The Park
Freed slaves lived on small scale farms in this area beginning in the early 1800s. The farming depleted the land and much of it was abandoned until the 1940s when the Maryland Department of Game and Fish bought 500 acres of the Toth farm for a State Game Refuge. Now Millington has grown to 3,800 acres of public hunting area.

The Walks
Canine hiking here is a rustic affair on flat woodlands, consisting primarily of hardwoods. No maps or wayfinding aids are available.
> **Where The Paw Meets The Earth:** Natural wooded surface
>
> **Workout For Your Dog** - Flat, easy terrain
>
> **Swimming** - Not easily found
>
> **Restrictions On Dogs** - None

Something Extra
One of the primary attractions in Millington are the presence of Carolina Bays or "whale wallows." These series of shallow depressions, filled with water in rainy times, are found only in Millington Wildlife Management Area and across the line in Delaware's Blackbird State Forest. Their origins are a mystery; local lore maintains that they are the result of struggling whales, stranded after the biblical flood receded. Other theories suggest glacial scraping or even meteorites. Whatever their origins, when wet these "living museums" support rare plants and abundant wildlife.

Monocacy National Battlefield

Phone - (301) 662-3515
Website - http://www.nps.gov/mono/
Admission Fee - No for grounds
Directions - *Frederick, Frederick County; From I-70, take Exit 54 (Market Street), then turn south on MD 355. The Gambrill Mill Visitor Center is located one-tenth of a mile south of the Monocacy River bridge.*

The Park

In 1847 a farm was cobbled together here from several small tracts that was purchased in 1862 by John Worthington. This farm saw withering action on July 7, 1864 when Union general Lew Wallace, better known as the author of *Ben Hur: A Tale of The Christ*, took up a defensive position with 2,700 men at Monocacy Junction, planning to check the advance of General Jubal Early and his 18,000 Confederates. The bloody battle that came two days later was a decisive defeat for the outnumbered Federals, but the delay it caused Early probably kept Washington from falling into Confederate hands.In 1928, Glenn Worthington petitioned Congress to create a National Military Park at Monocacy. The bill passed but acquisition of land for preserving the battlefield did not take place for another half-century.

The Walks

Much of the battlefield is in private hands but there is still plenty to see in the farm land that is virtually unchanged since the Civil War. At the park Visitor Center an interpretive half-mile trail in light woods leads to the Monocacy River. Down the road, a stacked loop explores the Worthington farm. There is a mix of open field canine hiking and hardwood forests on two stacked-loop trails. The park is devoted as much to the natural evolution of the landscape as to remembrance of battles fought. Of particular interest are the gnarly Osage-orange trees that were grown as natural fences. The terrain grows steep in places but overall this is a relaxed hike for your dog on natural trails and graveled farm roads. All told there are more than three miles of trails at Worthington Farm.

> **Where The Paw Meets The Earth:** Natural trails and gravel roads
> **Workout For Your Dog** - Quiet, easy canine hiking
> **Swimming** - Your dog will enjoy the Monocacy River
> **Restrictions On Dogs** - None

Something Extra

The mill on the property, located near Bush Creek, was one of the area's most productive. Built in 1830, James H. Gambrill bought it in 1856 and began cranking out sixty barrels of flour a day. He had to employ up to eight coopers just to build barrels for the mill output. A race was built to bring water across the field to power the undershot waterwheel.

Monocacy River NRMA

Phone - None
Website - None
Admission Fee - None
Directions - *Dickerson, Frederick County; parking east of town on MD 28 on the immediate east side of the Monocacy River bridge.*

The Park
If your dog isn't partial to things like trail maintenance and maps, he's likely to love these 1,800 acres of natural areas and farmlands along the Monocacy River. The paths are unmarked and many exist only from the passing of hunters, fishermen, and the occasional horse or deer. Plan on some bushwhacking and stream crossings so this may not be the choice after a soaking rain.

The Walks
The main trail leading from the parking lot is an old wagon road that provided access to a quarry and lime kiln used in building the nearby Chesapeake & Ohio Canal almost 200 years ago. This is not a place for a casual 30-minute stroll; the double track road leads out for several miles with many side paths to explore, including some that lead to the river for a swim.

> **Where The Paw Meets The Earth:** Natural surface
> **Workout For Your Dog** - Trails are not stenuous but long
> **Swimming** - Access to the river is usually problematic even though it is nearby
> **Restrictions On Dogs** - None

Something Extra
If you seek them out you can find remnants of the quarry days on the site.

Morgan Run Natural Environment Area

Phone - None
Website - None
Admission Fee - None
Directions - *Westminster, Carroll County; south of town, just off MD 97. After a left on Bartholow Road, turn left on Jim Bowers Road after .1 mile and another immediate left on Ben Rose Lane to the parking lot at the end in .6 mile. The hiking and angler trails are in the north section at the end of Jim Bowers Road off Nicode-mus Road from MD 97.*

The Park

The land that would eventually be preserved as the Morgan Run Natural Environment Area was settled in the early 1700s when a stagecoach road (now Liberty Road) was established between Baltimore and Frederick. Carroll County leads Maryland in agricultural preservation and these 1,400 acres of natural land are slated to grow to more than 3,000 in the future.

The Walks

Step out of the car onto the gravel parking lot and this looks like a place to walk the dog. Wide grass trails cut into rolling fields dip and dart across the horizon into woodlands. There are many intersecting trails cut through the grass (sometimes high) to extend the canine hiking experience here. When the trails reach the wooded areas at the cold, clear waters of Morgan Run they continue to be a paw-friendly, hard-packed dirt. There are unconnected trails on either side of Morgan Run in the flood-plain. Although these are hiker-only trails they are narrow and can be over-grown; a special trip to try them is not recommended.

> **Where The Paw Meets The Earth:** Wide, dirt paths through woods
> **Workout For Your Dog** - Long hikes and many hills
> **Swimming** - Morgan Run is a premier trout stream, especially in the winter, a modest five yards across in most places, it occasionally sports a canine swimming hole; a small pond can also sustain a doggie dip.
> **Restrictions On Dogs** - None

Something Extra

Hiking with the dog and the horse? Carroll County offers several equestrian trails but none with the feeling of vast open spaces like Morgan Run.

Naylor Mill Park

Phone - None
Website - None
Admission Fee - None
Directions - *Salisbury, Wicomico County; take US 13 and turn onto Naylor Mill Road north of Salisbury, heading west. The park is on the right after a mile in the Henry S. Parker Athletic Complex.*

The Park
Salisbury gets some of its drinking water from the Paleo Channel Aquifer here, drawing water from between 160 and 195 feet below the earth's surface. The park is a cooperative of the water company, Maryland's Open Space Pro-gram and the citizens of Wicomico County. When you enter the park athletic fields will be on your right and the wooded trail system on your left. There are no signs but drive to back parking lot and enter the trails there.

The Walks
Your dog will love the mixed sand and soft dirt surface of these paths that show a surprising amount of elevation change for the heart of the Eastern Shore. You'll actually be working along a ridge above swampy wetlands for awhile. The trails are narrow and tight, designed by the local mountain biking community that cut them. You'll find more than an hour of exploring at Naylor Mill Park, all under a mixed-forest canopy.

> **Where The Paw Meets The Earth:** Soft sandy dirt
> **Workout For Your Dog** - Enough rolls and dips to keep things interesting
> **Swimming** - A little fun in the creek but nothing to make a special trip for
> **Restrictions On Dogs** - None

Something Extra
A great stop for a quick hike on the way to the beach.

North Park

Phone - None
Website - None
Admission Fee - None
Directions - *Havre de Grace, Harford County; in town on Conesteo Street, off Water Street. Follow signs for the Lockhouse Museum.*

The Park
On June 12, 1764 Charles Mason and Jeremiah Dixon walked into Alexander Bryan's cornfield near Newark, Delaware and planted a small concrete pillar that cemented their names in American history. The survey the English mathematicians began that day would establish the border between Maryland and Pennsylvania and forever separate the "North" from "South" in America. Today the *Mason Dixon Trail* connects Chadds Ford, Pennsylvania with the Appalachian Trail 190 miles away using local parks and public roads. The well-marked *Mason Dixon Trail* begins its jaunt up the western bank of the Susquehanna River in Havre de Grace.

The Walks
You can pick up the blue blazes of the *Mason Dixon Trail* on a telephone pole in the parking lot for the Susquehanna Lockhouse Museum. Across a footbridge and past a small playground, the trail leads under the US 40 Hatem Memorial Bridge and picks up an abandoned rail line used in the building of the Conowingo Dam (trees growing in the middle of the tracks should ease worries of oncoming trains). This is easy going on level ground that passes through wetlands and a mixed hardwood forest. In about one mile the trail ends for canine hikers at the base of a large rockpile - an athletic dog might make the top but the risk dwarfs the reward. The return trip can be made on a wide dirt trail - wide dirt trail - probably the former towpath - on the edge of the Susquehanna River.

> **Where The Paw Meets The Earth:** Rocky surfaces and smooth dirt
> **Workout For Your Dog** - Level ground but not always a clear path
> **Swimming** - There is plenty of good access to the Susquehanna River
> **Restrictions On Dogs** - None

Something Extra
At this point the 444-mile Susquehanna River is busy emptying 19 million gallons of fresh water every minute into the Chesapeake Bay. It has drained that water from 13 million acres of land.

North Point State Park

Phone - (410) 329-0757
Website - http://www.dnr.state.md.us/publiclands/central/north-point.html
Admission Fee - Yes
Directions - *Edgemere, Baltimore County; from I-695 east of Baltimore, take Exit 40 to Route 151 south; from the west, use Exit 43. Follow signs to Fort Howard on North Point Road (MD 20). The park entrance is on the left, 1/2 mile from Miller Island Road.*

The Park
Notoriety came to the North Point area during the War of 1812 when local Free Staters engaged British invaders. Happier times arrived a century later with the establishment of a small amusement park known as Bay Shore Park. Bethlehem Steel purchased the land in the 1940s and tore down the park to establish a private hunting preserve for its executives. The public was invited back in 1989 after the State of Maryland acquired the property for conversion into a 1310-acre park with more than 6 miles of shoreline along the Chesapeake Bay, Back River and Shallow Creek.

The Walks
More than half the park consists of the Black Marsh Wildlands, considered to be one of the finest examples of a tidal marsh on the Upper Chesapeake. Unfortunately your dog will not see this unique landscape - dogs are not permitted in the Wildlands. You can hike around the short *Wetlands Trail Loop* which is a hard-packed dirt path. Also available is a hike/bike trail that skirts some of the fields at the park. The stone surface is not paw-friendly but does have wide grass shoulders. The old trolley line has been paved over in spots to form a nature trail. All the walking at North Point is flat and easy.

> **Where The Paw Meets The Earth:** Mostly macadam
> **Workout For Your Dog** - All canine hiking is flat and easy
> **Swimming** - A small wading beach at the Visitor Center was opened in 1999 and dogs are welcome to dive in
> **Restrictions On Dogs** - Dogs are not allowed in the wilderness area

Something Extra
Although only 20 acres, Bay Shore Park was considered one of the finest amusement parks ever built along the Chesapeake Bay. Opened in 1906, the park featured an Edwardian-style dance hall, bowling alley and restaurant set in among gardens and curving pathways. Most of the park was torn down after its closure in 1947 but you and the dog can explore the remains of a turn-of-the century amusement park including the wood-framed trolley station and the restored ornamental fountain. Complete your tour with a hike down the old Bayshore Pier that juts almost a quarter-mile into the wind-swept Bay - a diving board once operated where benches rest today.

Northern Central Railroad Trail

Phone - (410) 592-2897
Website - http://www.dnr.state.md.us/greenways/ncrt_trail.html
Admission Fee - None
Directions - *Ashland. Baltimore County; from York Road (MD 45) turn right on Ashland Road. Stay on Ashland as main road bears left on Paper Mill Road and continue to parking lot at end.*

The Park

The Northern Central Railroad began carrying passengers in 1838 but the road was known mostly to farmers and coal miners until November 18, 1863 when Abraham Lincoln boarded a regular coach, sitting with other passengers, headed for Gettysburg to dedicate a new national cemetery (contrary to popular folklore he did not scribble out the Gettysburg Address on the back of an envelope on the train). Less than two years later the President's funeral train would travel the same route. Passenger service would continue until 1972 when Hurricane Agnes finished the fading line by washing out bridges and tearing up track. The state of Maryland took possession of the NCRR in 1980 and after removing 600 tons of trash opened the first segment of the rail-trail in 1984.

The Walks

The 19.7-mile *Northern Central Railroad Trail* is the prettiest of the Baltimore area rail trails. Much of the route is decorated by isolated forests and meadows, occasionally dropping in on rustic farm towns. The first half of the trail roughly parallels the Big Gunpowder Falls (the Gunpowder Falls State Park administers the trail). The trail is broken up by nine parking lots so canine hikers with a two-car system can reduce the trail to manageable 2-3 mile segments. The crushed stone and clay path follows a gentle 1% grade to an imperceptible rise of 400 feet from south to north.

> **Where The Paw Meets The Earth:** Crushed stone and clay
> **Workout For Your Dog** - Easy grade throughout
> **Swimming** - Opportunities for a a quick doggie dip are easier to come by along the southern stretches
> **Restrictions On Dogs** - None

Something Extra

The Northern Central Railroad's legacy of 135 years of passenger service is one of the longest in the world. Traces of that heritage can be seen in iron mile markers, old railroad signals, and the historic train station at Monkton. Put in operation in 1898 as a Pennsylvania Railroad Company stop, there are now railroading artifacts on display in the station which serves as a rest stop for trail users.

Oregon Ridge Park

Phone - (410) 887-1815
Website - http://www.oregonridge.org/
Admission Fee - None
Directions - *Cockeysville, Baltimore County; from I-83 take Exit 20B west on Shawan Road. After one mile make a left on Beaver Dam Road and immediately take right fork into the park.*

The Park

An active mining community thrived at Oregon Ridge in the mid-19th century. Irish immigrants and emancipated slaves did most of the hard work pulling first Geothite, containing iron ore, and then high-grade Cockeysville marble from the hills. The iron was smelted in a furnace along Oregon Branch and the marble was used to build the United States Capitol and the Washington Monument. The Oregon Ridge Iron Works supported a company town of 220 workers and their families before the business died away in the 1870s. Today Oregon Ridge Park is Baltimore County's largest park with more than 1000 acres of woods and meadows.

The Walks

Although you get under way with a pleasant stroll into the forest across the wooden bridge spanning the Grand Canyon of Oregon Ridge (an aban-doned open pit mine), it doesn't take long to realize you have signed on for a serious hike here. The *Loggers Red Trail* pulls you to the top of the ridge - elevated enough to launch hang gliders - and your pick of nine short trails. The full loop of the property leads south along the yellow trails and will add 4 stream crossings and serious hill climbs to your outing. All told there are 6 miles of trails at Oregon Ridge. All are wooded and almost uniformly wide and soft to the paw. The lone exception is the rocky slopes of the *S. James Campbell Trail* which are a trade-off for the scenic trekking in the ravine. Be sure to make your way to the half-mile *Lake Trail*, a rollicking romp above the green waters of the 45-foot deep Oregon Lake, a flooded old iron quarry.

> **Where The Paw Meets The Earth:** Natural surface throughout
> **Workout For Your Dog** - Some good climbs on long trails
> **Swimming** - Baisman Run is simply for splashing but Ivy Pond is a delightful stop for a dip
> **Restrictions On Dogs** - Dogs are not permitted in the beach area at Oregon Lake

Something Extra

An interpretive trail leads to exhibits on the bountiful natural re-sources that Oregon Ridge provided to settlers in the region: water, timber, iron, marble and rich farmland. The trail begins at recreated tenant houses of the Oregon Ridge Iron Works just below the Nature Center.

Patapsco Valley State Park

Phone - (410) 260-8835
Website - http://www.dnr.state.md.us/publiclands/central/patapscovalley.html
Admission Fee - Only in developed areas; no dogs allowed
Directions - *Ellicott City, Baltimore County; see below*

The Park

Maryland's state park system began with the establishment of Patapsco State Forest Reserve in 1907. Today the park sprawls across 14,000 acres and four counties. The linear park traces the Patapsco River for 32 miles from southeastern Carroll County to tidewater in Baltimore Harbor.

The Walks

The widespread prohibitions against dogs in developed areas of Patapsco Valley State Park are a prime frustration for Maryland dog owners. But there is plenty of lemonade to be squeezed from the lemons served up by the State of Maryland. Four undeveloped areas are recommended by the park service to take the dog:

Feezer's Lane (gravel road on west side of Marriottsville Road just north of the bridge over North Branch of Patapsco River);

Henryton Road (off MD 99 at the end of the road at the washed out bridge over South Branch Patapsco River);

Daniels Area (at end of Daniels Road off Old Frederick Road, east of the intesection of Routes 29 and 99);

Hilltop Road at Hilton Area (off Frederick Road, Md 144, between Catonsville and Ellicott City).

> **Where The Paw Meets The Earth:** A variety of natural trails
>
> **Workout For Your Dog** - Long trails with good moderate climbs
>
> **Swimming** - There is great canine swimming in the Patapsco River in all four park areas, save Feezer's Lane
>
> **Restrictions On Dogs** - Dogs are not allowed in the Avalon, Orange Grove, Glen Artney, Hilton, Hollofield, Pickall and McKeldin day-use areas, as well as the Hilton campground. One camp loop for visitors with pets is available in the Hollofield campground.

Something Extra

When the trail crosses a section of Baltimore & Ohio track in the Henryton Road section look to the west at the Henryton Tunnel. Opened in 1850, it is the second-oldest tunnel in the world that remains in active railroad use. Look to the east and find a short concrete post by the side of the track. It is a vintage whistle post used to warn of the upcoming Marriottsville Road grade crossing around the bend. Few whistle posts survive today.

Patterson Park

Phone - None
Website - http://www.pattersonpark.com/
Admission Fee - None
Directions - *East Baltimore City; exit I-95 onto Eastern Avenue and follow to park on the right, bounded by Park Avenue, Baltimore Street and Eastern Avenue. Parking is on the street.*

The Park
This patch of ground in East Baltimore was notorious long before 75-year old merchant William Patterson donated five acres of land to the city in 1827. In 1808 thousands of Baltimore protesters boarded the brigantine Sophia and carted 720 gallons of gin here to fuel a patriotic bonfire. The official public park was not a decade old when the 7th Maine Regiment camped on the grounds during the Civil War. During its golden years Patterson Park sported spectacular ornamental iron gates by the local firm of G. Krug & Son, flower gardens and fountains. City and volunteer restoration efforts are rehabilitating the 2.6-acre waterfowl pond, Tudor buildings, and well-trod grounds.

The Walks
Many of the brick and asphalt paths winding through the 155-acre park are walkways based on plans drawn by brothers John Charles and Frederick Law Olmsted, Jr. in 1904. Scattered along the walkways and grassy slopes are magnificent trees dating to the original plantings when the park opened in 1853. Some of the scars and humps on the hillsides are remnants of the trenches dug during the War of 1812.

> **Where The Paw Meets The Earth:** Asphalt and brick pathways
>
> **Workout For Your Dog** - The park is essentially on one big hill
>
> **Swimming** - None
>
> **Restrictions On Dogs** - None

Something Extra
Standing on the highest rise in the park where Commander John Rodgers amassed 12,000 troops to protect the city during the Battle of Baltimore in the War of 1812 is the Patterson Park Observatory. Designer Charles H. Latrobe, grandson of the designer of the U.S. Capitol, built the orange-and-yellow tower in 1891 when he was Superintendent of Parks. Latrobe embellished the tower with three tiers of balconies and enough fantail windows, lattice work and Oriental flourishes that the Observatory is more commonly known as the "Pagoda." Recently restored, visitors can climb the spiral stairs on Sundays but the view from dog's eye level outside is none to shaggy either. And you never know what you may see - in 1937 a small plane safely crash-landed in Patterson Park.

Patuxent Research Refuge -North Tract

Phone - (301) 497-5580
Website - http://www.fws.gov/northeast/patuxent/
Admission Fee - None
Directions - *Laurel, Anne Arundel County; from the Baltimore-Washington Parkway, exiting to the east on Savage Road (MD 32). Make a right on Fort Meade Road (MD198) and after .7 miles a left on Bald Eagle Drive (marked by refuge sign).*

The Park

A scrawl of the pen by Franklin Roosevelt in 1936 established the Patuxent Research Refuge as America's only refuge to support wild-life research. The original 2,670 acres swelled to its current size of 12,750 acres with the addition of 8,100 acres formerly belonging to adjacent Fort Meade (visitors must sign a waiver regarding possible live ammunition encountered on the grounds - don't let your dog dig in strange holes!). It is said that the Patuxent Research Refuge is the largest patch of undeveloped green space that can be seen from the air on the east coast between Boston and Raleigh. There are two sections of the refuge open to the public: the National Wildlife in Prince Georges County and the North Tract.

The Walks

There are some 20 miles of trails in the North Tract, including the paved 8-mile Wildlife Loop access road which is lightly traveled. Another 9 miles of trails are on former access roads closed to vehicular traffic. The hiking on these pebbly roads cuts through the woods and, while quiet and solitary, the scenery seldom changes on the long, straight stretches. The best hiking at the North Tract is on the *Forest Habitat Trail*, opposite the visitor center. The wide, soft trail contours pleasantly as it circles for 2.5 miles through mature forest with limited understory. Two other hiker-only trails of less then a mile are available: the *Little Patuxent River Trail* which loops through the moist ground by the river and the sandy *Pine Trail*.

> **Where The Paw Meets The Earth:** Sandy dirt roads and natural trails
> **Workout For Your Dog** - Long trails with good moderate climbs
> **Swimming** - Several alluring ponds await canine swimmers including Rieve's Pond off the *Blue Trail* and the Cattail Pond at Bailey's Bridge and the Little Patuxent River a few feet from the pond has a deep pool as well
> **Restrictions On Dogs** - None

Something Extra

The wide diversity of habitats at Patuxent support at least 40 on-going research studies. The most famous research done here was conducted on the pesticide DDT that led to the banning of the chemical and launched the modern environmental movement.

Paw Paw Tunnel

Phone - (301) 678-5463
Website - http://www.nps.gov/choh
Admission Fee - None
Directions - *Paw Paw, Allegany County; Take I-70 to Hancock and go south on Route 522 to Berkeley Springs, West Virginia. Turn west on Route 9 and go 28 miles to Paw Paw.*

The Park
The biggest obstacle to the completion of the Chesapeake and Ohio Canal was five miles of crooked Potomac River water known as the Paw Paw Bends. It was decided to bypass the curves with a tunnel, destined to be the largest man-made structure on the 184-mile canal. Rosy-eyed planners began work on the tunnel in 1836 with a goal of 7-8 feet gained a day. Instead, the pace was more like 12 feet a week. Fourteen years later - with a cost overrun of 500% - the 26-foot high tunnel was opened. Encased in the six million bricks used to build the Paw Paw Tunnel at Mile 155 are tales of unpaid wages, immigrant worker abuse, labor unrest and even murder. The canal finally closed in 1924 after several devastating floods crippled commerce on the waterway.

The Walks
This is the most unique hike you can take with your dog in Maryland. The first thing you need to know is bring a flashlight - there are no lights in the tunnel and it is long enough to envelop you in complete darkness. This canine hike starts in a national park service campground and travels a short distance on the well-maintained towpath of the canal until you reach the Paw Paw Tunnel. At this point you can plunge directly into the 3,118-foot tunnel (more than a half-mile long) or veer to your right and lead your dog on a hardy hike over the top of the tunnel on the *Tunnel Hill Trail*. You will rejoin the towpath on the opposite side of the tunnel and complete your loop by returning through the darkness.

> **Where The Paw Meets The Earth:** Naural dirt and small cinder trails
> **Workout For Your Dog** - Short energetic climbs
> **Swimming** - Access at the Potomac River canoe launch
> **Restrictions On Dogs** - None; dogs allowed in campground as well

Something Extra
The tunnel and the nearby town take their name from the preponderance of Pawpaw trees, also known as a prairie banana or Ozark banana, in the area. This small tree with large leaves bears the largest edible fruit native to North America. The fruit is a plump berry that can be two feet long with numerous seeds; it is green when unripe, maturing to yellow or brown. The paw-paw has a flavor somewhat similar to both banana and mango.

Piney Run Park

Phone - (410) 795-3274
Website - None
Admission Fee - Yes
Directions - *Sykesville, Carroll County; From Exit 76 of I-70 take MD 97 North. After 5 miles look for Obrecht Road and make a right. Go 1 mile and make a left on White Rock Road. After another mile make a right on Martz Road and follow to park at end. To reach the equestrian trails, stay on White Rock Road to Liberty Road (MD 26). Make a right and another right on Martz Road and go 1 mile to parking area.*

The Park

In 1975 Piney Run was dammed to provide drinking water for Sykesville. The resulting reservoir covers 298 acres and the surrounding park that grew up around the lake is another 200 acres.

The Walks

Piney Run Park features more than 5 miles of wooded lakeside trails. The marquee trail here is the 3.5-mile *Inlet Trail* but canine hikers may want to start explorations on the .7-mile *Field Trail Loop*, especially for early arrivers. Dogs are allowed on this trail off-leash and under voice control until 8:00 a.m. Despite its name, most of this trail is under groves of Norway Spruce, Scotch Pine and White Pine. The *Field Trail* also has the best access to the Piney Run shoreline of any of its four trails.The *Inlet Trail* is essentially a long lasso of a trail with three scenic paths intersecting the loopthat take in both cultivated farm fields and a variety of forest habitats. Near the trailhead the *Inlet Trail* connects to the *Indian Trail* loop and then the *Lake Trail*, both wooded paths less than 1/2 mile long. The *Lake Trail* is a flat, semi-arc trail that features snatches of pretty lakeviews through the trees; the *Indian Trail* is a narrower pick-your-way hike in the deciduous forest. Across the lake are nearly 4 miles of equestrian trails for hikers who prefer their trails a bit less groomed, but free of charge. The southern trail is a linear trail along the shoreline; the northern section features more loops. Again, these Piney Run trails are wooded.

> **Where The Paw Meets The Earth:** Paw-friendly grass and soft dirt
> **Workout For Your Dog** - Mostly easy going
> **Swimming** - The trails seldom touch Piney Run Lake but when they do the dog paddling is excellent
> **Restrictions On Dogs** - None

Something Extra

Nailed to a post along the *Indian Trail* is a dugout canoe. No longer seaworthy, the wooden canoe is still an unexpected reminder of how transportation used to take place at Piney Run before dams and power boats.

Pocomoke River State Park

Phone - (410) 632-2566
Website - http://www.dnr.state.md.us/publiclands/eastern/pocomokeriver.html
Admission Fee - None
Directions - *Snow Hill, Worcester County; take Route 13 south from Salisbury to the traffic light at Dividing Creek Road (Route 364). Turn left and stay on Route 364 to Milburn Landing entrance on the right.*

The Park
The Pocomoke River flows out of the Great Cypress Swamp in Delaware and moseys 45 miles across Maryland into the Cheaspeake Bay. The Pocomoke - from the Indian word for "black water" - has long been an important travel route and was believed to be an important link in the Underground Railroad where escaped slaves could hide in the swamp until nightfall when they could safely resume their journeys north. The Pocomoke River State Forest and Park protects mre than 15,000 acres of woodlands more commonly seen in the Deep South - towering loblolly forests, eerie baldcypress swamps and great swaths of black gum trees.

The Walks
Pocomoke River State Park is divided into two sections about a half-hour's drive apart - you will want to take your dog to Milburn Landing since your best trail companion isn't permitted at Shad Landing. A trail using grassy fire roads and woodsy trails loops for 4.5 miles around the Pocomoke River Wildlands. The star canine hike here is the leafy *Bald Cypress Nature Trail* that departs from the first parking lot at the Mattaponi Pavilion. To find the trailhead, turn right onto Mattaponi Road opposite the campground and make your first left. The trail is barely maintained in the early going and it takes awhile to reach the baldcypress swamp but there is extended walking along this unique natural treasure. All the walking in Pocomoke State Park is level and easy for any dog.

> **Where The Paw Meets The Earth:** Soft, paw-friendly dirt
> **Workout For Your Dog** - Flat just about everywhere
> **Swimming** - Pocomoke River is a fine place for your dog to swim
> **Restrictions On Dogs** - Dogs are allowed at Milburn Landing but not at Shad Landing

Something Extra
The slackwater of the Pocomoke River begs for a canoe journey with your dog. On the *Corkers Creek-Blackwater Canoe Trail* paddlers quickly descend into the still world of the cypress swamp - look for river otters as you travel along. Canoes can be rented at the park.

Point Lookout State Park

Phone - (301) 872-5688
Website - http://www.dnr.state.md.us/publiclands/southern/pointlookout.html
Admission Fee - Yes
Directions - *Scotland, St. Mary's County; take MD 5 all the way down the peninsula to the park.*

The Park

Captain John Smith explored Point Lookout, a peninsula formed by the confluence of the Chesapeake Bay and the Potomac River, in 1612. The government built a lighthouse here in 1830 and William Cost Johnson bought most of the land on the peninsula in 1857 to develop as a resort. The Civil War upset those plans and a hospital for Union soldiers was built here and in 1863, after the Battle of Gettysburg, Confederate prisoners were sent to the remote spit of land.

The Walks

Dogs are restricted at Point Lookout - they are not allowed beyond the causeway where the Civil War fort was located. But dogs can stay in the campground and there are loops you can share with your dog. You wouldn't want to drive all the way down to Point Lookout for it but if you are nearby there is a superb sandy dog beach north of the causeway. The Chesapeake Bay waves are frisky enough to delight any water-loving dog.

> **Where The Paw Meets The Earth:** Natural surface footpaths
> **Workout For Your Dog** - Easy going through the woods
> **Swimming** - One of the best places for your dog to swim
> **Restrictions On Dogs** - Pets are allowed in all areas of Malone Circle, Tulip Loop, Green's Point Loop, Hoffman's Loop, and on the paved portion of the causeway and on the beach (north of the causeway) to the entrance of Tanner's Creek. They are NOT permitted in any other day use area or trail, including the beach or picnic area.

Something Extra

Thanks to its history as a Civil War Camp, Point Lookout is rumored to have an active ghost community - pay attention to your dog to alert you to the presence of wandering poltergeists.

Potomac State Forest - Backbone Mountain

Phone - None
Website - None
Admission Fee - None
Directions - *Oakland, Garrett County; from the town go south on Route 219 and cross over the intersection of Route 50 at Red House to Silver Lake, West Virginia. Staying on Route 219, go one mile south to an old logging road and park along the road.*

The Park

At 3,360 feet above sea level Backbone Mountain, a long slab of rock in the Allegheny range, is the highest point in Maryland, the 32nd highest "highpoint" in the United States. When you reach the summit you and your dog will actually be standing on the point of Hoye-Crest, named for Captain Charles Hoye, a prominent chronicler of Maryland lore and founder of the Garrett County Historical Society. Backbone Mountain is the Eastern Continental Divide - rain that falls on the eastern slope drains into the Atlantic Ocean via the Potomac River and water on the western side eventually finds it way to the Gulf of Mexico.

The Walks

The highest point in Maryland is less than two football fields from West Virginia and the easiest way to get to Hoye-Crest is to start across the state line in the Monongahela National Forest. You will use an old logging road to reach the ridge of Backbone Mountain; it is steep enough to get your dog panting but not so arduous you will need to pull over and rest. Once you reach the ridge it is a short ways to the high point. The trail on the ridge is more of a hiking trail and has some interesting features the short time you are on it. Once your dog is through soaking in the experience of being on the roof of Maryland the way down is the same as the way up - a two-mile round trip. There are plenty more trails to explore across Backbone Mountain but there won't be any wayfinding aids at the trailhead. Your dog can go off leash in Potomac State Forest.

> **Where The Paw Meets The Earth:** Rocky fire roads and rocky paths
> **Workout For Your Dog** - Straight up but short
> **Swimming** - There is no water on the canine hike to Hoye-Crest
> **Restrictions On Dogs** - None

Something Extra

At Hoye-Crest you will find a mailbox with a register so you can ink your dog's accomplishment at reaching the highest point in Maryland. You can also pick up a certificate authenticating your climb. On the aesthetic side there are views to enjoy from the top of Backbone Mountain through the trees.

Prettyboy Reservoir

Phone - None
Website - None
Admission Fee - None
Directions - *Middletown, Baltimore County; go west from Exit 31 off I-83. Middletown Road will lead to several roads with trailheads including Spooks Hill Road, Beckleysville Road and Gunpowder Road.*

The Park
In 1775 William Hoffman, recently arrived from Frankfurt, Germany, hacked his way through the wilderness to the West Branch of Great Gunpowder Falls to build Maryland's first paper mill. Hoffman's Clipper Mill is said to have produced paper for Continental currency during the Revolution. The state's paper industry thrived here for a century before giant mills in the West usurped its business. The river was dammed in 1933 to create Prettyboy Reservoir for a thirsty Baltimore. The colorful name survives from a local farmer's favorite horse that perished in a nearby stream.

The Walks
Baltimore City controls 7,380 heavily timbered acres along 46 miles of shoreline in the Prettyboy watershed. Most of the trekking is done high above the water level and the reservoiris only rarely glimpsed. Instead, it is the richness of differing forest types and not lake views that is the enduring beauty of Prettyboy. The reservoir slopes have been regularly logged and the forests are in differing stages of succession.

> **Where The Paw Meets The Earth:** Dirt and rocky fire roads mostly
> **Workout For Your Dog** - Long climbs and descents
> **Swimming** - Some splashing and dog paddling available in Gunpowder Falls but there are long stretches without water here
> **Restrictions On Dogs** - None

Something Extra
The best hiking at Prettyboy is out of sight of the reservoir and along the Gunpowder Falls, accessed by pull-offs on Gunpowder Road. Here you'll find walks through dense hemlock forests, none more special than the hike back in time to Hemlock Gorge. For this one, leave the fire roads behind and walk down a narrow dirt path on the northeast side of the bridge over the river. After crossing a tumbling stream the towering hemlocks begin in earnest, blocking out all other plants except the mosses clinging to the rock outcroppings on the steep slopes. When the river bends 90 degrees to the right, it serves up one lasting impression of Hemlock Gorge before the trail fades away. Scarcely, a half-mile long there is a good amount of rock scrambling and log-hopping for a fairly robust dog to follow the river.

Quiet Waters Park

Phone - (410) 222-1777
Website - http://www.aacounty.org/RecParks/parks/quiet_waters_park/
Admission Fee - Yes, closed Tuesdays
Directions - *Annapolis, Anne Arundel County; on Quiet Waters Park Drive off Forest Drive in the southern part of the city.*

The Park
Traces of human habitation dating back 5000 years have been found along Harness Creek. The water's name descends from Englishman William Harness who claimed a tract of land here in 1652. For the next three centuries the original land was divided and sold into various estates until 1976 when the entire property was deeded to Mary Parker by the Simplicity Land Company. In 1987 Anne Arundel County purchased 336 acres of woodland on the banks of the South River and Harness Creek to create Quiet Waters Park, which opened in 1990.

The Walks
The dominant trail at Quiet Waters is an eliptical multi-use path that circles the many cultural and recreational amenities of the park from end to end. The east side of the path traverses grassy fields and wetlands while the west side is a curving exploration of the woodlands. There are so many contours that even on a crowded day you can find a bit of solitude on the trail. Several loops lead off the main 4-mile trail to views of the water. The walking is fairly easy and level throughout. You may be tempted to step away from the wheeled traffic on this bike path and head down narrow dirt paths that radiate off the asphalt but do so only with an explorer's heart. The unmarked trails in the woods may or may not lead back to the main trail and may take you right off park property. Some of these natural trails roll up and down hills overlooking Harness Creek.

> **Where The Paw Meets The Earth:** Paved paths and natural ones
>
> **Workout For Your Dog** - Easy rolling for your dog here
>
> **Swimming** - Through the trees behind the dog park is a secluded stretch of South River beach just for swimming dogs; the waves are gentle enough to entice even the wariest dog into the water
>
> **Restrictions On Dogs** - None; Anne Arundel County's first dog park is here

Something Extra
The natural beauty of elegant Quiet Waters Park is augmented by the outdoor sculptures that grace the grounds. Sculptures are chosen by jury from national and international artists working with a variety of material and installed on a rotating basis.

Rachel Carson Conservation Park

Phone - None
Website - http://www.mc-mncppc.org/parks/park_maps/map_pages/rachelcarsoncp/rachelcarsoncp.shtm
Admission Fee - None
Directions - *Brookeville, Montgomery County; take New Hampshire Avenue (Route 650) past Georgia Avenue (Route 97) and make a left on Sundown Road. Turn left on Zion Road and parking is on the left.*

The Park
The park remembers the work of Rachel Louise Carson, a product of southern Pennsylvania farms who lived in Silver Spring. Her seminal work, *Silent Spring*, was published a decade later and introduced Americans to the dangers inherent in widespread use of chemical pesticides. Rachel Carson died of breast cancer shortly thereafter and is buried in Rockville, just south of the conservation area.

The Walks
There is a lot for your dog to love about Rachel Carson Conservation Park. First, it is close enough to Washington and Baltimore that you can get there without having your dog bounce around the car for hours but not so close to civilization that the trails are clogged with locals taking their dogs out for a quick 15-minute spin. Second, the terrain rolls just enough to keep your dog's interest without setting tongues to panting. Third, there is a nice mix of grassy, open-field canine hiking to soak in the sunshine and shady woods. Toss in some scenic rock-outcroppings and the gurgling meanderings of the Hawlings River. The 650 acres of the park were settled by Quaker farmers who were gentle stewards of the land. The mature chestnut oak forest is one of the best examples of its type in Maryland but before you reach the woods your dog can enjoy the grassy trails of the *Equestrian Loop*. If your dog has a taste for the grass under paw down the ways on Zion Road is the 1.25-mile *Blue Mash Nature Trail*, favored by birders.

> **Where The Paw Meets The Earth:** Wide grassy paths and wooded dirt
> **Workout For Your Dog** - Some small ups and downs
> **Swimming** - The Hawlings River is best suited for splashing
> **Restrictions On Dogs** - None

Something Extra
Maryland is home to 42 species of orchids and Rachel Carson Conservation Park is a good spot to come hunting these delicate flowers.

Robert E. Lee Park

Phone - None
Website - None
Admission Fee - None
Directions - *Baltimore County; just north of the city. The entrance to Robert E. Lee Park is on Lakeside Drive off Falls Road (MD 25), just north of Lake Avenue.*

The Park

Lake Roland was created in 1862 as Baltimore's first city water reservoir, eventually named for Roland Run, a feeder stream from the north that got its name from 17th-century settler Roland Thornberry. The water system was abandoned in 1915 due to silting in the lake. In the 1940s the 456-acre property was converted into a Baltimore city park (although outside the city limits) using funds bequeathed to the city for a statue honoring Confederate General Robert E. Lee.

The Walks

Robert E. Lee Park lacks a public entrance, has no signage, no amenities - in short, a perfect place to take a dog. And you will see more dogs per hour here than anywhere in Baltimore. Improvements will mean more visitation and more restrictions on dogs. Until that time, however, Robert E. Lee can provide just about any type of outing you want with your dog. Interested in a quick walk with a swim? Circle the old *Lakeside Park Loop* above the Lake Roland dam. Looking for a long, solitary hike? Cross the light rail line and explore a maze of hard-packed dirt trails through the woods. Some push into marshy areas along the lake for a bit of Baltimore's best bird watching. Warblers, ducks, geese and herons ply the reed-choked wetlands. Desire a walk around a lake? Cut across the lake on a narrow path beside the rail line (not for skittery dogs - a passing train will be only a few unfenced feet from the trail) and pick up a rollercoaster lakeside path across Lake Roland. Your dog will delight in bounding up the short slopes in happy anticipation of what the other side holds.

> **Where The Paw Meets The Earth:** Wooded dirt paths
>
> **Workout For Your Dog** - Mostly level trotting
>
> **Swimming** - There are many great places for a canine swim in Lake Roland on the dam side of the railroad bridge; across the tracks access to the lake is more limited; look for a dip in the wide, but shallow, Jones Falls over here.
>
> **Restrictions On Dogs** - None

Something Extra

After a long hike at Lake Roland you can sit on top of the Greek Revival valve house completed in 1862 and look over the stone dam. Lake Roland was created after plugging up Jones Falls.

Rock Creek Park

Phone - (202) 282-1063
Website - http://www.nps.gov/rocr/
Admission Fee - None
Directions - *Washington DC; the park abuts the western edge of 16th Street, MD 29, running north to south. The main road through the park, Beach Drive, can be picked up from the north on the East West Highway, Route 410.*

The Park
Although technically a national park, Rock Creek Park is more like a city park administered by the National Park Service. How many other national parks boast of ballfields and 30 picnic sites? It was the Army Corps of Engineers that first proposed the creation of Rock Creek Park when they considered moving the White House out of the mosquito-infested lowlands of down-town Washington after the Civil War. In 1890 Congress carved 1,754 acres from the Rock Creek Valley to establish the park, mostly in Washington, but spilling over to Montgomery County.

The Walks
The Rock Creek Valley runs from Lake Needwood outside of Rockville down through the main park in Washington D.C. An asphalt Rock Creek Hiker-Biker Trail travels the 13.6 miles through the scenic valley. In Rock Creek Park you'll find two main parallel hiking trails running the length of the park from north to south on either side of Rock Creek. The wiser choice for canine hikers is the *Valley Trail* (blue blazes) on the east side. In contrast with its twin, the *Western Ridge Trail* (green blazes), there are fewer picnic areas and less competition for the trail. Each is a rooty and rocky frolic up and down the slopes above Rock Creek, a superb canine swimming hole. Numerous spur trails and bridle paths connect the two major arteries that connect at the north and south to create a loop about ten miles long.

>**Where The Paw Meets The Earth:** Rooty and rocky dirt and paved paths
>**Workout For Your Dog** - Moderate climbs
>**Swimming** - Rock Creek is usually better for splashing than swimming but there are some good spots for dog paddling
>**Restrictions On Dogs** - None

Something Extra
The nation's capital was protected with a ring of 68 forts during the Civil War and Rock Creek Park administers several military sites. Your dog can visit the remnants of Fort De Russy, an earthworks fortification returned to its natural state just east of the *Western Ridge Trail* on a bridle path at Oregon Avenue and Military Road. Also near Military Road, three blocks east of the main park on 13th Street, is Fort Stevens.

Rock Creek Regional Park

Phone - (410) 592-2897
Website - http://www.mc-mncppc.org/parks/facilities/regional_parks/rockcreek/index.shtm
Admission Fee - None
Directions - *Rockville, Montgomery County; from Norbeck Road (MD 28) take Muncaster Mill Road west. Lake Frank and Meadowside Nature Center are on the left; Lake Needwood is down on Needwood Road.*

The Park
In 1965 an earthen dam was built creating Lake Needwood to prevent small stream flooding and control sediment. In 1967 another earthen dam was constructed down the road on the north branch of Rock Creek to create Lake Bernard Frank for the same reasons. Together the two lakes are the centerpieces of the 2,700-acre Rock Creek Regional Park.

The Walks
The two sections of Rock Creek Regional Park each radiate different personalities. Lake Needwood is a bit more rough-and-tumble with picnic shelters on the shore and boaters - including an outboard powered pontoon boat that cruises the lake on weekends - out on the water. The most-favored route for canine hikers here is a trip around the 75-acre lake partly on an old access road and partly on dirt paths. This is a shady, sometimes hilly circuit that hugs the shoreline and gives your dog plenty of opportunity for a swim. Lake Frank is given over to quiet, passive recreation. Aside from fishing on the lake the primary activity to take place here is hiking. Eight miles of well-maintained trails spread out from the Meadowside Nature Center. To stretch your dog's legs you can tour Lake Frank for over three miles on the *Lakeside Trail* or for those hounds with short attention spans you can jump from trail to trail on the many short, themed paths. There are many delights to found around the corners here: an old mill site, a restored log cabin, and even a covered bridge built by Rockville High School students.

> **Where The Paw Meets The Earth:** Mostly natural
> **Workout For Your Dog** - Modest climbs here and there
> **Swimming** - Excellent, don't disturb the fishermen
> **Restrictions On Dogs** - None

Something Extra
Don't leave without taking your dog for a stroll through the *Raptor Walkway* at Meadowside Nature Center, home to permanently injured, non-releasable birds of prey. At one time or another the park has hosted every species of owl native to Montgomery County, hawks, turkey vultures and a bald eagle.

Rockburn Branch Park

Phone - (410) 313-4955
Website - http://www.co.ho.md.us/RAP/RAP_HoCoParksRock-burn.htm
Admission Fee - None
Directions - *Elkridge, Howard County; two entrances to the park. The South area is on Montgomery Road off US Route 1 west and the North area is accessed from Landing Road off Montgomery Road.*

The Park
In pre-Revolutionary times the Patapsco River was deep enough to welcome ocean-going ships as far upriver as this point, known as Elkridge Landing. Tobacco grown in Anne Arundel County fields (Howard County was formed in 1851) was housed and shipped here. The river was silting steadily, however, and the port was gone by 1800. Only the name plates of Landing Road in the 390-acre Rockburn Branch Park hints at the area's rich maritime heritage.

The Walks
There is plenty of dogwalking to be had in both the North and South areas of Rockburn Branch. The South area features a 4.25-mile trail that slips through a wooded natural area. This amiable hike rolls up and down hills that represent the last gasp of the Piedmont plateau before it gives way to the coastal plain. Do not cross the power lines since the trails on the other side are part of Patapsco Valley State Park where dogs are not allowed.The hiking in the North area is less formal, including lightly forested trails in and around the disc golf course. Also here is an open field walking loop and the former bridle paths of the Clover Hill plantation.

> **Where The Paw Meets The Earth:** Natural dirt
> **Workout For Your Dog** - Easy rolling hills
> **Swimming** - Rockburn Branch is a scenic, meandering little stream but not deep enough for canine aquatics; no ponds are in the park
> **Restrictions On Dogs** - No dogs in the sports or picnic areas

Something Extra
Howard County preservationists have established the Rockburn Heritage Center as a depository for historic county buildings to join Clover Hill, a brick and frame mansion from the late 18th century that stands in the park. Currently its only companion is the Aaron McKenzie Bank Barn, a Civil War-era log barn. A third historic remnant, a 300-year old settler's barn was burned by arsonists in 2001.

Rocks State Park

Phone - (410) 557-7994
Website - http://www.dnr.state.md.us/publiclands/central/rocks.html
Admission Fee - Yes, for picnic areas
Directions - *Jarretsville, Harford County; the park office is in the Chrome Hill Road section, eight miles northwest of Bel Air on MD 24.*

The Park
The trails through dense forests along the Deer Creek are on the first Maryland lands purchased specifically to become a state park, back in 1951. The area was originally settled by the Susqehannock Indians who staged ceremonial gatherings at the massive 190-foot rock outcroppings known as the King and Queen Seat. Today Rocks State Park encompasses 900 acres of land in three separate parcels.

The Walks
Chrome Hill Road. The trails at the signature section of Rocks State Park all lead eventually to the top of King and Queen Seat. The views of the lush forestland from the top of the rock pile are spectacular but the outcroppings are unfenced and great care is required for dogs near the cliffs. The *White Trail* is a sporty loop trail up and down and around the mountainous knob; it accounts for most of the four miles of trails at Chrome Hill Road. A low-lying *Nature Trail* loop is a short, pleasant walk opposite the Hills Grove Picnic Area on St. Clair Bridge Road.

Falling Branch. In this 67-acre sanctuary a path leads to the base of Kilgore Falls, Maryland's second-highest vertical waterfall. At the falls, trails cross to the base and climb to the top of the 30-foot downspout.

Hidden Valley Natural Area. Quiet! That is what awaits you in this un-developed tract of woods about five miles north of Rocks. Your one-mile stroll along level ground beside Deer Creek will end at an idyllic spot beneath a jagged rock crag protecting dark pines. While you drink in the serenity your dog will enjoy the spa-like rapids in the shallow stream.

> **Where The Paw Meets The Earth:** Natural surface dirt
> **Workout For Your Dog** - Challenging climbs with narrow passages at times
> **Swimming** - Plenty of access to Deer Creek from the parking lots but not the trails; at Kilgore Falls are wonderful pockets of water
> **Restrictions On Dogs** - None

Something Extra
The chance to watch rock climbers tackle the namesake rock outcroppings of the King and Queen Seat which rule over the waters of the Deer Creek as they have for centuries.

Rocky Gap State Park

Phone - (301) 722-1480
Website - http://www.dnr.state.md.us/publiclands/western/rock-ygap.html
Admission Fee - Yes
Directions - *Flintstone, Allegany County; take Exit 50 off I-68.*

The Park
In season this is a busy resort-type park and you will be taking your dog past a campground, a lodge, pavilions, a golf course, tennis courts...and all the people using the facilities.

The Walks
The main canine hike here is the *Lakeside Loop* that travels for four miles around Lake Habeeb. There are stretches of memorable mountain scenery and, save for some rocky patches, relatively easy hiking for your dog. An alternate route leads to Evitts Mountain and the overgrown homesite of the original white settler who came to the area in the 1700s, supposedly to live out his life as a hermit after a disastrous love affair. History doesn't remember if he at least brought a dog with him. Rock hop down into the canyon on the challenging five-mile long *Evitts Homesite Trail* and find yourself surrounded by Hemlock, Laurel and Rhododendron. Cross the small cascading stream on the footbridge and begin to climb Evitts Mountain. This is an ambitious trail that climbs about 1,000 feet in elevation in 2.5 miles.

> **Where The Paw Meets The Earth:** Mostly rock-free
> **Workout For Your Dog** - Moderate going around the lake but you can really ratchet up the exercise on Evitts Mountain
> **Swimming** - Plenty of great access to Lake Habeeb
> **Restrictions On Dogs** - None

Something Extra
A magnificent view of the one mile long gorge is the gift hikers will get when they reach the overlook on the one-quarter mile long *Canyon Overlook Trail.*

Rosaryville State Park

Phone - None
Website - http://www.dnr.state.md.us/publiclands/southern/rosaryville.html
Admission Fee - Yes
Directions - *Upper Marlboro, Prince George's County; off US 301, just south of Osborne Road.*

The Park

Charles Calvert, the Third Lord of Baltimore built a hunting lodge here in 1660 - a large 50-foot room with fireplaces on either end. Mount Airy Mansion was converted into a proper manor house in the 1750s. The State of Maryland acquired the mansion and 982-acre grounds in 1972.

The Walks

Rosaryville is primarily a picnic park although the 7.5-mile *Perimeter Trail* circumnavigates the grounds. The frequent short hills will keep your dog guessing as to what's ahead on this wooded circuit. A network of unmaintained dirt trails can also be used if you don't want to circle the park.

> **Where The Paw Meets The Earth:** Wooded natural surface footpaths
>
> **Workout For Your Dog** - Rolling terrain
>
> **Swimming** - None
>
> **Restrictions On Dogs** - None

Something Extra

Mount Airy is one of the oldest Calvert mansions in Maryland and is rich in history. The oldest section of the mansion is the restored remains of that hunting lodge. The oldest section consisted of one 50-foot room with fireplaces on each end. A few years later the north and south wings were added to the original structure. Then during the 1750s the main section of the mansion was added to accommodate Benedict Swingate Calvert's family, making the stately building guests see today. On February 4, 1774 George Washington attended his stepson's, John Park Custis, wedding to Eleanor Calvert. Washington had opposed the marriage due to their youth but finally gave in and joined the festivities in the Calvert room at Mount Airy. He later became a frequent visitor and is said to have given the Calverts the boxwood in front of the home.

St. Mary's City

Phone - (800) 762-1634
Website - http://www.stmaryscity.org/
Admission Fee - No for grounds
Directions - *St. Mary's, St. Mary's County; located on MD 5.*

The Park
In the early 1600s King Charles I granted what is now the state of Maryland to Cecil Calvert, the second Baron of Baltimore with the expectation that Calvert would build trade with Mother England and profit to the Calvert family. In November 1633 two ships, the *Ark* and the *Dove*, set sail under Governor Leonard Calvert's command and eventually sailed up the Potomac River. After discussions with the indigent tribes the newcomers put down along the St. Mary's River, using land already cleared by the Yaocomaco Indians, who were preparing to leave. St. Mary's was the fourth permanent English settlement in North America. As more and more people took Lord Baltimore up on his offer of land the area's population grew and spread across the northern Potomac. In response, he chartered the town of St. Mary's in 1668. Community leaders were already meeting in Leonard Calvert's home and now Maryland had its first capital. When Annapolis won the tussle for state capital in 1695 St. Mary's was simply abandoned. Nothing ever came to take its place, just nature and some agriculture. The remains of Maryland's first established colony settled under the dirt, waiting to be reidscovered by archaelogists.

The Walks
Your dog is welcome to explore St. Mary's City as it is resurrected - the outdoor museum is certainly one of the most attractive of active historical sites. Serpentine walking paths connect exhibits ranging from an Indian longhouse to Maryland's first assembly house to a reconstructed chapel. The trail winds for three miles in open fields atop the wooded banks of the river and back to the former Splay Tobacco Plantation.
> **Where The Paw Meets The Earth:** Crushed stone paths
> **Workout For Your Dog** - Quiet, easy canine hiking
> **Swimming** - None
> **Restrictions On Dogs** - None

Something Extra
This is your dog's chance to hike through the 17th century. Check out farming techniques, look over some building methods without power tools and even look over a replica of the Dove that stands in the harbor. In season, costumed interpreters bring Maryland's first settlement to life.

St. Mary's River State Park

Phone - None
Website - http://www.dnr.state.md.us/publiclands/southern/st-marysriver.html
Admission Fee - None
Directions - *Great Mills, St. Mary's County; three miles south on Route 5 and turn right on Camp Cosoma Road to park.*

The Park
St. Mary's River State Park has two sections: one, a thickly wooded section that looks like it would be teeming with trails is actually undeveloped; the second, a 250-acre lake, is your destination.

The Walks
Come down near to southern Maryland is one of the longest walks around a lake you can take with your dog in the state. The narrow trail follows the shoreline for 11.5 miles although you can cut the route by about three miles. The trail is used mostly by bikers and equestrians but is lightly used at any time. If you want to fill an afternoon with easy hiking with your dog beside a scenic lake, St. Mary's is for you. And don't come on a time constraint - the unmarked trails that bop off the main drag make it easy to find yourself on one you never intended to start down.

> **Where The Paw Meets The Earth:** Natural surface
> **Workout For Your Dog** - It is a long way around that lake
> **Swimming** - Your dog will find a way into the water
> **Restrictions On Dogs** - None

Something Extra
For dogs who like to fish, the lake has been designated a trophy bass lake.

Savage Park

Phone - (410) 313-4682
Website - http://www.co.ho.md.us/RAP/RAP_HoCoParksSavage.
htm
Admission Fee - None
Directions - *Savage, Howard County; west of US 1. To reach the Wincopin Trails, exit US 1 to Guilford Road west. Make a left on Vollmerhausen Road to parking lot on left past schools. The Savage Loop is in town at the end of Baltimore Street. Parking for the Savage Mill Trail is on Foundry Street.*

The Park

Amos Williams and three brothers built a cotton works on the Patuxent River in 1822, naming it for John Savage, a director of the Bank of the United States who backed the project with $20,000. A major cloth producer for 125 years, the business declined rapidly after World War II due to a glut of canvas from returning war supplies and was gone by 1947. A visionary named Harry Heim bought the entire company town for $450,000 with dreams of a year-round Christmas village called Santa Heim, Merryland. Perhaps ahead of his time, the scheme suffered a quick death and the old mill was used mainly for warehouses until renovated for shops and offices and a park in 1988.

The Walks

Three unconnected areas surrounding the confluence of the Middle Patux-ent and Little Patuxent rivers conspire to form Savage Park. Although the *Wincopin Neck Trails* are the prime destination of the canine hiker, you may want to warm up on the *Savage Historic Mill Trail*. This wide, level wooded path traces the boulder-pocked stream below the confluence for 3/4 of a mile. Up the road are the hilly *River Trail* and *Lost Horse Trail* behind the recreation area.

> **Where The Paw Meets The Earth:** Most hiking is along wide pathways, save for rocky and narrow stretches near the Middle Patuxent
> **Workout For Your Dog** - Some steep descents
> **Swimming** - Pools in the falls are the prettiest canine swimming holes in the Baltimore region
> **Restrictions On Dogs** - None

Something Extra

On Foundry Road, at the trailhead for the *Historic Mill Trail*, is the last remaining Bollman Truss bridge in the world. Your dog can trot across the first successful iron bridge used by railroads, patented by Wendell A. Bolman in 1852. This example, a National Historic Civil Engineering Landmark, originally carried traffic on the B&O main line but was disassembled and put into service here for Savage Mill in 1887.

Savage River State Forest

Phone - (301) 895-5759
Website - www.dnr.state.md.us/publiclands/western/savageriver.html
Admission Fee - None
Directions - *New Germany, Garrett County; in central and eastern Garrett County, off I-68.*

The Park
On May 1, 1755, British General Edward Braddock led a 2,400-man expedition - George Washington and Daniel Boone among them - along an Indian trail through this area. Their mission was to reach Fort Duquesne at the forks of the Ohio in what is now Pittsburgh - 122 miles distant. To do so the men needed to hack the trail to a width of 12 feet to allow horse-drawn wagons hauling cannons to pass. Progress was slow, averaging just two miles a day with the men scrounging for wild game and rattlesnake meat for sustenance. Braddock's men were within seven miles of Fort Duquense when they were ambushed by a raiding party and vanquished. The rough road they carved out of the wilderness eventually became the main route west for settlers crossing the Eastern Continental Divide to reach the Ohio Valley. Today a small piece of the original road survives on Big Savage Mountain, in Maryland's largest public space - the 54,000+ acres of Savage River State Forest.

The Walks
The gem of the Savage River State Forest trail system is the *Big Savage Trail* that traipses 17 miles through upland forests and old farmsteads across the crest of Big Savage Mountain. This popular backpacking trail, nationally acclaimed for its beauty and challenge, suffered damage from ice storms in 2002 but is back open to test your dog. If you don't have a car shuttle or overnight backpacking gear for the *Big Savage Trail* there are day hikes on Meadow Mountain and Negro Mountain in the western sections of the park. The Negro Mountain system is an 8-mile horseshoe with steep slopes and stream crossings and Meadow Mountain features rocky canine hiking along its crest.

> **Where The Paw Meets The Earth:** Natural woodsy trails
> **Workout For Your Dog** - Moderate to strenuous
> **Swimming** - The fast-moving Savage River does not allow much
> **Restrictions On Dogs** - None

Something Extra
The Savage River is famous for its wild trout fishing as it makes its way to the Potomac River. These natives will test even the most accomplished fly fishermen.

Seneca Creek State Park

Phone - (301) 924-2127
Website - http://www.dnr.state.md.us/publiclands/central/seneca.html
Admission Fee - None
Directions - *Gaithersburg, Montgomery County; on Clopper Road North off Exit 10 of I-270. For dog owners, pass the park entrance, cross Germantown Road and take an immediate left on Schaeffer Road. Go two miles to the trailhead on the left.*

The Park
The Seneca Valley possessed everything European settlers craved upon arriving in the late 1600s: rich soil for crops, more fish and game than could be hunted in a lifetime, and tumbling streams to power their mills. The plentiful red Seneca Sandstone was quarried for building, including the Chesapeake & Ohio Canal and the original Smithsonian Institution "Castle" on the National Mall.

The Walks
Seneca Creek State Park preserves more than 6,000 acres of open space, including the beautiful area around Clopper Lake. Your dog, regrettably, will see little of it. Dogs are shuffled off to the *Schaeffer Farm Trail System*, 10 miles of dirt paths designed, built and maintained by local mountain bike clubs. And it shows. The trails all leave a single trailhead and the shortest loop is an easy 15-minute bike ride but one that will take 45 minutes by paw. There are no great destinations here - just hours of trail time with your dog.

> **Where The Paw Meets The Earth:** Dirt farm roads and trails
> **Workout For Your Dog** - Long hikes on the menu but not strenuous
> **Swimming** - No
> **Restrictions On Dogs** - No dogs in Clopper Lake area

Something Extra
The Seneca Schoolhouse, located on Route 190 west of Seneca, is a restored 19th century one-room schoolhouse, originally built for children of the Seneca Sandstone quarries along the Potomac River.

Schooley Mill Park

Phone - (410) 313-4700
Website - http://www.co.ho.md.us/RAP/RAP_HoCoParksS-chooleyMill.htm
Admission Fee - None
Directions - *Clarksville, Howard County; southeast of Highland on Hall Shop Road between Clarksville Pike (MD 108) to the west and Skaggsville Road (MD 216) to the east.*

The Park
Schooley Mill is a multi-use star in the Howard County park system. Much of its 192 acres is given over to equestrian activities and recreational pursuits.

The Walks
The simple trail system at Schooley Mill circles the perimeter of the property in two concentric loops. The outer loop is a mulch and dirt path through woodlands and wetlands; the inner loop uses old "carriage" roads, often on grass. There are 2 miles of wooded trails and 2 1/2 miles of roads through open meadows. Much of the hiking is easy going as the outer trail leads downhill to a stream valley where tulip poplars tower in the bottomlands. It follows the gurgling stream for a good distance and visits a secluded beaver pond. The trail system leads off-park for additional hiking in several places.

> **Where The Paw Meets The Earth:** Mulch and dirt under paw
> **Workout For Your Dog** - The park slopes away gradually down to the boundary stream
> **Swimming** - The beaver pond, which is packed into tight quarters, lures swimming dogs when the water dams up deep enough.
> **Restrictions On Dogs** - No dogs in the picnic or sports area

Something Extra
On a hilltop in the center of the park is the James Marlow House. Built around 1840 as a two-story home with one room on each floor, it stands as an historic example of the agrarian vernacular architecture that once permeated Howard County. The log and chink exterior walls were covered with clapboard when the house was later enlarged.

Soldier's Delight NEA

Phone - (410) 922-3044
Website - http://www.dnr.state.md.us/publiclands/central/soldiers.html
Admission Fee - None
Directions - *Owings Mills, Baltimore County; from I-795 take Franklin Boulevard West to Church Road. Go right and left on Berrymans Lane and left on Deer Park Road to the Visitor Center on the right.*

The Park
Soldiers Delight NEA's 1900 acres are part of a prairie-like grassland that rests on igneous rock that is one of only three such formations in North America. Early settlers called the area of Blackjack Pines and Post Oaks "The Barrens" because its low nutrient level was unfriendly to cultivation. The distinctive green rock was named "serpentine" for its resemblance to a snake native to northern Italy. This arid soil has produced a landscape more common in the American West than suburban Baltimore. Here you will find rare insects, rocks and at least 39 endangered plant species.

The Walks
The thing that makes Soldiers Delight so unique and visually appealing - the serpentine barrens - does not do hiking dogs any favors. The green-tinted stone is embedded in probably half of the park's seven miles of trails, jutting through the soil in hard ridges. So little soil accumulates in the barrens that the Maryland Geological Survey locates its seismic recording station here because such ready access to the bedrock makes it a simple matter to record vibrations during earthquakes. Soldiers Delight, so easy on the eye, can be tough on the paw. The trail system is essentially two loops connected at the Deer Park Road Overlook, While the terrain rolls up and down there are no tough climbs on these hikes. The woods are airy - and will become more so. The Virginia pines and Eastern Red Cedar you see are invasive species being removed by prescribed burning.

> **Where The Paw Meets The Earth:** Some rocky trails
> **Workout For Your Dog** - Long loops and hills will tire any dog
> **Swimming** - The streams are rarely more than knee-high to a dogleg
> **Restrictions On Dogs** - None

Something Extra
The first chromium mines in America were opened here in 1808 and from 1828 to 1850 just about every scrap of chrome in the world came from Soldiers Delight. Along the *Choate Mine Trail* you can stand in front of the entrance to the Choate Mine and look into the slanting holes kept open by half-timbered posts. So close the cool air wafting up from the mine will rustle your dog's fur.

Sugarloaf Mountain

Phone - (301) 874-2024
Website - http://www.sugarloafmd.com/index.html
Admission Fee - None
Directions - *Dickerson, Frederick County; follow Route I-270 South to the Hyattstown exit, follow MD 109 to Comus, then right on Comus Road to the Stronghold entrance.*

The Park

Gordon Strong, a wealthy Chicago businessman, who became captivated by Sugarloaf Mountain on a bicycle trip in 1902. He and his wife Louise began acquiring tracts of land on the mountain to preserve it for the enjoyment of the public. In 1924 he consulted with Frank Lloyd Wright to construct a monument of a building on the summit that would be an automobile destination for millions to enjoy the mountain. Wright designed an innovative spiral building that would complement the twisting road by Strong ultimately rejected the plan in favor of a traditional park. Wright used his sketches for the Guggenheim Museum. During the Franklin Roosevelt administration Interior Secretary Harold Ickes tried to purchase Sugarloaf as a Presidential retreat but Strong - a Republican - would not sell and the search moved to Camp David to the northwest. Instead Gordon Strong set up a private foundation, Stronghold, to manage the mountain for the enjoyment of the public - free of charge. A rare gift indeed.

The Walks

How would you like to enjoy the views and forests of Sugarloaf Mountain with your dog? Just about any way you can think of has been anticipated. For the canine hiker who is looking for a long ramble around the mountain before heading to the top there are three mostly concentric routes available at different elevations. None of these hiking loops actually reach the 1,282-foot summit - that is left to short - but steep - trails from the overlooks.

> **Where The Paw Meets The Earth:** Rocky dirt paths
> **Workout For Your Dog** - Yes, some tough climbs on the mountain
> **Swimming** - None
> **Restrictions On Dogs** - None

Something Extra

Unless you are a guest you can't stop and admire Strong Mansion or its neighbor, Westwood, but you can drive s-l-o-w-l-y past on your way off the mountain.

Susquehanna State Park

Phone - (410) 557-7994
Website - http://www.dnr.state.md.us/publiclands/central/susquehanna.html
Admission Fee - None
Directions - *Havre de Grace, Harford; take I-95 to MD 155, Exit 89. Go west on MD 155 to MD 161. Turn right and right again on Rock Run Road to the park.*

The Park
The first European to set eyes on the Susquehanna River was English explorer John Smith. He was suitably impressed. "Heaven and earth seemed never to have agreed better to frame a place for man's commodious and delightful habitation," he wrote. While sailing in this area, Smith met the native Susquehannocks, who gave the river, the longest of any waterway on the East Coast, its name. Industry came early to the area - the Lapidium community in the park traces its beginnings to 1683 and the park's restored Rock Run Grist Mill dates to 1794. The water-powered mill grinds corn into meal on summer weekends. Today Susquehanna State Park, opened in 1965, encompasses 2,500 inviting acres.

The Walks
Susquehanna State Park is a winning combination of history, scenery and wildlife. Among its 15 miles of trails the park features several loop trails in the hills above the Susquehanna River Valley. Most are around two miles in distance. If using the green-blazed *Deer Creek Trail* be on the look-out for a magnificent spreading white oak in the middle of the walk. Be aware that there are few streams on the slopes to refresh your dog on a hot day. The *Lower Susquehanna Heritage Greenways Trail*, which connects the park at Deer Creek with the Conowingo Dam is as pleasant a hike as you can take with your dog. Tracing the route of the 160-year old Susquehanna and Tidewater Canal towpath, the wide dirt path stretches 2.2 shaded miles along the water.

> **Where The Paw Meets The Earth:** Wooded dirt paths
> **Workout For Your Dog** - Short and challenging trails
> **Swimming** - The rock-strewn Susquehanna is full of clear pools for your dog to paddle around in with many points of access from the trail
> **Restrictions On Dogs** - No dogs in Deer Creek Picnic

Something Extra
The chance to see bald eagles, especially in the winter. The great piscavorious birds favor massive nests in the 100-foot treetops along the banks of the Susquehanna River from which they dive and pluck stunned and splattered fish from the spillways beneath the Conowingo Dam, America's longest concrete-slab dam.

Swallow Falls State Park

Phone - (301) 387-6938
Website - http://www.dnr.state.md.us/publiclands/western/swal-lowfalls.html
Admission Fee - None
Directions - *Oakland, Garrett County; from I-68 take Exit 14 at Keysers Ridge and go south on Route 219 for 19.5 miles to Mayhew Inn Road (2 miles past Deep Creek). Turn right on Mayhew Inn Road, travel 4.5 miles to end of road. At the stop sign turn left onto Oakland Sang Run Road, travel 0.3 miles to first road on the right which will be Swallow Falls Road. Turn right and travel 1.3 miles to the park.*

The Park
By 1900, it was highly unusual to see any big tree in Maryland that had escaped a logger's saw, unless it was too costly to reach. That was the case with the grove of white pines and hemlocks at Swallow Falls. The giants are the oldest in Maryland - some trees are estimated to be 360 years old. Philanthropist Henry Krug refused to allow the trees to be logged in the gorge and when a World War I plan to dam the Youghiogheny River fell through their suvival was assured. America's most famous car campers of the early 20th century - industrialists Henry Ford, Thomas Edison and Harvey Firestone camped here at Muddy Creek Falls and during the Depression the Civilian Conservation Corps created the campsite enjoyed by thousands today.

The Walks
This is the best single-trail park in Maryland. The *Falls Trail* is easy going for your dog through the river canyon under cool, dark hemlocks. Muddy Creek Falls, Maryland's highest single water plunge at 53 feet, arrives quickly on your canine hike and shortly you arrive at the confluence of Muddy Creek and the Youghiogheny River. Here you'll travel past several more hydrospectaculars before turning for home. This gorgeous loop covers about one mile. If your dog is hankering for more trail time there is a 5.5-mile out-and-back trail to Herrington Manor State Park (no dogs allowed). You'll get more water views and more giant hemlocks - be advised that this canine hike involves a stream crossing that may not be doable in times of high water.

> **Where The Paw Meets The Earth:** Soft pine straw/dirt
> **Workout For Your Dog** - Moderate canine hiking
> **Swimming** - Doggie swimming holes beneath the falls
> **Restrictions On Dogs** - Dogs not allowed in day-use area Memorial Day through Labor Day; yes for campground

Something Extra
At the Upper Falls on the Youghiogheny River you will find the source of the park name: a rock pillar where cliff swallows once nested by the hundreds.

Terrapin Nature Park

Phone - (410) 758-0835
Website - None
Admission Fee - None
Directions - *Stevensville, Queen Annes County; from I-83 take Exit 20B west on Shawan Road. After one mile make a left on Beaver Dam Road and immediately take right fork into the park.*

The Park
The Terrapin Nature Park occupies almost one mile of Chesapeake Bay shoreline from the Chesapeake Bay Bridge northward. With its open dunesland, tidal ponds and oyster-shell paths this 276-acre park manages to exude a certain beach feel despite being hemmed in by its industrial neighbors. The park is also the western terminus for the six-mile Cross Island Trail Park that spans Kent Island to the Kent Narrows.

The Walks
The stacked-loop trail system pushes through a combination of light woods and meadows towards the 4,000 feet of shoreline. The trail is sometimes gravel, sometimes oyster chaff and sometimes soft sand. There is a grassy shoulder if your dog finds the oyster shells uncomfortable under paw. The paths twist for slightly over three miles and the going is easy over the flat terrain. Along the way are blinds to observe visiting waterfowl in the wetlands an an interpretive gazebo on the beach to gaze out on the open waters of the Chesapeake Bay. If you are not looking for a complete crossing of Kent Island a good choice on the *Cross Island Trail* is old Love Point Park, a little more than one mile away. If you have a car shuttle there are several parking lots, including one at the Chesapeake Exploration Center that makes for a comfortable five-mile canine hike.

> **Where The Paw Meets The Earth:** Oyster shells, grass, dirt, asphalt
> **Workout For Your Dog** - Level terrain throughout
> **Swimming** - If your dog shies away from the waves in the Chesapeake there is a cement barrier that creates a calm-water pool
> **Restrictions On Dogs** - None

Something Extra
Some of the best views of the Chesapeake Bay Bridge anywhere can be found at Terrapin Nature Park. The world's largest continuous over-water steel structure was completed in 1952. Each year more than twenty million vehicles make the 4.35-mile crossing.

Triadelphia Recreation Center

Phone - None
Website - None
Admission Fee - None
Directions - *Brighton, Howard County; from Roxbury Mills Road (MD 97) cross the river and turn left on Triadelphia Lake Road to the parking lot.*

The Park

Triadelphia was once a leading Maryland mill town with a bustling population of 400. Meaning "three brothers," for the trio of brothers-in-law who married Brooke sisters and built the original mills, Triadelphia was destroyed by the same 1889 rains that ignited the famous Johnstown flood in Pennsylvania. Already in decline before the deluge, the village was not rebuilt and it was a ghost town that was drowned under the reservoir that bears its name in 1942.

The Walks

The Triadelphia Recreation Area was developed in the Patuxent Watershed for waterside picnicking and recreation. At the top of the boat launch steps lead to a linear trail that rises high above the reservoir and drops down along the Patuxent River to its terminus in a parking lot on MD 97. The route in Patuxent River State Park dips and rolls through the airy woods - few of the trees are old growth behemoths. The trail is narrow and easywalking as it skips along.

> **Where The Paw Meets The Earth:** Dirt trails
> **Workout For Your Dog** - A little rollercoaster of a canine hike
> **Swimming** - The Patuxent River provides some of the best dog paddling in the Baltimore area with easy access from grassy banks to pools and spilling water
> **Restrictions On Dogs** - None

Something Extra

Growing unobtrusively beside the parking lot is one of the rarest native ornamental trees in the world, the *Franklinia Alatamaha*. A relative of the camelia, this flowering tree is prized at any time of the year - in the winter for its striped bark, in the summer for its palm-sized snow white flowers, and in the fall for its deep red leaves. The Franklinia was discovered by Philadelphia botanist John Bartram in 1765 in a remote corner of Georgia along the Alatamaha River and named for his friend Benjamin Franklin. It has not been found growing in the wild since 1790. Just to the left of these botanical marvels is the historic spring which was used as Triadelphia's water supply when the town was founded in 1809.

Truxtun Park

Phone - None
Website - None
Admission Fee - None
Directions - *Annapolis, Anne Arundel County; between Spa Road and Bay Ridge Avenue. The main entrance is on Primrose Road off Hilltop Lane.*

The Park
Truxtun Park remembers Thomas Truxtun, a privateer in the American Revolution who impressed George Washington enough to be brought into the new United States Navy. Truxtun, the 8th recipient of the Congressional Gold Medal, outfitted the U.S.S. Constellation and was the earliest known user of signal flags aboard ship in the American navy. Looking down on Spa Creek, Truxtun Park is the Maryland state capital's largest park, covering 70 acres.

The Walks
At Truxtun Park you'll be trading the sculptures, manicured grounds and forced walkways of nearby Quiet Waters Park for rusting hulks of abandoned autos and free-flowing, hard-packed dirt trails - which suits most dog owners just fine. The trails roll over two large wooded hills separated by a ravine. In the recreational part of the park the Annapolis Striders have constructed a crushed stone path with built-in steps to navigate the slopes and help arrest erosion. Natural trails, including one route on the ridge above Spa Creek, cross the more isolated back section of the park. An extended canine hiking opportunity here is the *Spa Creek Trail*. This 1.5-mile route leaves Truxtun on a wooden bridge through high reeds and heads towards Spa Creek Conservancy and on to the former Bates High School.

> **Where The Paw Meets The Earth:** Bare dirt paths
> **Workout For Your Dog** - Lots of small hills
> **Swimming** - In a few spots the trails dip down to the waterline of Spa Creek for deep water canine aquatics
> **Restrictions On Dogs** - None

Something Extra
What dog doesn't enjoy the action of a good up-and-down-the-court basketball game? Some of the best outdoor basketball courts in Maryland can be found at Truxtun Park, including permanent bleachers to stop and watch the games.

Tuckahoe State Park

Phone - (410) 820-1668
Website - http://www.dnr.state.md.us/publiclands/eastern/tuckahoe.html
Admission Fee - Yes, for the Adkins Arboretum
Directions - *Queen Anne, Queen Anne's County; from the US 50/301 split on the Eastern Shore, bear to the right on US 50. Make a left at Route 404. Go approximately 8 miles and make a left on MD 480. To your immediate left take Eveland Road to the park.*

The Park
The easy-moving waters of the Tuckahoe Creek have long attracted settlers on its banks from the Nanticoke Indians through Colonial villagers as it flowed into Choptank River. A grist mill operated here in the late 1700s with millstones imported from England. Frederick Douglass, who escaped slavery and became the abolitionist movement's most eloquent speaker, was born in 1818 on Holmes Hill Farm along the banks of the Tuckahoe. Harriet Tubman was rumored to have established a number of safe houses on the Underground Railroad along the river. The mill was destroyed in 1924 when a dam burst and was never rebuilt. The State of Maryland began acquiring land along the Tuckahoe in 1962 and the park opened to the public in 1975. Today Tuckahoe State Park contains 3,800 acres of land.

The Walks
The backbone of a potpourri of canine hiking is the *Tuckahoe Valley Trail* that travels 4.5 easy miles through a climax deciduous forest. The route is well-hydrated with tiny streams. For more varied terrain try the *CreekSide Cliff Trail* that explores the high banks cut by the Tuckahoe. The best place to take your dog at Tuckahoe, however, is the 400-acres of the Adkins Arboretum in the center of the park. Dogs aren't often welcome in these living museums and this one is a real treat. The well-groomed trails work the upland forests around three creeks and after wandering under towering tulip poplars and loblolly pines your dog can luxuriate in the grassy paths of two meadows.

> **Where The Paw Meets The Earth:** Dirt, sand and pine straw
>
> **Workout For Your Dog** - Minimal elevation change
>
> **Swimming** - Check out the boat ramp at Crouse Mill Pond
>
> **Restrictions On Dogs** - Dogs are allowed throughout the park and in the campground except on the *Lake Trail*

Something Extra
The *Little Florida Trail* visits the remains of an old sand-and-gravel operation that gives your dog the feel of the New Jersey Pine Barrens on sandy soils. The scarred depressions from the quarrying provide excellent habitat for frogs and other amphibians.

Turner's Creek Park

Phone - None
Website - None
Admission Fee - None
Directions - *Kennedyville, Kent County; turn off MD 213 in the center of town onto MD 448 (Turner's Creek Road). There is no sign for either the road or the park - turn at the sign for Kent Museum. Follow to the park at the end of the road.*

The Park
John Smith is believed to have met with the Tockwogh Indians here in 1608 during his voyage of exploration around Chesapeake Bay. Francis Child received the first land grant along the Sassafras River in 1671 and the surrounding land remained as family farms for the next three centuries. Private donations triggered matching fnds from the state and federal governments to create the park in 1972.

The Walks
The barely discernible *Lathim Trail* - John Lathim built ships at Child's Harbour and his house circa, 1700, is now a restroom facility on the river - and *Cattail Trail* trip along Turner's Creek among massive beech and sassafras trees. There is a weathered mapboard at the parking lot that will help keep you oriented. You can use the barely-traveled Turner's Creek Road to close canine hiking loops on these out-and-back trails.

> **Where The Paw Meets The Earth:** Natural surface footpaths
> **Workout For Your Dog** - It can be on these often overgrown trails
> **Swimming** - Take your dog down the small hill for superb canine swimming in the Sassafras River at the boat ramps
> **Restrictions On Dogs** - None

Something Extra
For extended trail time visit the Sassafras River Natural Management Area, a former cattle farm, next door.

Watkins Regional Park

Phone - (301) 218-6700
Website - http://www.pgparks.com/places/parks/watkins.html
Admission Fee - None
Directions - *Upper Marlboro, Prince George's County; From the Capital Beltway (I-495), take Exit 15A onto Central Avenue, heading east. After three miles turn right onto Watkins Park Drive (MD 193) to park. Parker Athletic Complex.*

The Park

This is a big recreational park with plenty to offer - in addition to the requisite athletic fields, playground and picnic shelters visitors can find a working farm, nature center, campground, miniature golf course and a miniature train. There is still room for your dog, however, on several miles of trails.

The Walks

The *Spicebush Trail* circles the activity centers in its course of three miles. The *Beaver Pond Trail* and *Overlook Trail* escape the hustle and bustle into the deciduous forest at the southern end of the park. These are out-and-back canine hikes with your highlight being a small woodland pond.

> **Where The Paw Meets The Earth:** Wooded dirt paths and macadam
>
> **Workout For Your Dog** - An occasional rolling hill
>
> **Swimming** - Not the highlight of a canine visit
>
> **Restrictions On Dogs** - None

Something Extra

Located within Watkins Regional Park, the Chesapeake Carousel is believed to have been constructed by Gustav Dentzel at the turn of the century. The carousel operated at Chesapeake Beach through 1972. Restoration has been ongoing since it's acquisition in 1974; it was re-opened to the public here in July 1977. The carousel is open seasonally.

Wheaton Regional Park

Phone - (301) 680-536
Website - http://www.mc-mncppc.org/parks/facilities/regional_parks/wheaton/
Admission Fee - None
Directions - *Wheaton, Montgomery County; from Georgia Avenue (MD 97) go east onto Randolph Road. Parking for the Brookside Nature Center is on the right.*

The Park
Rhode Island-born Frank Wheaton was one of the few American military officers to attain the rank of major general without attending West Point. During the Civil War he received several battlefield promotions and was entrusted with the command of the defense of Washington from Fort Stevens just down Georgia Avenue from the park. Five years later the sparsely populated countryside nearby took the general's name. Almost any way you can think to get around a park can be found in Wheaton. Horesback riding, cycling, skating are all on tap here. A replica of an 1863 C.P. Huntington steam engine pulls a miniature train on a 10-minute tour of the park. There is even a treasured 1915 carousel built by the legendary Herschell Spillman Co. of North Tonawanda, New York. The carousel was operated on the National Mall in the District from the 1960s to 1980s before finding a home in the park.

The Walks
Wheaton Regional Park was not put together on a whim - wide, crushed-gravel trails lead to the five distinct areas of the park. There are four miles of these paths but you will want to start your dog on the natural surface trails at the Brookside Nature Center. These well-groomed paths are a pleasure for any dog and even the bridle paths in the system are not unduly torn asunder. At the nature center make sure to take your dog on the brief - but highly informative - *Woodland Walk*. Don't forget to try the bird calls to see the quizzical look on your dog's face.

> **Where The Paw Meets The Earth:** Crushed gravel and dirt
> **Workout For Your Dog** - Small undulations in terrain
> **Swimming** - Pine Lake is an attractive 5-acre lake with flat, unvegetated banks for your dog to take a swim
> **Restrictions On Dogs** - None

Something Extra
Near the Nature Center you can view the Thomas Harper cabin, built in 1870. The house is typical of those that sprung up in freed slave communities across Maryland following the Civil War. This hut was originally in Jonesville, a hamlet in western Montgomery County. It was sold in 1935 to Harry Willard who donated it to the county and it was reconstructed here.

Wye Island NRMA

Phone - (410) 827-7577
Website - http://www.dnr.state.md.us/publiclands/eastern/
wyeisland.html
Admission Fee - None
Directions - *Queenstown, Queen Anne's County; from Route 50
turn south onto Carmichael Road. Travel 5.1 miles on Carmichael
Road until you cross the Wye Island Bridge. From the Wye Island
Bridge, travel south on Wye Island Road for approximately 4.2
miles. Numerous public parking areas are available along Wye
Island Road.*

The Park
For more than 300 years Wye Island was privately owned and covered
with tobacco and wheat fields. Farms passed in and out of the hands
of a succession of interesting owners, including William Paca, third
governor of Maryland and a signer of the Declaration of Independence.
In the 1770s Charles Beale Bordley left a prosperous law career to
devote himself to farming and converting Wye Island into a private
fiefdom. Under his stewardship the island became self-sufficient with
its own vineyards, orchards, textile mills, brick foundry and brewery.
Over the decades the island fragmented under disparate ownership
and in the mid-1970s the State of Maryland purchased the island to
ensure its future in a natural state.

The Walks
Wye Island featues about six miles of mostly multi-use trails that
explore the tidal recesses betwen the Wye River and the Wye River
East. Several of the trails are built around unique destinations. The
Holly Trail leads to an American holly tree that was growing here
before the Revolution. The *Ferry Landing Trail* was once the only
access road to the island. Now it is a mile-long path that ends at a
small, sandy beach. Another similar length canine hike is along the
Schoolhouse Woods Nature Trail that rambles through one of the
largest old-growth forests on the Eastern Shore. The water trails at
Wye Island are as attractive as the land ones. There are three soft
landing sites that enable canoeists with dogs to stop and explore
the land trails.

> **Where The Paw Meets The Earth:** Paw-friendly grass
> and dirt paths
> **Workout For Your Dog** - Easy, level passages
> **Swimming** - Sure, it is an island after all
> **Restrictions On Dogs** - No dogs at Duck House

Something Extra
Each November Wye Island hosts several field trial championships
for sporting dogs. Different breeds are featured each year and some
trials crown a national championship. The general public is encouraged to watch or participate in these events.

NEW JERSEY

Abram S. Hewitt State Forest

Phone - None
Website - http://www.state.nj.us/dep/parksandforests/parks/abram.html
Admission Fee - None
Directions - *Hewitt, Passaic County; take I-287 to Exit 57 and continue on Skyline Drive to its western end at Greenwood Lake Turnpike in Ringwood. Turn right and proceed for 8.4 miles to a Y intersection with Union Valley Road. Take the right fork and continue ahead for 0.3 mile on Warwick Turnpike. Just past a short concrete bridge, there is a turnout on the right side of the road. Park here.*

The Park
Abram S. Hewitt owned the great ironworks at Ringwood and was regarded as America's greatest ironmaster. In 1867 he introduced the open-hearth process for manufacturing steel into the United States. Abram Hewitt's interest in iron began to wane and he became involved in New York politics, winning election to the United States House of Representatives and eventually becoming New York City mayor as part of the progressive movement. He is often called the Father of the New York Subway for his initiatives in public underground transportation, although the subway system wasn't actually built until 10 years after he left office.

The Walks
The 2,001 acres of Abram S. Hewitt State Forest are accessible only on foot and paw. Most of that walking is done to get to the exposed open rock trails of the Bearfort Ridge. You will need to climb about 600 feet to reach the ridge with its long exposed views of Greenwood Lake and beyond. A common destination is Surprise Lake, which can be circled before the return trip. Two long-distance trails cross the ridge: the *Appalachian Trail* and the *Highlands Trail*, a 150-mile work-in-progress that will eventually link the Hudson River north of Bear Mountain to the Delaware River.

> **Where The Paw Meets The Earth:** Dirt and rocks
> **Workout For Your Dog** - Yes, a good done
> **Swimming** - Your dog will come to hike, not to swim
> **Restrictions On Dogs** - None

Something Extra
Puddingstone is a type of sedimentary rock in which white speckles of quartz sand has cemented itself together over millions of years. Mixed with it is a combination of other pebbles and stones of various sizes, shapes and colors. Some may even contain fossils from ancient river beds. Much of your dog's walking will be on Bearfort Ridge will be across good-gripping, purplish puddingstone. Tightly cemented puddingstones make a good ornamental stone when cut and polished properly.

Allaire State Park

Phone - (732) 938-2371
Website - http://www.state.nj.us/dep/parksandforests/parks/allaire.html
Admission Fee - Yes, Memorial Day to Labor Day but for trail use you can park outside the main lot
Directions - *Farmingdale, Monmouth County; from the Garden State Parkway take Exit 98 and follow the well-marked signs to the park. From I-195 use Exit 31B.*

The Park
James Peter Allaire was born in Nova Scotia in 1785 where his family, loyal to the crown of King George III, fled in exile during the American Revolution. The Allaires returned to New York City in 1806 and the 21-year old James Allaire opened a brass foundry. In 1822 Allaire came to the wilds of New Jersey and bought the 5,000-acre Monmouth Furnace to supply his engine works. The isolation of his new Howell Works caused him to build a self-sufficient village around it. The ironworks thrived until 1850 when Allaire retired. Legendary newspaper editor Arthur Brisbane bought the property as a retreat and maintained much of the old village. His estate deeded 800 acres to the State of New Jersey and the park today covers more than 3,000 acres.

The Walks
Thanks to the Manasquan River the trail system is a bit disjointed; to reach all of it you need to drive to various parking lot trailheads on either side of the water. From the parking area at the Allaire Village you can access a 4.5-mile walking trail that tours the historic building and joins up with the stacked loop *Red Trail* at the Nature Center. The *Yellow Trail* slips out of the village and explores the Manasquan River floodplain. The canine hiking is easy on these wide, pedestrian-only trails and the pace is relaxed away from the village. Allaire State Park is laced with sand roads and an abandoned railroad have been converted into multi-use trails. Jump on any of these well-marked pathways for hours more of comfortable canine hiking in the northernmost reaches of the Pine Barrens.

> **Where The Paw Meets The Earth:** Paw-friendly sand and dirt
> **Workout For Your Dog** - Flat, easy trotting
> **Swimming** - The Manasquan River is about 30 feet wide but only averages about two feet deep
> **Restrictions On Dogs** - No dogs in the campground

Something Extra
The Pine Creek Railroad in the park dates to 1953 and is the oldest continuously operating steam preservation railway in the country. Narrow-gauge trains like this hauled bog iron more to the furnace and moved finished goods out to market.

Allamuchy Mountain State Park

Phone - (908) 852-3790
Website - http://www.nj.gov/dep/parksandforests/parks/alla-much.html
Admission Fee - None
Directions - *Hackettstown, Warren County; from I-80 take Exit 19 and head south on Route 517, following the signs for Stephens State Park. Go two miles looking for a small sign (maybe) and an unimproved road on the leftthat passes through some houses to a clearing that doubles as a parking lot. If you care to challenge a rugged dirt road you can access lots deeper into the park.*

The Park

Most of the 8,000+ acres that comprise Allamuchy Mountain State Park were once the estate of Rutherford Stuyvesant - a direct descendant of Peter Stuyvesant, the last governor of Dutch New Amsterdam. He established a 1000-acre game preserve here and introduced the English pheasant to America. The State of New Jersey purchased the land in the 1970s.

The Walks

It's a beautiful day in central New Jersey and you want to go for a long hike with your dog but you don't want to spend the day dodging other trail users. Where do you go? Allamuchy Mountain State Park. Even though the park abuts busy I-80 few people are familiar with it. The State of New Jersey is in no hurry to rectify the situation. The park is undeveloped, save for a 15-mile trail system, and lacks signage. If you really want to disappear with your dog there are another 25 miles of unmarked trails across I-80 in the northern chunk of the park. This trail system is accessed on Waterloo Road, where the parking lot is the southern terminus for the 21-mile *Sussex Branch Trail*.

> **Where The Paw Meets The Earth:** Dirt roads and softer dirt footpaths
> **Workout For Your Dog** - Long hikes with some good climbs
> **Swimming** - There is fine dog paddling in Deer Park Pond
> **Restrictions On Dogs** - None

Something Extra

Have you ever driven across New Jersey on I-80 and seen the sign for the Scenic Overlook approaching the Pennsylvania state line? Did you stop or were you too busy and just flew past? Well, if you've always wondered what the fuss was about you can reach the overlook from the Allamuchy State Park trail system. The view looking towards the Delaware Water Gap was suggested in the 1960s when the highway was built by Mrs. Lyndon Johnson as one of the best vistas in New Jersey.

Bass River State Park

Phone - (609) 296-1114
Website - http://www.state.nj.us/dep/parksandforests/parks/
bass.html
Admission Fee - Yes, in summer
Directions - *Tuckerton, Ocean County; the state forest is six
miles west on Stage Road. From the Garden State Parkway South
take Exit 52 or North take Exit 50 and follow brown signs.*

The Park
When Governor Edward Stokes instigated the purchase of 597 acres
of woodlands along the Bass River in 1905, New Jersey had its first
state forest. The Civilian Conservation Corps set up camp in the forest
in 1933 and stayed for a decade building roads, bridges and various
shelters and cabins. They also impounded two streams to create 67-
acre Lake Absegami, the park's feature attraction.

The Walks
Although the Bass River State Forest covers 26,700 acres, the marked
trails are all short and are centered at the park office. The feature trail
is the one-mile *Absegami Trail* that winds through a small Atlantic
white cedar bog. Some of this trip is across a wooden boardwalk.
Some of the best canine hiking is across the street from the park
office on the *Pink* and *Green* trails. These adjacent loops, partly on
wide sand roads, travel beneath thick pines for 2.2 and 3.2 miles,
respectively. This is easy going for your dog on soft surfaces. The Bass
River State Forest is also the southern terminus for the pink-blazed
Batona Trail that runs through Wharton State Forest and Byrne State
Forest for 50 miles. The wilderness path through the Pine Barrens was
begun in 1961 and fully linked the three state forests in 1987.

> **Where The Paw Meets The Earth:** Soft dirt and
> pine straw
> **Workout For Your Dog** - Mostly level ground all around
> **Swimming** - Lake Absegami is a doggie swimming hole in
> the off-season
> **Restrictions On Dogs** - No dogs in the campgrounds

Something Extra
Fire is a way of life in the Pine Barrens - an average of one fire a day
occurs here. In 1930 one wildfire burned a record 267,000 acres.
In 1936 the Bass River Forest ignited and, in a fire that lasted four
days, three Civilian Conservation Corps were killed when the winds
shifted while they were setting a backfire. Two State Fire Wardens
also perished in the blaze. A memorial to the men who died stands
along the Pink Trail at the spot of their camp. It was dedicated in
1976 and ironically the next year four volunteer firefighters from the
Eagleswood Fire Company were killed when their engine was burned
over on a fire several miles from this memorial, and in 1982 a plaque
was added for them.

Batona Trail

Phone - None
Website - None
Admission Fee - None
Directions - *The trail runs through Lebanon, Wharton and Bass River State Forests where information on finding a parking lot can be found. Some commonly used starting points are on Routes 563 at Evans Bridge, 542 at Batsto Village at Route 72 at Four Mile.*

The Park

The *Batona Trail* is a wilderness trail that begins at Ongs Hat to the north and ends at Lake Absegami in Bass River State Forest. The original 30 miles of the Batona Trail were routed and cleared through white cedar and pitch pine forests by volunteers in 1961. Today the total length of the trail is 50.2 miles with many road crossings that make different lengths of canine hikes possible. The distinctive pink blazes on the *Batona Trail* were selected by Morris Burdock, then president of the Batona Hiking Club and chief advocate for the building of the trail.

The Walks

The *Batona Trail* is easy walking on paw-friendly sand for most of its length. Despite the over-whelming flatness of the surrounding countryside, there are undulating elevation changes on the trail itself. Any dog could walk end to end with no problem, if that was the goal. The high point on the trail is Apple Pie Hill, soaring 209 feet above sea level (there is a fire tower you can scale - the steps are too open for dogs - and literally scan the east-to-west entirety of New Jersey from Atlantic City to Philadelphia). A superb canine hike is the four-mile walk here from the Carranza Memorial. For the most part, however, there are no vistas beyond what you see around you - cedar swamps and millions of pine trees. In season wild blueberries and huckleberries can be gobbled along the trail.

> **Where The Paw Meets The Earth:** Packed sand roads and sandy soil
> **Workout For Your Dog** - Long walks on sandy will do the trick
> **Swimming** - The route of the trail is well-lubricated by tea-colored streams and an occasional pond
> **Restrictions On Dogs** - None

Something Extra

Mexico's greatest aviator, Emilio Carranza Rodriguez, crashed and died in the Pine Barrens in 1928. A memorial, paid for with pennies collected by schoolchildren, marks the location of his death, along the *Batona Trail*.

Bear Swamp

Phone - None
Website - None
Admission Fee - None
Directions - *Red Lion, Burlington County; Hawkins Road off Route 206 south of Route 70.*

The Park

The original settlers were people by the name of Parks. Bear were plentiful once through this locality and were hunted, in season and out of season, by earlier inhabitants. This town, before it had any definite name, was supposed to be a base for such hunters. They used the settlement at the crossroads as a sort of headquarters for their expeditions. One day a Parks family member went in search of a bear and actually stumbled on a mountain lion, crouched at the edge of a cedar swamp. Parks shot at the lion and wounded it. Then his gun failed and he was forced to fight the big cat by hand. He clubbed at its head and it clawed at him. Blood flowed freely. The yellow beast, covered with gore, seemed to turn red, as it expired. Parks finally brought his kill to town and the town became Red Lion.

The Walks

A labyrinth of unmarked and unmaintained trails provide access to hundreds of protected acres of mixed hardwoods and pine trees. The soft dirt and sand trails are generally wide but there are places that will require bushwhacking and picking your way through muddy low spots. Look for trails leading into the woods on the north side of Hawkins Road, that switches from a macadam to dirt surface in the region of Bear Swamp. One such entrance is on the east side of a small bridge across Little Creek on the western edge of the hard surface/soft surface switchover.

> **Where The Paw Meets The Earth:** Natural surface trails and dirt roads
> **Workout For Your Dog** - Flat terrain
> **Swimming** - The wetlands are not deep enough for swims
> **Restrictions On Dogs** - None

Something Extra

Bear Swamp is a noted birding area. Both Barred Owls and Red Shouldered Hawks are endangered species in New Jersey that can be seen here.

Belleplain State Forest

Phone - (609) 861-2404
Website - http://www.state.nj.us/dep/parksandforests/parks/belle.html
Admission Fee - None
Directions - *Woodbine, Cumberland County; the park is roughly situated between major Routes 47 and 49. The park office is on Belleplain-Woodbine Road (Route 550 that connects Route 9 to the east and Belleplain Road (Route 605 to the west).*

The Park
Belleplain State Forest was established in 1928 for, as the state says, "recreation, wildlife management, timber production, and water conservation." To achieve these goals, cranberry production in the region just south of the Pine Barrens was the odd man out. During the Great Depression the Civilian Conservation Corps converted Meisle Cranberry Bog into Lake Nummy, the popular recreation area at the center of the Belleplain Forest's 21,034 acres today.

The Walks
Belleplain offers up over 17 miles of non-motorized trails, plus an additional 24 miles of motorized trails if you are inclined to dodge the occasional truck or motorcycle. The marquee canine hike for dog lovers is the *East Creek Trail*, a meaty seven-mile loop that connects Lake Nummy to East Creek Pond. Expect to hit soupy spots in the trail along the way, although this is more of a hindrance to you than your dog. As you do creative stepping through these mucky areas keep your eyes open for the white blazes to keep going in the right direction. You will cross active roadways on this trek and to complete the loop you must walk a short distance on busy Route 347. But the shoulder is wide and should be of little consequence to even a skit-terish dog. If you come to Belleplain State Forest with two vehicles, you can use them for shuttle hikes. One such canine hike is along the 2.2-mile *Ponds Trail* that links East Creek Pond with the Pickle Factory Pond in the southwesternmost part of the forest.

> **Where The Paw Meets The Earth:** Soft dirt and sand with pine straw
> **Workout For Your Dog** - Long, flat trails
> **Swimming** - The four main ponds in the state forest will set any water-loving dog's tail to wagging
> **Restrictions On Dogs** - No dogs in the campground

Something Extra
Lying just south of the Pine Barrens, Belleplain enjoys better soil conditions and a correspondingly richer variety of trees. You can enhance your arboreal education with interpretive signs at both the Nature Center and the East Creek Group Cabin.

Berlin Park

Phone - None
Website - http://www.camdencounty.com/government/offices/ parks/pk_berlin.html
Admission Fee - None
Directions - *Berlin, Camden County; between White Horse Pike, New Freedom Road and Park Drive.*

The Park
The Berlin Train Station is the oldest existing station in New Jersey and is is listed on the New Jersey and National Registry of Historic Places. Originally called the Long-A-Coming Station (a bungling of a Lenni Lenape Indian word), it was built in 1856. In 1929 the 161-acre Berlin Park was added to the Camden County park system.

The Walks
Several miles of densely wooded trails course through the park behind the Environmental Studies Center at the corner of Broad Street and Park Drive. The main pathway through the spine of the park is wide and composed of pebbly sand; it runs alongside the Great Egg Harbor River. Designated a Wild and Scenic River, the Great Egg Harbor is narrow, dark and forboding. Unmarked dirt trails branch from the trunk in narrow slivers through the thick woods. Also available is a short nature loop inside a wired path.

> **Where The Paw Meets The Earth:** Pebbly sand and dirt
> **Workout For Your Dog** - Flat terrain
> **Swimming** - Every now and then the Great Egg Harbor River pools deep
> enough for a little swim
> **Restrictions On Dogs** - None

Something Extra
When the White Horse Pike (Route 30) was opened in 1922, connecting Camden and Atlantic City through downtown Berlin Borough, it was the longest concrete-paved highway in the world.

Branch Brook Park

Phone - 973-268-2300
Website - http://www.branchbrookpark.org/
Admission Fee - None
Directions - *Newark, Essex County; downtown; I-280 to Exit 15 and north on Bloomfield to park.*

The Park
This four-mile linear park, a block or two wide for most of its length, became the first county park in the United States when it was authorized in 1895. It was conceived as a natural space in a valley of a brook flowing into the Passaic River known as Old Blue Jay Swamp but additional land donations and gifts transformed the open space into a recognizable park of lakes, flower gardens, and ballfields.

The Walks
Expect easy canine hiking on paved paths and dirt scars across grassy lawns and patchy woodlands. You'll cross pedestrian bridge, observe historic Newark buildings, pass park sculptures and see a variety of architecturally significant bridges. The meadow in the northern area of the park is one of the largest recreaitonal open spaces in Essex County and a great place for playing with your dog.

> **Where The Paw Meets The Earth:** Asphalt, dirt and grass
> **Workout For Your Dog** - More for strolling than panting
> **Swimming** - The park features a large centralized lake
> **Restrictions On Dogs** - None

Something Extra
The highlight at Branch Brook Park each year is the flowering of more than 2,000 dogwood trees during April. The residents of "Cherry Blossomland" are more numerous and more varied than the famous cherry trees in Washington, D.C.

Brendan T. Byrne State Forest

Phone - (609) 726-1191
Website - http://www.state.nj.us/dep/parksandforests/parks/byrne.html
Admission Fee - None
Directions - *New Lisbon, Burlington County; From the NJ Turnpike, take Exit 7 and follow Route 206 south to Route 38 east, to second traffic light, then turn onto Magnolia Road (Route 644). Follow Magnolia Road until you come to the Four-Mile Circle. From the circle take Route 72 east, at mile marker 1 make a left. There is a forest entrance sign on your left as you turn in. Take the first right and the office is on the left.*

The Park
It is hard to imagine this vast 32,000-acre forest was stripped, barren land a little more than a century ago. The Lebanon Glass Works, from which the forest takes its name, set up shop in 1851 and within 16 years had devoured every stick of timber for miles in every direction. With its supply of wood depleted the furnace was shut down and abandoned. The state began buying the land that ultimately became Lebanon State Forest in 1908 (and Brendan T. Byrne State Forest a century later) and once again the sandy soil is blanketed with stands of pine, oak, maple, gum and Atlantic white cedar.

The Walks
Ongs Hat, at the western tip of the park, is the northern terminus for the *Batona Trail* and about 9 miles of the 49-mile route slice across the lower edge of the state forest. The Batona can be used to create large canine hiking loops with other forest trails. Another good walking choice is the *Cranberry Trail* which runs 5 miles to Pakim Pond. Pakim Pond, from the Lenni-Lenape word for "cranberry" was once used as a reservoir for an adjacent cranberry bog, now a swamp. For the more adventurous canine hiker there are over 20 miles of wilder-ness trails and if your restless spirit is still not sated it is easy to get off the grid here: Lebanon State Forest features 400 miles of unpaved roads.

> **Where The Paw Meets The Earth:** Packed sand and soft dirt
> **Workout For Your Dog** - Miles and miles of flat trotting
> **Swimming** - Many small ponds and creeks
> **Restrictions On Dogs** - None

Something Extra
Atlantic white cedar - prized in shipbuilding for its water-resistant wood - once dominated thousands of acres here. Decimated by years of logging, the state has worked diligently to reforest several cedar swamps in the Lebanon State Forest. The 735-acre Cedar Swamp Natural Area at the headwaters of Shinns Branch is one such diverse habitat.

Cape May National Wildlife Refuge

Phone - (609) 463-0994
Website - http://www.fws.gov/northeast/capemay/
Admission Fee - None
Directions - *Cape May Courthouse, Cape May County;*
the Headquarters Office is west of town on Kimbles Beach Road,
directly off Route 47.

The Park
The Cape May National Wildlife Refuge became one of the newest refuges in the federal system when a modest 90 acres were acquired in 1989. The vision for the refuge calls for 21,200 acres to be brought under protection in this key location along the Atlantic Flyway. The U.S. Fish and Wildlife Service is about half way to realizing that goal. Included in its more than 11,000 acres is a five-mile stretch along the Delaware Bay. Faced with 12 miles of open water to cross during their seasonal migration songbirds and raptors spend extra time on Cape May Point resting and feeding. So many shorebirds linger here during migration that it is second only to Copper River Delta in Alaska as a shorebird staging area.

The Walks
Cape May National Wildlife Refuge is divided into three divisions. The Cedar Swamp Division has no maintained trails and the Two-Mile Unit does not allow dogs so canine hikers will want to head to the Delaware Bay Division at the Headquarters. There is a short, winding crushed gravel trail at the Headquarters but dog owners will start here only to pick up a trail map. The prime destination is the next road south at Woodcock Lane. The *Woodcock Trail* is a one-mile stacked loop trail that skirts a woodland habitat. The mown grass path is wide enough to keep your dog centered and out of the reach of hitchhiking ticks in the tall grasses.

> **Where The Paw Meets The Earth:** Soft dirt and grass
> **Workout For Your Dog** - Easy, flat hikign for your dog
> **Swimming** - The swimming is for the birds, not dogs
> **Restrictions On Dogs** - No dogs in the Two-Mile Unit

Something Extra
The refuge hosts more than 300 species of birds but none is more celebrated than the red knot. The shorebirds' arrival in May and early June coincides with the horseshoe crab spawning season which gives these long-distance flyers a chance to gorge on high-energy crab eggs. In May virtually every red knot on the North American continent can be found on a Delaware Bay beach.

Cattus Island County Park

Phone - (877) 921-0074
Website - http://www.co.ocean.nj.us/parks/cattus.html
Admission Fee - None
Directions - *Toms River, Ocean County; from the Garden State Parkway use Exit 82 - Route 37 East/Seaside Heights. Take the jughandle to Fischer Boulevard and head north. Turn right at the fourth light onto Cattus Island Boulevard. The parking lot is on the left.*

The Park
At the turn of the 20th century, John V.A. Cattus, a New York importer, purchased the property to use as a hunting and boating retreat. In 1914, he became the charter Commodore of the Barnegat Bay Racing Association.Private owners bought Cattus Island in 1961 but before it could be developed the New Jersey Wetlands Act of 1970 saved it for open space. The county began construction of the trail system in 1977.

The Walks
A paved and unpaved road runs for one mile down the spine of the 500-acre Cattus Island peninsula. Two main trails loop across the road and a smaller loop radiates off it near the end for a total of five miles of walking paths. Come here for relaxed canine hiking on level paths through the maritime forests and salt marshes. The *Island Loop* snakes around for a little more than two miles under a wooded canopy. Stop along the way at a bird blind to check on activity at one of several osprey poles in the marshes. At the parking lot is the 1.7-mile *Maritime Forest Loop* that is a landlocked exploration for your dog. The *Hidden Beach Loop* at the end of Cattus Island uses a boardwalk to cross onto a small island of forest. The Boy Scouts have sculpted a paw-friendly trail of wood shavings and soft dirt that makes an ideal destination for a canine hike.

> **Where The Paw Meets The Earth:** Soft natural trails and roads
> **Workout For Your Dog** - Flat and easy throughout the park
> **Swimming** - The swimming for your dog in Barnegat Bay and Silver Bay is as good as it gets
> **Restrictions On Dogs** - None

Something Extra
The Cattus Island Butterfly Garden was created in 2005 with plants selected to attract a wide range of native butterlies not commonly seen in New Jersey backyards. While most plants lure butterflies with the promise of sweet nectar, others play host to butterfly larvae. The best time to catch butterfly activity is on a bright summer's day.

Cheesequake State Park

Phone - (732) 566-2161
Website - http://www.state.nj.us/dep/parksandforests/parks/cheesequake.html
Admission Fee - None
Directions - *Cheesequake, Middlesex County; from the Garden State Parkway take Exit 120 and follow signs for the park through residential streets.*

The Park

Located between northern and southern plant communities, this area has long been recognized for its botanical value. The State of New Jersey began acquiring land for the park in 1938 and opened a picnic grove and hiking trails two years later. The name Cheesequake is commonly believed to derive from a Lenni Lenape Indian term roughly translating to "upland village." But the area does rest atop a tetonic fault and one of the earliest earthquakes on record that shook the metropolitan New York area in 1779 was centered in Cheesequake.

The Walks

The agreeable canine hiking at Cheesequake State Park is concentrated in the western section of its 1,274 acres. Four trails all launch from the same trailhead just past the park entrance. Another trail designed for mountain bike use but open to foot traffic is also available hard by the Garden State Parkway. The star trek here is along the *Green Trail* that will introduce your dog to just about every forest type in New Jersey - scrub pine barrens, Atlantic white cedar swamp, red maples in saltwater marshes and upland hardwood forests. There is just enough elevation changes to keep your dog interested on these paw-friendly trails.

> **Where The Paw Meets The Earth:** Soft dirt for the most part
>
> **Workout For Your Dog** - Expect hilly stretches but not severe
>
> **Swimming** - The *Yellow Trail* drops down to Hooks Creek Lake for a quick chance at a doggie dip
>
> **Restrictions On Dogs** - No dogs in the campground

Something Extra

Henry David Thoreau wrote about beach heather after visiting Cape Cod in 1849, describing how local residents called the low-growing mossy plants "poverty grass" because it grew where nothing else did. Island Beach State Park is home to the greatest expanse of beach heather in New Jersey. In late May the heather balds, as patches of the plant are called, explode in a carpet of yellow in the secondary dunes.

Clayton Park

🐾 🐾 🐾 🐾

Phone - (609) 259-5794
Website - http://www.monmouthcountyparks.com/parks/clay-tonpark.asp
Admission Fee - None
Directions - *Upper Freehold,Monmouth County; from I-195 Take Exit 11 (Imlaystown/Cox's Corner) and head south on Route 43 that will soon reach Route 526. Turn left and make an immediate right on Davis Station Road (there is a small park sign).Go through the village and after one mile make a left onto Emley's Hill Road and follow to the parking lot on the left.*

The Park

For most of the 20th century Paul Clayton shunned modern farming methods, working his fields by hand with his five horses growing potatoes, tomatoes, grains and corn until 1971 when he retired at the age of 87. For years he turned down lucrative offers to harvest the trees on his property along Doctor's Creek. Instead he sold his 176 acres to Monmouth County in 1978 for a price below market value. The county has since doubled the size of Clayton Park to its current 421 acres of hardwoods.

The Walks

Clayton Park is a true jewel for New Jersey canine hikers with about eight miles of sandy dirt paths traipsing through airy stands of towering beech, black oak and tulip poplar. The trail system is neatly divided into two stacked-loops by a wide ravine so you can bring your dog for a satisfying loop of less than one hour or carve out a longer hiking day. You will start on the *Bridges Trail* that rolls around ridges and through valleys; the ups and downs go down easy on these well-maintained paths. If you choose a big canine hiking day you will penetrate deeper into the core of the Clayton forest on the 1.5-mile *Old Forge Trail* or finish the Bridges loop by skirting farm fields. Either way you will spend time along the wetlands of Doctor's Creek that will eventually drain in the Delaware River.

> **Where The Paw Meets The Earth:** Soft natural trails
> **Workout For Your Dog** - Moderate climbing around wooded hills
> **Swimming** - Look for a small pond along the *Bridges Trail*
> **Restrictions On Dogs** - None

Something Extra

Clayton Park is one of the best spring wildflower sites in central New Jersey. In the open understory look for jack-in-the-pulpit, trout lily, wild geranium and even the seldom seen trillium and wild ginger in April and May. Come back in mid-summer and enjoy spotted jewelweed with its tiny blood-red droplets.

Cooper River Park

Phone - None
Website - None
Admission Fee - None
Directions - *Pennsauken, Camden County; traversed by Park Drive North and Park Drive South. Access is from Cuthbert Boulevard to the east and Crescent Boulevard (Route 130) to the west.*

The Park
People began settling along the Cooper and Newton creeks in the 1690s as the waterways became busy conduits for goods to and from a young Philadelphia. Through the decades the free flow of water became strangled by all manner of debris and waste tumbling from the industrializing banks. In 1936 workers from the Works Project Administration waded into the putrid Cooper River swamp to build a dam, shove around mountains of dirt and shaped the creek into the slender lake that is the centerpiece of Cooper River Park.

The Walks
A 3.8-mile paved pathway loops around the active lake. The serpentine route features almost continually unobstructed views of the water, which on most days will be sprinkled with sailors from the Cooper River Yacht Club on the south shore. Long stretches of the walk, especially in the eastern end of the park, are bereft of recreational activity, leaving you alone with other dog walkers and joggers. A number of war memorial monuments and statues grace the route.

> **Where The Paw Meets The Earth:** Paved asphalt
> **Workout For Your Dog** - Easy going
> **Swimming** - There is access to the water at many points
> **Restrictions On Dogs** - None

Something Extra
A generation ago the waters of the Cooper River were so polluted from sewage that it was not safe for dogs to drink. Boaters who accidentally fell into the river rushed for hepatitis shots. Thanks to the Clean Water Act of 1972 the rejuvenated waters of the Cooper River have emerged as a world-class competitive rowing venue. The 2000-meter straightaway, protected from crosswinds and current, is ideal for competition. The course has hosted three national championships, including an Olympic Trials regatta, and a lucky dogwalker can watch these graceful sculls upon the glassy water.

Corson's Inlet State Park

Phone - (609) 861-2404
Website - http://www.state.nj.us/dep/parksandforests/parks/corsons.html
Admission Fee - None
Directions - *Ocean City, Cape May County; from the Garden State Parkway use Exit 82 - Route 37 East/Seaside Heights. Take the jughandle to Fischer Boulevard and head north. Go right at the fourth light onto Cattus Island Boulevard; parking lot is on the left.*

The Park
Corson's Inlet was established in 1969 before every last inch of Jersey shorefront became developed. With its undisturbed sand dune systems and marine estuaries this is one of your last opportunities to experience the Atlantic oceanfront in New Jersey as it was before people discovered the shore.

The Walks
There aren't many places where the hiking public is invited to walk across protected ocean dunes but Corson's Inlet is one. Even rarer still is to find a dune system that permits dogs and again Corson's Inlet is the place - from September 16 through March 31. The main trail (Yellow) leading away from the small parking lot beside the Rush Chattin Bridge between Ocean City and Strathmere and its two spur paths (Orange, then Red) all lead to the beach that can be used to create loop hikes on the hook-shaped peninsula. All canine hiking is on deep sugar sand and the trails are just long enough to be enjoyable without becoming laborious. If you come to Corson's Inlet in late September or October on a hot day make sure to bring plenty of fresh water for your dog. Even though the trails aren't long there is little shade among the dunes.

> **Where The Paw Meets The Earth:** Sand
> **Workout For Your Dog** - Yes, with ocean swimming and running in sand
> **Swimming** - If the excitement of the Atlantic surf is too intimidating try the expansive crescent beach along the inlet with its calm, inviting waters
> **Restrictions On Dogs** - No dogs between April 1 and September 15

Something Extra
America's second-worst fire took place on a steamship called the *General Slocum* on New York's East River in 1904 - more than 1,000 people perished. The steamer was salvaged and put back into service as a barge called the *Maryland* that sank off Corson's Inlet on December 11, 1911. Buried beneath several feet of shifting sand searchers believe they have located the infamous General Slocum but there has been no definitive recovery.

Crow's Woods

Phone - None
Website - None
Admission Fee - None
Directions - *Haddonfield, Burlington County; From King's High-way West head towards the Hi-Speed Line overpass and make a left on Warwick Road. After one mile make a left onto Upland Way and make a right just past the underpass into the park. Follow the park road to the end.*

The Park
The area was first settled in 1682 but things didn't really get going until 21-year old Elizabeth Haddon arrived in 1701 to establish her father's claims here. It wasn't until 1875 that Haddonfield Borough was officially established and the natural area south of town has been known as Crow's Woods for nearly as long. For years part of the area was used as a landfill which was converted into playing fields following the 1967 construction of the PATCO Hi-Speed Line which abuts the park. Today, the grounds at Crow's Woods encompass more than 65 acres.

The Walks
Crow's Woods packs plenty of topographical diversity into its short, intermingling trails. In fact, so many dog walkers have come from outside Haddonfield to enjoy the park's ravines and hills that borough commissioners have considered imposing a "use tag" system similar to New Jersey beaches. The wide, soft dirt paths wind through dense woodlands of scrub oak, pitch pine and mountain laurel. An asphalt jogging track around the perimeter of the sports fields is also available.

> **Where The Paw Meets The Earth:** Dirt and asphalt
> **Workout For Your Dog** - Plenty of short, quick hills in the woods
> **Swimming** - There are small swimming holes in the woods that are more suited for a refreshing splash than sustained dog paddling
> **Restrictions On Dogs** - None

Something Extra
Also in Haddonfield, in the north end of the borough, is the heavily wooded Pennypacker Park where dinosaur bones were discovered in 1838 in a steep ravine carved by the Cooper River. When a full excavation was initiated by William Parker Foulke in 1858 nearly 50 bones of a plant-eating, duck-billed dinosaur were discovered. Haddonfield was suddenly famous as the site of the most complete dinosaur skeleton ever found. A small memorial marks the spot where *Hadrosaurus Foulkii* was unearthed at the end of Maple Street.

Deer Path Park

Phone - None
Website - http://www.co.hunterdon.nj.us/depts/parks/guides/ DeerPath.htm
Admission Fee - None
Directions - *Flemington, Hunterdon County; on Route 31, north of town. Exit onto Woodschurch Road and follow the signs to the park.*

The Park
Deer Path was originally owned by Alois and Berta Batz. Until 1967, the land was used for agriculture. That year, they established a summer camp on the property for children and the pond was expanded to it current size. The county acquired the property in 1977 for development and operation as an active park. Eight acres were subdivided from the property in 1980 for the construction of the Hunterdon County YMCA.

The Walks
The canine hiker at Deer Park will find a pleasing blend of meadow and woods walking and level hiking and climbing. The main attraction will be across Woodschurch Road, a 600-foot knob that exploded into existence in a volcanic eruption during the Triassic Period. After some cuppy going on horse trails through old farm fields (look for a natural fence of gnarled osage orange trees), the figure-eight *Nature Trail* heads up the verdant hillside. The entire path is 1.5 miles back to the trailhead but the *Peter Buell Trail* branches off the main trail to cross Round Mountain on its wasy to a different trailhead/parking lot. The recreational section of Deer Path Park should not be overlooked if it is not a busy day. This old farm, and later summer camp, is surrounded by two miles of open cross-country trails that are especially palatable to your dog on a sunny day.

> **Where The Paw Meets The Earth:** Natural surface
> **Workout For Your Dog** - It takes some effort to move across Round Mountain for your dog
> **Swimming** - Deer Path Pond is a 3-acre pond with super access to the water for dogs
> **Restrictions On Dogs** - None

Something Extra
During the winter months these trails are an excellent outing for your dog while cross-country skiing and snow shoeing.

Delaware & Raritan Canal State Park

Phone - (609) 924-5705
Website - http://www.dandrcanal.com/
Admission Fee - None
Directions - *Princeton, Mercer County; the canal towpath can be accessed many places; the canal office is at 145 Mapleton Road in Princeton.*

The Park
When canal building fever swept America in the early 1800s it didn't take much imagination to dream of a water route between New York and Philadelphia across central New Jersey. Ships could navigate up the Delaware River to Bordentown and to New Brunswick in the east so all that was required was to dig a ditch between the two villages. Construction began in 1830 and by 1834 the canal was open. The main artery - 75 feet wide and seven feet deep and all hand dug - stretched 44 miles and another feeder line ran down the Delaware River to Trenton for 22 miles. The Delaware and Raritan was one of America's busiest canals and staved off competition from the railroads at a profit until almost 1900. It remained open until 1932 until the last coal barge was grounded. The State of New Jersey took over the property as a water supply system and today the canal remains virtually intact. The state park is a 70-mile linear park connecting fields and forests along its route.

The Walks
Canine hiking along the old towpath uses natural and crushed gravel surfaces. Several mill buildings, wooden bridges and canal structures are reminders of the bustling times that were once routine here. The canal still brims with activity today - almost any time you can count on sharing the trail with joggers, fishermen, cyclists, horseback riders - and other dogs.
> **Where The Paw Meets The Earth:** Natural and crushed gravel stretches
> **Workout For Your Dog** - Flat, but long canine hikes possible
> **Swimming** - Many places to drop down and find a swim
> **Restrictions On Dogs** - No dogs in overnight areas

Something Extra
Hike back to another century with your dog along the canal route as you encounter wooden bridges and 19th century bridge tender houses, remnants of locks, cobblestone spillways and hand-built stone-arched culverts.

Delaware Water Gap NRA-Kittatinny Point

Phone - (570) 828-2253
Website - http://www.nps.gov/dewa/
Admission Fee - Only for recreation areas where dogs are not allowed
Directions - *Warren County; traveling west on I-80 exit into the rest area as you enter the Water Gap approaching Pennsylvania. You can park in the rest area but the actual parking lot is just beyond on the right.*

The Park
In the Lenni Lenape language Kittaninny means "endless mountain" which is quite ironic when looking at Mount Tammany where the 1,527-foot high Kittaninny Ridge ends abruptly by plunging 1200 feet into the Delaware River. It didn't take much imagination for early American entrepreneurs to dream of glorious resorts in the vicinity of one of New Jersey's great wonders. More recently U.S. Army engineers envisioned damming the gap and creating a giant reservoir for water supply and recreation. Amidst great controversy the Tocks Island Dam project was finally scuttled in 1992 and today the Delaware Water Gap National Recreation Area encompasses 70,000 acres for more than 30 miles along the Delaware River on both the New Jersey and Pennsylvania sides.

The Walks
The climb up Mount Tammany may be the steepest canine hike in New Jersey but not beyond the capabilities of a healthy dog. The *Red-Dot Trail* covers the 1200-foot elevation gain in 1.5 miles using switchbacks on an oft-times rocky path under paw. There is one 30-foot rock climb that will need to be negotiated. After enjoying the spectacular views push away from the Water Gap on the *Blue-Dot Trail*. A welcome respite in light woods on the level ridge begins a long, steady descent accentuated by groves of mountain laurel in the early summer. You will eventually reach the white-blazed *Appalachian Trail* along Dunnfield Creek that you'll use to close this four-mile loop.

> **Where The Paw Meets The Earth:** Dirt and rocks
> **Workout For Your Dog** - Maybe the best in the state
> **Swimming** - You will need to travel up Old Mine Road to get access into the Delaware River
> **Restrictions On Dogs** - Dogs are not allowed in the Kittatinny Point Visitor Center and picnic area or Watergate

Recreation Site in New Jersey

Something Extra
Dunnfield Creek brings many waterfalls on the tumbling brook and creates a perfect doggie swimming hole at the ideal time for refreshment - the first water encountered on this strenuous hike.

Dorbrook Recreation Area

Phone - (732) 542-1642
Website - http://www.monmouthcountyparks.com/parks/dor-brook.asp
Admission Fee - None
Directions - *Colts Neck, Monmouth County; take the Garden State Parkway to Exit 109 and head west on Route 520, Newman Springs Road. Turn left on Swimming River Road and right on Route 537 to park.*

The Park
The first land for this park was acquired from the estate of Murray Rosenberg, creator of Miles Shore stores. Later additions included Festoon Farm, a horse spread named for the English import, Festoon, who won the One Thousand Guinea Stakes at Newcastle, first contested in 1814.

The Walks
As active recreation areas go for hiking with your dog, this is one of the best. The park is big at 535 acres and there is plenty of room for 2.4 miles of paved trail on two loops.
>   **Where The Paw Meets The Earth:** Asphalt
>   **Workout For Your Dog** - Easy loping around the park
>   **Swimming** - None
>   **Restrictions On Dogs** - None

Something Extra
Dorbrook has been named the best place in Monmouth County for rollerbladers if your dog is so inclined.

Double Trouble State Park

Phone - (732) 341-6662
Website - http://www.state.nj.us/dep/parksandforests/parks/double.html
Admission Fee - None
Directions - *Bayville, Ocean County; travelling south on the Garden State Parkway take Exit 80 and turn left to Double Trouble Road. Follow to end in about four miles and cross the road into the park. Heading north use Exit 77 and turn left to park entrance in 1/4 mile.*

The Park
Sawmills have operated at this site on the Cedar Creek, processing dense stands of Atlantic White Cedar into shingles and shipmasts. Over time cranberries were planted in the swamps vacated by the harvested trees. In 1909 the entire area became the Double Trouble Cranberry Company. The name supposedly comes from problems with the dams used to sustain the bogs. One theory has two wash outs in a single spring rainy season inspiring the name and another traces it to two separate leaky holes gnawed in a dam by muskrats. Today the park centers around Double Trouble Historic Village, a cluster of 14 surviving structures from the late 1800s.

The Walks
The park preserves more than 8000 acres of natural Pine Barrens habitat but you will experience just a tiny slice of it on just a single trail in Double Trouble State Park. The 1.5-mile *Nature Trail* leaves on an old sand road along a series of cranberry bogs. You leave the open area around the ponds with a sharp right turn into a dark avenue of Atlantic Cedar. The trees were once thought to be limitless in the Pinelands when the sawmills were running full force. You and your dog will have experienced what lies beyond in millions of acres of the Pine Barrens in a short, exceedingly pleasant outing.

> **Where The Paw Meets The Earth:** Sandy dirt
> **Workout For Your Dog** - Long, flat hikes possible
> **Swimming** - Ponds, canals
> **Restrictions On Dogs** - None

Something Extra
The cranberry is a native American fruit that was harvested naturally in the Pine Barrens for centuries. Commercial production began around 1835 in New Jersey and today only Massachusetts and Michigan grow more cranberries, named because its flower resembles a craning neck. The restored cranberry sorting and packing house at Double Trouble park is the finest of its kind from the 19th century. The bogs are still producing and if you come in the fall you can see thousands of the buoyant berries bobbing on the surface; at other times of the year you will have to make do with looking at a few harvest escapees washing against the shoreline.

Eagle Rock Reservoir

Phone - None
Website - None
Admission Fee - None
Directions - *West Orange, Essex County; take I- 280 East to Exit 8B (Prospect Avenue /Cedar Grove) onto Prospect Avenue. Turn right onto Eagle Rock Avenue and left into the park.*

The Park
Shortly after Newark was settled in 1666 a surveying station was located on Eagle Rock, named for bald eagles that called the rock home. Although the park is undeveloped today it was a busy place through the early 1900s with trolley lines, vacationers and a casino (the non-gambling old-time kind). Automobile enthusiasts of that period held races up the cobblestone roadway of Eagle Rock Avenue terminating in Eagle Rock Park.

The Walks
The deciduous forest of the 408-acre reservation is striped with bridle trails and footpaths, some marked and some not. The park is most known for its direct views into New York City.

> **Where The Paw Meets The Earth:** Rocky and dirt roads
> **Workout For Your Dog** - Moderate trotting in store here
> **Swimming** - None
> **Restrictions On Dogs** - None

Something Extra
This area overlooking the New York City skyline is now the site of the newly dedicated Memorial to the 3,000 people murdered by terrorists on September 11.

Edwin B. Forsythe National Wildlife Refuge

Phone - (609) 652-1665
Website - http://www.fws.gov/northeast/forsythe/
Admission Fee - None
Directions - *Oceanville, Atlantic County; follow Route 72 to Route 9 North. Take Route 9 North to Lower Shore Road. Turn left. At second fork, turn right (Collinstown Road). Continue on road.*

The Park
Forsythe Refuge's Brigantine and Barnegat Divisions were originally two distinct refuges, established in 1939 and 1967 respectively, to protect tidal wetland and shallow bay habitat for migratory water birds. In 1984 they were combined under the Edwin B. Forsythe name, in honor of the late conservationist Congressman from New Jersey.

The Walks
The pristine Holgate Unit in the Barnegat Division at the tip of Long Island is the star attraction at the Atlantic seashore refuge but it is off-limits to dogs. But there is still lemonade to be made from the lemons dished out here by the U.S. Fish & Wild-life Service - dogs are welcome to enjoy the nature trails in the Brigantine Division. There are four short trails that will take you into woodlands and salt marshes along the leisurely eight-mile Wildlife Drive. This is a quiet place to bring your dog for relaxed canine hiking.

> **Where The Paw Meets The Earth:** Natural surface, boardwalks and pavement
> **Workout For Your Dog** - Level, easy canine hiking
> **Swimming** - No
> **Restrictions On Dogs** - No dogs in Holgate Unit

Something Extra
If you come between December and March you may find the wetlands afire. At Forsythe they use fire to control Phragmites, an invasive species that grows so fast and densely that it chokes off the productivity of marshes. Fire removes dry, dead plant matter that has built up over the years, opening up space for new plant growth and providing better cover and food for wildlife. The burn allows nutrients locked up in the dried plants to be returned to the soil to be used by new plants. Not too long ago the dikes were covered with Phragmites but no longer.

Eno's Pond County Park

Phone - (877) 627-2757
Website - http://www.ocean.nj.us/parks/enos.html
Admission Fee - None
Directions - *Lacey, Ocean County; take Exit 74 off the Garden State Parkway, going east on Lacey Road. Cross over Route 9 onto East Lacey Road for another mile and park entrance on left past the Captains Inn.*

The Park

With the advent of the tourism in the late1800s Lacey became a summer destination for the wealthy. Several large hotel resorts sprang up in the township. In 1889 Byron E. Eno purchased The Riverside House and built a dam to enlarge the Colonial-era pond adjacent to his hotel. He used the pond to harvest ice in the winter to store for his summer guests. By the 1940s beach houses were replacing seasonal hotels and the Riverside House declined until it was finally destroyed by a fire in 1952. Eno's ice pond remains and has become the centerpiece for a county park at the along the south shore of Bridge Creek. The casino that was part of Eno's resort still stands and operates as the Captain's Inn.

The Walks

Eno's Pond County Park abuts the Forsythe National Wildlife Refuge and the two have joined forces to create a trail system through a regenerative forest. One of the two trails is handicapped-accessible and canine hikers will want to concentrate on the *Self-Guided Nature Trail* that swallows much of its fellow trail anyway. This is an exceedingly pleasant 1.1-mile hike with your dog, enhanced by one of the better trail guides to be found in New Jersey parks. This is easy-going on a variety of surfaces completely in a shaded loop.

> **Where The Paw Meets The Earth:** Paw-friendly sandy dirt and boardwalk
> **Workout For Your Dog** - Very easy canine hiking
> **Swimming** - Your dog can slip into Eno's Pond for some refreshing dog-paddling
> **Restrictions On Dogs** - None

Something Extra

In front of the parking lot is a large open playing field that is ideal for a spirited game of fetch after your hike with your dog on days when the park is not crowded.

Estell Manor Park

Phone - (609) 645-5960
Website - http://www.aclink.org/PARKS/mainpages/estell.asp
Admission Fee - None
Directions - *Mays Landing, Atlantic County; located on Route 50, 3.5 miles south of town.*

The Park
The first deed granting land to the Estell family in this area appeared in 1677. During Colonial times the Estells were among the largest landowners in Atlantic County. In 1825 a glassworks was established by the Estells using the bottomless supplies of Jersey sand to best advantage. During World War I industry came to the Great Egg Harbor River in a big way. The Bethlehem Loading Company munitions plant churned out more than 50,000 large caliber shells in little more than one year before shutting down in 1919. A complete town of 3,000 people sprung up to support the bustling plant. For nearly a century the forest has been reclaiming the area and today the 1,700-acre Estell Manor Park is the most popular in the Atlantic County Park System.

The Walks
There is plenty of to do in this busy park and canine hikers will do best to turn north and leave the ballfields and exercise trail and fishing docks to others. The trail system in the North End is built largely upon many of the 24 miles of abandoned railway built by the Bethlehem Loading Company. These leveled paths are soft and wide and perfect for any dog. Almost all of your canine hiking here will be under the canopy of a shaded, mature forest. Estell Manor maintains about 13 miles of trail, including almost two miles of elevated boardwalk across a cedar swamp. Back near the Nature Center you can pick up a 1.5-mile loop that visits the ruins of the Estellville Glassworks. The Nature Center and trail guide are among the most informative you will find in New Jersey.

> **Where The Paw Meets The Earth:** Soft sandy dirt and boardwalk
> **Workout For Your Dog** - Only in time, not in difficulty
> **Swimming** - The best place to get your dog some paddling time is in the South River at the end of Artesian Well Road
> **Restrictions On Dogs** - None

Something Extra
The rich history of this property has created a multitude of surprises awaiting the canine hiker along the trail: an ancient cemetery, ruins from the munitions plant, an artesian well, observation decks in hardwood swamps.

Farny State Park

Phone - (973) 962-7031
Website - http://www.state.nj.us/dep/parksandforests/parks/farny.html
Admission Fee - None
Directions - *Newfoundland, Morris County; Take I-80 West to Exit 37 (Hibernia/Rockaway). At the bottom of the ramp, turn left onto Green Pond Road (County 513). Follow Green Pond Road north through the town and turn right onto Upper Hibernia Road (opposite the Marcella Community Center). After a mile turn left go 1.2 miles to a large dirt parking area on the left side of the road, just after crossing the dam of the Split Rock Reservoir.*

The Park

Farny State Park, despite its location in the center of North Jersey, is one of the least-used parks in the state. There are no spectacular must-see destinations and the canine hiking is quite rugged with plenty of climbs and stream crossings that can be tricky when waters run high.

The Walks

This forested wilderness connects watershed lands and is crossed by an old logging road. Streams, mixed oak-hardwood forest and swamps comprise the park. Trail entry is through the Farny Natural Area. Split Rock Reservoir is adjacent to the park. Much of your day here will be on the blue-blazed *Split Rock Loop Trail* and the *Four Birds Trail*, named for North American wild turkeys in the deciduous forests, red-tailed hawks above the cliffs, osprey along the lake shores, and great blue heron in the beaver meadows.

> **Where The Paw Meets The Earth:** Rocky, dirt trails
> **Workout For Your Dog** - This is a rugged place to take your dog
> **Swimming** - Split Rock Reservoir is an off-the-grid place for canine swims
> **Restrictions On Dogs** - None

Something Extra

Look for remnants of mining that once took place around Split Rock Reservoir as you work these trails.

Forest Resource Education Center

Phone - (732) 928-2360
Website - http://www.state.nj.us/dep/parksandforests/forest/njfs_frep.html
Admission Fee - None
Directions - *Jackson, Ocean County; from I-195 take Exit 21 (527/528 South) for 6.2 miles and turn right onto Bowman Blvd. After .9 miles turn right onto Don Connor Boulevard. The Interpretive Center is on the right.*

The Park

The Forest Resource Education Center is exactly what it sounds like - a living outdoor classroom to teach New Jersey residents about trees. The State of New Jersey has 660 acres to teach and practice forest stewardship. In addition the New Jersey Forest Tree Nursery uses 45 acres for the propagation and production of more than 300,000 seedlings each year to supply community forestry programs throughout the state.

The Walks

Dogs are welcome to use the interpretive trails across the Education Center property. You may even be able to linger behind a passing class group and learn a few things about New Jersey forests. Several of the trail subjects are not your typical nature center fare: fire ecology and forest products, for instance. There are a total of about five miles of formal trails and plenty of sand roads to wander around. This is all easy going for any dog, flat and paw-friendly surfaces. Of course there is plenty of shade on hot summer days.

> **Where The Paw Meets The Earth:** Grass and dirt paths around the woods and logging roads
> **Workout For Your Dog** - Mostly level terrain here
> **Swimming** - Not a major feature of this park
> **Restrictions On Dogs** - None

Something Extra

Maple sugaring is just one of the things your dog can learn about how to use the woods here.

Fort Mott State Park

Phone - (609) 935-3218
Website - http://www.state.nj.us/dep/parksandforests/parks/
fortmott.html
Admission Fee - None
Directions - *Pennsville, Salem County; from Exit 1 of I-295, take Route 49 East to Fort Mott Road. Turn right onto Fort Mott Road and travel 3 miles. Park is located on right.*

The Park
Fort Mott was envisioned as part of a three-fort defense of Philadelphia that dangled across the Delaware River. Following the Civil War, work began on 11 gun emplacements but only two were completed when the fort was abandoned in 1876. In preparation for the Spanish-American War in 1896, Fort Mott, named to honor Major General Gershom Mott, a native of Bordentown, was completed and outfitted with three 10-inch and three 12-inch guns. The fort remained active until 1943, although during its last two decades the guns were dismantled and shipped elsewhere. In 1947 the State of New Jersey purchased Fort Mott as an historic site and opened the state park on June 24, 1951.

The Walks
Fort Mott features a walking tour through the 19th century defensive position that enables your dog to ramble through the gun batteries and ammunition magazines and to clamber on top of the massive protective parapet. This concrete wall was built of concrete poured 35 feet thick with an additional 60 feet of earth piled in front. Landscaping made the fort look like a big hill from the Delaware River. In additon to this unique dog walk there is a groomed trail that winds through twelve-foot high swamp grasses to Finn's Point National Cemetery, the final resting place for 2,436 Confederate soldiers who perished in a Civil War prisoner of war camp at Fort Delaware.

>   **Where The Paw Meets The Earth:** Grass and concrete and gravel
>   **Workout For Your Dog** - Easy moving around
>   **Swimming** - The beach at the Delaware River is a super place for dogs to swim
>   **Restrictions On Dogs** - None

Something Extra
Your dog has the chance to wander into gun parapets, bunkers, cells and other wondrous nooks and crannies.

Garret Mountain Reservation

Phone - (973) 881-4832
Website - http://www.passaiccountynj.org/ParksHistorical/Parks/garretmountainreservation.htm
Admission Fee - None
Directions - *West Paterson, Passaic County; from I-80 exit at Squirrelwood/West Paterson (Exit 56 westbound, Exit 56A east-bound) and continue through the traffic light and pass Berkeley College where the road becomes Rifle Camp Road. Make your first left onto Mountain Avenue and the park entrance on the right.*

The Park
The Lenni-Lenape Indians who once lived here used this mountain as a hunting grounds, chasing deer off the cliffs. Excitement on the mountain around the turn of the 20th century came in the form of an amusement park. In 1892 Catholina Lambert, one of the Silk Kings of Paterson - the Silk City - spent a half million dollars to build his Lambert Castle here from sandstone quarried on the mountain. Labor unrest led to financial difficulties for Lambert in 1914 and forced him to be mortgage his home. He died in 1923 at the age of 88 and several years later his son sold the castle to the City of Paterson for $125,000. Passaic County combined the Lambert estate with land purchased from the shuttered amusement park to create the 568-acre Garret Mountain Reservation.

The Walks
The main canine hiking at Garret Mountain is found along a yellow-blazed path that loops the park for about three miles. The highlight of this circuit are the unobstructed views to the east from the edge of the ridge 500 feet above sea level. Paterson spreads out directly below and the Manhattan skyline is clearly visible in the distance. The Verrazzano-Narrows Bridge can even be seen on a bright day. There are no severe climbs to reach these spectacular vistas that makes for an enjoyable walk for your dog. Many folks shun the bridles paths and foot trails and use the winding park roads to hike with their dogs in the jogging/bike lanes.

> **Where The Paw Meets The Earth:** Natural and asphalt paths
> **Workout For Your Dog** - Plenty of fun winding around the mountain
> **Swimming** - Barbour's Pond is available for a doggie dip
> **Restrictions On Dogs** - None

Something Extra
Lambert Castle was lovingly restored over five years and was rededicated 2000. It is open for tours at the base of Garret Mountain. On top of the mountain Lambert's 70-foot observation tower still stands but is closed to visitation. Still you can stop along the trail and enjoy the views here.

Gateway NRA-Sandy Hook Unit

Phone - (732) 872-5970
Website - http://www.nps.gov/gate/
Admission Fee - None
Directions - *Highlands, Monmouth County; north of town at the end of Route 36.*

The Park
Ships sailing into New York harbor have always needed to navigate around the shifting sands of Sandy Hook. The first lighthouse was built from lottery funds in 1764. The strategic peninsula has been fortified since the War of 1812 and the Hook was the site of the first United States Army Proving Ground. The last active military base, Fort Hancock, closed in 1974 but the United States Coast Guard still maintains an active presence at Sandy Hook.

The Walks
The best canine hiking in the 1,655-acre Sandy Hook Unit is on the seven miles of ocean beach. The open sands of North Beach curl around to reveal views of the Brooklyn skyline and the Verrazano Narrows Bridge, the longest suspension bridge in the world when it opened in 1964. Open all year to dogs are short nature trails through a 264-acre maritime forest that holds the greatest concentration of American Holly on the East Coast. When hiking around sand trails, steer your dog clear of low-lying prickly pear cacti that grow in abundance on the peninsula. In addition to the unspoiled natural areas at Sandy Hook, there are plenty of places to explore with your dog through historic Fort Hancock, much of which is used for educational purposes today. Interpretive trails describe missile testing sites, anti-aircraft defenses, and lead into overgrown gun batteries.

> **Where The Paw Meets The Earth:** Sand and concrete
> **Workout For Your Dog** - Miles and miles of flat canine hiking
> **Swimming** - As much Atlantic Ocean time as your dog wants
> **Restrictions On Dogs** - Dogs are not allowed in the recreation area from March 15 to Labor Day to protect nesting shorebirds, dogs are also not allowed on the *Old Dune Trail*

Something Extra
The Sandy Hook Lighthouse has been guiding ships through the sandy shoals for 240 years. You can walk your dog around the grassy base of the National Historic Landmark and well-behaved dogs can even sit in on the short video history of the illumination of New York harbor. While looking at the old brick sentinel, you can grasp the dynamics of land-building at Sandy Hook - when first built, the lighthouse was a mere 500 feet from shore and today is more than one and one-half miles from the northern end of the peninsula.

Great Falls of the Passaic River

Phone - None
Website - None
Admission Fee - None
Directions - *Paterson, Passaic County; From I-80 take Exit 57 B-A. Follow signs for "Downtown Paterson" and make the 1st left onto Cianci Street. Go one light to Market Street and turn left. Market Street ends at Spruce Street. Turn right onto Spruce Street. Go one block to McBride Avenue Extension and turn right. The Great Falls parking area is on the right.*

The Park

The thundering Great Falls roar over a 280-foot crest, plunging 77 feet with more water volume than any Eastern waterfall not named Niagara. Two hundred million years ago hot magma erupted from the earth and cooled to become the basaltic First Watchung Ridge, oblivious to erosion. The trapped Passaic River began poking around for a way around the ridge and finally found it here. Alexander Hamilton was the first to link the power of the Falls to industry after dining at its base during the Revolutionary War. His vision of a great industrial city here was not quite realized but over the years the water turned machines for textiles, steam locomotices, revolvers and other paterson industries.

The Walks

This is certainly not a vigorous hike, more of an interesting place to walk your dog. The Great Falls can be viewed from Overlook Park and Hamilton Park on either side of the river. You walk your dog across the chasm between the two parks on the eighth bridge built at the Falls.

>**Where The Paw Meets The Earth:** Macadam
>**Workout For Your Dog** - No
>**Swimming** - None
>**Restrictions On Dogs** - None

Something Extra

Sam Patch, known as The Yankee Leaper, was the first famous U.S. daredevil. He first gained recognition in September 1827 he jumped off the 70 foot Passaic Falls in New Jersey, pleasing a large crowd that had gathered.Patch continued his career jumping from bridges, factory walls, and ship's masts. He became the first of Niagara Fall's famous daredevils when he jumped from a 125-foot ladder rigged for a jump over the gorge below Goat Island opposite the Cave of the Winds. He perished in 1829 after he jumped into the 99-foot high Upper Falls in Rochester, New York. For whatever reason he did not enter feet first, broke both shoulders and drowned. His body was found frozen in the ice the next spring.

Hacklebarney State Park

Phone - (609) 861-2404
Website - http://www.state.nj.us/dep/parksandforests/parks/hackle.html
Admission Fee - None
Directions - *Chester, Morris County; from town follow Route 24/513 west for one mile to State Park Road for two miles. Turn right onto Hacklebarney Road and travel 1/2 mile. The entrance is on the left. From Pottersville, take Pottersville Road (partially paved) right of the Black River and turn left on Hacklebarney.*

The Park

In the 1800s settlers mined this area for veins of iron ore exposed by the retreating glaciers. It is believed by some that the colorful name for the park came from workmen in a mine who heckled a petulant foreman named Barney Tracey. "Heckle Barney eventually morphed into Hacklebarney. Others believe the name has Lenni-Lenape Indian origins based on the word for ground, "Haki." Park staff apparently buy into this theory since there is a *Haki Trail* and no Tracey Trail. Adolph E. Borie (who also has no trail) donated the first 32 acres of land in 1924 as a memorial to his mother and niece, a Titanic survivor. The Civilian Conservation Corps helped develop the park during the 1930s and today it consists of nearly 1000 acres of Black River glacial valley.

The Walks

There are some five miles of sporty canine hiking in Hacklebarney State Park to enjoy with your dog. Most of the park can be experienced on the red-blazed *Main Trail* that sweeps down the ravine to the Black River and comes back up the opposite side. The trail drops about 200 feet in elevation to the water and this is negotiated on wide, graded gravelly footpaths.Along the rollicking Black River the trail is narrow and rocky with a different angle of footfall on every step. Your dog can take a misstep here as easily as you can so take care.

> **Where The Paw Meets The Earth:** Dirt and gravel
> **Workout For Your Dog** - Hilly almost everywhere
> **Swimming** - The rushing Black River waters slow into pools a few times
> to provide a refreshing doggie dip
> **Restrictions On Dogs** - None

Something Extra

If you are looking for a place to picnic with your dog in New Jersey this is it! Picnic tables and benches have been spotted on spectacular locations throughout the park, perched on rocks atop racing river waters or tucked deep into secluded wooded grottoes. Some of these sites are quite a hike away from the parking lot so try and avoid cooler duty!

Hammonton Lake Natural Area

Phone - None
Website - None
Admission Fee - None
Directions - *Hammonton, Burlington County; at North Egg Habor Road and Park Avenue.*

The Park

During the War of 1812, William Coffin built a sawmill along what later became known as Hammonton Lake. Upon his death, his sons John Hammond Coffin and Edward Winslow Coffin inherited the factory and the settlement became known as "Hammondton." The lake is now the centerpiece of an attractive park.

The Walks

The Natural Area is a wooded area next to the park, a duck-billed peninsula surrounded by the lake on three sides. For canine hikers who want a taste of the Pinelands without the vast forests this is a pleasant option. An unclean Hammonton Lake has been closed to swimmers at times in recent years but that won't stop your dog from a refershing dip.

Where The Paw Meets The Earth: Soft sandy dirt

Workout For Your Dog - No

Swimming - Hammonton Lake is the main attraction here

Restrictions On Dogs - No dogs in the swimming area

Something Extra

Each spring a United States Triathlon-sanctioned event takes place around Hammonton Lake.

Hartshorne Woods Park

Phone - (732) 872-0336
Website - http://www.monmouthcountyparks.com/parks/harts-horne.asp
Admission Fee - None
Directions - *Middletown, Monmouth County; take the Garden State Parkway south to Exit 117. Bear left beyond the toll booths and continue on Route 36 for 11.5 miles. Turn right at the exit for Red Bank Scenic Road, then turn right at the stop sign onto Navesink Avenue. Continue for 0.3 mile to the Buttermilk Valley parking area on the left. To reach Rocky Point continue on Route 36 and turn right on Portland Avenue before crossing the Highlands-Sea Bright Bridge and follow to end.*

The Park

In 1677, Richard Hartshorne came to the Native Indians with crates of guns, beads and liquor and purchased 2,320 acres that included Sandy Hook on the Atlantic Ocean beach and the land where the park that today carries his name is today. During World War II, concrete batteries were built as part of the Atlantic Coast Defense System. The military abandoned the facility in the 1970s, and in 1973 Monmouth County purchased 736 acres of wilderness for use as an undeveloped open space.

The Walks

Hartshorne Woods is indeed undeveloped, save for its more than 15 miles of trails. The park is divided into three segments, each with a feature trail. From the Buttermilk Valley lot the main loop is the *Laurel Ridge Trail* in the Buttermilk Valley Section, a 2.5-mile romp through - surprise - thick stands of mountain laurel. The center of Hartshorne Woods is the Monmouth Hills Section, disected by the *Grand Tour Trail*. These moderate elevation changes are a welcome find for canine hikers at the shore. In the eastern part of the park the *Rocky Point Trail* swings through the remains of the old military installation. Short connectors link these main trails to expand your dog's time here.

> **Where The Paw Meets The Earth:** Dirt, crushed stone, paved roads
> **Workout For Your Dog** - Yes, plenty of hill hiking here
> **Swimming** - At Blackfish Cove Fishing Pier is a sandy beach with fantastic swimming in the Navesink River
> **Restrictions On Dogs** - None

Something Extra

The Atlantic Highlands, the highest point on the Atlantic Coast in the United States, were first spied by a European in 1524 when explorer Giovanni de Verrazano sailed by. In the Rocky Point section of the park, beyond Battery Lewis you can linger and enjoy the views from this highpoint over the ocean.

Hedden County Park

Phone - None
Website - http://www.morrisparks.net/parks/heddenmain.htm
Admission Fee - None
Directions - *Dover, Morris County; the park adjoins the town. From Route 10 take Dover-Chester Road north to a t-interesection. Make a left and a right on Concord Road and follow into the park or make a right on Reservoir Avenue and left on Hawthorne Street into the park.*

The Park
The local Hedden family of Dover donated the original 40 acres for this park in 1963. Over the years Morris County has increased the size of Hedden Park to 380 acres west of Dover. There are two distinct sections: the pond section with a fishing pier, boathouse and outdoor fireplace for ice skaters and the Concord Road section with an open playing field and a forested hiking area.

The Walks
This is an unexpected canine hiking paradise in a residential setting. From the Concord Road lot you can jump in the middle of the feature trail in the park, the white-blazed *Hedden Circular Trail*. From a rather benign beginning this surprisingly sporty two-mile loop gets interesting in a hurry as you and your dog work along the curves of a rocky hillside. The truly adventurous dog will want to cut the loop short and try the red-blazed *Mountain Trail* that it picks its way straight up the slope. The paths are studded with rocks but of the worn-down, smaller variety, not the monstrous boulders of some neighboring parks. For more relaxed canine hiking take your dog along the *Indian Falls Trail* and the *Jackson Brook Trail* that trace the lively stream through a shady glen. These two are both out-and-back affairs but well worth retracing your pawprints. Indian Falls is Hedden Park's best-known attraction.

> **Where The Paw Meets The Earth:** Rocky dirt trails
> **Workout For Your Dog** - Yes, especially if you churn up the *Mountain Trail*
> **Swimming** - Jackson Brook provides a refreshing respite and a small six-acre pond is at the end of the *Indian Falls Trail*
> **Restrictions On Dogs** - None

Something Extra
Even though you can just about toss a meatbone and hit a house, the park's pond is home to an active beaver colony. Look for the lodge near the boathouse; the best time to see the beavers is on a quiet evening.

Herrontown Woods

Phone - None
Website - http://www.princetontwp.org/herron.html
Admission Fee - None
Directions - *Princeton, Mercer County; take Route 27 (Nassau Street) from the center of town to Snowden Lane. Make a left and follow Snowden to the parking lot.*

The Park
Herrontown Woods was the former home of Oswald Veblen, an Iowan-born mathematician whose work in geometry at Princeton University was internationally acclaimed. Veblen spent many an hour in his private sanctuary and probably blazed some of the the park's trails. The top academic prize in geometry awarded each year is named for Oswald Veblen, who deeded this land to Mercer County in 1957. In the 1970s the county acquired additional property to bring the park to its current size of 142 acres.

The Walks
Your dog will be completely surrounded by the smells of easter de-ciduous forest in Herrontown Woods. Oak, gum, tulip and red maple are the dominant trees here. Start with a tour of the property on an outer ring that rises about 150 feet in elevation. The trails alternate between paw-friendly dirt (the soft paths can be muddy through wetland areas) and rockier ground. Watch for rooty spots. Once you have completed the outer loop you can continue your canine hike on the various inner trails. All told there are about three miles of woody paths here.

> **Where The Paw Meets The Earth:** Natural surface wooded footpaths
> **Workout For Your Dog** - Steady but not strenuous going
> **Swimming** - Seasonal streams offer up a splash or two at best
> **Restrictions On Dogs** - None

Something Extra
As you hike with your dog through Herrontown Woods keep a look out for quarry holes. The diabase, or traprock, formed when molten magma pushed its way through cracks in the surface. Among the many uses for the hard stone is roadbuilding.

Higbee Beach WMA

Phone - (609) 628-2103
Website - http://www.njfishandwildlife.com/ensp/higbee.htm
Admission Fee - None
Directions - *Cape May, Cape May County; from Route 9 south, turn onto Route 626. Cross the bridge and turn right onto New England Road (Route 641). The road deadends at Higbee Beach into a wildly rutted dirt parking lot.*

The Park
Higbee Beach, the last remaining dune forest along the Delaware Bay, was acquired by the State of New Jersey in 1978, thwarting plans to build a campground here. The Higbee Beach Wildlife Management Area today is jointly administered by the state and the U.S. Army Corps of Engineers. For years Higbee Beach was known as the area's "nude beach" but now your dog is the only visitor legally allowed to hit the beach without a swim suit.

The Walks
You can't beat the canine hiking at Higbee Beach for diversity. From the parking lot at land's end on the Cape May Peninsula you have your choice of open fields, woodlands or dune forest. Of course, your dog will want to sample all three. The sandhills are not covered with windswept grasses as is seen along most of the Jersey shore but with resilient red cedars and holly trees. There is about a mile of trails meandering through this dunesland. To stretch those leg muscles there are several miles of more trails behind the dunes in the woods and fields of the wildlife management area that reaches all the way to the Cape May Canal.

> **Where The Paw Meets The Earth:** Mostly sand with some dirt paths
> **Workout For Your Dog** - Plowing through the sandy dunes will qualify
> **Swimming** - The best in New Jersey on the Delaware Bay
> **Restrictions On Dogs** - None

Something Extra
The beach next door to Higbee is the similarly dog-friendly Sunset Beach, famous for its Cape May Diamonds. The "diamonds" are actually pieces of quartz crystals that have been eroded from the Upper Delaware River and been polished by a 200-mile journey of churning and jostling that can last a millennium or two. The stones, that can be cut and faceted to do a passable imitation of a diamond, are found in abundance here because the tidal flow bounces off a unique concrete ship that rests offshore. The Atlantus was built to transport soldiers during steel-short World War I. The reinforced-concrete ship worked but the recovery of post-war steel supplies made her obsolete and the Atlantus was being towed to Cape May to serve as a ferry slip when an accident dumped her on a sand bar where she remains today.

High Point State Park

Phone - (973) 875-4800
Website - http://www.state.nj.us/dep/parksandforests/parks/highpoint.html
Admission Fee - None
Directions - *Sussex, Sussex County; travel on Route 23 for seven miles north of town to the park entrance.*

The Park
Colonel Anthony Kuser, founding member of the New Jersey Audubon Society and director of more than 50 corporations, and his wife Susie Dryden, daughter of Senator John Fairfield Dryden, founder of the Prudential Life Insurance Company, made the largest land donation in the history of New Jersey when they deeded 11,000 acres for High Point State Park in 1923. The Kusers had purchased the High Point Inn in 1910 and transformed it into a transcendent wildlfe sanctuary. To help complete the transition from country estate to public park the Olmsted Brothers, sons of Central Park creator Fredeick Law Olmsted, were retained to landscape the mountaintop.

The Walks
The park maintains an 11-trail system around the 1,803-foot summit at the top of New Jersey. You can choose to hike with your dog on wide, manicured paths or take off on rock-strewn mountain trails. Leaving from the far end of the parking lot at the High Point Monument, the trail tops the ridge in light woods with abundant views east and west. The narrow path is rocky as it rolls along but completely manageable for any dog. Below the ridge you will find the 1,500-acre Dryden Kuser Natural Area, created in 1965 and site of some of the most pleasant canine hiking in the state. The Atlantic white cedars here are normally found only in the Pine Barrens of south Jersey. This cedar swamp is at the highest elevation of any of its kind in the world. The swamp trail is level and wide and shouldn't be missed by any dog who visits the roof of New Jersey. There is also extended canine hiking available on the *Appalachian Trail* that crosses through the park.

> **Where The Paw Meets The Earth:** Rocky dirt on slopes
> **Workout For Your Dog** - Only a very few small hills
> **Swimming** - Not the dominant feature of canine hiking here
> **Restrictions On Dogs** - None

Something Extra
In 1927 Kuser commissioned the construction of a 220-foot obelisk on the state's high point to honor all war veterans. A scramble up 291 steps leads to panoramic views of the Pocono, Catskill, and Kittatinny mountains. The monument, crafted of grey New Hampshire granite and local quartzite, was dedicated on June 21, 1930, just months before Colonel Kuser died.

Holmdel Park

Phone - (732) 946-9562
Website - http://www.monmouthcountyparks.com/parks/holmdel.asp
Admission Fee - None
Directions - *Holmdel, Monmouth County; take Garden State Parkway to Exit 114. Southbound, turn right onto Red Hill Rd; northbound, turn left onto Red Hill Rd. Follow Red Hill Rd. to Everett Rd., turn right (heading west). Follow Everett Rd. to Roberts Rd., turn left. Follow Roberts Rd. to Longstreet Rd., turn right to Park on left.*

The Park
The land here was first cleared for subsistence farming around the time of the American Revolution. In 1806 Hendrick Longstreet pieced together several small farms totalling 495 acres. While much of what was grown here was used on his farm, potatoes were a cash crop. The farm preserved today as a living history farm remained in family hands until Monmouth County bought it in 1962.

The Walks
Canine hikers visiting Holmdel Park will want to drive past Longstreet Farm and turn right to head up the hill to Parking Lot 3, which is at the center of the trail system. The trails are a series of loops, most around one mile, that you can use to build a canine hiking day. There are 8 miles of trails through beech, hickory, oak, tulip, spruce and pine trees. There is not much understory in this agriculture field-turned forest so you get a big feel to these dog walks. The most demanding canine hike in the park is the *Cross-Country Trail* that circles the property for 3.1 miles.

> **Where The Paw Meets The Earth:** Big dirt trails
> **Workout For Your Dog** - The terrain is hilly but the trails work around the slopes rather than pushing straight uphill
> **Swimming** - Small streams hydrate the ravines and glens and old farm ponds
> **Restrictions On Dogs** - No dogs in Longstreet Farm

Something Extra
Holmdel Park is an excellent place to study Dutch architecture from the earliest days of European settlement in central New Jersey. At Longstreet Farm is the oldest Dutch barn in Monmouth County. Dating to 1792, the barn is immediately recognized as Dutch by the high wagon doors placed in each end of the gables that slope near the ground. Surrounded by the park but not in it, the Holmes-Hendrickson House is snuggled in a grove of trees. The red frame house was built in 1754 by William Holmes, who ignored the fashionable trend of symmetrical Georgian house-building in favor of his traditional Durch design.

Huber Woods Park

Phone - (732) 872-2670
Website - http://www.monmouthcountyparks.com/parks/huber.asp
Admission Fee - None
Directions - *Locust, Monmouth County; the park is east of the Garden State Parkway. Take State Highway 35 to Navesink River Road. Travel east for 2.8 miles and turn left onto Brown's Dock Road (unimproved). The park entrance is on the right at the top of the hill.*

The Park

Joseph Maria Huber sailed for New York City from his native Bavaria in 1883 as a sales agent for his family's ink-pigment business. Once in America it didn't take him long to see opportunities for a hard-working ink supplier. Before the decade was out Huber was so successful that he bought out the American stake of the business from his German relatives—and launched J.M. Huber Corporation. Four generations later the multinational supplier of engineered materials is one of the largest family-owned companies in the United States. Huber Woods Park is the result of a 118-acre gift of land from the Huber family in 1974. Ongoing acquisition in the same spirit of land preservation has doubled the size of the present-day park.

The Walks

It is hard to imagine a more pleasant place to hike with your dog in New Jersey than at Huber Woods. The six-mile trail system offers any length of outing from a half-hour to a half-day. You can stay completely within an airy, mixed hardwood forest or cross Brown's Dock Road to include open fields on the *Meadow Ramble Trail*. In spring on the short *Nature Loop*, azaelas and later mountain laurel bursts into bloom. The trails roll up and down hills but never in a way that will leave your dog panting. Once you have explored the hollows and valleys of the woodlands cross to the other side of the parking lot and try the *Farm Path*, an equestrian trail that passes through fields managed to maintain the pastoral feel of the Huber farm.

> **Where The Paw Meets The Earth:** Paw-friendly dirt
> **Workout For Your Dog** - Just hilly enough to keep your dog's interest
> **Swimming** - None
> **Restrictions On Dogs** - None

Something Extra

The Environmental Center in the park is the former manor house of Hans Huber, son of the company founder. Its distinctive appearance is German-Swiss in inspiration with a central block of brick with half-timbering. Additional wings are covered in stucco.Three massive chimneys sprout from a red tile roof dominated by a plump turret.

Hunterdon County Arboretum

Phone - (973) 875-4800
Website - http://www.co.hunterdon.nj.us/depts/parks/guides/Arbortum.htm
Admission Fee - None
Directions - *Flemington, Hunterdon County; 5 miles north of town on the east side of Route 31.*

The Park

George Bloomer opened a commercial nursery on this location in 1953. The core of his business were the spruces and hardwoods commonly known to backyards throughout New Jersey but he also grew exotic trees like Amur cork trees from Manchuria and dawn redwoods, an ancient tree known only through fossils until 1941 when a botany student tracked down living specimens in rural China. Bloomer's wife Esther founded the Hunderdon County SPCA in 1965. He sold his 73-acre site to the county in 1974 to be used for public education. Across the road behind the Arboretum are 32 additional acres that were once the property of J.C. Furnas, writer, historian and biographer. His most famous work was a case for safe driving, published in Reader's Digest in August 1935. It became perhaps the most widely circulated article ever written with eight million reprint copies distributed. Furnas left the land to the county after his death in 2001 at the age of 95. It is currently undeveloped.

The Walks

Dogs are often banned from arboretums so it is a treat to be able to enjoy this living tree museum with your dog. There are two miles of easy canine hiking on wide and flat dirt trails that are broken into small segments. In addition to the wide variety of trees and shrubs there are display gardens of native and non-native flowers. A good way to approach the Arboretum is to take your dog on a circuit of the 1.1-mile *Outer Loop Trail* that visits tree plantations and wetlands. With this overview you can then re-visit some of the short connecting trails.

> **Where The Paw Meets The Earth:** Paw-friendly dirt and grass trails
> **Workout For Your Dog** - Level, easy canine hiking
> **Swimming** - The pond and stream across the property are not for dogs
> **Restrictions On Dogs** - None

Something Extra

Dominating the display garden - and your first impression - upon entering the trail system is a rare two-story gazebo. Constructed of red cedar in 1892 it is considered the oldest such structure in New Jersey. The gazebo was moved from a Raritan Township farm in 1979 and renovated in 1997.

Island Beach State Park

Phone - (732) 793-0506
Website - http://www.state.nj.us/dep/parksandforests/parks/island.html
Admission Fee - Yes, higher in summer
Directions - *Seaside Park, Ocean County; from the Garden State Parkway use Exit 82 - Route 37 East/Seaside Heights. Once on the island make a right onto Route 35 South to the park entrance.*

The Park
Henry Phipps, compatriot with Andrew Carnegie in U.S. Steel, purchased the island in 1926 with visions of a grand shore resort but the stock market crash halted his assault after erecting a handful of rambling houses. The Phipps estate sold the property to New Jersey in 1953 and the park opened to the public in 1959. Island Beach State Park protects 10 miles of dunesland that have survived virtually untouched as they have always been.

The Walks
There are a series of short nature trails (less than one mile) as you drive down the main park road to its end at Barnegat Inlet but once your dog gets that whiff of salt air in her nose, she may not be in any mood to tarry. Get to the beach! This is one of the few places in New Jersey you can enjoy the Atlantic Ocean with your dog in the summer. Parking is limited, however, and if you don't arrive early enough you will be shut out. In the off-season this is not a problem so don't confine your visits to the novelty of summer at the beach with your dog. There is some shade for your dog in the dunes and the thickets behind the dunes when it is hot but make sure you bring plenty of fresh water. From the last parking lot to the southern tip of the island is a hike of over one mile on the piles of white sand.

> **Where The Paw Meets The Earth:** Sand everywhere
> **Workout For Your Dog** - Long hikes on soft sand are tough
> **Swimming** - Ocean swims are why you come
> **Restrictions On Dogs** - No dogs in the swimming areas or near shorebird nesting areas

Something Extra
Henry David Thoreau wrote about beach heather after visiting Cape Cod in 1849, describing how local residents called the low-growing mossy plants "poverty grass" because it grew where nothing else did. Island Beach State Park is home to the greatest expanse of beach heather in New Jersey. In late May the heather balds, as patches of the plant are called, explode in a carpet of yellow in the secondary dunes.

Jenny Jump State Forest

Phone - (908) 459-4366
Website - http://www.state.nj.us/dep/parksandforests/parks/
jennyjump.html
Admission Fee - None
Directions - *Hope, Warren County; take I-80 to Exit 12
to Hope. Turn onto Route 519 north at blinking light. At the third
right, turn onto Shiloh Road. After aproximately one mile turn right
onto State Park Road.*

The Park

Mile-thick glaciers did the carving of ridges and valleys in this forest
and littered giant boulders about for decoration. There are several
legends surrounding the name "Jenny Jump." The most dramatic has
little Jenny out picking berries with her father when they were surprised by hostile Indians. Preferring the fate of a leap off an exposed
cliff to capture by Indians for his daughter, the father yelled for Jenny
to jump. And so she did, to her death.Kinder, gentler versions have
Jenny and her father transporting a wagon of homemade beer and
Jenny jumping off the kegs and fleeing to safety or Jenny leaping
from a precipice to avoid an unwanted suitor and being rescued at
the base of the cliff by her true love.

The Walks

The main canine hiking in Jenny Jump State Forest is along the *Summit Trail* that rambles up and down along a 1,090-foot high ridge.
The trailhead is almost at that elevation so the climb will scarcely get
your dog panting. Several trails intersect the ridge with its views to
the west and many dog walkers will want to use the *Orchard Trail* to
complete a loop hike through a picnic area built by Civilian Conservation Corps workers in the 1930s. Adventurous canine hikers can
drop off the ridge on the *Ghost Lake Trail* that leads to a man-made
lake fed by an artesian well. This lake is only about ten feet deep and
becomes choked with vegetation, including yellow-blooming water
lilies in the summer. This trail doesn't loop so you will have to climb
about 400 feet back up the mountain unless you have employed a
car shuttle linked to the Ghost Lake parking lot.

> **Where The Paw Meets The Earth:** Paw-friendly dirt
> **Workout For Your Dog** - It can be if you leave the ridge
> **Swimming** - Ghost Lake provides a venue for canine
> aquatics
> **Restrictions On Dogs** - No dogs in the campground

Something Extra

At the Ghost Lake parking lot on Shades of Death Road you can take
your dog along a short, rocky trail along the lakeshore to a steep
rocky slope.Here you will find a cave known as Faery Hole. The cave
room has a flat floor and enough headroom for a Great Dane to stand
on two legs.

John A. Roebling Park

Phone - None
Website - http://www.mercercounty.org/parks/parks.htm
Admission Fee - None
Directions - *Trenton, Mercer County; from Route 206 (South Broad Street), turn onto West Park Avenue. Make a left turn onto Wescott Avenue. After passing under high tension wires, make an immediate right turn onto the lane that leads to the park.*

The Park
John Augustus Roebling was born in Prussia in 1806 and came to Pittsburgh at the age of 25. Although a trained engineer, he and his brother came to America to farm. His agrarian pursuits were none too successful and he began doing engineering work for the state of Pennsylvania when he hit upon the idea of twisted metal wire to suspend long bridge spans. Roebling completed his first suspension bridge in 1845 and became succesful enough to expand his business. He purchased 25 acres in Trenton for his wire factory in 1850. After winning the contract to build the Brooklyn Bridge, Roebling never recovered from an injury suffered early in the construction and died in 1869. His son Washington completed the masterwork and the family business continued to expand. The land for the John A. Roebling Park was donated by the family in the 1950s.

The Walks
There are two disparite trail systems in the park. The *Watson Woods Trail* and the *Abbott Brook Trail* move through some scruffy, wooded wetlands. Your dog may have to pick his way through some blowdowns and overgrown vines on these barely maintained paths. A dirt road can be used for elbow room and to complete a canine loop hike. In the opposite direction is open walking into the marshes on the *Spring Lake Trail*. Don't be put off by the trash, old tires and power lines as you hike past Rowan Lake. Things improve as you shortly reach Spring Lake and get better still as you circle the lake and cross into the North Marsh.

> **Where The Paw Meets The Earth:** Natural surface and macadam
> **Workout For Your Dog** - Level, easy canine hiking
> **Swimming** - There is open water but not that attractive
> **Restrictions On Dogs** - None

Something Extra
In 2008 the stone house on a bluff looking over Roebling Park will have been standing for 300 years. Trenton wasn't even called Trenton yet when it was built in 1708. The inside has been altered but if Isaac Watson showed up today he would still recognize his house. The Watson House, open for tours, is the oldest house in Mercer County.

Ken Lockwood Gorge WMA

Phone - None
Website - None
Admission Fee - None
Directions - *High Bridge, Hunterdon County; from Route 513, take Hoffmans Crossing (about 1.5 miles north of Voorhees State Park) across an iron bridge - easily spotted from the main road - and make an immediate right on River Road. Continue past several houses to a small parking area at the end of the pavement.*

The Park
This 2 1/2-mile section of the South Branch of the Raritan River was purchased by the state in 1948 through what monies raised from the sale of hunting and fishing licenses. It was named for the long-time outdoors columnist for the *Newark Evening News*. Considered one of the prettiest spots in New Jersey, the gorge is an apt memorial to one of the earliest advocates of preserving vanishing wild spaces for the benefit of the public.

The Walks
This canine hike covers about two miles along the banks of the South Branch, that gets extremely frisky in the gorge. The entire route is on a deeply rutted dirt road that is occasionally braved by a car and also used by cyclists and off-road vehicles. The gorge is not completely straight but twists a bit so you will need to keep a close eye on your dog around bends in the road - admittedly a tough task to take your gaze off the mesmerizing clearn brown-green waters of the river and the hemlock-studded gorge. Chances are you won't hear approaching vehicles either as you will be listening to the roaring waters.

> **Where The Paw Meets The Earth:** Hard dirt road
> **Workout For Your Dog** - Fairly easy trotting through the gorge
> **Swimming** - If there isn't a fly fisherman working a deep pool in the river your dog can test the swift-flowing South Branch
> **Restrictions On Dogs** - None

Something Extra
You will encounter an impressive tri-trestle bridge over the river but it is not the structure for which the town is named. THE high bridge a 1,300-foot long, 112-foot high span across the South Branch was built by the Central Railroad Company. It was, unfortunately, not safe enough for heavy locomotives and in 1859 it was decided to support it with an dirt embankment.The project took five years to complete and left a double-arch culvert. You can take your dog to visit the original bridge in the Arches section of the South Branch Reservation at Arch Street in High Bridge.

Kittatinny Valley State Park

Phone - (973) 786-6445
Website - http://www.state.nj.us/dep/parksandforests/parks/kit-tval.html
Admission Fee - Yes, during summer
Directions - *Andover, Sussex County; from I-80, take Route 206 nrth for 8 miles through Andover Borough. Turn right onto Goodale Road and follow it to the park entrance on the right.*

The Park
Fred Hussey's family made their money in whaling in early America. In the mid 1900s Hussey owned a company called Aeroflex that developed an ingenious rubber camera mount that was the first way to take steady photograhs from the air. The company started in producing aerial maps but the camera mount was invaluable to the military in identifying targets for bombing raids. In the late 1950s Hussey built an airport here to maintain his private collection of WWI aircraft, antique cars, and military surplus cars. For its time, the facility was state-of-the-art; almost everything was custom-built. After his death in the mid-1970s, the LoRae family acquired the land at auction and converted several buildings into stables to house their beloved Arabian horses. The State of New Jersey acquired the property in 1994 and created Kittatinny Valley State Park. The airport still operates today under the New Jersey Forest Fire Service. It is the only state-owned and operated airport in New Jersey. The former Hussey home on Lake Aeroflex has been converted into the new park visitor center.

The Walks
Just about any type of canine hike your dog is after can be crafted in Kittatinny Valley State Park. The *Sussex Branch Trail*, the remnants of the Sussex Branch Line of the Erie-Lackawanna Railroad, runs down the spine of the park providing relaxed, peaceful trotting on cinder based paths moving on mild grades. It can be used to create hiking loops of varying lengths.For a more energetic pace there are miles of are miles of short, interlaced tails that roll on small hills through woods and around rock outcroppings. Four lakes are a prominent feature of Kittatinny Valley State Park but the trails just skirt the water occasionally.
> **Where The Paw Meets The Earth:** Natural and cinder surfaces
> **Workout For Your Dog** - Long, flat trails with gentle hills
> **Swimming** - You can seek out a canine swimming pool here
> **Restrictions On Dogs** - None

Something Extra
The long, gentle grades of the Sussex Branch Trail and the Paulinskill Valley Trail are ideal for dog sledding in the winter. Check with the park for any scheduled events or bring your own team.

Lewis Morris County Park

Phone - (973) 829-8257
Website - http://www.state.nj.us/dep/parksandforests/parks/belle.html
Admission Fee - None
Directions - *Morristown, Morris County; take I-287 into Morristown. From Morristown Green turn right onto Washington Street. Go 3.5 miles west towards Mendham and Chester on Route 510 West/Route 24. The park entrance is on the left.*

The Park
When it opened in 1958 this was the first park to be created by Morris County in a public park system that now features over 17,000 acres - New Jersey's largest. The original park was 350 acres but has tripled in size over the past half-century. The park, as is the county, was named in honor of Lewis Morris, a wealthy landowner born near the present-day Bronx in 1671. Morris became a Colonial official and was instrumental in achieving the separation of New Jersey from New York in 1638. Morris was named the first governor of the State of New Jersey and served until his death in 1646. His family lost all their land and great wealth in New York City during the American Revolution.

The Walks
With six picnic areas, a recreational lake, a group camping area and several ballfields most people don't think "hiking" when they think about Lewis Morris County Park. But there are many miles of woodsy trails that leave all the recreational amenities behind. The terrain is hilly but never taxing - many of the trails slide around the hills rather than charge right up them. There is little understory and the airy woods give this canine hike a big feel. Parking in the Mendham Overlook Area provides central access to the trail system. The *Green Trail* and *Red Trail* are connected loops that are more or less surrounded by the Yellow Trail. They all explore the same ridges and valley so it is no problem to bounce back and forth. If your dog is having too good a time to return to the car there are connectors to the *Grand Loop* and hours more walking in Morristown National Historical Park.

> **Where The Paw Meets The Earth:** Dirt
> **Workout For Your Dog** - Big, easy hills
> **Swimming** - In the off-season when no one is around Sunrise Lake can make a fine canine pool but there is no swimming along the trails
> **Restrictions On Dogs** - None

Something Extra
Lewis Morris County Park does have a dog park. The surface is blacktop, however, so it is not a prime choice on a hot day.

Lincoln Park

Phone - None
Website - http://www.njcu.edu/programs/jchistory/Pages/L_Pages/Lincoln_Park.htm
Admission Fee - None
Directions - *Jersey City, Hudson County; Lincoln Park is divided into Lincoln Park East and Lincoln Park West; the East Park entrance is at Kennedy Boulevard and Belmont Avenue.*

The Park
Hudson County has seven parks and Lincoln Park, in Jersey City, is the largest. The park grounds were laid out by landscape architects Daniel W. Langton and Charles N. Lowrie in 1907.

The Walks
Lincoln Park is a good choice to show your dog a classic urban park with promenades and gazebos and large grassy spaces suitable for a game of fetch. Walking paths set you off on a canine hike around the perimeter of the 273-acre city park.

> **Where The Paw Meets The Earth:** Paved surfaces
> **Workout For Your Dog** - No
> **Swimming** - No
> **Restrictions On Dogs** - None

Something Extra
Lincoln Park is notable for a restored 53-foot fountain decorated with spouting frogs and allegorical figures, designed by Pierre J. Cheron in 1911, and a 20-foot statue of a seated, Abraham Lincoln, designed by James Earle Fraser, best remembered for his design of the buffalo nickel.

Loantaka Brook Reservation

Phone - (732) 542-1642
Website - http://www.morrisparks.net/parks/loantakamain.htm
Admission Fee - None
Directions - *Morristown, Morris County; from I-287 take Exit 35 onto Madison Avenue and head east. Turn left on South Street to park on left.*

The Park
The genesis of the park is from the Seaton Hackney Farm and the stables are a dominant feature of today's activities. Seaton Hackney Farm, a focal point of the "horsey set" during the 1900's, was donated by Mr. and Mrs. Paul Moore of Convent Station. With the addition of Helen Hartley Jenkins Wood, a gift of Mr. and Mrs. M. Hartley Dodge, the park evolved into four distinct areas along the Loantaka Brook. The Reservation includes Seaton Hackney Stables, South Street Recreation Area, Loantaka Brook Park at Kitchell Road and the Loantaka Way trail access area. It encompasses more than 570 acres.

The Walks
There are nearly five miles of trails in this narrow neck of a park but this is not the place to come to lose yourself in nature with your dog. The canine hiking is easy and you have your choice of curvy, paved paths or bridle paths winding through light forest and wetlands. The flat terrain brings out the inline skaters and strollers to roll alongside the horses.

> **Where The Paw Meets The Earth:** Asphalt
> **Workout For Your Dog** - Great leg-stretchers but not anything difficult
> **Swimming** - If no one is using the duck pond there is the chance to slip in for a swim; the Loantaka Brook is deep enough only for splashing
> **Restrictions On Dogs** - None

Something Extra
If you are looking for a place to hike with yor dog and push a baby stroller, this is the place.

Mahlon Dickerson Reservation

Phone - (973) 326-7631
Website - http://www.morrisparks.net/parks/directions/mahlon-dir.htm
Admission Fee - None
Directions - *Milton, Morris County; from I-80 exit onto Route 15 North. Proceed for 5 miles to the Weldon Road Exit and travel approximately 4 miles east. Signed parking lots can be found on both sides of the road.*

The Park

This park is the largest facility in the Morris County Park System, and with more than 3,000 acres can easily be mistaken for a rustic state park. It is named for one of the Garden State's most accomplished citizens, Mahlon Dickerson, born in Hanover Township in 1770. Dickerson graduated from Princeton in 1793, having mastered several foreign languages and was soon admitted to the New Jersey Bar. He owned and operated iron mines and was widely known for his work in botany. Dickerson was appointed to the New Jersey Supreme Court in 1813 and before his political career was over he had served as governor and United States Senator.

The Walks

This is a canine hiker's trail system. Your dog can stretch his legs on the wide old logging roads that make up most of the 20 miles of trails. Save for Headley Overlook (beware of false overlooks if you approach from the south!) and its east-facing views there are no great destinations at Mahlon Dickerson, just miles of rambling under a solid canopy of mixed forest. On the way you'll pass through interesting rock formations, dank hemlock groves and thick stands of laurel. Although the average elevation in the park is over 1,200 feet the ups and downs are never grueling. The high point tops out at 1,388 feet along the *Pine Swamp Trail* but there are no views here. Several stream crossings add flavor to your dog's expedition in Mahlon Dickerson. If you start your explorations at Saffin Pond she will have an ideal pool to cool off in after the hike.

> **Where The Paw Meets The Earth:** Natural surface and old woods roads
> **Workout For Your Dog** - Yes, a good walk
> **Swimming** - Saffin Pond is centralized and convenient for a doggie dip but out on the trails there is only splashing in streams
> **Restrictions On Dogs** - None

Something Extra

A large slice of trail at Mahlon Dickerson runs on the old Ogden Mine Railroad right of way. The only remaining structure of the railroad is a stone arch bridge on Sparta Mountain Road at the northern edge of the park.

Manasquan Reservoir

Phone - (732) 919-0096
Website - http://www.monmouthcountyparks.com/parks/
manasquan_park.asp
Admission Fee - None
Directions - *Howell, Monmouth County; from Exit 195 take Exit 28 onto Route 9, heading north. Make a right onto Georgia Tavern Road and another right on Windeler Road to the Visitor Center.*

The Park
Manasquan Reservoir was completed in the late 1980s, the realization of a water supply plan to provide up to 30 million gallons of fresh water a day. Water is actually pumped through a five-foot diameter pipe for over five miles from the Manasquan River and stored in the 4-billion gallon capacity reservoir. In 1990 Monmouth county entered into a 99-year agreement to manage recreation activities around the reservoir. Most of those activities center around the 770 acres of water that dominate the 1,200-acre property.

The Walks
In a state of few natural lakes, this is one of the longest walks you can take with your dog around water in new Jersey. The canine hiking here is performed mostly on a crushed gray gravel multi-use path that circumnavigates the reservoir for five miles. Of course, once you sign on for this journey you are in for all five miles. If you do want to just walk out and turn around, concentrate your explorations to the southwestern section of the trail. There are three access points to the perimeter trail, all in this area. There is a good deal of diversity despite the confined spaces of the trail. You will take your dog through wetlands and grassy plains and airy woodlands. Of course you will get your share of long views across open water. The terrain is mostly level throughout to promote a pleasant pace.

> **Where The Paw Meets The Earth:** Crushed stone
> **Workout For Your Dog** - Circling the reservoir would qualify as a good workout
> **Swimming** - Most of the time you are traveling above the water line
> **Restrictions On Dogs** - None

Something Extra
More than 200 species of birds have found their way to this relatively new body of water, including bald eagles. Manasquan Reservoir is the best site to view bald eagles in Monmouth County. Bald eagles mate for life and a nesting pair has taken residence in the western area of the park. During the early summer, baby eagles can be seen near the nest practicing their flying and hunting abilities as they mimic their parents.

Manumuskin River Preserve

Phone - None
Website - http://www.co.cumberland.nj.us/tourism/manu-muskin/
Admission Fee - None
Directions - *Bricksboro, Cumberland County; take Route 55 to Exit 21 onto Schooner Landing Road. Turn left at the stop sign. Follow the road to the gate at the end; the preserve is on the right.*

The Park
Europeans settled along the 12-mile long Manumuskin River in 1720; remains of chimneys and foundations can be seen along the river trail. The river corridor has remained nearly undisturbed under a rich forest canopy producing superb water quality for nine miles from its headwaters in Atlantic County until it encounters tides from the Delaware Bay. The preserve started in 1983 with a donation of 6.65 acres - a couple of big backyards. Today it covers more than 3,500 acres, the largest Nature Conservancy in New Jersey. Dogs are typically not permitted on conservancy lands but they can hike on the bridle trails here.

The Walks
Dogs are typically not permitted on conservancy lands but they can hike on the bridle trails here.

> **Where The Paw Meets The Earth:** Sandy dirt roads
> **Workout For Your Dog** - Very easy canine hiking
> **Swimming** - Make your way to the Maurice River for canine fun
> **Restrictions On Dogs** - Only on horseback riding trails

Something Extra
The pure water supports a host of threatened New Jersey species, most notably a population of sensitive joint vetch. This member of the bean family is found nowhere else in the state and the stand here is the largest and healthiest in the world.

Mercer County Park

Phone - (609) 726-1191
Website - http://www.mercercounty.org/parks/parks.htm
Admission Fee - None
Directions - *Edinburg, Mercer County; from Route 206 (South Broad Street), turn onto West Park Avenue. Make a left turn onto Wescott Avenue. After passing under high tension wires, make an immediate right turn onto the lane that leads to the park.*

The Park
This is the flagship of the Mercer County park system with about 2,500 acres. Just about any recreation idea you can come up will be satisfied here: a dozen ballfields, top-notch tennis courts, miles of bike paths and, out on Lake Mercer, world class sculling.

The Walks
Most of the hikable trails at Mercer County Park are south of the lake. The main paved trail that hugs the shoreline on a peninsula to the left of the marina is one choice for canine hikers. Another is the mountain bike trail system that runs for miles through the wooded areas around the lake. There are some ups and downs but apparently not enough to make this a biking hotbed so you may be able to find some relaxing canine hiking here. North of the lake, across the power line, is dominated by the *Blue Trail*. The trail system is not as elaborate on the north side and once you sign on to the *Blue Trail* you will have to take it the whole way. Perhaps the best route for canine hikers in Mercer County Park is one of your own design. There are plenty of islands of green space that alternate with stands of trees and you can take your dog on your own adventure.

> **Where The Paw Meets The Earth:** Natural surface and asphalt
> **Workout For Your Dog** - Easily rolling terrain
> **Swimming** - There are plenty of places for a doggie swim in Mercer Lake
> **Restrictions On Dogs** - No dogs in the recreational areas

Something Extra
The Mercer County Bark Park is a prominent feature of the park, not shuffled off to some forgotten corner. There are fenced-in runs for large and small dogs. There is no shade for the dog players on a hot day on top of the hillside, however.

Merrill Creek Reservoir

Phone - (908) 454-1213
Website - http://www.merrillcreek.com/
Admission Fee - None
Directions - *Washington, Warren County; Route 57 to Mountain Road to Richline Road to Merrill Creek Road.*

The Park
Since it opened in 1989 Merrill Creek Reservoir has become a popular destination for wildlife enthusiasts. The resevoir was built to store water for release into the Delaware River during periods of low flow. When the river is high, water flows back to the reservoir through a 3.5-mile pipe.

The Walks
An exceptionally attractive trail system runs through a plump peninsula on the eastern side of the lake. There is open space aplenty and airy woodlands, including a pine plantation. The black-marked *Perimeter Trail* sweeps around the water for 5.5 miles, mostly on old farm roads. If you are the type who likes to let your dog off the leash when no one is around, Merrill Creek Reservoir is not the place for you. A sign warns that anyone seen with a dog off the leash will be escorted off the property and forever banned.

> **Where The Paw Meets The Earth:** Paw-friendly dirt with a rocky patch here and there
> **Workout For Your Dog** - Yes, for the entire trip around the water
> **Swimming** - No dogs allowed in the water
> **Restrictions On Dogs** - Still no dogs in the water

Something Extra
Bald eagles often use Merril Reservoir as a pit stop on their travels around the East Coat. In 1998 one pair decided to make the body of water their home and have been nesting on the shore ever since.

Mills Reservation

Phone - None
Website - None
Admission Fee - None
Directions - *Montclair, Essex County; take Exit 151 off the Garden State Parkway onto Watchung Avenue and head west. Continue to end at Upper Mountain Avenue and turn right. Turn left in 1.7 miles at Normal Avenue to entrance on the left. Parking is also available on Edgecliff Road for a handful of cars.*

The Park
A gift of 119 acres from the Davella Mills Foundation in 1954 got the ball rolling for this greenspace in heavily suburbanized Cedar Grove-Montclair. The original donation stipulated the hillsides be kept in a natural state and the only development - no buildings at all - at Mills Reservation are three miles of curving paths designed by the Olmsted family. Their minimally intrusive design was the last of many projects the historic landscape archtitecture firm did for Essex County.

The Walks
If you are seeking a communal canine hike, Mills Reservation is your place to come in New Jersey. The parking lots fill early and having a dog in tow almost seems a requirement to use the trails. Although you are squeezed into housing developments on every side these wooded trails do manage to radiate an air of the great outdoors. Most folks are trekking on wide crushed gravel paths that roll easily around the hills but narrow ribbons of dirt can provide some relief. There are no navigation aids and most likely you will bang into a residential street at a park boundary at some point. Keep at the trails, however, until you reach a flat rock outcrop at Quarry Point with its views of migratory birds and eastern New Jersey.

> **Where The Paw Meets The Earth:** Mostly crushed gravel and dirt paths
> **Workout For Your Dog** - Easy going on the park's hills
> **Swimming** - None
> **Restrictions On Dogs** - None

Something Extra
Although the park is undeveloped there is one building on the property. Off the main trail, near the Edgecliff side of the park, there is the skeleton of a tipi. It is about as unexpected a discovery as you will find along a trail in New Jersey.

Monmouth Battlefield State Park

Phone - (732) 462-9616
Website - http://www.state.nj.us/dep/parksandforests/parks/monbat.html
Admission Fee - None
Directions - *Manalapan, Monmouth County; from I-95, from the Garden State Parkway, take Exit 123 to Route 9 South for 15 miles to business Route 33 West. Park is located 1.5 miles on the right.*

The Park
The American Army came of age in 1778 in the Battle of Monmouth, forcing the British from the field in a brilliant counterattack led by George Washington. The General had planned a support role for himself, hoping to deliver a final, fatal blow to the British Army but when he started for the battle he instead discovered 5,000 of his best troops in a confused retreat. A stunned Washington immediately took personal command from Charles Lee, the general he had entrusted the attack to, and stopped the retreat. Eagerly his troops, hardened from their experience at Valley Forge, rallied to rout the British in record June heat. It was the last major battle of the Revolution in the north and Washington's finest hour in the field.

The Walks
Trails, unadorned with historical markers, traverse the scene of some of the most desperate fighting. Most of the canine hiking in the historical park is across open fields with plenty of soft grass for your dog's travels.

> **Where The Paw Meets The Earth:** Grass and sandy dirt roads
> **Workout For Your Dog** - Easy rolling terrain
> **Swimming** - None
> **Restrictions On Dogs** - None

Something Extra
The Battle of Monmouth Reenactment is an annual event at the park. Walk your dog through camp and pass pacing sentries, see enlisted men clean their weapons or idle away their time gambling, and watch the women of the army cook, mend, and wash. You may encounter a drum major drilling his musicians or the court martial of a rebel. At the parade ground, watch soldiers drill or artillerists fire their cannon.

Morristown National Historic Park

Phone - (973) 543-4030
Website - http://www.nps.gov/morr/
Admission Fee - Yes
Directions - *Morristown, Morris County; the park is located along I-287. Traveling south on I-287, use Exit 36; traveling north on 287, exit at 36A. Look for the signs for Jockey Hollow.*

The Park
Morristown, a village of 250, was a center of iron supply for the American Revolution and even though it lay only 30 miles west of the main British force in New York it was protected by a series of parallel mountain ranges. It was the twin luxuries of a defensible position and close proximity to the enemy that twice brought General George Washington to camp his main army here, first in 1777 and again in 1779-1780. The park was created in 1933 as America's first national historic park.

The Walks
Canine hiking at Morristown National Historic Park is found at the Jockey Hollow Encampment Area. When here, nothing could have prepared the Continental Army for the worst winter of the 18th century. Twenty-eight blizzards pounded the slopes and whipped through the wooden huts that were cut from 600 acres of hardwood forests here. The forest has grown back and is open and airy with long views through the trees from the trail. Four main trails circle the Jockey Hollow Encampment. The 6.5-mile *Grand Loop Trail*, blazed in white, circles the park but doesn't visit any historical attractions without a detour. It is also the only trail that cannot be accessed from the centrally located Trail Center. The *Aqueduct Loop Trail* and the stacked loop *Primrose Brook Trail* are two of the prettiest rambles in the park as they trace some of the many gurgling streams that once served the Colonial Army. The long-distance *Patriot's Path* traces its lineage back to 1966 and links Jockey Hollow to the New Jersey Encampment Area and neighboring parks and contributes mightily to the total of 27 well-groomed miles of Morristown trails.

> **Where The Paw Meets The Earth:** Natural dirt trails
> **Workout For Your Dog** - Long, rolling canine hikes possible
> **Swimming** - A few streams do not a canine swimming mecca make
> **Restrictions On Dogs** - None

Something Extra
The trails lead directly into reconstructed Revolutionary-era huts that you can explore with your dog.

Mount Hope Historical Park

Phone - None
Website - http://www.morrisparks.org/parks/mhmain.htm
Admission Fee - None
Directions - *Dover, Morris County; from I-80 take Exit 35B and turn right onto Mt. Hope Avenue. Turn onto Richard Mine Road to Teabo Road and park.*

The Park
The first iron ore was pulled from the ground in this area almost 300 years ago. There were three plump veins or ore, known as the Brennan, Mount Pleasant, and Richard veins. John Jacob Fresch, a Swiss immigrant, built the Mount Hope Furnace in 1772 and the forge was kept busy during the Revolutionary War producing shot, shells and cannon for the Continental Army. The park is on the site of three of the most productive mines in the state. The furnace fired for the last time in 1825 but high grade magnetite iron ore was mined here from the early 1800s to 1978.

The Walks
From an unpromising start up a rock road and under utility wires this turns into a fine ramble through the remnants of some of the score of 18th century iron mines that once operated in Mount Hope. Working on a wide, somewhat rocky trail you will twist past old building foundations and yawning open pits that nature is rapidly taking back from almost three centuries of mining activity. There are several trails through the airy woods but you will want to use the Red Trail first. After a short tail this walking path takes in most of the mining relics at Mount Hope as it moves down a hillside in a counterclockwise loop for 1.5-miles. This trail is joined by another moderate-length loop, the *Orange Trail*, that will expand your dog's time at Mount Hope to over an hour. The *Blue Trail*, short but steep, goes to the Old Teabo mine and the *White Trail*, another quick one, goes to the Brennan mine. All told there are about four miles of quiet trails through this once-bustling series of hills.

> **Where The Paw Meets The Earth:** Rocky dirt trails
> **Workout For Your Dog** - Moderate climbs to the old mines
> **Swimming** - None
> **Restrictions On Dogs** - None

Something Extra
The landscape has been churned up form the mining operations at Mount Hope bringing the minerals from the earth and leaving them on the surface.You can still find pieces of magnetite iron ore on the trails; look for small black stones with angular shapes that feel heavier than normal rocks.

Mountain Lakes Preserve

Phone - (609) 924-8720
Website - http://www.princetontwp.org/mtnlakes.html
Admission Fee - None
Directions - *Princeton, Mercer County; take Route 206 North out of town. Look for the sign for Mountain Avenue and exit into the jughandle. Cross over 206 and the parking lot is immediately on the right.*

The Park
In the 1880s the Margerum family constructed a system of earthen and concrete dams to create the two namesake lakes and began selling ice. Look closely and you can see foundations of large barns used for ice storage on the western slopes of the lakes. The bustling ice business continued until 1930. The original park was created in 1987 when the Friends of Open Space helped purchase a 70-acre private estate. Additional parcels of land were welded onto Mountain Lakes to create Princeton's "Central Park." The eastern section includes part of the Tusculum estate, home of John Witherspoon, who added his name to the Declaration of Independence.

The Walks
There are seven miles of rambles with your dog here spread across three   distinct segments of property, each with its own personality. The blue-blazed *James Sayen Trail* system circumnavigates the mountain lakes on dirt and mown grass trails that are easy-going for any dog. In the northern end of the park reached with some mild climbing into the John Witherspoon Woods, drops into an old-growth forest that has sprung up in a boulder field created by a volcanic intrusion that formed Princeton Ridge. Your dog will find the going a bit more challenging through this section. Returning to the parking lot through Community Park North you descend into a nicely-spaced scented pine grove before crossing a grass-covered sewer line into a garden area to finish your canine hike.

> **Where The Paw Meets The Earth:** Soft dirt and rocky patches in the northern stretches
> **Workout For Your Dog** - A hilly piece of property
> **Swimming** - There is easy access for dogs into the mountain lakes for playful canine aquatics
> **Restrictions On Dogs** - None

Something Extra
In the Pettoranello Gardens in the Community Park North section a natural slope by the lake has been fashioned into an ampitheatre. Among other events, the Princeton Rep Company puts on an outdoor Shakespeare production in the summer.

Musconetcong River Reservation

Phone - (908) 782-1158
Website - http://www.co.hunterdon.nj.us/depts/parks/guides/MusconetcongGorge.htm
Admission Fee - None
Directions - *Holland Township, Hunterdon County; Travel west on I-78 to exit 7 and proceed to route 173 west. On route 173, drive 1.3 miles to route 639. Turn left on to Route 639 and travel 4 miles. At the stop sign, bear left on 519, then turn left and cross the Musconetcong River, staying on Route 519. Take the next left onto Dennis Road, a gravel road, and go 0.2 of a mile to the parking area located on the left side of the road.*

The Park
There are two tracts of land in this park encompassing over 1,100 acres. The Musconetcong Gorge land was originally owned by the Warren Glenn Paper Mill that started production in 1873 and still operates today as Fibermark Inc. Point Mountain, at 935 feet the third highest spot in Hunterdon County, was added to the park in 1995. The name refers to the prominent crest that the silhouette of the property projects.

The Walks
The *Nature Trail* at the Gorge is a scenic amble that leads into the mossy ravine. It was the result of an Eagle Scout Project and the path is smooth and well-maintained - a joy for any paw. Continue on the *Railroad Trail* for more easy canine hiking but extended time in the Gorge will necessitate a climb to the *Ridge Trail*. Point Mountain is reached with a steep and rocky scramble up the *Ridge Trail* to the *Overlook Trail*. You can then make a big loop of over two miles to return to the Musconetcong River or retrace your steps back down. Looping around the parking area is the bounding *Riverwalk Trail* that indeed spends plenty of time along the sycamore-edged streamside. This jaunt also has its share of open field canine hiking.

> **Where The Paw Meets The Earth:** Natural surface trails
> **Workout For Your Dog** - Turn up the energy dial here
> **Swimming** - The Musconetcong River will keep your dog cool
> **Restrictions On Dogs** - None

Something Extra
Along the trails at Musconetcong Gorge every now and then you will pass flat, open areas that appear out of place in the lush woods. These are "charcoal landings" where mill workers would stack timber for conversion into charcoal.

New Brooklyn Park

Phone - None
Website - http://www.camdencounty.com/government/offices/
parks/pk_newbrook.html
Admission Fee - None
Directions - *New Brooklyn, Camden County; on New Brooklyn Road north of the Atlantic City Expressway and east of Route 536.*

The Park
The park is the terminus of the Great Egg Harbor River where it feeds into New Brooklyn Lake.

The Walks
On the north shore of the lake there are unmarked trails and dirt roads in the woods of the 758-acre park. The trails are paw-friendly sand and dirt. A small sand beach offers access to the shallow waters of the 100-acre lake. A paved multi-purpose trail winds through the developed sections of the park.

    Where The Paw Meets The Earth: Sandy dirt and asphalt
    Workout For Your Dog - Flat terrain
    Swimming - New Brooklyn Lake is calling your dog's name
    Restrictions On Dogs - None

Something Extra
The wooden bridge over New Brooklyn Lake on CR 536 was built in 1926 and is considered an historic American bridge.

North Brigatine Natural Area

Phone - None
Website - None
Admission Fee - None
Directions - *Brigantine, Atlantic County; take Route 30 into Atlantic City from Route 9 and head north on Brigantine Boulevard through town and all the way to the end.*

The Park

The Brigantine Bay and marsh complex includes the open water and tidal wetlands of, from north to south: Little Bay, Reed Bay, Somers Bay, Absecon Bay and Channel, Lakes Bay, and Scull Bay between the mainland coast of New Jersey and the barrier islands from Little Egg Inlet southwest to Great Egg Harbor Inlet. The complex includes the undeveloped segments of Little Beach and northern and southern Brigantine Island. This portion of the New Jersey backbarrier lagoon estuarine system is very significant for migrating and wintering waterfowl, colonial nesting waterbirds, migratory shorebirds, and fisheries.

The Walks

It may change due to concerns about nesting plovers but this undeveloped area at the northern tip of Brigantine is open to dogs. You can hike north on the shore, ducking out of the way of surf fishermen, and take the hook along the inlet and head back. If the Atlantic waves are too intimidating for your dog, the gentle surf of the bay will be a perfect place to swim. This entire hike up and back - completely on sand - will take about an hour if you keep moving and don't linger for too many swims.

> **Where The Paw Meets The Earth:** Sand
> **Workout For Your Dog** - Racing on sand and jumping in the ocean will tire any dog
> **Swimming** - Absolutely
> **Restrictions On Dogs** - None

Something Extra

This is a rare Jersey shore destination for dogs throughout the year.

Norvin Green State Forest

Phone - (973) 835-2160
Website - http://nj.gov/dep/parksandforests/parks/norvin.html
Admission Fee - None
Directions - *Bloomingdale, Passaic County; take I-287 to Exit 57. Follow Skyline Drive to Greenwood Lake Turnpike to West Brook Road to Snake Den Road. Follow signs to Weis Ecology Center. Park in the lot before the center or along Burnt Meadow Road and Glen Wild Road.*

The Park
This area supported active mining through the 1800s but officials began eyeing the Wanaque River as a potential water source as far back as the 1870s. Construction on the Wanaque Dam began in 1920 and a decade - and $25 million and 70 homes - later New Jersey communities began tapping into the some 30 billion gallons of water held in Wanaque Reservoir. The state forest is named for its donor, Norvin Hewlett Green. Most of the trails across the 4,210 acres of forest were cut by the members of the Green Mountain Club in the early 1920s.

The Walks
The attraction at Norvin Green are numerous viewpoints on hilltops ranging to 1,300 feet, most reached via some of the best, albeit rugged, canine hiking in New Jersey. There are many places to spend the day with your dog in the northern highlands and if this isn't first on your list it should be in the discussion. Past the mines the climbing begins on sometimes rocky and rooty woods trails. High Point, at 960 feet far from the tallest peak in the park, rewards you with 360-degree views after a steep last ascent. If you choose to penetrate deeper into Norvin State Forest there is a Coney-Island type rollercoaster trail to Carris Hill and more views in every direction. Down the hill on the White Trail is the split plunge of Chikahoki Falls.
> **Where The Paw Meets The Earth:** Rock-spiked dirt
> **Workout For Your Dog** - Many energetic climbs
> **Swimming** - The mountain streams are suitable only for splashing but a detour can lead to the shore of Wanaque Reservoir
> **Restrictions On Dogs** - No dogs on the Weis Environmental trails

Something Extra
The nearest destinations to the parking lot are the remainders of the mining era of the 1800s along the *Red/Yellow Trail*. A short detour climbs to Roomy Mine that you can actually explore with your dog in the warmer months when bats are not hibernating. Bring a flashlight and you can enter for 50 feet or so. Up the trail is the flooded Blue Mine that produced tons of ore before the encroaching water could not be abated in 1908.

Ocean County Park

Phone - (877) 921-0074
Website - http://www.co.ocean.nj.us/parks/ocp.html
Admission Fee - None
Directions - *Lakewood, Ocean County; east of town on Ocean Avenue (Route 88) between Route 9 and the Garden State Parkway.*

The Park
In 1879 a New York banker named Charles Henry Kimball stopped in town to stay with a friend. During his visit he noticed his weak lungs flourished in the pine-studded community. He decided to move to the area and develop a resort that soon was attracting socially prominent visitors, many who decided to stay. One who returned to live was John D. Rockefeller who built a 610-acre estate on Ocean Avenue. After his death in 1937 his son John, Jr., who would donate $537 million (in World War II money) over his lifetime, gave his father's summer playground to Ocean County for its first park in 1940. The park has played host to a variety of recreational pursuits, including a stint as spring training home to the New York baseball Giants. Today the park's 323 acres attracts fishermen, picnickers, tennis players, softball players, swimmers, cyclists and more.

The Walks
A phalanx of majestic silver-green pine trees immediately separate Ocean County park from the hub-bub of its surroundings. You can hike with your dog around the former Rockefeller grounds on the main paved park roadway or by dirt paths around the perimeter. Regular visitors can take advantage of a fee-supported dog park that covers five acres in the back of the park. There is a gated, fenced-in area mostly for small dogs and an off-leash open field and wooded area for more spirited romps. If walking your dog around the main road look for a small cemetery for dogs that have served Ocean County, located just before the roadway to the dog park.
> **Where The Paw Meets The Earth:** Grass and asphalt
> **Workout For Your Dog** - Not much hill-climbing here
> **Swimming** - When it is not crowded you dog can jump in Lake Fishigan
> for a refreshing swim
> **Restrictions On Dogs** - No dogs in the beach area of the swim area

Something Extra
Rockefeller purchased the Ocean County Hunt and Country Club in 1902 for his Lakewood estate and played on his private course every day, on the tee precisely at 10:15. He played golf into his 90s and in later years he rode a bicycle pushed by caddies to conserve his energy for his shots. Today, Ocean Park retains a driving range that is yardage-marked and free to use.

Palisades Interstate Park

Phone - (201) 768-1360
Website - http://www.njpalisades.org/
Admission Fee - None
Directions - *Alpine, Bergen County; from I-95 take the exit for Fort Lee / Palisades Interstate Parkway (Exit 72, after the last toll on the New Jersey Turnpike). Turn left at the light at the top of the ramp. Go through several lights in succession, then the entrance to the northbound PIP is on right.*

The Park
If millions of Americans didn't already live in the area by the time we got around to setting aside land for parks it is not hard to imagine the 500-foot sheer cliffs of the Palisades being a national park right now. The cliffs formed 200 million years ago when molten volcanic material cooled and solidified before reaching the surface. Subsequent water erosion of the softer sandstone substrate left behind the columnar structure of harder rock that exists today. Today's park meanders about 12 miles along the river - never more than a half-a-mile wide - and preserves 2,500 acres of wild Hudson River shorefront and uplands, including some of the most impressive sections of the Palisades.

The Walks
Two long-distance trails - the aqua-blazed *Long Path* atop the Palisades   and the white-blazed *Shore Path* along the river - traverse the length of the park. Occasional, and very steep, connectors (sometimes using steps) connect the two that enable canine hiking loops. Every now and then the Long Path touches on the edge of the impressive cliffs and there are spots an overly-curious dog could squeeze under the fence, so be careful. On top of the Palisades the going is mostly easy but does roll through varied woodlands that will distract you from the spectacular views at times. You can also find extra trail time for your dog on cross-country ski paths if you don't want to walk for miles along the cliffs.
Where The Paw Meets The Earth: Mostly dirt
Workout For Your Dog - Very demanding
Swimming - Small beaches at the Hudson River
Restrictions On Dogs - None

Something Extra
The iconic hike at Palisades is "The Giant Stairs" located beneath State Line Lookout. The Giant Stairs are massive boulders that have piled up at the foot of the cliffs from thousands of rock slides over millions of years. You need to scramble for over a mile to complete a 3.5-mile loop at the north end of the park. Unless your dog is light enough to lift DO NOT attempt this with your dog. Is it possible? Yes. Is it fun. NO.

Parvin State Park

Phone - (609) 358-8616
Website - http://www.state.nj.us/dep/parksandforests/parks/parvin.html
Admission Fee - None
Directions - *Pittsgrove, Salem County; six miles west of Vineland on Route 540, just east of the intersection with Route 553.*

The Park

The first landowner of these diverse pinelands was John Estaugh, husband of Elizabeth Haddon, who lived in present-day Haddonfield. Estaugh was granted 2,928 acres on March 31, 1742, by the Proprietors of West Jersey. Development began in 1796 when Lemuel Parvin purchased the property with the intention of operating a sawmill. He created Parvin Lake by constructing an earthen dam across Muddy Run on its journey to the Maurice River.The State of New Jersey's stewardship began in 1930 with the acquisition of 918 acres of forest and the 108-acre lake. During the Depression of the 1930s the Civilian Conservation Corps established a camp at Parvin, building campgrounds and cabins and carving trails. In 1944, German prisoners of war from Fort Dix were housed in Parvin while working on local farms and food processing plants. The POWS were captured from German Field Marshall Erwin Rommell's marauding Afrika Corps. Many of the facilities built by the Civilian Conservation Corps are still in use in the park today.

The Walks

A variety of loops and linear trails slice across Parvin State Park's 1,135 acres, about evenly divided between a recreational area and a natural area. The canine hiking is easier in the recreational area with its wide, packed-sand trails; paths narrow in the oak-pine forests, cedar swamps and laurel thickets of the natural area. These scenic woodlands on the fringe of the Pine Barrens are home to 40 known types of trees and 61 different woody shrubs as southern United States ecosystems collide with northern species at the southern tip of their natural range. All the hiking with your dog is on nine named trails, totalling more than 15 miles, and is easy-going for any dog.

> **Where The Paw Meets The Earth:** Soft dirt and maybe mud
>
> **Workout For Your Dog** - Mostly level terrain
>
> **Swimming** - Excellent dog paddling in the attractive Parvin Lake and the smaller Thundergast Lake
>
> **Restrictions On Dogs** - No dogs in beach area or campgrounds

Something Extra

For the dog who favors entering the water with a well-executed belly flop there are boat docks available, including a wide wooden pier stretching 25 yards into Lake Parvin for Dock Diving practice.

Penn State Forest

Phone - None
Website - http://www.state.nj.us/dep/parksandforests/parks/penn.html
Admission Fee - None
Directions - *Jenkin's Neck, Burlington County; take Route 563 to Lake Oswego Road in Jenkins Neck, and follow for three miles.*

The Park
There are over 3,000 undeveloped acres in Penn State Forest; most canine hikers start their explorations at Lake Oswego that sports a picnic and canoe-launch site.

The Walks
You say you've already taken your dog to Wharton State Forest and saw one person a four-hour hike and thought your dog was feeling a little crowded? Try Penn State Forest, over to the east a ways. You will still be in the Pine Barrens, the largest contiguous swath of greenspace between Boston and Washington. Canine hiking is down unmarked sand roads.

>**Where The Paw Meets The Earth:** Packed sand roads
>**Workout For Your Dog** - Long canine hikes possible
>**Swimming** - Lake Oswego is the best part of this adventure for your dog
>**Restrictions On Dogs** - None

Something Extra
The highlight of Penn State Forest is its Pygmy Pine Forest in an area known as the Plains. The trees rarely grow over four feet and you may mistake this for a young forest but these survivors have been trying to suck sustenance out of the sandy, acidic soil for decades. No one knows why the trees don't grow but theories center on the active fire cycle in the Pine Barrens, where on average a fire occurs every day of the year.

Poricy Park

Phone - (732) 842-5966
Website - http://www.monmouth.com/~poricypark/index.html
Admission Fee - None
Directions - *Middletown, Monmouth County; The Nature Center is located on Oak Hill Road, just west of Route 35. There are directional signs posted on Route 35 and the Parkway exits.*

The Park

Poricy Park is a nature preserve owned by Middletown Township. The 250-acre park includes woodlands, fields, stream and marsh ecosystems, and a bed of Cretaceous fossils, known to collectors throughout the Northeast. Joseph Murray farmed this land in Colonial times. In 1780 Murray, a member of the Monmouth Militia, was shot down by British loyalists in his cornfield in what is now Poricy Park's New Jersey State Historic Site. The Murray Farmhouse in the park dates to 1777. The farm remained in the Murray family until 1861 and was farmed continuously thereafter. In 1969 a plan to reroute a sewer line through the brook triggered a citizen outrage that saved these 250 acres from further development.

The Walks

There is a nice mix of open field and light woods canine hiking across the wedge of land the makes up Poricy Park. The fields are paw-friendly mown grass that support a meadow habitat. There are many short, intersecting trails cut into the grassland maze that suggest extra time should be devoted to exploration with your dog. This is all easy canine hiking. Other spots to visit include Sassafras and Nut Grove with nut-bearing trees, a natural marsh area that is about 10 degrees warmer in winter than other areas in the park and a butterfly garden planted outside the Nature Center. The garden features a variety of feeders.

> **Where The Paw Meets The Earth:** Natural dirt and grass
> **Workout For Your Dog** - The gentlest of hills
> **Swimming** - There is a pond at the base of a small cliff that you can make your way down to; but be careful of its muddy shore
> **Restrictions On Dogs** - None

Something Extra

The Poricy Brook Fossil Beds date to the Cretaceous period of the Mesozoic era, 145 to 65 million years ago, when coastal New Jersey was a shallow ocean. You can find fossils by sifting the sand and gravel of the stream bed (fossil screens can be rented at the nature center). The stream continuously exposes new fossils; the best time of the year to find fossils is in the early spring.

Princeton Battlefield State Park

Phone - (609) 921-0074
Website - http://www.state.nj.us/dep/parksandforests/parks/princeton.html
Admission Fee - None
Directions - *Princeton, Mercer County; from I-80 exit onto Route 15 North. Proceed for 5 miles to the Weldon Road Exit and travel approximately 4 miles east. Signed parking lots can be found on both sides of the road.*

The Park
Having finally achieved an important victory at Trenton in late December 1776, George Washington was in no mood to remain on the western side of the Delaware River. He came back to New Jersey after the new year hoping to surprise the British at Princeton. His army was spotted at daybreak by an alert British sentry and the Americans were pushed back through a field of frozen cornhusks. Washington, however, counterattacked and chased the British down the road. Major General Cornwallis had hoped to have all of New Jersey under his control by this time but instead had only the ports around New York City. The American Revolution was saved at Trenton and Princeton but little has been done to develop the sites historically. The terrain of the main fighting at the Battle of Princeton has remained virtually unchanged since that pivotal January day in 1777.

The Walks
The explorations on the Princeton Battlefield are around a sloping open field that suggests the terrain on which the armies met. The real canine hiking begins when you slip behind the Clarke House and enter the 588-acre Institute Woods. The trails carve the woodlands into a checkerboard with the first east-west *Trolley Track Trail* marking the route Washington's troops took during the battle. If you hike straight back you'll reach the open paths of the *Cornfield Trail*.

>**Where The Paw Meets The Earth:** Wide paths of grass and dirt
>**Workout For Your Dog** - Easy going for your dog
>**Swimming** - There is access to Stony Brook
>**Restrictions On Dogs** - None

Something Extra
Brigadier General Hugh Mercer became one of the most celebrated American casualties of the Revolution when he fell on this field. Mercer was bayonetted seven times but refused to leave the battle and was laid under a white oak tree. He would die nine days later in the Clarke House. The famous Mercer Oak lasted awhile longer - until March 3, 2000 when a windstorm toppled the beloved tree.

Pyramid Mountain Natural Historic Area

Phone - (973) 334-3130
Website - http://www.morrisparks.net/parks/pyrmtnmain.htm
Admission Fee - None
Directions - *Boonton, Morris County; from I-287 take Exit 45 onto Wooten Street, turning left from northbound or onto Myrtle Avenue and turning right southbound. Go up the hill to the blinking red light and turn right onto Boonton Avenue (Route 511). Proceed to the park entrance on the left after 2.5 miles.*

The Park
Hikers had been coming to Pyramid Mountain for decades to enjoy the wilderness but it wasn't until 1987, when the spectre of expanding suburbia raised its ugly head, that grassroots efforts led to the creation of a permanent public open space. The Pyramid Mountain Natural Historic Area now protects more than 1,500 acres of varied trails, fields, forests and wetlands.

The Walks
There is quite a menu for canine hikers at Pyramid Mountain. Looking for views? Exposed promontories will provide long looks to the mountains in the west or as far as New York City to the east. Want a waterside ramble? Check out the Orange Trail that works the slopes under a rocky ridge along the Taylortown Reservoir. Like to poke around ruins? You'll find old homesteads and the remains of stone cottages along the Pyramid Mountain trails. Seeking a leafy ravine to escape to with your dog? You can do it here.Across Boonton Avenue there is actually more parkland than the Pyramid Mountain side. The terrain is less flashy but you will find picturesque wetlands, views of the New York skyline and long, uninterrupted stretches of easily rolling woods walking. Depending on your route - and there are many choices - you can get five miles or so of canine hiking on the east side of the park.

> **Where The Paw Meets The Earth:** Mostly soft dirt
> **Workout For Your Dog** - Plenty of short, steep climbs
> **Swimming** - The *Orange Trail* drops to the lake for some excellent dog paddling and Botts Pond is a good swimming hole on the east side
> **Restrictions On Dogs** - None

Something Extra
Pyramid Mountain is best known for its glacial erratics - boulders that were sprinkled across the landscape by retreating ice sheets from the last Ice Age. The most famous is Tripod Rock, a boulder various estimated at between 150 and 200 tons, that is suspended heroically off the ground by three smaller stones. Nearby notable neighbors include two massive monoliths: Whale Head Rock and Bear Rock.

Ramapo Valley County Reservation

Phone - None
Website - None
Admission Fee - None
Directions - *Mahwah, Bergen County; from I-287 take Exit 66 onto Route 17 South and then Route 202 South. Drive about two miles and turn right into the parking area (about .5 of a mile south of Ramapo College).*

The Park
Ramapo translates roughly to "round ponds." There are hydro-delights aplenty in this Bergen County park - lakes and waterfalls - as well as great views across Bergen County to New York City. These forested mountains were a strategic route drung the Revolution and later a favorite camping spot for the Boy Scouts before the county began acquiring the land for the 2,000-acre park.

The Walks
There are at least 15 miles of marked trails across Ramapo Mountain, doled out in trail segments in the system. The choice of loops - or even a long car shuttle - is yours. One of the more popular - if ambitious - destinations is Bear Swamp Lake where you can see the scars of a modern day battle. Developers were the loser in this war and you can poke around chimneys and foundations and abandoned patios as remnants of the defeat. If some of the popular trails seem too popular there are many options on these wide woods roads and footpaths created under many a Boy Scout hoe. The Ramapos only rise to about 1,200 feet and your dog won't find much in the way of strenuous trotting here so you may want to spend extra time on these trails, maybe even exploring neighboring parks like Ramapo State Forest.

> **Where The Paw Meets The Earth:** Rock-studded dirt
> **Workout For Your Dog** - Moderate pulls to the top of the hill
> **Swimming** - Absolutely - plan a route to visit at least one lake
> **Restrictions On Dogs** - None

Something Extra
New Jersey is not thought of as a place of waterfalls - there are plenty of places with lively rapids but not many dramatic plunges. Of the 30 or so waterfalls in the state, two are easily reached in Ramapo Valley Reservation, courtesy of Bear Swamp Brook. The Bear Swamp Falls is a dual drop that can be found by walking up the closed Bear Swamp Road about one mile from U.S. Route 202. Buttercup Falls spills over a rock ledge to tumble nearly 25 feet. It is easily reached via the wide trail from the park entrance.

Rancocas State Park

Phone - (609) 726-1191
Website - http://www.nj.gov/dep/parksandforests/parks/ranco-cas.html
Admission Fee - None
Directions - *Mount Holly, Burlington County; from the Mount Holly Bypass go west on Marne Highway (Route 537) and make first right on Deacon Road to end after 1.3 miles.*

The Park
The main branch of the Rancocas Creek, the largest watershed in south-central New Jersey, fractures into tributaries at this spot. The major tribes of the Lenni-Lenape found their way to the Rancocas, probably named for one of the sub-tribes, sometime after the 1400s. European settlement - and diseases - eventually displaced the Lenni Lenape. In the late 19th century members of the Powhatan Renape Nation, descended from the Nanticoke of southern Delaware and the Rappahannocks of Virginia, began trickling into a tiny hamlet known as Morrisville to establish a community. As a state park, Rancocas is so underfunded that it once had to close for several years in the 1970s. It's a park again but still far from robust. The New Jersey Audubon Society leases part of the park's 1,252 acres to help it survive.

The Walks
Active dog owners are a lot that can appreciate a shabby park. The lack of visitation is typically accompanied by a similar lack of restrictions against dogs. When you arrive at Rancocas don't expect to be greeted by any typical state park amenities such as entrance signs, visitor centers or trail maps. Just perfect for a dog ready to explore. And there is plenty to escape to at Rancocas. A tangle of unmarked paths and sand roads provide access to freshwater tidal creeks, dark forests, open meadows, and reedy marshes. Expect to encounter an overgrown patch here and there - a small price to pay for the uncrowded trails.

> **Where The Paw Meets The Earth:** Paw -friendly soft dirt and sand
> **Workout For Your Dog** - Mostly level terrain
> **Swimming** - Fishermen's trails often lead from the sand roads along the waterways and offer good swimming opportunities in the Rancocas Creek branches
> **Restrictions On Dogs** - No dogs on the trails of the Rancocas Nature Center

Something Extra
A portion of the park is leased to the Powhatan Renape Nation. A replica of an Indian village of the 1600s has been constructed on theit reservation, along with an interpretive nature trail. The annual Powhatan Indian event is a festival of music, performances and crafts.

Ringwood State Park

Phone - (973) 962-7031
Website - http://nj.gov/dep/parksandforests/parks/ringwood.html
Admission Fee - None outside rec areas
Directions - *Ringwood, Passaic County; from I-287 take Exit 55 and head north on Greenwood Lake Road (Route 511) heading north. Make a right at Sloatsburg Road (it is not marked) to the park. If you go completley past Wanaque Reservoir, you've gone too far.*

The Park
The Ringwood Company put a dam across the Ringwood River and used the water power to operate blast furnaces and forges. For the next 200 years some of America's most famous ironmasters toiled here. In the mid-1800s Ringwood came under control of Abram S. Hewitt, the pre-eminent American ironmaster. His descendents deeded the Ringwood Manor House and property to the State of New Jersey for a park in 1936.

The Walks
The Ringwood trail system ties into the Ramapo Mountain State Forest system to the west and into Bergen County parkland to the east. Volunteers have carved so many trails into the New Jersey highlands your dog could start out sampling them as a puppy and return a senior dog before hiking them all. Some trails serve to connect the two sections of the park, Ringwood and Skylands. Some of the more popular canine hikes explore the areas around the manor houses while those in search of rocky vistas can try the yellow-blazed *Cooper Union Trail* that explores Governor Mountain. The original trail was laid out by members of the Cooper Union Hiking club from the prestigious Manhattan college founded by one of New Jersey's largest landowners, Peter Cooper.

> **Where The Paw Meets The Earth:** Natural surface and old roads
> **Workout For Your Dog** - As tough as your dog want to make it
> **Swimming** - Many ponds in the extensive forest
> **Restrictions On Dogs** - None

Something Extra
Ringwood Manor is considered to have at least two ghosts in residence. One is believed to be Robert Erskine, the original owner of the property. The other may be Jackson White, a strange and restless spirit. His ancestry was parts black, Indian, and white, the descendant of runaway slaves that settled in this valley during the Civil War. The ghosts' distinctive footsteps can be heard throughout the house. No word on sightings out on the trails but if your dog's ears perk up for no apparent reason on your hike you may know why.

Round Valley Recreation Area

Phone - None
Website - http://www.state.nj.us/dep/parksandforests/parks/round.html
Admission Fee - Yes, in summer
Directions - *Clinton, Hunterdon County; take I-78 to Exit 18 (Route 22 East) and follow the signs to the park.*

The Park
A natural horseshoe-shaped basin enclosed on three sides by Cushetunk Mountain attracted the attention of the New Jersey Water Supply Association in the mid-1900s and the task of moving people and houses out of the deep, natural ravine and building two dams was completed by 1965. The reservoir has no natural drainage and is filled by pumping water up from the Raritan River. Since this is a costly proposition water is drawn from the 55-billion gallon reservoir only in emergencies. Thus the water level in Round Valley is consistently high, and the clarity exceptional. From the beginning Round Valley was created with recreation in mind. A campground was ready by 1972 and an earthen dam was constructed to form a swimming area. Today the park manages almost 4,000 acres, half of which are covered in water.

The Walks
Canine hiking in Round Valley is conducted on the *Cushetunk Trail*, a nine-mile natural surface path that leads to the wilderness camping sites. This is an out-and-back affair - you can not hike completely around the lake. Many canine hikers use a small beach about five miles in as a turning-around point. Aside from the potential for many hours of trail time, the workout for your dog here is provided from some daunting ascents (and descents in the opposite direction). The trail dips in and out of wooded areas and views of the lake from different angles help inject variety into this trek.

> **Where The Paw Meets The Earth:** Natural surface and woods road
> **Workout For Your Dog** - It is a long way along the reservoir
> **Swimming** - The trail touches down to the shoreline
> **Restrictions On Dogs** - No dogs in the campgrounds

Something Extra
With an average depth of 70 feet and its lowest point covered by 180 feet of water, this is the deepest lake in New Jersey. Scuba divers are attracted to the clear waters to explore the mud, rocks, snails, and huge stands of water plants later in the season. Snorkeling is also a popular underwater activity in the reservoir.

Schooley's Mountain Park

Phone - None
Website - http://www.morrisparks.net/parks/directions/schooleysdir.htm
Admission Fee - None
Directions - *Schooley's Mountain, Morris County; take I-80 West to I-287 Southand Exit 22. Go north on Route 206 to the Route 24 intersection. Turn left onto Route 24, heading west up Schooley's Mountain, past Washington Township Municipal Building. Turn right at park sign onto Camp Washington Road. Continue on same, which becomes Springtown Road, to the park is on the right side.*

The Park
The quiet, spacious woods and cloistered waterfalls on Schooley's Mountain belie a very active past. Stone has been quarried here to build area houses. The iron ore ripped from the ground was so magnetic the workers could not use metal tools to extract it. The pent-up power of the rushing waterfalls was tapped to generate electricity. Before that, in the early 1800s, Joseph Heath had opened a spa and touted the waters as the purest in America, able to heal whatever was ailing you. Folks came in stagecoaches and then railroads to take the waters. After the spa came a boarding school, then a YMCA camp. Through it all the mountain retained the name of the Schooley family who lived here in the 1700s. Morris County opened the 797-acre park, mostly on wooded hillsides, in 1974.

The Walks
Rarely will a canine hike turn as wild and wooly as fast as the one at Schooley's Mountain. Just minutes past starting down well-maintained wooden steps by the lodge and stepping through the serenity of a forested oudoor chapel you and your dog are traipsing past waterfalls and scrambling across boulders as the trail seems to disappear. You are just yards from the roadway and neighborhoods but you may as well have descended into the wilderness of the early 1700s when all this land was just referred to as The Great Forest. Soon enough your dog is trudging uphill on a somewhat road that will eventually lead to scrambled boulder fields and overlooks of more trees and the countryside. The excitement now gears down as the rest of your dog's outing is spent on old roads and footpaths under an attractive forest. The loop to return to Lake George covers about two miles.

> **Where The Paw Meets The Earth:** Dirt, rocky slopes
> **Workout For Your Dog** - Serious hiking in the Electric Brook gorge
> **Swimming** - Lake George is your ticket
> **Restrictions On Dogs** - No dogs in the recreation areas

Something Extra
You can take your dog one of the more unique quick walks in New Jersey when you cross a 470-foot floating bridge across Lake George.

Shark River Park

Phone - (732) 922-4080
Website - http://www.monmouthcountyparks.com/parks/shark_park.asp
Admission Fee - None
Directions - *Wall, Monmouth County; from the Garden State Parkway take Exit 100 (Route 33 East). At Schoolhouse Road turn right and follow to the park. The main trail system is across the road from the parking lot.*

The Park
The wetlands and floodplains of the Shark River were the site of Monmouth County's first park, created in 1961. Shark River's 588 acres are neatly divided into a recreational area that attracts picnickers and fishermen and ice skaters and an isolated trail system of almost seven miles.

The Walks
The *Hidden Creek Trail* loops the trail system and visits most of the diverse landscapes packed into Shark River Park. The passage is surprisingly undulating although terms like "moderate" and even "challenging" used by the park to describe trails here is a bit of a stretch. Your dog will enjoy these packed sand and dirt paths through a dense mixed forest. The out-and-back *Pine Hills Trail* provides a sporty detour into some of the deeper undulations in the park and the *Rivers Edge Trail* drops into the floodplain to twist along the Shark River for thhe better part of a mile. This is not the Shark River of a few miles downstream at the Atlantic Ocean with marinas and open water. At this point the fast-flowing water can just about be stepped across and carries a strange industrial-hued tint.

> **Where The Paw Meets The Earth:** Soft dirt and sand with pine straw
> **Workout For Your Dog** - Long, flat trails
> **Swimming** - The four main ponds in the state forest will set any water-loving dog's tail to wagging
> **Restrictions On Dogs** - No dogs in the campground

Something Extra
The prime attraction of the interior *Cedar Trail Loop* is an Atlantic White Cedar bog where you can chance to see a carnivorous pitcher plant. The nutrient-challenged bog doesn't provide enough sustenance for these ewer-shaped plants so they must lure insects into a deadly trap for consumption by a cocktail of digestive fluids in the pitcher. Tiny hairs pointing downward prevent the trapped insects from crawling out to freedom.

Six Mile Run Reservoir Site

Phone - (609) 924-5705
Website - http://www.dandrcanal.com/interest.html#sixmile
Admission Fee - None outside rec areas
Directions - *Somerset, Somerset County; from Route 514 West take a left onto Route 533. Make a left on Blackwell Mills Road in about 2.5 miles. Cross the canal and make a right on Canal Road; the parking lot is on the left.*

The Park
In 1970 the State of New Jersey acquired more than 3,000 acres with an eye towards creating a reservoir site. That day never came and in 1993 alternative water sources were discovered and the Division of Parks and Forestry became the new stewards of the land. The park is administered as a part of the Delaware and Raritan Canal State Park. Much of the land is leased to the public but there is plenty of hiking space left to entice visitors to make the journey to this out-of-the-way natural area.

The Walks
Of the three color-coded trails to try with your dog, you will most likely push away on the *Blue Trail* behind the parking lot. The longest of the trio starts in open fields before eventually ducking into the woods. A good choice for the canine hiker is to come back on the *Yellow Trail* that traces the Six Mile Run before finishing at the old park office after a short field walk. The 1.5-mile *Red Trail* serves up what could be called rugged fare at Six Mile Reservoir Site. There are stream crossings and an occasional scamper up a slope through open fields and groves of cedar trees. The Red Trail also connects with the *Blue Trail* to form a 5.3-mile loop. For extended canine hiking you can cross the road and take off on a jaunt down the Delaware and Raritan Canal towpath. This is a relaxed rural stretch of the popular canal trail that runs from New Brunswick to Bordentown.

> **Where The Paw Meets The Earth:** Paw-friendly soft dirt and grass
> **Workout For Your Dog** - Only a very few small hills
> **Swimming** - Small dogs might find some dog paddling in the Six Mile Run but it's mostly for splashing or a great spot to lie in on a hot summer day
> **Restrictions On Dogs** - None

Something Extra
This was once Dutch farming country, a region of New Netherlands that stretched from central New Jersey through eastern New York in the 1600-1700s. Mostly grain farms, the hub of activity was the Dutch barn. These increasingly rare structures are identified by their low walls and steep gables.The boxy barns were supported by a handful of massive beams, joined in an H-pattern. You can still see examples of Dutch barns as you drive to Six Mile Run Reservoir Site.

Sourland Mountain Preserve

Phone - None
Website - http://www.somersetcountyparks.org/activities/parks/sourland_mt.htm
Admission Fee - None
Directions - *Hillsborough, Somerset County; from Route 206 (South Broad Street), turn onto West Park Avenue. Make a left onto Wescott Avenue. After passing under high tension wires, make an immediate right turn onto the lane that leads to the park.*

The Park

Sourland Mountain is at the northeast point of a ridge of sedimentary and igneous rock that was deposited between 150 and 180 million years ago and stretches to the Delaware River. It is hard to believe walking the thickly wooded mountainside but this was once a tree-less farm. After picking your way through the boulders strewn across the Preserve it is easy to imagine that the name "Sourland" comes from the farmers who abandoned growing crops in favor of grazing cows but it actually is believed to derive from the term "sorrel-land" to describe the reddish-brown colored soils.

The Walks

Sourland Mountain features three blazed trails, the star being the 5-mile Ridge Trail. The trail pushes uphill away from the parking lot - not too strenuously but expect to see your dog start panting - until it reaches a picturesque cluster of boulders. The elevation gain is about 300 feet. After this the trail flattens out and is a comfortable walk with your dog in airy woodsland on a wide path. The *Ridge Trail* can be aborted with a walk down a cut-away for a pipeline. This is the only open-air hiking at Sourland Mountain and you can enjoy the views on the way down. On a clear day it is possible to see New York City. If the 300-foot climb seems more hike than your dog is looking for, you can still enjoy Sourland Mountain. The *Maple Flats* and *Pondside* trails break off from the Ridge Trail before heading up the mountain. The two form a stacked-loop trail that together totals less than two miles.

> **Where The Paw Meets The Earth:** Rocky trails
> **Workout For Your Dog** - Moderate pulls to the top of the hill
> **Swimming** - You bet, see below
> **Restrictions On Dogs** - None

Something Extra

Down below the parking lot is the best canine swimming hole in New Jersey. The pond has level, unobstructed access all the way around. It is deep enough that your dog will be swimming in two steps and it is just big enough that you can't throw a stick all the way across. Situated right beside the trail exit, it is a perfect way to end a hardy canine hike. The only thing missing is a towel rack.

South Branch Reservation

Phone - None
Website - http://www.co.hunterdon.nj.us/depts/parks/guides/
SouthBranch.htm
Admission Fee - None
Directions - *many locations in Hunterdon County; to Echo Hill Environmental Education Area, take Route 31 north of Flemington 5.6 miles from circle. Make a right onto the jug handle for Stanton Station Road. Travel .4 mile to Lilac Drive and turn right to park entrance.*

The Park
The South Branch of the Raritan River drains over 1,100 miles - more than any river in New Jersey. The South Branch Reservation is a pack of twelve parks and preserves that highlight the historic and natural delights along the river. A good way to spend a day with your dog is to drive through the watershed in Hunterdon County, stopping at the various sections and enjoying a short hike or swim.

The Walks
Clumped together, the dozen parks total more than 1,000 acres. Several are old farms and offer pleasant open-field canine hiking; others serve up wooded trails. At Echo Hill, home of the South Branch Watershed Association, the Civilian Conservation Corps cut down the original orchard and blanketed the property with 200,000 evergreens in 1939.

> **Where The Paw Meets The Earth:** You'll find some gravelly paths, grass passages and dirt trails
> **Workout For Your Dog** - Many short walks available
> **Swimming** - Plenty of access to the South Branch
> **Restrictions On Dogs** - None

Something Extra
A journey down the South Branch is a wonderful education in bridge engineering with the river crossed by stone arch bridges, iron truss bridges and pier-and-deck spans.

South Mountain Reservation

Phone - None
Website - None
Admission Fee - None
Directions - *South Orange, Essex County; from I-78 take Exit 50 and head north on Millburn Avenue to Brookside Drive and the park. To reach the trail to Washington Rock, turn right on Brookside, right on South Orange Avenue and right on Washington Rock Drive to parking area.*

The Park

In 1895 Essex County began buying land that would become South Mountain Reservation. They retained Central Park creator Frederick Law Olmsted to design the new park. Olmsted was in the twilight of his career, about to turn the business over to his sons, but surveyed the property and declared it one of the choicest park sites he had ever seen. It was the first of more than two dozen projects the Olmsteds would design for Essex County. South Mountain has remained in its wild state. Working from Olmsted site plans the Civilian Conservation Corps built trails, bridges and picnic shelters in the 1930s. Today's park is the largest in the Essex County Park Commission system at 2,047.14 acres, to be exact.

The Walks

Water is the star at South Mountain. The Rahway River makes a pleasant canine hiking companion and there are cascades and even a 25-foot plunge over bare basalt rock to enjoy. You'll get an occasional steep ascent but most of the going on South Mountain trails will be easily devoured by any dog. Crest Drive has been closed to vehicular traffic and makes a pleasant start to an outing here, either on the curling roadway or an adjacent footpath with Washington Rock the most common destination. Beyond Lookout Point, much of your day will be spent on the yellow-blazed *Lenape Trail* with a return on the white-blazed *Rahway Trail*. This loop will take the better part of two hours with much more available.

> **Where The Paw Meets The Earth:** Dirt and asphalt and gravel
> **Workout For Your Dog** - You can find some tiring stretches
> **Swimming** - Yes, in the river
> **Restrictions On Dogs** - None

Something Extra

George Washington stood here. With his army camped in Morristown in 1777, General Washington ordered 23 beacons constructed to observe British troop movements in New York City. Beacon Signal Station 9 was built here. As you stand on Washington Rock today remember that the mountain had by this time been stripped of most of trees, providing unobstructed views.

Stokes State Forest

Phone - (973) 948-3820
Website - http://www.state.nj.us/dep/parksandforests/parks/stokes.html
Admission Fee - Yes, in the summer in the recreation aeas
Directions - *Branchville, Sussex County; take Route 206 north of town for four miles to the park office on the right.*

The Park
The State of New Jersey began buying land for Stokes Forest in 1907 - sometimes paying a whole dollar an acre. The forest is named for Edward Casper Stokes who served one term as Republican governor from 1905 until 1908, forming the New Jersey Forest Commission during his tenure. He donated the first 500 acres. After he left office Stokes remained active in politics, failing in three bids to win a U.S. Senate seat and another term as governor. In 2001, lightning struck his mausoleum in the Mount Pleasant Cemetery in Millville. The lightning blasted through the mausoleum's roof and littered the floor with shattered marble, blowing a 6-inch hole in the governor's crypt. His casket was not damaged.

The Walks
Stokes Forest is the chunk of land between the Delaware Water Gap National Recreation Area to the south and High Point State Park to the north providing 30 miles of uninterrupted parkland along the Kittatinny Ridge of the Appalachian Mountains. With 25 named trails, any type of canine hike is possible here - you could fill up a day just walking on beginner-to-moderate type trails that explore attractive streams, visit old mine sites or just disappear with your dog in a remote patch of woodsland. But most visitors will point their dogs in the direction of Kittatinny Ridge and 1,653-foot Sunrise Mountain. Four trails lead to the Appalachian Trail atop the ridge in the vicinity of Sunrise Mountain enabling you to create hiking loops of between four and ten miles, depending on how long you want to walk on the ridge soaking in the views.

> **Where The Paw Meets The Earth:** Dirt trails can be rocky
> **Workout For Your Dog** - Absolutely
> **Swimming** - Plenty in the valley, not on the ridge
> **Restrictions On Dogs** - No dogs in the campgrounds

Something Extra
To cap off your dog's day at Stokes Forest head to Tillman Ravine for easy walking through a dark, shady evergreen forest of eastern hemlock. The Tillman Brook that carves this moist ravine is one of the prettiest in the state.

Swartswood State Park

Phone - (973) 383-5230
Website - http://www.state.nj.us/dep/parksandforests/parks/swartswood.html
Admission Fee - Yes
Directions - *Smartswood, Sussex County; from I-80, take Exit 25, Route 206 north to Newton, about 12 miles. From Newton, make a left at the second traffic light (Route 206 and Spring Street) then make a left at the next light onto Route 519. Follow 519 for approximately 1/2 mile, then make a left onto Route 622 at Sussex County College sign. Follow Route 622 for about 4 1/2 miles. Turn left onto Route 619. The park entrance is about 1/2 mile south on Route 619.*

The Park

This is New Jersey's first state park. The entire state park system grew from a 12.5-acre gift from George M. Emmans, made with "an inent that people may have use of the premises herein conveyed as a public park forever." New Jersey's first ever state park land is now the Emmans Grove Picnic Area.

The Walks

There are two hiking options for canine hikers in Swartswood State Park. Across from the park entrance is a multi-use trail system consisting of *Duck Pond Trail* (paved for its half-mile length) and leading to the 2.8-mile *Spring Lake Trail*. Dogs are rewarded for completing this hilly loop with a dip in the secluded Spring Lake. Most dogs probably won't take not of the impressive old growth hemlock stands along the way. A better first choice would be the *Grist Mill Trail* in the isolated western section of the park. This hearty 40-minute loop uses switchbacks to advance on a cedar forest on the upper slopes.

> **Where The Paw Meets The Earth:** Natural surface and asphalt
>
> **Workout For Your Dog** - A lot more than it looks when you set out
>
> **Swimming** - Of course - but even better than you may think; at the boat ramp for Little Swartswood Lake and the boat ramp at Snake Island on the westen shores of Swartswood Lake both have piers that are ideal for a little dock diving practice
>
> **Restrictions On Dogs** - No dogs in the campground or swim area

Something Extra

Milling has gone on around Swartswood Lake since Colonial times. Keen's Mill at the trailhead dates to 1830, built from native attractive limestone and slate. The dam is much newer - it was built by the Army Corps of Engineers in the 1980s.

Tatum Park

Phone - (732) 671-1987
Website - http://www.monmouthcountyparks.com/parks/tatum.asp
Admission Fee - None
Directions - *Middletown, Monmouth County; take Exit 114 from the Garden State Parkway onto Red Hill Road heading east. You can continue to the Red Hill Activity Center on yourleft but the better choice is tohead for the Holland Activity Center by turning left on Van Schoick Road and right on Holland Road to the entrance on the right.*

The Park
Charles Tatum was a prominent glass manufacturer with factories in Keyport and Millville. He selected this land as a summer home in 1905 and his family continued to farm 170 acres here until 1973. A portion of the farm was then donated to Monmouth County and additional acreaged has since been acquired to push the current park size to 368 acres.

The Walks
Tatum Park serves up as nice a mix of open field and mixed-hardwood canine hiking as you are liable to find in New Jersey. You can start your explorations from either the Holland Activity Center or the Red Hill Activity Center but the centrally located Holland Center offers a greater variety of trail options.Two parallel trails lead away from the parking lot. If you want to start your dog with a jaunt down old farm roads and through blossoming meadows start off down the *Tatum Ramble Trail* and pick up the *Meadow Run Trail* for a three-mile easy loop. The other choice, the Indian Springs Trail is another old road that once served as the main entrance to the farm. It will eventually lead to the twisting *Dogwood Hollow Trail* or the *Holly Grove Trail* - both narrow, rolling dirts paths through vibrant woodlands.

> **Where The Paw Meets The Earth:** Dirt paths and farm roads
> **Workout For Your Dog** - Some easy hills on the old farm
> **Swimming** - Your dog can splash in some old farm ponds or slender streams in the hollows of the park but little more
> **Restrictions On Dogs** - None

Something Extra
In 1885, Clinton Heath, once a slave in North Carolina, became the first black farmer in Middletown Township. He and his wife Mary would raise 13 children and 3 foster children and their youngest, Bertha, donated an addition to the Red Hill Activity Center where you can view a permanent exhibit of the black community's ties to the land.

Taylor Wildlife Preserve

Phone - None
Website - None
Admission Fee - None
Directions - *Riverton, Burlington County; east of town, off River Road (Route 543). The main entrance is on Taylors Lane and the trails can also be accessed from Inman Street.*

The Park

In 1720 Joshua Wright purchased land along the Delaware River known to the local Indians as "the island" since it often remained dry during the periodic flooding of the river, which rises and falls as much as five feet between high and low tides. The land has remained in his family ever since. In 1975 Sylvia and Joshua Taylor donated 89 acres of their 130-acre property to the New Jersey National Lands Trust and opened the Taylor Wildlife Preserve to the public.

The Walks

One of the few remaining accessible open spaces remaining along the heavily industrialized Delaware River is at Taylor Wildlife Preserve. As it is, the preserve is squeezed against the water by four neighboring industrial parks. A 12-step interpretive trail has been carved around a vibrant freshwater marsh. For the most part the trails are dirt and stony. Several benches have been provided overlooking the marsh and the Delaware River. The walk along the river is one of the longest in the area and dogs can easily reach the water for a swim.

> **Where The Paw Meets The Earth:** Soft dirt and small stones
>
> **Workout For Your Dog** - Easy going on the park's hills
>
> **Swimming** - There is easy access to the Delaware River for good dog paddling
>
> **Restrictions On Dogs** - None

Something Extra

The view south from the trail at Taylor Wildlife Preserve is an un-obstructed panorama of the Tacony-Palmyra Bridge with the higher landmarks of the Philadelphia skyline thrusting above its arch. The truss and girder span, that opened in 1929, was once known as the Nickel Bridge when the toll was dropped to 5 cents in 1955 after the structure was paid for.

Teetertown Ravine Nature Preserve

Phone - None
Website - http://www.co.hunterdon.nj.us/depts/parks/guides/
Teetertown.htm
Admission Fee - None
Directions - *Califon, Hunterdon County; from I-78 proceed north
on Route 31 for 1.7 miles to Route 513 North. Turn right through
High Bridge toward Califon for about 6.5 miles. Just past the A&P,
turn left onto Sliker Road. Turn right onto Teetertown Road. Follow
the left fork of the road about 1 mile to the stop sign at Hollow
Brook Road. Turn left and proceed 0.1 mile up the ravine. There
are vehicle pull-offs near the trailheads.*

The Park
German immigrant John Teeter purchased a mill here in 1814, giving
his name to the town the mill supported. In 1953, the Watchtower
and Bible Tract Society of New York, Inc. (Jehovah's Witnesses) took
ownership of the site as a communal farm, calling it "Mountain Farm."
However, due to economics, the farm was considered surplus and was
sold to the County in 1999. Tht same year, the adjoining 155 acres,
which is now called Mountain Farm Section, was purchased adding
large fields and two ponds to the diversity of the park. The preserve
now totals 682 acres.

The Walks
This park offers the solitude of a densely wooded area, including a
variety of hardwoods, shrubs, and animal life, and the contrast of
a spectacular rushing stream winding its way through the Ravine's
dramatic rock outcroppings. A plethora of shortish trails provide great
variety in open fields and diverse woodlands. An old farm serves up
ponds and an old peach orchard. Be prepared for some steep hilly
areas - your reward being a pleasing view of the valley.

> **Where The Paw Meets The Earth:** Natural surface trails
> **Workout For Your Dog** - Short but spirited hiking here
> **Swimming** - There is access to the water at many points
> **Restrictions On Dogs** - None

Something Extra
The house built by pioneer John Teeter still stands 150 years later
and Merv Griffin once lived in it.

Thompson Park

Phone - (732) 842-4000
Website - http://www.monmouthcountyparks.com/parks/thompson.asp
Admission Fee - None
Directions - *Lincroft, Monmouth County; from I-287 take Exit 35 onto Madison Avenue and head east. Turn left on South Street to park on left.*

The Park

This 665-acre park was established in 1968 with a donation of 215 acres from the estate of Geraldine Livingston Thompson. Mrs Thompson's beloved "Brookdale Farm" was a premier thoroughbred race horse breeding/training facility.

The Walks

The centerpiece of Brookdale Farm, a 32-room Colonial revival mansion built in 1896 by Lewis and Geraldine Thompson, was ravaged by fire in February 2006 forever altering the character of this park. You can still bring your dog to this beautiful former thoroughbred farm to tour old roads and exercise trails. A paved jogging path trips the length of the park for 1.8 miles in open fields and tickles woodlands.

> **Where The Paw Meets The Earth:** Pavement and dirt roads
> **Workout For Your Dog** - Easy hiking for your dog here
> **Swimming** - None
> **Restrictions On Dogs** - None

Something Extra

The Three Barn section is named for the two large horse barns (now Theatre Barn and Activity Barn) and a cow barn (now the Creative Arts Center). The Three Barn area is also where the extremely popular off-leash dog area is located.

Timber Creek Park

Phone - None
Website - http://www.bigtimbercreek.org/big_timber_creek_park.htm
Admission Fee - None
Directions - *Almonesson, Gloucester County; on the southeast corner of Hurffville Roud (Route 41) and Cooper Street/Almonesson Road.*

The Park

Timber Creek Park was purchased by Deptford Township with New Jersey Green Acres funding with the help of the New Jersey Conservation Foundation. It contains 18 acres of wetlands and forested uplands. The wetlands include a thick red maple swamp that contains many wetlands species such as ferns, sweet pepperbush, bay magnolia, and skunk cabbage. The uplands contain a mature hardwoods forest with many large beech, oak, mocker nut and tulip poplar trees and mountain laurel.

The Walks

This small park offers an eyehook trail whose highlight is a view of the wetlands of the Big Timber Creek estuary, home to ducks, geese, herons and kingfishers. The wide, soft dirt and sand trails follow a rolling, wooded path along the slopes above the marsh. This pleasant stroll takes less than one half hour but there is more at the Old Pine Farm (end of Rankin Avenue).

> **Where The Paw Meets The Earth:** Paw-friendly dirt
> **Workout For Your Dog** - Small bluffs to climb but nothing difficult
> **Swimming** - None
> **Restrictions On Dogs** - None

Something Extra

There is and impressive stand of Virginia pine near the trailhead. Virginia pine has only recently been used as a Christmas tree. It tolerates warmer temperatures and has been developed as a southern alternative to Scotch pine. The tree has to be mechanically formed into shape; the foliage is dark green to gray in color; the limbs are stout with woody branches; Virginia pine is one of the most often purchased Christmas trees in the Southeastern United States.

Tourne County Park

Phone - (973) 326-7631
Website - http://www.morrisparks.net/parks/tournemain.htm
Admission Fee - None
Directions - *Mountain Lakes, Morris County; from I-80 take Exit 38 for Denville. Follow Route 46 east through Denville to Mountain Lakes. Turn right onto the Boulevard and go through Mountain Lakes. Bear left onto Powerville Road. Take the first left onto McCaffrey Lane to the park.*

The Park
Tourne, roughly translated from Dutch as "mountain" or "overlook," is the last remaining undeveloped chunk of land from the Great Boonton Tract that was purchased by David Ogden, Colonial Attorney-General of New Jersey, in 1759. This was a mining area and McCaffrey Lane that runs into the park was designed in 1767 to haul iron ore from Hibernia's mines to the Ogden ironworks in Old Boonton.Clarence Addington DeCamp owned most of the land that is now Tourne Park in the first half of the 20th century. With just hand tools and levers, DeCamp - a conservationist before there was such a term - built two roads to the top of the hill for people to enjoy the views. Morris County came into possession of the land after DeCamp's passing and opened the 545-acre park for the public in 1960.

The Walks
The must-do canine hike at Tourne County Park is the 370-foot climb to the 897-foot namesake summit, a 2-mile round trip. Your dog will be using the same roads that Clarence DeCamp carved a century ago (the *DeCamp Trail*). There are views in every direction by the time you crest the summit and head down the opposite side. Across the road the *Hemlock Trail* is a sporty push up a hill under exceedingly pleasant woodlands. The trail system here also meanders along Rigby's Brook in airy woods. More blazed foot trails can be found for your dog in the western areas of the park; what they lack in views they compensate for in elbow room.

> **Where The Paw Meets The Earth:** Rocky roads and natural surfaces
> **Workout For Your Dog** - Some excellent climbs here
> **Swimming** - Rigby's Brook is a great stream for splashing but not deep enough for dog paddling
> **Restrictions On Dogs** - No dogs allowed in *Wildflower Trail* area

Something Extra
A short detour from the summit leads to a gravity-defying glacial erratic called Nouse Cradle Balancing Rock. Clarence DeCamp named it in 1897when he discovered a mouse nest in a nook in the rock. The 54-ton boulder is balanced on two points of a ledge rock and a hidden wedge stone.

Turkey Swamp Park

Phone - (732) 462-7286
Website - http://www.monmouthcountyparks.com/parks/turkey.asp
Admission Fee - None
Directions - *Freehold, Monmouth County; from the New Jersey Turnpike take Exit 7A and head east on I-195. Take Exit 22.Turn left and go north on Jackson Mills Road. Turn left at the light for Georgia Road and continue to park/campground entrance on the left.*

The Park

The first human habitation of this land was by the Lenni Lenape, an Algonquian group of Indians who lived in loosely-knit family groups in the greater Delaware area. The tribecamped along the Metedeconk River and excavations are ongoing to learn more about their life here. Turkey Swamp Park is a combination woodland park and family campground. Don't come looking for turkeys - the park is named for the village of Turkey, now called Adelphia.

The Walks

There are two distinct options for canine hikers at Turkey Swamp. The *Old Lenape Trail* skips off through the pitch pine and blueberry bush landscape common in the northern reaches of the Pine Barrens. The sandy soil is easy on the paws - too easy in wet times as the trail turns swampy. In the other direction is the orange-blazed *Alder Trail* that circles a 17-acre man-made lake. The route links picnic areas and provides several access points to superb dog paddling, especially when the campground is closed. This is also an easy hike for your dog, alternating between open fields and light woods.

> **Where The Paw Meets The Earth:** Sandy dirt and grass
> **Workout For Your Dog** - Easily rolling terrain
> **Swimming** - In the lake when there are no fishermen, this is an excellent dog swimming pool
> **Restrictions On Dogs** - None

Something Extra

A feature of many Monmouth County parks not typically found elsewhere is a large grassy field. These roomy open spaces are not developed as ballfields, just grass. They are ideal for a big game of fetch.

Voorhees State Park

Phone - (908) 638-6969
Website - http://www.aclink.org/PARKS/mainpages/estell.asp
Admission Fee - None
Directions - *High Bridge, Hunterdon; from I-78 take Route 31 North. Turn right on Route 513 North. After passing through the town of High Bridge, the park entrance will be on the left.*

The Park
Former New Jersey governor Foster M. Voorhees donated his 325-acre Hill Acres estate to the state for a park in 1925. The honorable Governor Voorhees died in 1927 and in another decade he wouldn't recognize his old farm. Beginning in 1933 a Civilian Conservation Corps unit of 200 men set up camp in Voorhees State Park, cutting trails, building stone picnic shelters, carving roads and planting thousands of trees to create the park of 1,000 wooded acres.

The Walks
The trail system at Voorhees is built around seven out-and-back trails that can be cobbled together to form canine hiking loops such as the orange-blazed *Brookside Trail* and the green-blazed *Tanglewood Trail* around the main drive.with the *Blue Trail* to form a 5.3-mile loop. Two of the premier paths at Voorhees link the two main segments of the park: the blue-blazed *Hill Acres Trail* leads to a scenic view through a cut in the trees and the *Cross Park Trail*, the only footpath-only trail here, leads to the astronomical observatory.

> **Where The Paw Meets The Earth:** Mostly gravelly multi-use trails
> **Workout For Your Dog** - Moderate hills throughout
> **Swimming** - There is a pond here but this is not a swimming dog's park
> **Restrictions On Dogs** - No dogs in the campground

Something Extra
Never miss the chance to exceed your dreams. The New Jersey Astronomical Association was founded in 1965 by seven men looking to make 10-inch telescopes. Instead they would up with a domed observatory housing a 26-inch Newtonian reflector, one of the largest privately owned star-gazers in the state. The Edwin E. Aldrin Astronomical Center, named for the second man to walk on the moon from Montclair leases land in Voorhees State Park and offers regular skywatching programs on weekends.

Washington Crossing State Park

Phone - (609) 737-0623
Website - http://www.state.nj.us/dep/parksandforests/parks/ washcros.html
Admission Fee - None
Directions - *Titusville, Mercer County; from I-95, take Route 29 north. Parking is available along the Delaware River just past Route 546.*

The Park
These sleepy, tree-lined banks along the Delaware River became immortalized in American mythology on the icy night of December 25, 1776 when General George Washington led a demoralized Continental Army across the river to score a surprise victory over unsuspecting Hessian troops in Trenton. Land was eventually preserved on both the New Jersey and Pennsylvania sides of the river to commemorate one of the turning points in the battle for independence.

The Walks
There are dog-walking opportunities on both sides of the Delaware; the more historic explorations can be found on the Pennsylvania side, the more natural trails in New Jersey. Quiet paths meander through an historic village at the scene of the American disembarkment in Washington's Crossing Historic Park. On the New Jersey side, the terrain instantly becomes rolling and wooded beyond the Johnson Ferry House where the troops landed in what is now Washington Crossing State Park. The many miles of trails are carved through a mixed hardwood and spruce forest, often times plunging into and out of wide ravines. Washington Crossing State Park can also be used as a jumping off point for hikes up and down the towpath along the 70-mile Delaware and Raritan Canal.

> **Where The Paw Meets The Earth:** Mostly paw-friendly dirt with some crushed stone paths and a sandy dirt towpath
> **Workout For Your Dog** - Lots of dips and rolls in the woods
> **Swimming** - There is no good access to the Delaware River at this point
> **Restrictions On Dogs** - None

Something Extra
You and your dog can follow the route of Washington's troops by walking across the Delaware River on a steel bridge. The bridge affords long views of the river as well.

Washington Valley Park

Phone - None
Website - http://www.somersetcountyparks.org/activities/parks/washing_valley_pk.htm
Admission Fee - None
Directions - *Bridgewater Township, Somerset County; from I-78 take Exit 33 for Route 525, heading south. Go 3.1 miles to Washington Valley Road. Turn left and go to Vosseler Avenue and make a right on Miller Road to the park OR turn right on Washington Valley Road and make a quick left onto Newman's Lane to the parking area on left.*

The Park
The 705-acre park is located between the first and second Watchung Mountains at the geographic center of Somerset County. It consists of pine and hemlock forests, open freshwater wetland marshes, impressive rock outcroppings, numerous historic features and a 21-acre former Bound Brook Reservoir.

The Walks
Washington Valley Park offers two park areas. At Miller Road the canine hiking here is rugged - both on the hills and on the paws across rocky trails. With more than seven miles of trails in Washington Valley Park, it is best to leave this yellow-blazed trail system to the mountain bikers who frequent the park. Newman's Lane is the jumping off point for three different trail systems, two that run on either side of the picturesque Washington Valley Reservoir. Your dog can spend hours touring these pine and hemlock forests between the First and Second Watchung Mountains. Hopefully, you'll be able to get a trail map to decipher the trails in this spread-out park; if not there is a mapboard to study at Newman's Lane.

> **Where The Paw Meets The Earth:** Dirt trails and stony roads
> **Workout For Your Dog** - You bet, on many trails
> **Swimming** - None
> **Restrictions On Dogs** - None

Something Extra
The Miller Road parking lot leads to a Hawk Watch overlook that is one of the East Coast's premier locations to watch raptors migrate south each fall.

Watchung Reservation

Phone - (908) 789-3670
Website - http://www.unioncountynj.org/trailside/index.html
Admission Fee - None outside rec areas
Directions - *Mountainside, Union County; from I-78 East take Exit 44 (New Providence/Berkeley Heights). At the light turn left onto Glenside Avenue and go 1.2 miles. Turn right into the Reservation (Rt. 645). From I-78 West use Exit 43 (New Providence/Berkeley Heights). Turn right at the first light onto McMane Avenue. At the T-intersection, turn left onto Glenside Avenue to the park.*

The Park
The land was first settled in the 1730s and George Washington took advantage of this natural defensive barrier to twice winter his troops as the British occupied New York City. The Civilian Conservation Corps did work here during the Depression, including planting an impressive pine plantation, and in 1941 the first natural history museum in New Jersey opened on the 2,060-acre preserve. Today this well-developed park features a riding stable, picnic areas, playgrounds, large open play fields, a greenhouse, trailside museum, scout camp and planetarium. And you can bring your dog too.

The Walks
The beast of the Watchung Reservation trail system is the white-blazed *Sierra Trail* that circles the park for 10 miles, although there are ample opportunities to cut your canine hike short. Overlooks and scenic views are not on the hiking menu but there is a variety of attractions that are not ordinarily expected in such a developed area. Your dog will pass a cemetery from the 1700s, old mill ruins and several ponds and bubbling streams. The full route utilizes roomy bridle paths and footpaths and does involve several road crossings. There are also several short trail loops near the Trailside Center at the center of the park to sample.

> **Where The Paw Meets The Earth:** Mostly dirt
> **Workout For Your Dog** - The *Sierra Trail* is a match for the most energetic of dogs
> **Swimming** - Lake Surprise, a slender body of water in a depression between ridges isa great place for a dog to swim with its bare dirt banks
> **Restrictions On Dogs** - None

Something Extra
In 1845, Daniel Felt founded Feltville as a small company village for workers of his specialty paper business. He created his town in the Utopian image. In 1882 Feltville became a middle class resort called Glenside, and the cottages were remodeled like rustic Adirondack cabins. By 1916 the resort was in decline as automobiles carried city vacationers well beyond the Watchung Mountains. The "Deserted Village" stands today on the *Sierra Trail*.

Wawayanda State Park

Phone - (973) 853-4462
Website - http://www.state.nj.us/dep/parksandforests/parks/wawayanda.html
Admission Fee - Yes, in summer
Directions - *Hewitt, Sussex County; take Route 23 north to Union Valley Road and go about six miles to stop sign. From the stop sign, go to second traffic light. Turn left, travel to fork in road (about 2 miles) and go left about 1/2 mile to Warwick Turnpike. Turn left. The park entrance is four miles on the left.*

The Park

When the New Jersey Zinc Company was here they saw the miles of trees as fuel for timbering their mines. When Fred Ferber, an Austrian immigrant who helped pioneer the ballpoint pen, bought 6,800 acres of timberland from New Jersey Zinc he saw wilderness that needed to be preserved. Not as a public park. Ferber chased hunters from the land and railed against such facilities as toilets and campgrounds in the woods. When Ferber ran into financial reversals he was forced to sell portions of his land to the state over the years that would become exactly what he hated - Wawayanda State Park, a recreational mecca for boaters, fishermen, campers, picnicers, swimmers, hunters and, yes, hikers.

The Walks

Spread across 16,679 acres are more than 40 miles of trails, many on old logging roads that make for easy, although often active, canine hiking. There are three major destinations in the park:

Wawayanda Hemlock Ravine Natural Area. There is only one trail through this hemlock/hardwoods preserve, a stretch of the *Appalachian Trail* so you will need to retrace your steps on any explorations here.

Wawayanda Swamp Natural Area. This is the dominant central section of the park with Laurel Pond, a small glacial lake, a quick destination on an old gravel road.

Bearfort Mountain Natural Area. The most famous hike at Wawayanda State Park, the 4-mile loop to Terrace Pond, is here. Prepare your dog for very serious rock-hopping on this memorable journey.

> **Where The Paw Meets The Earth:** Natural surfaces
> **Workout For Your Dog** - Some of the most challenging hikes in New Jersey
> **Swimming** - Ghost Lake for canine aquatics
> **Restrictions On Dogs** - No dogs in the campground or swimming areas

Something Extra

Wawayanda Lake was dammed in 1846 to provide power for an iron furnace and mills. An entire town grew up on the lake shores. All that remains are foundations and the old 1846 charcoal blast furnace.

Wells Mills County Park

Phone - (609) 971-3085
Website - http://www.ocean.nj.us/parks/wellsmills.html
Admission Fee - None
Directions - *Wells Mills, Ocean County; the park is on Route 532, west of the Garden State Parkway.Northbound, take Exit 69 and make a left going west on Route 532. Southbound, use Exit 67 onto Route 554 West and continue to Route 72. Make a right and another right on Route 532 to the park entrance on the right.*

The Park

James Wells won the land that would become this county park at auction. Wells dammed Oyster Creek to build a sawmill to process the large stands of Atlantic white cedar found here. The Estlow family acquired the property in the late 1800s and built adjacent sawmills, hence the pluralistic park name. Possession of the land passed to the Conrads, a prominent local business family, in 1936. When the tax burden of the land became too onerous in the late 1970s the New Jersey Conservation Foundation took control, beginning the process that insured protection of this slice of Pine Barrens as a public park.

The Walks

The queen of Ocean County parks at over 900 acres, Wells Mills is also on the top of any list for canine hikers. The trails trip through a rich variety of habitat from cedar swamps to thick pine-oak woodlands. Most of the going is on paw-friendly sand or soft dirt covered in pine straw. But what truly sets Wells Mills apart from its Pine Barrens neighbors is elevation change. Nothing grueling but in the western part of the park the trails roll joyously up and down across small ridges and sandhills. The namesake mound of sand on the *Penns Hill Trail*, the longest of the park's routes at 8.4 miles, reaches 126 feet. That white-blazed trail circles the perimeter of the park; a simliar shorter route is the green-blazed Estlow Trail at 3.5 miles. Additional loops up to 1.3 miles can be hiked near the Nature Center. All told Wells Mills maintains more than 16 miles of trails.

> **Where The Paw Meets The Earth:** Paw-friendly sand and dirt
> **Workout For Your Dog** - Some long hikes possible
> **Swimming** - Spurs from the *Estlow Trail* reach out and tickle the shore
> of Wells Mills Lake for a doggie dip
> **Restrictions On Dogs** - No dogs in the campgrounds

Something Extra

The Wells Mills Nature Center is a standout among its kind with three stories and 1400 square feet of exhibit space. Climb up to the observation deck for a splendid view of the Pine Barrens and Wells Mills Lake.

Wenonah Woods

Phone - None
Website - None
Admission Fee - None
Directions - *Wenonah, Burlington County; the town is on Route 553. The trails are accessed from several points around town including Hayes Road at East Mantua Avenue; the west end of West Cedar Street; and the east end of Pine Street.*

The Park
Wenonah grew out of a resort community that was founded in 1872, carved from the surrounding Deptford area. It was later the location of a junior-high and high-school level military academy, until the late 1930s. Interconnected wooded trails loop around the southern half of the town from northwest to east.

The Walks
From the north, across from Wenonah Lake, the first trail is Break Back Run, winding along wooded stream valleys and ridges. Next is the *Clay Hill Trail* where the walking is level save for the namesake hill by a bend in the stream. The well-maintained *Glen Trail* connects the paths on both sides of the railroad. A brief side trail to Clinton Street leads to a tiny, stone fish pond, a quaint remnant of Wenonah's 19th century resort days. Continuing onto the *George Eldridge Trail*, the path features many streams and wooden bridges. Side trails lead to more hiking on the *Deptford/Sewell Trails* and the *Monongahela Brook Trail*, a half-mile loop that rolls along the south shore and drops to a flat creekside return trip. Some of the biggest trees in the Wenonah Woods can be found here. The last trail is *Covey's Lake Trail*, a 3/4-mile loop along the quiet tree-lined shore. The lake was once a center for leisurely recreation at the resort, sporting a boathouse and a teahouse.

> **Where The Paw Meets The Earth:** Dirt paths through town
> **Workout For Your Dog** - Mostly easy trotting
> **Swimming** - At the northern terminus of *Break Back Run Trail*, across N. Jefferson Avenue is Davidson's Lake, a super canine swimming hole; Comey's Lake is algae-encrusted but there is access to clear water near the wooden dock
> **Restrictions On Dogs** - None

Something Extra
An elaborate, reinforced wooden railroad trestle bridges a ravine on the *Glen Trail*. The trail runs by a stream under the trestle and there are sweeping views of Wenonah Woods from the top.

Westcott Nature Preserve

Phone - None
Website - http://www.state.nj.us/dep/parksandforests/parks/penn.html
Admission Fee - None
Directions - *Rosemont, Hunterdon County; take Route 29 North along the Delaware River to Route 519, past Stockton. In Rosemont make a left on Raven Rock-Rosemont Road to the park.*

The Park

Wescott Nature Preserve was donated to Hunterdon County by Mr. and Mrs. Lloyd Wescott in 1966. This denotation created the first county park and predates the County Parks Department which was established in 1973. The 80 acre park is bisected by the Lockatong Creek. The Lenni Lenape Indians had settlements in this area and took pride in the dense stones, called Argillite, which can be found in the streambed. The Lenape would strike these stones at acute angles against other stones to fashion tools and weapons.

The Walks

While less than a mile long there is plenty for your dog to experience on this loop that makes it a worthy detour when traveling along the Delaware River. This easy canine hike begins and ends in an open meadow that abuts a diverse woodland of red maple, oak, ash - and hemlock. Along the lively Lockatong Creek, in terrain too difficult for loggers to negotiate, grows a magnificent stand of hemlock. Although the trail works atop the creek there is an opportunity for your dog to climb down and enjoy the spa-like rapids.

> **Where The Paw Meets The Earth:** Dirt and grass
> **Workout For Your Dog** - Not much roll to this streamside property
> **Swimming** - Only the smallest of dogs will find Lockatong Creek more than a refreshing diversion
> **Restrictions On Dogs** - None

Something Extra

A small building stands on the property. Constructed in 1861, it served as the John Reading School or District Schoolhouse #97. Historically, a school was located on this site since 1796. Today, the building currently serves as a private residence.

Wharton State Forest

Phone - (609) 561-0024
Website - http://www.state.nj.us/dep/parksandforests/parks/wharton.html
Admission Fee - Yes, weekends at Batsto
Directions - *Hammonton, Burlington County; at Batsto Village on Route 542, eight miles east of Hammonton, and at Atsion Recreation Area on Route 206, eight miles north of Hammonton.*

The Park

The area's bog ore once supported a booming iron industry which supplied much of the weaponry for the American Revolution. Many of the indecipherable sand roads through the Pine Barrens date to that time. When the foundries followed the discovery of America's massive upper midwestern iron ranges in the mid-1800s, the area's economy became so depressed that Philadelphia financier Joseph Wharton was able to acquire over 100,000 acres of land here. That land now makes up the state forest - the largest single tract of land in the New Jersey state park system.

The Walks

The main hiking trail through Wharton State Forest is the *Batona Trail* but for dogs who feel cramped by the rigidness of a narrow 50-mile band there are more than 500 miles of unpaved sand roads in Wharton State Forest. If that is too much choice, bring your dog to Batsto Village. Thirty-three wooden structures have been restored to this bog iron and glassmaking industrial center which flourished from 1766 to 1867. There is a self-guided one-mile nature walk around the lake at Batsto Village, that includes stops at the Batsto Mansion and an operating gristmill and sawmill.

> **Where The Paw Meets The Earth:** Soft sand on the trails and packed sand on the roads
> **Workout For Your Dog** - Very long canine hikes possible
> **Swimming** - The slow-moving Batsto River is stained the color of tea by cedar sap, adding to the region's mystique; it makes an excellent canine swimming pool - or a wonderful water trail in a canoe
> **Restrictions On Dogs** - None

Something Extra

The chance to see New Jersey's version of Bigfoot, the legendary winged creature known as the "Jersey Devil." The Jersey Devil is a creature with the head of a horse supported by a four-foot serpentine body with large wings and claws. He lives in the Pine Barrens and perhaps your dog can sniff one out.

Worthington State Forest

Phone - (908) 841-9575
Website - http://www.state.nj.us/dep/parksandforests/parks/worthington.html
Admission Fee - None
Directions - *Millbrook, Warren County; take I-80 West to the last exit in New Jersey (Millbrook/Flatbrookville), getting in the right lane as the higway bends right. At the bottom of the ramp, turn right onto Old Mine Road. The park office is three miles on the left.*

The Park
In 1903, Charles C. Worthington, President of the Worthington Pump Company, laid plans for his own transportation system. He would build a pipeline to bring water down from Sunfish Pond at the top of Kittatinny Ridge to his farm on Shawnee Island. Worthington owned more than 8,000 acres of land around the mountain that the State of New Jersey acquired the first parcels of land that would become the 6,000-acre Worthington State Forest.

The Walks
Trailheads for a potpouri of 26 miles of canine hiking spring up along Old Mine Road. The first you come to is the *Karanac Trail*, an easy canine hike to the sandy shores of the Delaware River. Next come a series of trails that lead to the top of the mountain starting with the *Douglas Trail* that climbs 980 feet to Sunfish Pond in two miles. The blue-blazed path is named for Supreme Court Justice William O. Douglas who participated in a protest hike in 1967 over management practices proposed for the glacial pond. Another hike to the *Appalachian Trail* at the top of the mountain is the *Coppermines Trail* that passes two ancient open-faced mines before meandering up the slopes. Once on top a 5-mile loop to Rattlesnake Swamp is possible - be careful as you cross to the eastern edge of the ridge as your dog will be walking on exposed cliff faces. Farther up the road you reach Van Campens Glen and an out-and-back trail leading to a sparkling waterfall in about 30 minutes. Finally at the end of Old Mine Road you reach the preserved Millbrook Village where your dog can trot down an old logging road.

> **Where The Paw Meets The Earth:** Soft dirt to rocky dirt
> **Workout For Your Dog** - Oh yes
> **Swimming** - The ponds on the ridge and the river below
> **Restrictions On Dogs** - No dogs in Watergate Recreation Area

Something Extra
Worthington fenced in his property with an eleven-mile fence and imported whitetail deer from Virginia to replace deer that had become extinct in New Jersey. When he tore down the fence, the roaming deer became the ancestors of deer herds across the state.

PENNSYLVANIA

Andorra Natural Area/Fairmount Park

Phone - (215) 685-9285
Website - http://www.fairmountpark.org/WissahickonEC.asp
Admission Fee - None
Directions - *Philadelphia; at the boundary of the city with Montgomery County on Northwestern Avenue between Ridge Avenue and Germantown Avenue (Route 422).*

The Park
America's first public park began with 5 acres in 1812. Today, Fairmount Park is the largest contiguous landscaped municipal park in the world with nearly 9,000 acres. It is the bucolic home to an estimated 2,500,000 trees.The Andorra Natural Area evolved from a 19th century private nursery into the East coast's largest after World War II. Ownership of the property dates to 1840 when Richard Wistar named it "Andorra" from a Moorish word meaning "hills covered with trees."

The Walks
The main trail at Andorra is a 20-station Nature Hike. There are also a dozen other named trails that branch off this loop. The *Forbidden Drive* begins its 7-mile journey along the Wissahickon Creek to the Schuylkill River here. So named when it was closed to automobiles in the 1920s, your outing on the *Forbidden Drive* can be shortened by several bridges across the Wissahickon. A natural dirt trail rolls along the opposite bank to create hiking loops. The best canine hiking comes on these dirt trails when you leave the paved Forbidden Drive and climb out of the gorge. These narrow ribbons of dirt crossing the hillsides are a dog's delight time and again.

> **Where The Paw Meets The Earth:** Dirt and macadam
> **Workout For Your Dog** - Yes, on the slopes of the gorge
> **Swimming** - The Wissahickon is deep enough for great dog swims
> **Restrictions On Dogs** - None

Something Extra
In 1855, a hotel entrepreneur built a new inn on Rex Avenue. To draw attention to his hostelry he constructed an Indian from old barn boards and propped it up on top of a rock overlooking the Gorge. In 1902, when the Indian Rock Hotel was long gone but with the silhouette still there, artist Massey Rhind was commissioned to make a representation of a "Delaware Indian, looking west to where his people have gone." The kneeling warrior has gazed up the Wissahickon Gorge ever since. A switchback trail leads to the Indian Statue where you can get close enough to pat his knee.

Anson B. Nixon Park

Phone - (610) 388-1303
Website - http://dsf.chesco.org/ccparks/cwp/view.
asp?A=1550&Q=616010
Admission Fee - None
Directions - *Kennett Square, Chester County; from Route 1, exit onto State Street and make a right at the bottom of Miller's Hill (the first one heading into town) onto N. Walnut Street. Make a left into the park at the fork 1/4 mile ahead. You can also access the park by taking Route 82 South from Route 1 and make your first left onto Leslie Road, past the Saint Patrick Cemetery. A small parking lot is by the ballfield at the end of the lane.*

The Park
The land here, featuring a 22-foot drop in the East Branch of the Red Clay Creek, was bought in 1795 by William Chambers to build a mill. He was looking to clean wool. Chambers named his property and fine mansion "Bloom-field," in honor of Brigadier General Bloomfield who drilled 3000 troops on his brother's adjoining property in preparation for the War of 1812. The first organized school in the borough was conducted in a grove of trees here in 1830, a quarter-century before Kennett Square was incorporated. The property remained in the Chambers family for more than a century. The mansion burned and the 82-acre park was established in 1982.

The Walks
The park is essentially carved into three main segments, each featuring a walking loop. The *Beechwood Trail* in the Beech Woods slips between rare umbrella magnolias and tupelos dressed in gnarly trunks deformed from a bacterial infection. Also here is the signature Kennett Beech which stood when William Penn came from England to claim his land grant more than 300 years ago. The *Otherplace Trail*, named for the home of Cyrus Chambers, penetrates the Pine Woods on the eastern side of the park. Informal spur trails also run through Nixon Park.

> **Where The Paw Meets The Earth:** Sandy dirt roads and gravelly paths
> **Workout For Your Dog** - Easy going on dips and rolls
> **Swimming** - The Red Clay Creek is not deep enough for anything beyond splashing; ponds are set below the level of the trails, providing tricky access
> **Restrictions On Dogs** - None

Something Extra
A small remnant of the forests that blanketed southeastern Pennsylvania at the time of 17th century European settlement remain in the park. It retains the species diversity of the original woodland, with a mix of native trees rarely found in this area. The area's biodiversity is described on interpretive signs along the trails.

Apollo County Park

Phone - (717) 840-7440
Website - http://ycwebserver.york-county.org/Parks/Apollo.htm
Admission Fee - None
Directions - *Brogue, York County; southeast of York on the Susquehanna River, just upstream from Safe Harbor Dam. Take Route 74 South through Red Lion and make a left on Burkholder Road after town. Continue on Burkholder when it becomes Route 425 in New Bridgeville. Continue east for 3.5 miles and turn left on Boyd Road. Go to bottom of the hill and a Y-intersection with two gravel roads. Bear left to end of Boyd and the small parking lot.*

The Park
Paper manufacturer P.H. Glatfelter donated 149 acres for this park in 1969 that was christened "Apollo" for the moon landing on July 20 of that year. The park is quite possibly the first public facility named to honor the men who walked on the moon. The park remains undeveloped. In 2001, when a parking lot was first built, county officials estimated visitation at three people per day. The tiny lot scarcely accommodates three cars so it is unlikely that visitation has exploded since the building of the lot.

The Walks
Apollo County Park is a lesson in not judging a trail by the parking lot. The sliver of dirt leading up a hill through a small opening in the trees holds little promise but soon the woods open up to reveal a thick carpet of ferns as you reach the trail loop that begins at the junction with the Mason-Dixon Trail. It is best to enter the loop going downhill in a clockwise direction. At the bottom you make the first of two stream crossings of Wilson Run and soon you reach the second and begin the prettiest stretch of trail in York County as tumbling water rushes all about you in a hemlock-filled ravine. To complete the loop on this *#1 Trail*, a scramble up a rock-filled stream cut is required. There is additional canine hiking available on the Mason-Dixon Trail as it leaves county land. To the west, it is a short distance to the end of the ravine (much of it rock-hopping on often slippery boulders) and to the east it is about one mile to Boyds Run below the Safe Harbor Land. The trail runs atop a high river bluff in this direction.

> **Where The Paw Meets The Earth:** Dirt studded with rocks
> **Workout For Your Dog** - Sporty canine hiking here
> **Swimming** - Wilson Run is quick and shallow
> **Restrictions On Dogs** - None

Something Extra
The steep walls of the Wilson Run ravine house some of the most dramatic fallen trees you can see anywhere. Logs scattered on the slopes and massive trunks crashed across the stream when bases erode.

Awbury Arboretum

Phone - (215) 849-2855
Website - http://www.awbury.org/
Admission Fee - None
Directions - *East Germantown, Philadelphia County; on Washington Lane between Chew Avenue and Ardleigh Street.*

The Park
Awbury was originally the summer home of the Cope family. Henry Cope, a Quaker shipping merchant, purchased Awbury in 1852 and named the estate after the village, Avebury, England, from which his family originally emigrated. Awbury soon became a year-round home for members of the extended Cope family. Various Victorian and Colonial Revival houses were built between 1860 and the 1920s, forming a unique cultural landscape. Except for the Francis Cope House (1860) which is now the Arboretum headquarters, all of the houses are now privately owned. Awbury's grounds were laid out in the 19th century in the English landscape garden tradition with the advice of the celebrated horticulturalist William Saunders, designer of the National Cemetery at the Gettysburg Battlefield and of the Capitol grounds in Washington, D.C. Long vistas are framed by clusters of trees and shrubs which are interwoven with open space creating stunning visual contrasts. Concern for the preservation of this piece of open space led to the establishment of the Arboretum in 1916 by members of the Cope family. In 1984, the Awbury Arboretum Association was established as a non-profit organization.

The Walks
Across the 55 acres are plantings of groves and clusters of trees set amidst large swaths of grass fields in the English landscape garden tradition. You can investigate more than 200 species, mostly native, in your informal explorations of the grounds. Old macadam paths lead to most areas of the odd-shaped property. Also on the grounds are wetlands surrounding an artificial pond.

> **Where The Paw Meets The Earth:** Grass and macadam
> **Workout For Your Dog** - Awbury will not tire out your dog
> **Swimming** - None
> **Restrictions On Dogs** - None

Something Extra
Preeminent American author John Updike has included Awbury Arboretum in one of his novels, *Terrorist*.

Beltzville State Park

Phone - (610) 377-0045
Website - http://www.dcnr.state.pa.us/stateparks/parks/beltz-ville.aspx
Admission Fee - None
Directions - *Lehighton, Carbon County; five miles east, just off of US 209. From the Northeast Extension of the Pennsylvania Turnpike, take Exit 74 and follow the signs to the park.*

The Park

The 2,972-acre Beltzville State Park is developed around the U.S. Army Corps of Engineers flood control project, Beltzville Dam. Beltzville Lake is 949 acres with a shoreline of 19.8 miles. The park is along the Pohopoco Creek with recreation areas around the lake. The park officially opened in 1972.

The Walks

There are four areas to get your dog on the trail at Beltzville. For longer outings head for the south shore and Preachers Camp where long linear trails leave from both sides. Behind the dam on the west end are two short, stacked loops and there are short trails in the recreation area. But the prime spot to experience Beltzville is from the lot at the Wildcreek Trailhead. The trail pushes out on a wide woods road before fracturing into three segments. The picturesque *Falls Trail* drops off to the left and then you can continue onto the two-mile *Cove Ridge Trail* loop. If your dog hasn't gotten enough of the mature hemlocks and mixed hardwoods you can tie into the *Christman Trail* and finish a complete two-hour tour of the peninsula around Wild Creek Cove.

> **Where The Paw Meets The Earth:** Natural surface trails
> **Workout For Your Dog** - Rolling hills around the lake
> **Swimming** - Plenty of opportunity to get your dog in Beltzville Lake from the trail or boat ramps
> **Restrictions On Dogs** - No dogs in the swimming areas

Something Extra

At the suggestion of local residents, the original covered bridge, built across Pohopoco Creek in 1841 by local craftsman Jacob Buck, has been relocated between the picnic areas and the beach for public use and enjoyment. This bridge was first used by horse and buggy traffic and later by one-lane car traffic. It is now for pedestrian use only.

Big Pocono State Park

Phone - None
Website - http://www.dcnr.state.pa.us/stateparks/parks/bigpo-cono.aspx
Admission Fee - None
Directions - *Tannersville, Monroe County; the entrance to the park is from PA 715 and Exit 299 of I-80 at Tannersville. Turn left into the Camelback Ski Area and follow the road to the top of the mountain. The park is closed from just after deer hunting season in mid-December until mid-March.*

The Park
Big Pocono State Park is on land which was owned by Henry S. Cattell near the turn of the 20th century. In 1928, 12 years after Mr. Cattells death, the Pennsylvania Game Commission purchased the area. In 1950, a portion of the state land on the steep north slope of the mountain was leased to Big Pocono Skiing, Inc., for commercial ski development. Later named Camelback Ski Corporation, the facility has been developed into a major ski resort. In 1954, after the construction of restrooms, parking areas, picnic sites, fireplaces and a scenic drive around the summit, the area was opened to the public as Big Pocono State Park.

The Walks
You have a choice of three wooded loops atop Camelback Mountain. The toughest is to drop down the mountainside on the wide, rocky *North Trail* (red blazes) and climb back up on the more reasonably graded *South Trail* (yellow blazes). The entire loop will cover about three miles and 90 minutes.The *South Trail* can also be hike completely around the summit using the paved entrance road to close the loop. Inside the *North-South Loop* is the 1.3-mile *Indian Trail* loop that also drops off the summit but not as severely.

> **Where The Paw Meets The Earth:** Rocky fire roads, asphalt and dirt
> **Workout For Your Dog** - Yes, a great workout for your dog
> **Swimming** - None
> **Restrictions On Dogs** - None

Something Extra
Henry Cattell constructed a stone cabin on the summit of Camelback Mountain in 1908 and, knowing that many others shared his love for the area, left it unlocked for many years to be used as a shelter by anyone who wished. The Cattell Cabin served for many years as a park office and nature museum.

Black Rock Sanctuary

Phone - None
Website - http://dsf.chesco.org/ccparks/cwp/view.asp?a=1550&q=616465
Admission Fee - None
Directions - *Phoenixville, Chester County; northeast of town on Route 113.*

The Park
Black Rock Sanctuary is dedicated to wildlife habitat and public use. It consists of 119 acres of wetlands, woodlands and meadows. One of many desilting basins found along the Schuylkill River in Berks, Montgomery, Chester and Philadelphia Counties, Black Rock Sanctuary offers a wonderful opportunity to relax and discover the history, geology, wildlife, plant life and habitats of the basin.

The Walks
Occupying 133 acres on a thumb of land where the Schuylkill River bends back on itself, the Black Rock Preserve has recently been developed. Molded hillsides and rocky waterfalls have been sculpted around an impoundment marsh. The red-stone trail of nearly one mile connects interpretive kiosks scattered about the wetlands. Down by the Schuylkill River an unmarked linear dirt trail hugs the river for nearly a mile and continues for another mile outside the preserve below Black Rock Dam, a stone-filled timber crib structure 11 feet high and 370 feet long. There is excellent access to the river from this flat trail (stay clear of the dam) for a canine aquatic workout.

> **Where The Paw Meets The Earth:** Crushed stone in the preserve and dirt along the river to the Pennsylvania Fish & Boat Commission boat ramp
> **Workout For Your Dog** - Easy going
> **Swimming** - Yes, in the Schuylkill River
> **Restrictions On Dogs** - None

Something Extra
The observation deck at the "Bird" Station has been crafted out of sticks to actually resemble a giant bird nest.

Blue Marsh Lake Recreation Area

Phone - (610) 376-6337
Website - http://www.nap.usace.army.mil/sb/bm_guide.htm
Admission Fee - Yes
Directions - *Leesport, Berks County; northwest of Reading on Route 183 between Route 222 and I-78.*

The Park
In 1955, waters along the Delaware River and its tributaries poured over their banks and caused over $100 million in property damage, taking 90 lives. Blue Marsh Lake was the result of a federal initiative by the United States Army Corps on Engineers to bring that type of devastating flooding under control. An earthen dam was erected across Tulpehocken Creek, blocking its flow to the Schuylkill River. The resulting reservoir, developed in the 1970s, is designed to hold up to 11 billion gallons of water above normal wintertime depths. But most of the people who come to Blue Marsh Lake for recreation don't much think about that anymore.

The Walks
The *Blue Marsh Lake Trail* actually circles the lake in a 30-mile journey, designed for bicycles and equestrians. The best place for canine hikers to sample the lake views from this path is at Old Dry Road Farm, a national historic site operated by the Army Corps as a living history museum (on Highland Road off Brownsville Road, park at the first gate past the farm and walk the road or further along in the State Game Lands parking area at the second gate). Use Highland Road as a spine for exploring this area and follow it to the lake and the multi-use trail. This is one of the best country lane/rolling farmland walks with your dog in the area. Hiking-only trails at Blue Marsh Lake are located on opposite sides of the lake. The *Squirrel Run Nature Trail* loops around a small stream valley heading into the lake. The *Great Oak Nature Trail* at the Day Brooks Day Use Area dips and climbs to a wildlife viewing area and vistas of the lake. Both are secluded forested hikes of about one mile. Also at Day Brooks is the *Foxtrot Hiking Loop*, a lakeside amble that visits woodlands and farm fields.

> **Where The Paw Meets The Earth:** Natural surface trails for foot traffic
>
> **Workout For Your Dog** - Long, rolling canine hikes
>
> **Swimming** - High banks but the water's great when there is access
>
> **Restrictions On Dogs** - No dogs in the swimming area

Something Extra
A permanent orienteering course has been developed in the Dry Brooks Day Use Area to introduce trail users to the art of map and compass. Try it and you can challenge your dog's nose in a wayfinding contest.

Boyd Big Tree Preserve Conservation Area

Phone - (717) 567-9255
Website - http://www.dcnr.state.pa.us/stateparks/parks/boyd-bigtree.aspx
Admission Fee - None
Directions - *Fishing Creek, Dauphin County; north of Harrisburg. From Route 322, take the Fishing Creek Exit, turning on to Fishing Creek Valley Road. The park entrance is in an open field about 2.5 miles on the right.*

The Park

This swatch of about 1000 acres on Blue Mountain became one of Pennsylvania's newest state parks when Alexander Boyd, president of the Union Deposit Corporation, donated the land for the perpetual management and protection of big trees. For this act Boyd received a Conservation Landowner of the Year award.

The Walks

Once you leave the parking lot every step your dog takes here will be under a canopy of leaves. Most of those steps will be moving uphill or downhill. For those chasing an easy exploration of the large trees on the mountainside choose the *Lower Spring Trail* upon entering the woods. The toughest haul in the park is up the *Janie Trail* where the 2.5-mile footpath reaches the ridge of Blue Mountain. Up on the ridge are superior views of the annual hawk migration on the thermals swirling along the mountain. There are over 10 miles of trail in the Conservation Area but most, unfortunately, are rocky, old access roads that can be tough on your dog's paws on a long hike. In contrast to its nearby cousin, the Ibberson Conservation Area, these trails are rougher, longer and steeper. Also, about 800 of the park's acres are open to hunting so in-season it will be nearly impossible to take a canine hike of any duration without crossing into active hunting grounds.

> **Where The Paw Meets The Earth:** Dirt trails and rocky roads
> **Workout For Your Dog** - Long, tough climbs
> **Swimming** - A pond is on the *Pond Trail* straight out of the parking lot
> **Restrictions On Dogs** - None

Something Extra

At Boyd Big Tree park a small chestnut grove is planted by the parking lot where conservationists practice a technique known as backcross breeding. After an initial cross with an American Chestnut and a Chinese Chestnut - that is resistant to the blight - all subsequent generations are crossed only with American Chestnuts. The blight-resistant gene is carried forward as the young trees become closer and closer to the original prince of the American forest.

Capital Area Greenbelt

Phone - (717) 921-4733
Website - http://www.caga.org/
Admission Fee - None
Directions - *Harrisburg, Dauphin County; from York,
a linear park connecting and passing through Riverfront Park,
Cameron Parkway, Paxtang Park, Paxtang Parkway, Reservoir
Park, the grounds of the State Hospital, Harrisburg Area
Community College, and Wildwood Lake.*

The Park
Unique among Pennsylvania cities, Harrisburg's 20-mile Capital
Area Greenbelt was a century in the making. After a European tour
in 1900, naturalist Mira Lloyd Dock returned to Harrisburg with a
vision of an "emerald necklace" of parks and pathways to energize
the increasingly polluted city. An impassioned speech by Dock to the
Harrisburg Board of Trade led to a commitment to greenspace that
increased city park acreage from 46 in 1902 to 958 in 1915. Dock
lived into her 90s but her death in 1945 and suburban flight cost the
Greenbelt its leading voice and necessary tax funds. It would take
another half-century and a national revival in linear urban parks
to revive the Greenbelt. The park is maintained through a blend of
private activism and governmental action.

The Walks
Canine hiking on the Greenbelt is on paved or hard gravel surfaces.
The route travels along the Susquehanna River, industrial areas and
under shaded lanes at times. Most canine hikers new to Harrisburg
will want to try the stretch along the river - much of this land has
been recycled on layers of iron slag from local iron furnaces.
> **Where The Paw Meets The Earth:** Pavement or packed
> gravel
> **Workout For Your Dog** - Only if a long canine hike is
> involved
> **Swimming** - There is an occasional chance to slip into the
> water but that is not a feature of the Greenbelt
> **Restrictions On Dogs** - None

Something Extra
Off PA 441, west of the East Mall and the county prison, is the Five
Senses Garden, with plantings designed to stimulate your smell, taste,
touch, sight and sound (listen to the gurgling Spring Creek).

Central Park

Phone - (717) 299-8215
Website - http://co.lancaster.pa.us/parks/cwp/view.asp?a=676&q=518262&parksNav=|7871|
Admission Fee - None
Directions - *Lancaster City; south of center city. Take Duke Street south until Chesapeake Street. Turn right and enter the park on the left in 300 yards.*

The Park
People have been traveling through this land for centuries - the Great Indian Warrior Trading Path, the most heavily used in colonial America, passed through here. And Robert Fulton, inventor of the steamship, first practiced with a paddlewheel boat on the Conestoga River here. Much of the heart of today's park was once owned by Edward Hand, George Washington's Adjutant General. The first land to transfer to public use came in 1903 as a gift from businessman and philanthropist Henry S. Williamson to the City of Lancaster. He had earlier supplied the money for Franklin & Marshall's first athletic field. Central Park became Lancaster County's first park in 1966 with a purchase of 397 acres. Today the county showplace contains 544 acres of diverse activities.

The Walks
There is plenty of canine hiking for any taste on Central Park's nine miles of trails, including three miles of the Lancaster Hiking Club's *Conestoga Trail System*. Your first choice could be the 1.4-mile *Mill Creek Trail* through a natural area dominated by mature oak and beech trees. The going is easy on the paw-friendly natural trail (muddy when wet) that loops inside an oxbow of Mill Creek. To form circuit hikes you will need to combine the short spurs of the remaining named trails. The *CVA Trail* begins with a pull up a short hill to the dramatic Indian Rock before dropping to the banks of the Conestoga River and a level waterside ramble. For the most challenging canine hiking in Central Park, save some time for the *Conestoga Trail* as it rolls up and down the park's hills.

> **Where The Paw Meets The Earth:** Natural surface and some asphalt
>
> **Workout For Your Dog** - Moderate hills through the park
>
> **Swimming** - The Conestoga River and Mill Creek each provide the opportunity for canine aqautics
>
> **Restrictions On Dogs** - None

Something Extra
Central Park's covered bridge was originally built across the Conestoga Creek near Hinkletown in 1876. The wooden structure was nearly destroyed by Hurricane Agnes in 1972 and was rebuilt across Mill Creek.

Central Perkiomen Valley Park

Phone - (610) 287-6970
Website - http://www.montcopa.org/parks/cpvp.htm
Admission Fee - None
Directions - *Perkiomenville, Montgomery County; on Plank Road between Gravel Road (Route 29) and Skippack Pike (Route 73).*

The Park
Central Perkiomen Valley Park headquarters on Plank Road is situated along the scenic Perkiomen Creek in the center of Montgomery County. This 800- acre park extends over 10 municipalities.

The Walks
Central Perkiomen Valley Park consists of 30 parcels of woodlands, open grass and wetlands hopscotching from Collegeville to Perkiomenville. There are two walks at the55-acre park headquarters on Plank Road. A pedestrian trail snakes along the Perkiomen Creek, although there are not many water views once you leave the bridge area. An old Reading Railroad right-of-way has been converted into a trail along Plank Road. Both are very rocky under paw. The Perkiomen Creek is wide but shallow and a superb canine swimming hole. Central Perkiomen Valley park is also a jumping off point for the *Perkiomen Trail* that winds for 19 miles along the Perkiomen Creek.

> **Where The Paw Meets The Earth:** Rock encrusted dirt; the Perkiomen trail is paved asphalt
> **Workout For Your Dog** - Easy rambling around the park
> **Swimming** - Yes, in the Perkiomen Creek
> **Restrictions On Dogs** - None

Something Extra
The Old Mill House in the park dates to 1901 and is availble for rental for parties.

Chickies Rock County Park

Phone - (717) 299-8215
Website - http://www.co.lancaster.pa.us/parks/cwp/view.asp?a= 676&q=518276&parksNav=%7C7871%7C
Admission Fee - None
Directions - *Columbia, Lancaster County; north of town and Route 30. Take the Columbia/Route 441 Exit off Route 30 and head north. Heading uphill on the left will be the Breezy View Day-Use Area. The small parking lots (both sides of the road) for the Chickies Rock Overlook are at the crest of the hill.*

The Park
American Indians called this bend in the Susquehanna River turns "Chiquesalunga" - the "place of the crayfish." When settlers moved in, the crustaceans were forgotten and the area became an industrial and transportation center. The county began acquiring land for its second largest park in 1977. Its 422 acres are managed to preserve the area's natural resources, the most notable being the gigantic outcropping of quartzite rock that towers 200 feet over the river.

The Walks
The best canine hiking at Chickies Rock is at Breezy View Day-Use Area that travels through a reclaimed woodland and natural meadow that flows down Chickies Hill to the river, known as Kerbaugh Lake, a filled-in body of water. First timers will have to try the *Chickies Rock Overlook Trail* for the river views but this stony pathway holds no thrills for dogs. Skip the Clayton B. *Shenk Hiking Trail* on the east side of the road altogether - it is steep, narrow and scarcely discernible in most places.

> **Where The Paw Meets The Earth:** Stony road and rocky dirt trails
> **Workout For Your Dog** - Short, steep walks
> **Swimming** - None
> **Restrictions On Dogs** - None

Something Extra
Henry Haldeman operated a successful sawmill at Chickies Rock in the early 1800s. In 1845, to take advantage of the iron ore mined in open pits in the area, he built the first Chickies Furnace to refine iron on the same site. Before the end of the century seven blast furnaces and rolling mills would support a vibrant community. Remnants of this industrial heritage can still be seen in the quiet park today.

Codorus State Park

Phone - (717) 637-2816
Website - http://www.dcnr.state.pa.us/stateparks/parks/codorus.aspx
Admission Fee - None
Directions - *Hanover, York County; southeast of town. From I-83, take Exit 18 and stay on PA 216 all the way to the park.*

The Park
In a pioneering cooperative project between the Commonwealth of Pennsylvania and the P.H. Glatfelter Paper Company the Codorus Creek was impounded in 1966. The paper company paid $5.5 million to construct an earth fill dam 109 feet high, 750 feet thick and a third of a mile wide. The resulting lake that became the heart of the state park was named Lake Marburg for the small community that was covered by the trapped waters.

The Walks
The marquee Codorus hiking trail, the *Mary Ann Furnace Trail*, is tucked away in the western edge of the park. The Mary Ann Furnace that operated here (a common name for Colonial iron furnaces) was founded in 1761 by George Ross, a Lancaster attorney who would later ink his name on the Declaration of Independence, and Mark Bird. It was the first iron forge built west of the Susquehanna River, fueled by the abundance of chestnut trees in the area. The route is a trio of stacked loops that total about 3.5 miles. The wide walking paths meander along the water between Black Rock Flats and Wonder Cove - dropping down to the shore several times for superb canine swimming. The trails are shady throughout. A second hiking trail - the *LaHo Trail* - slips around a finger of the lake called Wildasin Flats for 1.5 miles. The path hugs the waterline and also affords excellent swimming opportunities for your dog. If you don't mind sharing trails you can also sample the seven miles of bridle trails on the western shore of Lake Marburg and the mountain biking trail system that is open on Sundays only during hunting season.

> **Where The Paw Meets The Earth:** Paw-friendly dirt and grass mostly
> **Workout For Your Dog** - Easy ups and downs
> **Swimming** - Just try to get your water-loving dog out of the park's lakes
> **Restrictions On Dogs** - None

Something Extra
Pennsylvania state parks are slowly warming to the idea of dogs in their campgrounds. A few parks set aside a few sites for pets as a trial and it has been well enough received that more campgrounds are opening to pets. In Codurus State Park about a dozen dog sites are available and several dog walking areas have been designated.

Conewago Recreational Trail/Lebanon Valley Rail Trail

Phone - (717) 299-8215
Website - http://co.lancaster.pa.us/parks/cwp/view.asp?a=676&
q=518283&parksNav=|7871|
Admission Fee - None
Directions - *Elizabethtown, Lancaster County; the trailhead is one
mile northwest of town along Route 230.*

The Park
First came the ore deposits - there are 82 different minerals in the
hills around Cornwall. Then came the furnace to smelt the ore into
iron. The first was built in 1742. Then came the rail lines to move
the ore from the mines to the furnace. There would be three - the
last built in 1883 by Robert H. Coleman to compete with the Cornwall Railroad operated by other members of his prominent family.
Coleman's Cornwall & Lebanon Railroad tracks often ran alongside
his competitors' and it was not unusual to see trains racing each
other to provide superior service. Automobiles gradually ate away at
the train business until Hurricane Agnes ripped up enough track in
1972 to close the Cornwall & Lebanon forever. The historic line was
preserved by the county of Lancaster in 1979.

The Walks
The 5.5-mile *Conewago Recreation Trail* is one of the best of the rail-
to-trail family of abandoned railroads, exuding a peaceful country
feel. You will slip under a tunnel of trees, past producing farms and
massive boulder fields. The meandering Conewago Creek is never
far away. The *Lebanon Valley Rail-Trail* extended down to its ninth
mile - including the 1000th mile of old Pennsylvania railroad track
coverted to footpath - and connected with the Conewago trail in 2002
to create extended canine hiking in this area.

>**Where The Paw Meets The Earth:** Mostly cinder paths
>**Workout For Your Dog** - Easy canine hiking
>**Swimming** - Conewago Creek can be accessed in several
>places and the waters can get frisky at time
>**Restrictions On Dogs** - None

Something Extra
Robert Coleman built a sylvan retreat called Mt. Gretna.Thanks to
the Cornwall & Lebanon's connection to the Reading and Pennsylvania railroad lines, his outdoor camp was accessible to vacationers
across the country. President Benjamin Harrison passed some time
here. Coleman created an early amusement park with a primitive
switch-back rollercoaster, a dancing pavilion, a fancy carousel and
other attractions. Today, Mt. Gretna is still a quiet retreat for those
looking for an escape.

Core Creek Park

Phone - (215) 757-0571
Website - http://www.buckscounty.org/government/depart-ments/ParksandRec/Parks/CoreCreek.aspx
Admission Fee - None
Directions - *Langhorne, Bucks County; east of Route 413 off Tollgate Road or Bridgeton Pike.*

The Park
Core Creek is a busy recreational park developed on more than 1000 acres around Lake Luxemborg.

The Walks
Between breaks in the activity on the athletic fields and playgrounds there are patches of woods crossed by narrow dirt trails and wider bridle paths. A paved bicycle path is also available for dog walking. Lake Luxemborg is one of the best places in Bucks County to take the dog for a swim.

> **Where The Paw Meets The Earth:** Dirt and asphalt
> **Workout For Your Dog** - Long canine hikes are possible across the gently rolling hills
> **Swimming** - Yes
> **Restrictions On Dogs** - None

Something Extra
A pair of bald eagles has taken up residency at Lake Luxemborg and their aerie is convenient to so many curious onlookers that the area around their nest is often restricted but it is still an excellent place to observe eagles.

Darlington Trail

Phone - None
Website - None
Admission Fee - None
Directions - *Lima, Delaware County; a small parking lot for the Darlington Trail is located on Darlington Road, 1/2 mile from Route 1. The parking lot is marked by a trailhead sign.*

The Park
The *Darlington Trail* was developed by Middletown Township, preserving space near the former Darlington Family Dairy Farm.

The Walks
Half of the yellow-blazed *Darlington Trail* hugs the heavily wooded Chester Creek valley and the other half traverses the meadows and fields of the former farmstead. The entire loop is approximately 2 3/4 miles long. The *Cornucopia Trail*, a shorter path blazed in orange, connects with the *Darlington Trail* and circumnavigates a residential area. The *Darlington Trail* also connects with the *Rocky Run Trail*, a scenic linear walk in open woodlands along the Chester Creek. The trails, for the most part, are wide and easy to negotiate. To do the entire loop will require several steep climbs away from Chester Creek. You can also treat the trail as an out-and-back linear hike along the creekbed that creates an easy walk.

> **Where The Paw Meets The Earth:** Paw-friendly dirt with some rocky stretches
>
> **Workout For Your Dog** - Away from the creek you are never moving on level ground
>
> **Swimming** - At a 270-degree turn in the Chester Creek behind the parking lot, the banks are sandy, giving your dog the opportunity for a rare Delaware County beach experience; Rocky Run, which joins the Chester Creek on the trail is more for splashing
>
> **Restrictions On Dogs** - None

Something Extra
In July 1920, Babe Ruth took his big four-door touring sedan on a Yankee roadtrip from Philadelphia to Washington. It was a jolly trip on the way back for Ruth, his wife and three teammates, including stops for bootleg liquor. Singing and driving much too fast past midnight, Ruth failed to negotiate a turn on Route 1 near here and flipped his car. No one was hurt and all walked to a nearby farmhouse to spend the night. Ruth returned the next day with a mechanic to look at the tangled wreckage in the daylight. When he saw it, he said simply, "Sell it." The entourage made their way to Philadelphia, greeted by newspaper headlines screaming, "Ruth Reported Killed In Car Crash."

Delaware State Forest

Phone - (570) 895-4000
Website - http://www.dcnr.state.pa.us/forestry/stateforests/delaware.aspx
Admission Fee - None
Directions - *Swiftwater, Pike County; for the headquarters take PA 447 north and turn right on Laurel Run Road.*

The Park
In 1899 the first forest tree planting on any state land in Pennsylvania was made in Pike County. One half acre of Carolina Poplar cuttings were planted, but the planting was later reported as a failure due to winter kill. Now the Delaware State Forest admininsters over 12,000 acres of land with hundreds of miles of trails.

The Walks
There are several popular natural area destinations in the state forest. Bruce Lake Natural Area covers 2,845 acres including two lakes visited by the trails system, Bruce Lake and Egypt Meadow Lake. Bruce Lake was formed during glaciation and is completely spring fed. Egypt Meadow Lake was constructed by the Civilian Conservation Corps in 1935. The *Blooming Grove 4-H Hiking Trail* covers nearly seven miles and features two loop trails encircling hardwood swamps and a meadow. The *Thunder Swamp Trail System* traverses 26 miles of southern Pike County. The trail is highlighted by mountain streams, swamps, varieties of forest types, forest management practices and other natural features found on the Pocono Plateau. This trail system offers short loop trails for day use and longer loops for overnight camping.

> **Where The Paw Meets The Earth:** Expect many rocks on your trails
> **Workout For Your Dog** - Long hikes on the menu but not much elevation change; Pennel Run is an exception
> **Swimming** - There are 13 lakes and ponds within Delaware State Forest - six glacial and seven artificial and scores of streams
> **Restrictions On Dogs** - None

Something Extra
The Tarkill Forest Demonstration Area was established in 1998 as an "outdoor textbook area." This 82-acre tract contains sites where several different forest management practices have been conducted. A self guided nature trail showcases the results of these practices and of various forest dynamics. A trail brochure, which describes each site, is available.

Evansburg State Park

Phone - (610) 409-1150
Website - http://www.dcnr.state.pa.us/stateparks/Parks/evansburg.aspx
Admission Fee - None
Directions - *Collegeville, Montgomery County; from Route 29, pick up Germantown Pike across the Perkiomen Bridge. Make a left on Skippack Creek Road; continue straight onto May Hill Road into the Main Park Area.*

The Park

This land was part of William Penn's American Province purchased from the Lenni Lenape Nation in 1684. The area developed rapidly; by 1714 settlers were sending goods to Philadelphia via the Skippack (from the Lenape word for "wetland") Pike. The agrarian ways of the Mennonites in the Skippack Valley began to evaporate in the years following World War II and plans began for setting aside the land that became Evansburg State Park. The park officially opened for public use on June 28, 1974.

The Walks

Although Evansburg comprises more than 3,000 acres, most of the property is set aside for hunting and trapping. There are 6 miles of hiking trails, primarily on the *Skippack Creek Loop Trail* which is essentially two linear trails on either side of the Skippack Creek. This is mostly easy walking with some moderate ups and downs, although the trail on the far side of the Skippack Creek can rise some 100 feet above the water. On the Main Park Area side the trail is wider and flatter, the far side is woodsier and more scenic. Another 15 miles of walking is available on equestrian trails.

> **Where The Paw Meets The Earth:** Dirt and mud where the horses roam
> **Workout For Your Dog** - Moderate hill-climbing
> **Swimming** - The Skippack Creek is seldom deep enough for sustained dog-paddling and there are no ponds in the park
> **Restrictions On Dogs** - None

Something Extra

Germantown Pike was the first road to be started in Montgomery County, dating to 1687 when funds were allocated for a "cart road" from Philadelphia to the Plymouth Meeting settlement. Later extended to present-day Collegeville, an eight arch stone bridge was built to span Skippack Creek in 1792. An equestrian trail crosses the bridge, which is the oldest bridge in continuous, heavy use in America.

Ferncliff Wildflower and Wildlife Preserve

Phone - (717) 392-7891
Website - http://lancasterconservancy.org/
Admission Fee - None
Directions - *Benton, Lancaster County; south of Lancaster on the Susquehanna River. Take Route 272 south past the intersection with Route 372. Continue for three miles to Chestnut Level Road and make a right.Make a left on River Road past the cemetery and a quick right onto Slate Hill Road. After a bend in the road, make a right on Harmony Ridge Road. In a couple miles look for Bald Eagle Road on th eleft. Turn and find the preserve at the bottom of the hill on the right.*

The Park

This wooded ravine is celebrated for its old growth forest, one of the last remaining in Pennsylvania's Piedmont region. In 1972 the Ferncliff Wildflower and Wildlife Preserve was named a National Natural Landmark. Today the 65 acres are managed by the Lancaster County Conservancy.

The Walks

The way in and out of the Ferncliff Preserve is on a closed county road. Gently sloping and comprised of dirt and gravel, it is a beautiful trail as it swings back and forth along the Barnes Run stream corridor. There are a couple of shallow water crossings that certainly won't trouble even the smallest dog. Past tiny waterfalls, beside jagged rock outcroppings, and under towering ash, oak and hemlock trees, the old road eventually reaches the railroad tracks that block the way to the Susquehanna River. A small sign on the north side of the road points the way to a *North Rim Trail* and this narrow footpath can be used for a return trip, picking along the valley slopes.

> **Where The Paw Meets The Earth:** Dirt road that is easy on the paw
>
> **Workout For Your Dog** - Easy unless you decide to try the slopes that may require some bushwhacking in the side ravine
>
> **Swimming** - Barnes Run is too shallow for real swimming
>
> **Restrictions On Dogs** - None

Something Extra

Ferncliff Wildflower and Wildlife Preserve is one of fewer than 600 sites designated as a National Natural Landmark. The program recognizes and encourages the conservation of outstanding examples of our country's natural history. There are 26 such sites in Pennsylvania. Ferncliff Preserve has been selected for its unique vegetation, thought to be virgin growth.

Fonthill

Phone - (215) 348-9461
Website - http://www.mercermuseum.org/fonthill/
Admission Fee - Not for the grounds
Directions - *Doylestown, Bucks County; at Swamp Road and E. Court Street, 1/2 mile east of Route 611.*

The Park

The Moravian Pottery and Tile Works was established by noted anthropologist, antiquarian, artist, writer, and tile-maker Henry C. Mercer, a leader in the turn-of-the-century Arts and Crafts movement, in an effort to recreate early Pennsylvania pottery manufacturing techniques. Mercer's factory produced tiles depicting Pennsylvania flora and fauna and was awarded a gold medal at the 1904 St. Louis Exposition and a 1921 gold medal from the American Institute of Architects. The Tile Works is owned by the Bucks County Department of Parks and Recreation and is open to the public as a museum illustrating Mercer's tile making techniques. Built of reinforced concrete with concrete buttresses, measuring approximately 120 feet by 100 feet with arcaded court, it resembles a medieval cloister. The factory is 2 ½ stories built in tiers with towers. The gable roofs have rounded ridges of brushed concrete with steep parapets at the gable ends. Irregular chimneys and windows with a variety of decorative tiles are set in both exterior and interior walls. The present building, built between 1911 and 1912, still functions as a manufactory of mostly architectural tiles, and was designated as a National Historic Landmark by the Secretary of Interior in 1985.

The Walks

Dog walkers can wander around the grounds and use the wide dirt trails through the woodlands on the estate. There is less than an hour of pleasant dog-walking here.

> **Where The Paw Meets The Earth:** Paw-friendly natural surface wooded paths
> **Workout For Your Dog** - Easy going
> **Swimming** - No
> **Restrictions On Dogs** - None

Something Extra

Henry Mercer (1856-1930) built Fonthill as his home between 1908 and 1912. The concrete castle boasts 44 rooms, 18 fireplaces and more than 200 windows of varying size and shape. The interior walls, floors and ceilings are elaborately adorned with an incredible array of Mercer's original handcrafted tiles.

Fort Washington State Park

Phone - (215) 591-5250
Website - http://www.dcnr.state.pa.us/stateparks/parks/fort-washington.aspx
Admission Fee - None
Directions - *Fort Washington, Montgomery County; between Fort Washington and Flourtown, two miles from the Pennsylvania Turnpike, Exit 26. To reach the Militia Hill Day Use Area, take Skippack Pike (Route 73) and turn onto Joshua Road to the entrance on the left.*

The Park
The 493-acre park is named for a defensive redoubt built by George Washington in the Fall of 1777. After being whipped at Germantown, Washington brought his 12,000 troops to this area on November 2 to regroup as he pondered whether to attack the British in Philadelphia. After five weeks, the General decided against an offensive assault and the British concluded the Americans had prepared their defenses too well to be attacked. Washington ended the stalemate by marching the Continental Army 15 miles to Valley Forge for the winter. In the early 1920s, Philadelphia's Fairmount Park Commission began acquiring land here, even though it lay outside the city limits. In 1953, the Commission turned the park over to the Commonwealth of Pennsylvania.

The Walks
There are 3.5 miles of wooded trails at Fort Washington, primarily in the Militia Hill Day Use Area. The interlocking trails, many on old vehicle roads, can be combined to form loop walks. None, however, escape the constant drone of traffic on the nearby Pennsylvania Turnpike. A segment of the *Green Ribbon Trail* passes through the park, connecting the Militia Hill and Flourtown areas.

> **Where The Paw Meets The Earth:** The old vehicle roads are stony and overgrown with grass; the cross-country trail is grass and dirt
>
> **Workout For Your Dog** - The trails across Joshua Road are hilly; the cross-country trail that circumnavigates the picnic area is less so
>
> **Swimming** - There is access to a deep stretch of the Wissahickon Creek along the *Green Ribbon Trail* at the edge of the park; there is no water anywhere else
>
> **Restrictions On Dogs** - None

Something Extra
A wooden observation deck has been constructed to observe the seasonal migration of raptors down the Wissahickon Valley.

Four Mills Nature Reserve

Phone - (215) 646-8866
Website - None
Admission Fee - None
Directions - *Ambler, Montgomery County; south of town at 12 Morris Road, east of Butler Pike.*

The Park
The Four Mills Nature Reserve comprises 55 acres of Wissahickon Creek floodplain, 50 of which were donated by former Philadelphia *Bulletin* owner, Robert McLean, in 1966. The original estate named Abendruh, German for "evening's rest," was created by Charles Bergner of Bergner and Engle Brewing Company, a 19th century Philadelphia brewery. McLean used the estate as a private hunting ground, stocking the property with pheasant and quail. Four Mills derives its name from four long-disappeared mills that once operated in the vicinity.

The Walks
The trails at Four Mills lie on islands in the Wissahickon Creek (if your dog shies away from open-grate bridges, you may have to carry him). As of this writing, storm damage had decimated some of the downstream trails. You can also access the *Green Ribbon Trail* here, including Tall Tree Woods. A good walk at Four Mills is to take the *Green Ribbon Trail* between water crossings upstream and downstream.

> **Where The Paw Meets The Earth:** Mostly soft dirt with some stony stretches
> **Workout For Your Dog** - Flat and level canine hiking
> **Swimming** - The normal level of the Wissahickon is not deep enough for dog paddling
> **Restrictions On Dogs** - None

Something Extra
Now the headquarters of the Wissahickon Valley Watershed Association, the Four Mills Barn was originally built in 1891. It was designed by prominent Philadelphia architect Horace Trumbauer, whose credits include the Free Library of Philadelphia and the Keswick Theater. How destructive can the Wissahickon Creek be when it floods? Stand in the Association's museum on the first floor of the Four Mills Barn and imagine it inundated with creek water, as happened during the record flood of 1955.

Frances Slocum State Park

Phone - (570) 696-3525
Website - http://www.dcnr.state.pa.us/STATEPARKS/parks/francesslocum.aspx
Admission Fee - None
Directions - *Wyoming, Luzerne County; five miles north of Dallas. From exit 170B of I-81, take PA 309 north about seven miles (7.2). Turn right (east) on Carverton Road and go about four miles (4.2). Turn left (north) on 8th Street Road and go about one mile (1.3). Turn left (west) onto Mt. Olivet Road and go one mile. The park entrance is on the left.*

The Park
On November 2, 1778, a small group of Delaware Indians entered the Slocum home and carried away Frances who was then just five years old. Frances was taken along as the American Indians moved westward and spent the rest of her life with them. Her brothers found her 59 years laer living on a reservation near Peru, Indiana. She had been married twice and had borne four children. Frances refused the pleas of her brothers to return to Pennsylvania and died in Indiana in 1847, at the age of 74. Frances Slocum Lake was created to control flooding. Picnicking areas and the dam were constructed and the only Pennsylvania state park named for a woman opened in the spring of 1968.

The Walks
There is a trail for any level of canine hiking available in the park. A good start is the red-blazed *Lakeshore Trail* that traipses around the boot-shaped peninsula that is surrounded on three sides by Frances Slocum Lake. After this easy warm-up you can test the trails on the wings on either side of the lake. The *Larch Trail* near the campground is a hilly loop that visits a vibrant stand of the coniferous tres known for shedding their needles. The *Deer Trail* is a series of interconnecting loops that can cover any canine hike up to four miles. These sporty paths - open to hunting - traverse the entire spectrum of habitats found in the park - hardwoods, marshes, thickets and hemlock groves.

> **Where The Paw Meets The Earth:** Dirt trails
> **Workout For Your Dog** - If you cover all 9 miles of trails in the park you will have one tired dog
> **Swimming** - The *Lakeshore Trail* provides access to the water in many places, although not constantly
> **Restrictions On Dogs** - None; dogs are allowed in the campground

Something Extra
The first night after her abduction was spent in a crude shelter under a rock ledge along Abraham Creek, found on the *Frances Slocum Trail*.

French Creek State Park

Phone - (610) 582-9680
Website - http://www.dcnr.state.pa.us/stateparks/parks/frenchcreek.aspx
Admission Fee - None
Directions - *Elverson, Chester County; north on Route 23; take Route 345 North to the south entrance of the park. From the Pennsylvania Turnpike the park is 7 miles northeast of the Morgantown Interchange (Exit 22).*

The Park
A wilderness fort once stood on the small stream flowing through these woods that was garrisoned by the French during the French and Indian War and thus "French Creek." The hillsides here were dotted with charcoal hearths throughout the 1800s, fueling the nascent American iron industry. The furnace was stoked for the last time in 1883. French Creek State Park was originally developed by the federal government during the Depression as a National Park Service Demonstration Area. The Civilian Conservation Corps built dams, roads and other recreational trappings. In 1946, the area was transferred to the Commonwealth of Pennsylvania.

The Walks
Approximately 40 miles of trails visit every corner of French Creek's 7,339 acres. There are nine featured hikes of between one and four hours' duration. The marquee walk is the *Boone Trail*, a six-mile loop connecting all the major attractions of the park. The *Mill Creek Trail* is a back-country hike that visits Millers Point, a pile of large boulders where you and your dog dog can easily scramble to the top. All the walks are heavily forested with hardwoods - keep an eye out for the ruins of the area's charcoal-burning past. Repeatedly timbered, there is little understory and the trails are almost universally wide and easy to walk. The park is hilly with the steepest - and rockiest - slopes blanketing the eastern section of French Creek.

> **Where The Paw Meets The Earth:** Dirt trails, rocky on the slopes
> **Workout For Your Dog** - Plenty of hills here
> **Swimming** - Easy access to two lakes, the 21-acre cold water Scotts Run Lake and 63-acre Hopewell Lake
> **Restrictions On Dogs** - None

Something Extra
Appended to French Creek State Park - and open to canine hiking - is Hopewell Furnace National Historic Site, one of the finest examples still remaining of a rural early American iron plantation. Ironmaster Mark Bird built the original blst furnace is 1771 and supplied cannon and ammunition to the Revolutionary Army during the struggle for independence. The buildings on the historic site include a blast furnace and the ironmaster's mansion.

Gifford Pinchot State Park

Phone - (717) 432-5011
Website - http://www.dcnr.state.pa.us/stateparks/parks/gifford-pinchot.aspx
Admission Fee - None
Directions - *Lewisberry, York County; from Harrisburg use the Lewisberry Exit (35) of I-83 south then PA 177 south; or by US 15 south to Dillsburg, then to PA 74 south. From York, take PA 74 north or I-83 north. From I-83, take the Newberrytown Exit (32), PA 382 west to PA 177 south.*

The Park

Gifford Pinchot studied in France and became the first American trained in forestry. As the first Chief Forester of the U. S. Division of Forestry he placed over 200 million acres of national forest came under scientific land management. Policies developed by Pinchot still help guide most national and state forests. In 1922 Pinchot began serving the first of two terms as governor of Pennsylvania. He created the first state budget and erased the state's debt, starting by cutting his own salary. This state park was dedicated in his honor in 1961, fifteen years after his death at age 81.

The Walks

The focal point of Gifford Pinchot State Park is a multi-fingered lake. The trail system, with nearly 20 miles of paths, is constrained by the water although a variety of canine hikes can be cobbled together. The *Lakeside Trail* covers 8.5 miles around the lake and numerous short trails in a network near the campground or latch on to the *Mason-Dixon Trail* as it nears its conclusion from the Brandywine Valley south of Philadelphia to the *Appalachian Trail* on South Mountain.

> **Where The Paw Meets The Earth:** Asphalt, gravel and natural trails
> **Workout For Your Dog** - Mostly gentle hill climbs
> **Swimming** - Super dog paddling in Pinchot Lake
> **Restrictions On Dogs** - None

Something Extra

The legacy of Gifford Pinchot is wide-ranging, but not without controversy. Although regarded as a pioneer in American land conservation his developmental policies were hotly contested in California and led to the formation of the Sierra Club, now the nation's leading voice for protecting our natural resources. During the Depression in the 1930s Pinchot established work camps throughout Pennsylvania that President Franklin Roosevelt used as a model for the national Civilian Conservation Corps. Pinchot's crews built 20,000 miles of paved roads for "taking the farmer out of the mud." His first hard-surfaced, high-crowned road is now PA 177, running across the northwest boundary of the state park.

Gouldsboro State Park

Phone - None
Website - http://www.dcnr.state.pa.us/stateparks/parks/goulds-boro.aspx
Admission Fee - None
Directions - *Gouldsboro, Monroe County; the park entrance is one-half mile south of the village on PA 507. PA 507 intersects with I-380 at Exit 13, two miles south of the park entrance, and with I-84, 13 miles north of the park entrance.*

The Park
The name Gouldsboro comes from the village north of the park that was named for Jay Gould (1836-1892). A native of New York, Gould acquired a very large fortune that by 1892 included ownership of ten percent of all railroad track in the country. One of the railroads he owned was the Erie-Lackawanna. This rail line parallels the eastern boundary of the park and is now a part of the Steamtown, USA railroad excursion route between Scranton and Pocono Summit. Gould was a co-owner of a leather tannery at Thornhurst, a small village 9.5 miles west of Gouldsboro. Raw hides shipped from Australia and the western United States came to Gouldsboro by railroad and then were taken in two-ton loads by horse drawn wagons over a plank road to Thornhurst for tanning. Gouldsboro State Park, in Monroe and Wayne counties in northeastern Pennsylvania, contains 2,800 acres of land, including the 250-acre Gouldsboro Lake.

The Walks
Canine hiking in the park is conducted on the *Prospect Rock Trail*, a large loop that features long, level stretches save for a topsy-turvy area around the namesake rock formation and a steady climb up the *Old Route 611 Trail*. The 5.8-mile trip is about evenly divided by trotting on woods paths and wide, old roads. The old concrete highway travels through the wide open Kistler Swamp.
> **Where The Paw Meets The Earth:** Dirt, concrete, rocks
> **Workout For Your Dog** - A few tough patches and the full circuit will provide a hearty canine hike
> **Swimming** - The trail doesn't touch Gouldsboro Lake but it isn't far away from the parking lot
> **Restrictions On Dogs** - None

Something Extra
You get to hike with your dog for more than one mile on the cracked concrete of the original Route 611 that was once the main thoroughfare to Philadelphia in a less congested time.

Governor Dick

Phone - None
Website - None
Admission Fee - None
Directions - *Lebanon, Lebanon County; six miles south of town, on the northeast edge of Mount Gretna. A trailhead and parking can be found on Route 117 and, one-half mile from town, on Pinch Road.*

The Park
When Cornwall Furnace impressario developed Mount Gretna as a resort destination in the late 1800s it was natural to provide access to a neighboring 1120-foot mountain top known as "Governor Dick." Not an influential government official, Governor Dick was the nickname of a former slave and later a woodsman and laborer at the Cornwall Furnace who worked the site in the late 1700s. Coleman built a narrow-gauge railroad (only two feet wide) to transport picnicers to the top. This type of railroad is generally constructed to reach tricky mines and timber stands on steep mountain slopes and this four-mile line was the only one of its type used for recreational purposes. In 1934 Clarence Schock, founder of the Schock Independent Oil Company (SICO), bought this land and in 1953 donated 1105 acres to "forever remain as playground and park." A half-century later the uniquely privately owned but publicly accessible Clarence Schock Memorial Park at Governor Dick   strains to hold true to that promise against developmental pressures.

The Walks
The most heavily-traveled route at Governor Dick is the main road up and over the summit of the mountain. The old rail bed is very rocky under paw but offers a steady pull up, rather than steep grind to the top. For additional canine hiking at Governor Dick, come with a mind to explore. Side trails marked with numbered signposts are impossible to decipher for the uninitiated and a forest left in a natural state means large tree blowdowns and thick underbrush rather than the groomed trails of a public park.

> **Where The Paw Meets The Earth:** Dirt road and trails and rocky paths
> **Workout For Your Dog** - A good one here
> **Swimming** - There will be no canine aquatics on Governor Dick
> **Restrictions On Dogs** - None

Something Extra
Every first-timer's visit to Governor Dick is sure to include a hike to the concrete-and-steel tower on the summit. The current 66-foot tower is a descendant of the original tower built in the 1800s as a geodetic survey signal station.

Green Lane Park

Phone - (215) 234-8684
Website - http://www.montcopa.org/parks/green%20lane.htm
Admission Fee - None
Directions - *Green Lane, Montgomery County; off Route 29.
There are several approaches to the trails. For the* Orange Trail,
*make a left on Snyder Road, drive through the recreation area to
the parking lot on Deep Creek Road. For the* Blue Trail, *make a
left on Park Road and a right on Hill Road to the trailhead on the
left. The* Red Trail *is just off Route 29 on Knight Road.*

The Park
Public recreation here dates to 1939 with the founding of Upper
Perkiomen Valley Park. Upon its wedding to Green Lane Reservoir
Park, the largest single open space purchase-easement in Montgomery County history, Green Lane Park, was created. The focal point of
the 3100-acre park is the Green Lane Reservoir, home to more than
a dozen species of freshwater fish.

The Walks
Four of the five trails here are open to dogs (four-legged friends are
not welcome on the *Hemlock Point Trail*). The *Red Trail*, designed as an
equestrian trail but not chewed up like so many other such surfaces,
winds through open fields and stands of trees for 10 miles, although
the entire length can be aborted in several places. The premier trail
at Green Lane Park is the heavily wooded *Blue Trail* on the western
edge of the reservoir where you pick your way across steep ravines
and narrow ridges for 6 miles. Watch for passages over loose rocks.
The full loop can be cut off at the Turn Around but you'll miss the
extravagant rock carvings of falling water at work. At the Hill Road
Office, and overlapping the Blue Trail, is the *Whitetail Trail*, a self-
guided nature walk. There are hilly climbs throughout Green Lane
Park; the gentlest terrain is found on the *Red Trail*.

> **Where The Paw Meets The Earth:** Dirt trails
> predominantly
> **Workout For Your Dog** - You can find some easy going
> but be prepared for long, hilly routes
> **Swimming** - There is excellent access to the reservoir
> from the *Blue Trail*; less so on the *Red Trail*
> **Restrictions On Dogs** - No dogs on the *Hemlock
> Point Trail*

Something Extra
On the *Red Trail*, there is an unexpected walk into a young stand of
cedar growing on red dirt and the feeling of Utah desert instantly
washes over you.

Grey Towers National Historic Site

Phone - (570) 296-9630
Website - http://www.fs.fed.us/na/gt/local-links/directions.shtml
Admission Fee - None for the grounds
Directions - *Milford, Pike County; take Interstate 84 to Exit 46. Turn left off ramp onto Highway 6 East toward Milford. At the base of the hill, make a sharp right just after the Apple Valley shops complex. The entrance to Grey Towers is about 1/4 mile on the left.*

The Park
The Pinchot family arrived in Milford in 1816 and opened a mercantile store, The French Store. In 1850 by the time 19-year old James was ready to enter the family business there was no room so he trundled off to New York City and made a fortune in the wallpaper trade. He retired after 25 years and by 1886 he had built the French-influenced Grey Towers in his hometown. At the time his son Gifford was 21 and instilled with a love of nature. When his friend Theodore Roosevelt became President in 1900, Gifford Pinchot was named the first Chief Forester of the United States Forest Service. During his tenure, national forests tripled in size to 193 million acres. Later, Pinchot became one of Pennsylvania's most popular and progressive governors.

The Walks
A collection of short trails designed to educate and experience nature surround the Grey Towers mansion. The *Trail of Time* snakes down a hillside to learn about the Pinchot land, lives and legacy. The *Forestry Trail* travels on well-groomed loop through the woods behind the house for almost one mile and the *Bluebird Trail* is a walk along the deer fence around the perimeter of the estate. Some of the most fun for your dog will be on the free-form *Tree Trail* where you are invited to "wander, walk, saunter, run, skip or hop" through the field along the estate driveway and learn about some of the trees of Grey Towers. Tree ID signs reveal the names and most popular uses of these trees. One oak tree in the yard is over 150 years old and 18 feet in diameter.

> **Where The Paw Meets The Earth:** Grass and paw-friendly dirt
> **Workout For Your Dog** - Easy loping around the hillsides
> **Swimming** - None
> **Restrictions On Dogs** - No dogs in the mansion

Something Extra
The Grey Towers mansion is open for tours; be sure to visit the historic gardens that includes the Fingerbowl, the Pinchot's unique outdoor dining table.

Heinz National Wildlife Refuge

Phone - (215) 365-3118
Website - http://www.fws.gov/northeast/heinz/
Admission Fee - None
Directions - *Philadelphia; from I-95 North take Exit 10, Route 291 (Philadelphia International Airport). At the first light make a left onto Bartram Avenue. At the third light make a left onto 84th Street. At the second light make a left onto Lindbergh Boulevard. Make a right into the refuge just past the stop sign. The parking area in Delaware County is on Route 420; take Exit 9B off I-95 for Route 420 North. The parking area is right there.*

The Park

There are more than 500 National Wildlife Refuges in the United States and only Philadelphia and San Francisco offer an urban environmental study. When the Swedes settled here in 1634, Tinicum Marsh measured over 5,700 acres. Three hundred years later the tidal marsh had been reduced to only 200 acres. The routing of I-95 in 1969 threatened to finish off the marsh but, in ironic fact, saved it. Congress authorized the purchase of 1,200 acres in 1972, establishing the Tinicum National Environmental Center and enabling the highway to roar through the area.

The Walks

You can cover about ten miles of trails here in two major loops. The more attractive of the two is around the Impoundment Marsh near the Visitor Contact Station. If you have a patient dog you can pause at the Observation Platform or one of the Observation Blinds and try to identify one of the 288 species of birds seen in the refuge. The western loop, that begins in Delaware County, leads onto a dike in the middle of the marsh and along the Darby Creek. The trail on the dike is narrow to the point of being overgrown during the spring and summer.

> **Where The Paw Meets The Earth:** Dirt roads and paths
> **Workout For Your Dog** - Easy going all the way around
> **Swimming** - The Darby Creek is accessible but the fish pulled from these waters are contaminated so you may want to limit water time here
> **Restrictions On Dogs** - None

Something Extra

There aren't many other places where you can walk along with the dog and scan the skies alternately for a Northern Goshawk and a McDonnell-Douglas or a Buff-Breasted Sandpiper and a Boeing.

Heritage Rail Trail County Park

Phone - (717) 840-7440
Website - http://ycwebserver.york-county.org/Parks/RailTrail.htm
Admission Fee - None
Directions - *York County; from downtown York the northern terminus for the rail-trail begins directly behind the Colonial Courthouse on West Market Street.*

The Park
The Northern Central Railroad began carrying passengers in 1838, rolling from Washington D.C. to Lake Ontario but the road was known mostly to farmers and coal miners until November 18, 1863 when Abraham Lincoln boarded a regular coach, sitting with other passengers, headed for Gettysburg to dedicate a new national cemetery (contrary to popular folklore he did not scribble out the Gettysburg Address on the back of an envelope on the train). Less than two years later the President's funeral train would travel the same route. Passenger service would continue until 1972 when Hurricane Agnes finished the fading line by washing out bridges and tearing up track. The 21-mile stretch of line from the Colonial Courthouse in York to the Maryland line, covering 176 acres was established in 1992 as the Heritage Rail Trail County Park. The trail connects with 20 miles of abandoned Northern Central bed in Maryland that the state opened in 1984 after removing 600 tons of trash along the right-of-way.

The Walks
The Heritage rail-trail is broken up by nine parking lots so canine hikers with a two-car shuttle system can reduce the trail to manageable 2-3 mile segments. The crushed limestone and clay more or less follows Codurus Creek with some stretches through private farm fields and some wooded lanes. Most of the going on the rail-trail is over gentle grade; if you are searching for a heartier workout for your dog try the New Freedom trailhead.

> **Where The Paw Meets The Earth:** Crushed stone
> **Workout For Your Dog** - Level or imperseptible grades
> **Swimming** - It is possible to slip into Codurus Creek at times
> **Restrictions On Dogs** - None

Something Extra
A bit past five miles from York the rail-trail runs through Howard Tunnel, thought to be America's oldest railroad tunnel in continuous service. Rather than continue laying track along the twisting Codorus Creek engineers opted to drill through 370 feet of rock to open the passageway in 1838. The stone facework you see as you pass through the tunnel today was completed two years later. In 1868 the brick-lined Howard Tunnel was rebuilt to accommodate a second track.

Hibernia County Park

Phone - (610) 383-3812
Website - http://dsf.chesco.org/ccparks/cwp/view.asp?A=1550&Q=616010
Admission Fee - None
Directions - *Wagontown, Chester County; from Route 30, take Route 82 North two miles to Cedar Knoll Road, turn left and travel 1.25 miles to the main entrance.*

The Park
Property deeds in this area date to October 1, 1765. In the 1790s, Samuel Downing built the first iron forge at Hibernia, along the West Branch of the Brandywine Creek. Downing lost his forge in a sheriff's sale in 1808 and the property then passed rapidly through many owners until Charles Brooke pur-chased the enterprise in 1821. He expanded its holdings to 1,710 acres and by the Civil War, the Hibernia Iron Works was churning pig iron into bar iron from two forges, two heating furnaces and a rolling mill. The forge went silent in the 1870s. In 1894, Colonel Franklin Swayne, a successful Philadelphia real estate lawyer, purchased the property and transformed Hibernia (the Roman name for Ireland) into a gentleman's country estate. In 1963 the old ironmaster's mansion and nearly 900 acres of surround-ing   grounds passed to Chester County for renovation as a park.

The Walks
Hibernia features 5 main trails, all wooded and none longer than 1.5 miles. Only the *Cedar Hollow Trail* loops so you will need to combine park roads and unmarked paths to avoid retracing steps in your walking day. A dirt trail along the Brandywine is one of the longest waterside walks in Chester County. Most of the walking is easy; there are slight hills down to the Brandywine Creek and the *Rim Trail* across the water requires a good climb to reach the ridge.

> **Where The Paw Meets The Earth:** Dirt and crushed stone
> **Workout For Your Dog** - Gentle slopes across the property
> **Swimming** - Dogs can enjoy a dip in the Brandywine Creek, a fishing pond or in Chambers Lake, where there is limited access to a 90-acre water reservoir created in 1994 with the damming of Birch Run
> **Restrictions On Dogs** - None

Something Extra
A long-time admirer of the English manor tradition, Colonel Swayne made 29 trips to the British countryside to collect ideas for his home. On one such trip he purchased the massive lion heads which adorn the pillar gate posts. It was the colonel who is thought to have cov-ered the stone exterior of the mansion with its distinctive coppery peach stucco.

Hickory Run State Park

Phone - (570) 443-0400
Website - http://www.dcnr.state.pa.us/stateparks/parks/hickory-run.aspx
Admission Fee - None
Directions - *White Haven, Carbon County; from I-80, take Exit 274 at the Hickory Run State Park Exit, and drive east on PA 534 for six miles. From the Northeast Extension of the Pennsylvania Turnpike, take Exit 95 and drive west on PA 940 for three miles then turn east on PA 534 for six miles.*

The Park
In 1918, Allentown millionaire General Harry C. Trexler began buying land for one purpose: "I would like to see Hickory Run developed into a state park where families can come and enjoy wholesome recreation." Trexler, who began his career as a farmer but soon branched into logging and other industries, opened his land to public hunting and fishing. Trexler died before his plans could be completed. The National Park Service purchased Hickory Run in 1935 to create a national recreation demonstration area and a decade later was transferred to Pennsylvania and became Hickory Run State Park.

The Walks
More than 20 trails covering over 40 miles in three natural areas await your dog in Hickory Run State Park. One thing he won't find is many hickory trees; one theory of the park's name origins is that it was based on one large, now-extinct hickory tree. The leading candidate for "prettiest trail" in the park is the intriguingly named *Shades of Death Trail* near the park office. It follows Sand Spring and meanders through unique rock formations and past dams and old logging-mill ruins that date to the 1800s. The thick rhodedendron forest is a une highlight.

> **Where The Paw Meets The Earth:** Rocky dirt trails
> **Workout For Your Dog** - Plenty of varied opportunities for a hearty hike
> **Swimming** - Hickory Run Lake and Sand Spring Lake and a hatfull of streams are idela for canine aquatics
> **Restrictions On Dogs** - None, dogs are also allowed in the campground

Something Extra
The Boulder Field, a striking boulder-strewn area, is a National Natural Landmark. Some 14 acres of jumbled stone deposited during the last Ice Age stretch across more than a quarter-mile. The unique slope of the terrain here is repsonsible for the glacial debris piling up here. The Boulder Field is reached on a relatively easy hike with your dog of 3.5 miles on the *Boulder Field Trail*. Across the road from the trailhead is a short trail leading to the picturesque Hawk Falls.

Indian Orchard/Linvill Trails

Phone - None
Website - None
Admission Fee - None
Directions - *Lima, Delaware County; just off Route 352 (Middletown Road). The parking lot for the Indian Orchard Trail is at the end of Copes Lane on the western side of Route 352. To reach the Linville Trail from Route 1, make a right on West Knowlton Road and take your first right on Linville Road to the parking lot.*

The Park
In 1986, Middletown Township began preserving significant portions of open space in Middletown in recognition of the Township's Tricentennial. These trails were carved from 157 acres of property acquired from the Linvill family.

The Walks
The *Indian Orchard Trail*, blazed in yellow, rolls through a woodland of mature hardwoods and conifers, crossing five bridges along its one-mile length. The *Linvill Trail* covers 3 1/2 miles over two sections; one, a long perimeter loop around the pasturelands and orchards, the other a fish-hook trail behind Linvilla Orchard. A short spur connects the two trails. These trails are easy hiking, with the *Linvill Trail* the flatter of the two. Indian Orchard features some sporty ups and downs. Take caution on the *Farm Fields Trail* which is sometimes cut from the crop stalks, leaving tiny spears that can injure a pet's paws.

> **Where The Paw Meets The Earth:** Natural surface trails
> **Workout For Your Dog** - Moderate ups and downs
> **Swimming** - Crum Run intercepts the *Indian Orchard Trail* several times although it is not deep enough for a full swim; the most water you'll encounter on the *Linville Trail* is at the Hidden Hollow Swim Club, which doesn't welcome dogs in its pools
> **Restrictions On Dogs** - None

Something Extra
Even into the 20th century indoor plumbing was not universal and the "necessary" or "outhouse" was a familiar sight on the rural American landscape. In the woods along the *Indian Orchard Trail* is a relic of these times - an abandoned two-seater necessary.

Jacobsburg Environmental Education Center

Phone - (610) 746-2801
Website - http://www.dcnr.state.pa.us/stateparks/parks/ja-cobsburg.aspx
Admission Fee - None
Directions - *Wind Gap, Northampton County; from PA 33 at the Belfast Exit. Follow signs to the meeting of Henry and Belfast roads. Turn left on Belfast Road and in less than a mile will be a parking lot on the left, just past Bushkill Creek.*

The Park
On the northern edge of the Lehigh Valley, the rolling terrain of Jacobsburg Environmental Education Center is near the foothills of the Pocono Plateau. The habitats range from fields in various stages of successional growth to mature hardwood forests dominated by oak trees. About 2.5 miles of the beautiful Bushkill Creek and its tributary, Sobers Run, wind through the center. The original land for the center was purchased by the Department of Forests and Waters from the City of Easton in 1959. In 1969, additional land was purchased using funds from Project 70. This brought the total land area of the center to its present size of 1,168 acres.

The Walks
The star canine hike in the park is a 4-mile loop through Henrys Woods linked by the *Homestead Trail* and the *Henrys Woods Trail*. This route is particularly attractive along the Bushkill Creek where luxurient hemlocks grow. The *Henry Woods Trail* is the only pedestrian-only trail in the park. Most of the more than 18 miles of wooded paths are equestrian trails. Short detours off this loop lead to the Henry homestead and other historic souvenirs.

>**Where The Paw Meets The Earth:** Rocky, rooty dirt trails
>**Workout For Your Dog** - Easy to moderate climbing around the woods
>**Swimming** - The trails tip onto Bushkill Creek for splashing
>**Restrictions On Dogs** - None

Something Extra
The Jacobsburg National Historic District lies almost entirely within the boundaries of Jacobsburg Environmental Education Center. William Henry II purchased land here from the heirs of Jacob Hubler, who in 1740 founded the community from which Jacobsburg draws its name, and built a gun manufactory. Three succeeding generations produced small arms and the Henry firearm became the most prominent weapon of the western frontier due to its durability, accuracy and relatively low cost. Only the foundations remain from the colonial village of Jacobsburg.

Joseph E. Iberson Conservation Area

Phone - (717) 567-9255
Website - http://www.dcnr.state.pa.us/stateparks/parks/josepheibberson.aspx
Admission Fee - None
Directions - *Dauphin County; the Ibberson Conservation Area straddles Peters Mountain, north of Harrisburg. The park entrance is on the north side of the mountain. From Route 322/22, take PA 225 north over the mountain and turn right on Hebron Road near the bottom of the other side, a distance of about 4.5 miles. Follow Hebron for another 4.5 miles, bearing right at the forks in the road, until reaching the Conservation Area on the right.*

The Park
Peter Allen built a stone house on the mountain that came to be named for him in 1726. The house, the oldest in Dauphin County, still stands at the interesection of PA 225 and PA 325. In 1962, Joseph Ibberson, a long-time Bureau of Forestry executive, began buying land here to create a tree farm and in 1998, the same year he was named Pennsylvania Tree Farmer of the Year, Ibberson donated his land to become the first conservation area in the Pennsylvania Bureau of State Parks.

The Walks
The trail system in this 350-acre swath of unbroken hardwood forest is a crown jewel for area canine hikers. The paths are wide, the woods are airy, and the choices are many. The only thing Ibberson Conservation Area lacks for canine superstardom is varied access to water sources. A pleasant woodland pond is encountered along the *Turkey Foot* and *Pine* trails. For those sniffing out a challenge, the *Victoria Trail* - utilizing the historic Victoria Road that was used to drag timber to the iron furnace - grinds for two miles up to the *Appalachian Trail* on top of Peters Mountain.

>**Where The Paw Meets The Earth:** Natural trails
>**Workout For Your Dog** - Moderate uphills on the mountain slopes but you can go for hours without setting your dog to excess panting
>**Swimming** - A small pond in the western area of the park
>**Restrictions On Dogs** - None

Something Extra
This is a good place to observe forest succession. Pioneering species are typically pines that require healthy doses of sunshine. The original white pines and hemlocks that populated these slopes were mostly cut and mostly hardwood trees grew up in their place.

Kellys Run Natural Area

Phone - (800) 354-8383
Website - http://pplweb.com/holtwood/
Admission Fee - None
Directions - *Holtwood, Lancaster County; the Holtwood Environmental Preserve stretches across both sides of the lower Susquehanna River. To reach Kellys Run turn on River Road (the first or last turn in Lancaster County) and make your first left onto Old Holtwood Road. The parking area for the preserve is on the right.*

The Park

The Pennsylvania Power and Light Company manages 5,000 acres of recreational land surrounding the Holtwood hydroelectric plant. You can camp, enjoy a picnic, play some ball, do a little fishing - or hike. There are 39 miles of marked trails along the lower Susquehanna, most on the long distance *Mason-Dixon* and *Conestoga* trails. Canine hikers will want to head for Kellys Run where the 6-mile trail system has been designated a National Recreation Trail.

The Walks

Starting out on the blue-blazed *Kellys Run Trail* you begin routinely enough at a picnic pavilion and drop quickly into airy woods of mature maples and poplar. Nothing special as you roll along. Then the trail drops abruptly and you are introduced to Kellys Run. Soon you are squeezing through thin avenues in a Wissahickon schist canyon as you follow the roiling stream down to the Susquehanna. In places where the rocks pinch the stream tightly enough, deep pools form to lure your dog in for a swim. After you reach the end of the run the character of this outing changes again. Old access roads are used to climb relentlessly back to your car. Benches appear in the woods as if by magic in this leg of the hike. Your final steps will be through rolling farm fields and, finally, ballfields. Near the parking area, circling around Kellys Run Trail, is the 3/4-mile *Oliver Patton Trail* that was also named a National Recreation Trail in 1992. This lively little track, named for the original farmer on these hills, traverses a stand of Norway spruce and white pine planted by the power company.

> **Where The Paw Meets The Earth:** Dirt woods and grass fields
>
> **Workout For Your Dog** - Some major climbs lurking on these trails
>
> **Swimming** - Kellys Run is mostly for splashing
>
> **Restrictions On Dogs** - None

Something Extra

Several routes will take you out of the Kellys Run gorge up to the Pinnacle, a grassy picnic spot on a bluff more than 507 feet above Lake Aldred. The best route is the *Conestoga Trail*, carved by the Lancaster Hiking Club along the river. At the Pinnacle you can fill your dog bowl with water in season.

Lackawac Sanctuary

Phone - (570) 689-9494
Website - http://www.lacawac.org
Admission Fee - None
Directions - *Lake Ariel, Lackawanna County; I-80 Exit 20 to Route 507 north for half a mile and left on Ledgedale Road. Follow to stop sign, then turn right (toward Hawley). Go one mile and turn right onto St. Mary Church Road to entrance on the right. Parking for the nature trail is just past stone gate on the right.*

The Park
This property has, at one time or another, been in the hands of many of the region's most powerful landowners, beginning with William Penn, whose family called its holding here Wallenpaupack Manor. The next owner was James Wilson, a signer of the Declaration of Independence, who, at his death in 1799, was the largest landowner in Wayne County. Then in 1849 came Burton G. Morss, whose sawmill and tannery dominated the area. At the turn of the century, coal baron William Connell bought the Lacawac property as a summer estate and a deer farm (at that time you actually had to import and breed deer in eastern Pennsylvania). When he died the property was acquired by Colonel Louis A. Watres, Scranton's leading businessman. His grandchildren sought to establish Lacawac as place of study and nature and formed the Lacawac Sanctuary Foundation in 1966.

The Walks
The sanctuary covers more than 500 acres and features a mature second-growth forest, a glacial lake, two ponds, several wetlands, and over one mile of shoreline on Lake Wallenpaupack. For the canine hiker the most important will be the woods, last lumbered in 1920. The *Maurice Broun Nature Trail* begins in an open field where nature is reclaiming an old apple orchard. After a short time the path drops down the hillside and begins a mile-long loop above Lake Wallenpaupack and meanders among weathered rock formations that inspired early settlers to give the town of Ledgedale its name.

> **Where The Paw Meets The Earth:** Dirt trail with not as many rocks as the typical Poconos path
> **Workout For Your Dog** - A little trotting down a hillside
> **Swimming** - None
> **Restrictions On Dogs** - None

Something Extra
If you spend any time in the woods in the spring, you are likely to encounter folks with a hiking stick and a mesh bag. These are morel mushroom hunters - passionate seekers of the storied fungus that sprouts in moist, dank woodlands. A prime spot for morel hunters are abandoned apple orchards like the one in Lacawac. Look near the trunks in late May.

Lackawanna State Forest

Phone - (570) 963-4561
Website - http://www.dcnr.state.pa.us/forestry/stateforests/lackawanna.aspx
Admission Fee - None
Directions - *Pleasant View Summit, Lackawanna County; from I-80 take Exit 284 and head north on PA 115. After 5.5 miles look for River Road (SR 2040) on the right and turn. Turn left on Bear Pond Road (SR 2016) to the forest headquarters.*

The Park
The Lackawanna State Forest, noted for its diverse recreational opportunities, contains a total of 8,115 acres of State Forest land in two separate tracts. The park consists of two tracts: the larger and more developed Thornhurst Tract (6,711 acres) and the wilder West Nanticoke Tract. Formal hiking trails have not been developed here.

The Walks
The 23-mile *Pinchot Trail System* is a large loop that was laid out by Frank Gantz, a retired truck driver, in the 1970s. It offers everything from a scenic overlook of expansive forests, a path sheltered by hemlocks next to a gurgling creek, to bog areas which contain some plants not common to Pennsylvania. You can do the entire orange-blazed trail across the Pocono Plateau in a day with your dog but if you aren't that ambitious a good sampler is the *Choke Creek Trail* in the southern swing of the system.

> **Where The Paw Meets The Earth:** Rocky dirt/grass roads and paths
> **Workout For Your Dog** - Long trails but not arduous climbing
> **Swimming** - Bear Lake and its tiny neighbor Grassy Pond are the best places to take your dog
> **Restrictions On Dogs** - None

Something Extra
This 87-acre Spruce Swamp Natural Area, located on the Thornhurst tract, is noted for its glacial bog where native spruce, balsam fir, and tamarack are found. Labrador Tea and Bog Roseary, not commonly found in Pennsylvania, also grow here. Surrounding the bog and acting as a buffer is a typical hardwood forest interspersed with hemlock and assorted pines.

Lackawanna State Park

Phone - (570) 945-3239
Website - http://www.dcnr.state.pa.us/stateparks/parks/lacka-wanna.aspx
Admission Fee - None
Directions - *Dalton, Lackawanna County; from I-81 north of Scranton take Exit 199 and travel three miles west on PA 524. Visitors coming via U.S. routes 6 and 11 should take PA 438 east about three miles to PA 407, then south. entrance.*

The Park
The price of water indirectly led to the creation of Lackawanna State Park on this former swath of farmland. In 1912, the D.L. & W. Railroad felt that they were being overcharged for water and began purchasing land to build their own reservoir. The Scranton Gas and Water Company lowered their price and the lake was never built. The land was leased to farmers until 1946 when Robert Moffat, a prominent Scranton coal operator, purchased the land and rented it to his employees. In 1968, the Commonwealth of Pennsylvania purchased the land and developed it into an outstanding recreation area whose primary attraction is Lackawanna Lake, the meeting place of many streams (Lacka-wanna is an American Indian word meaning "the meeting of two streams"). The park was dedicated on June 10, 1972.

The Walks
Over five miles of trails fold back on one another, mostly on the east side of the lake. Much of the second-growth forest in the 1,411-acre park was planted in rows of pine and hemlock trees. You can even cobble together a route to circle the lake cutting through the recreation area and using some short walks on paved roads.

> **Where The Paw Meets The Earth:** Rocky dirt trails mostly, plus some grass and paved roads
> **Workout For Your Dog** - Moderate climbing and many easy stretches
> **Swimming** - Lackawanna Lake and farm ponds
> **Restrictions On Dogs** - Dogs are not allowed in the campground

Something Extra
In 1898 several area farmers organized the Maitland Fair and Driving Park Association. Annual fairs and horseraces attracted large crowds for a dozen years. The site of the former racecourse is located in the park camping area on the *Woodland Ponds Trail*.

Lehigh Gorge State Park

Phone - (570) 443-0400
Website - http://www.dcnr.state.pa.us/stateparks/parks/lehigh-gorge.aspx#history
Admission Fee - None
Directions - *Jim Thorpe, Carbon County; Glen Onoko is the southern access area and may be reached by taking Exit 74 of the Northeast Extension of the Pennsylvania Turnpike. Follow US 209 south to Jim Thorpe. Then take PA 903 north across the river to Coalport Road. Turn off of Coalport to Glen Onoko.*

The Park

In the early 1800s, the need to transport increasingly large quantities of coal to markets down the Lehigh River river led to construction of 20 dams and 29 locks over the 26 miles between Mauch Chunk (now Jim Thorpe) and White Haven. It was called the Upper Grand Section of the Lehigh Canal because the locks and dams were larger and far more impressive than the locks of other canals. At the turn of the 20th century, railroads popularized the southern end of the canal as a resort called Glen Onoko. Hotel Wahnetah boasted 47 rooms, a dance pavilion, tennis courts, fresh air and hikes to the scenic Glen Onoko Falls. A fire in 1911 closed the hotel and a fire in 1917 ended the resort era. The gorge lay forgotten. In the 1970s, the Commonwealth of Pennsylvania began purchasing parklands and in 1980 the land was turned over to the Bureau of State Parks.

The Walks

The 26-mile *Lehigh Gorge Trail* is mostly for biking so canine hikers will want to cross under the railroad tracks and tackle the demanding *Glen Onoko Run Trail*. In about a mile the stream will tumble 900 feet over seven distinct waterfalls. Chamelon Falls, that drops 150 feet, is the highest and most colorful cataract. You will be moving almost straight up at times, hopping across the stream and picking your way to the top. The return trip can be down a less arduous side route to complete a loop or back down the way you came.

> **Where The Paw Meets The Earth:** Rocky dirt trails and slippery rocks
> **Workout For Your Dog** - Absolutely
> **Swimming** - Glen Onoko Run doesn't run very deep very often but the Lehigh River calms down enough at this point to offer some excellent canine swimming
> **Restrictions On Dogs** - None

Something Extra

When severe flooding in the mid-1800s destroyed the canal system, it was replaced with the new technology of railroads. Remains of locks, dams and towpath are still evident in the Lehigh River Gorge.

Lock 12 Historic Area

Phone - (800) 354-8383
Website - http://www.pplweb.com/holtwood/things+to+do/lock+12+historic+area.htm
Admission Fee - None
Directions - *Holtwood; York County, the park is on River Road at the Norman Wood Bridge on Route 372 over the Susquehanna River.*

The Park

In America's great canal-building age of the 1820s and 1830s there was obvious interest in creating an efficient waterway down the Susquehanna to the Chesapeake Bay. In 1835 the Susquehanna and Tidewater Canal Company was chartered to build a canal 45 miles from Wrightsville to Havre de Grace. Engineers had to overcome an elevation drop of 233 feet with the construction of 28 lift locks. The canal was ready for traffic by 1840 and until 1894 thousands of barges hauling coal, lumber, iron and grain maneuvered through the canal at speeds no greater than four miles per hour. The Pennsylvania Power & Light Company maintains the Lock 12 Historic Area.

The Walks

The Lock 12 Historic Area includes the 190-mile *Mason-Dixon Trail* as it enters York County on its peripatetic journey from Chadds Ford south of Philadelphia to the *Appalachian Trail* west of Harrisburg. The narrow band of trail is akin to walking atop a stone wall as it travels through the park. A satisfying canine hike is to take the *Mason-Dixon Trail* north until it swings across River Road ans south through the Lock 13 area.

> **Where The Paw Meets The Earth:** Dirt and rocks
> **Workout For Your Dog** - Expect some tough stepping
> **Swimming** - Much of the Susquehanna River bottom below the Holtwood Dam is exposed, creating small pockets of water that are ideal doggie swimming pools; heed the signs to evacuate the area if a water release from the dam is signaled
> **Restrictions On Dogs** - None

Something Extra

Lock 12 has survived in remarkably pristine condition and has been preserved by the power company. The walls, meticulously constructed of native schist-stone by hand, are still intact although the wooden gates that closed to seal in water and raise the barges 8.8 feet in less than 10 minutes have disintegrated. For those who prefer their historical ruins less groomed, walk a half-mile downstream to the remains of Lock 13. You can still see the fine craftsman that has enabled the stone walls to survive more than 100 years after they were abandoned, albeit in a much wilder states. Large trees even grown in the middle of the lock now.

Lorimer Nature Preserve

Phone - None
Website - None
Admission Fee - None
Directions - *Paoli, Chester County; themain entrance is on North Valley Road, north of Swedesford Road. Turn right into the small parking lot up the hill from the bridge across Valley Creek.*

The Park
The nature preserve, managed by the Open Land Conservancy, is named for George Horimer Lorimer, longtime editor of the Saturday Evening Post. Lorimer, a resident of Wyncote, was a passionate con-servationist during his lifetime.

The Walks
The Lorimer Preserve is an ideal spot for a walk of less than an hour. The short, interconnecting maze of trails offer a pleasing mix of open fields and woods. The walking is easy throughout with many flat streches, especially in the fields. There is no map or trail mark-ings but you should not need to call out the St. Bernards to help you back to the car.

>**Where The Paw Meets The Earth:** The paths are almost all paw-pleasing grass
>**Workout For Your Dog** - Two terrace-like park sections connected by short downhills
>**Swimming** - Two ponds are on the property; the woods pond is always filled and ready for your water-loving dog but the field pond, the larger of the two, is subject to the vagaries of drought
>**Restrictions On Dogs** - None

Something Extra
The best stick-fetching pond in greater Philadelphia. Tucked into a hollow in the woods, the pond is scarcely 25 yards across at any point. Your dog can swim across the pond to retrieve a stick and meet you on the other side as you circle the water on land.

Main Line Colleges

Phone - None
Website - None
Admission Fee - None
Directions - *From east to west: Haverford is on Route 30. Follow the signs to the Visitor Parking Lot where you can pick up a campus map and the trailhead. Bryn Mawr is three blocks north of Route 30 via Roberts Road. Parking is on the street. Rosemont College is on Montgmery Avenue; visitor parking is left of the entrance. Villanova is spread across Routes 30 and 321. The main parking is opposite the campus on Route 30.*

The Park
Several private colleges along the Main Line welcome responsible dog owners to visit campus.

The Walks
Bryn Mawr College Arboretum. This English-landscape style campus mixes massive trees with its gothic buildings. The campus grounds were designed by the firm of Frederick Law Olmsted, architects of many of America's greatest parks.

Haverford College Arboretum. The college dates to 1833, making it the oldest institution of higher learning with Quaker roots in the country. There are two walking choices here: a nearly three-mile loop around the perimeter of the campus (you'll barely see any school buildings) or an Arboretum tour highlighting 33 special trees.

Rosemont College. At 56 acres, the smallest of the Main Line grounds, Rosemont offers a quiet walk around the knob of a hill. At the center of campus is Rathalla, resplendent with its French Renaissance turrets. The original house on the Sinnott Estate, it once contained all college activities.

Villanova Arboretum. The oldest and largest Catholic university in Pennsylvania formally dedicated its arboretum in 1993 - more than 100 years after many of the school's 1,500 trees were well-established. The trees are easily identified from the paths.

> **Where The Paw Meets The Earth:** Dirt, grass and asphalt
> **Workout For Your Dog** - All easy going
> **Swimming** - There are small streams at Haverford and Rosemont but no canine swimming
> **Restrictions On Dogs** - None

Something Extra
These four colleges are close enough to one another that they all may be enjoyed in an afternoon.

Marsh Creek State Park

Phone - (610) 458-5119
Website - http://www.dcnr.state.pa.us/stateparks/parks/marshcreek.aspx
Admission Fee - None
Directions - *Downingtown, Chester County; the hiking trails at Marsh Creek are reached from Route 282 (Creek Road). From the south, make a right on Reeds Road North. From the north, make a left on Lyndell Road. Both feed into Marsh Creek Road and the parking lot.*

The Park
To counter frequent flooding in the Brandywine Creek watershed, plans for Marsh Creek Dam began in 1955. Work on the 89-foot earthen dam began in 1970. In 1974 the lake began to fill and six months later 535 acres of what used to be Milford Mills were under up to 73 feet of water. Gone were 42 residences and more than 70 old barns and other structures.

The Walks
Marsh Creek Lake dominates the 1,705 acres of the park. There is no hiking at the main entrance on the east side of the lake. All the hiking - six miles worth - lies on the western shores. The main loop (*Bridle Trail*) is interjected with three inner loops. The trail is on a hill overlooking the lake but water views are few. The trails are heavily wooded. The terrain is hilly leading from the trailhead but easy walking once the high hill is scaled; down the opposite side of the hill the trail hooks into an old railbed along the East Branch of the Brandywine Creek. This stretch of trail, the prettiest in the park, is flat. The trails are mostly dirt although there are long patches of rocky ground on the slopes that are tough on foot and paw.

> **Where The Paw Meets The Earth:** Rocky dirt
> **Workout For Your Dog** - Long flat stretches intermingled with hill climbs
> **Swimming** - Accessed from the parking lot, Marsh Creek Lake offers the best lake swimming in Chester County; the Brandywine Creek here is usually too shallow for anything more than splashing
> **Restrictions On Dogs** - None

Something Extra
Theodore Burr built a bridge spanning the Hudson River at Waterford, New York in 1804. He added an arch segment to the multiple truss bridge popular at the time, attaining a longer span. Patented in 1817, the Burr Arch Truss became one of the most common in the construction of covered bridges. The Larkin's Bridge, a 65-foot long, 45-ton "Burr Arch" covered bridge erected in 1854 and rebuilt in 1881, was relocated to the northeast section of the park in 1972. Larkin's Covered Bridge is the only remaining legacy of Milford Mills.

Mauch Chunk Lake Park

Phone - (570) 325-3669
Website - http://www.carboncounty.com/park/index.htm
Admission Fee - Yes, daily rate or seasonal
Directions - *Jim Thorpe, Carbon County; from the Pennsylvania Turnpike take the Lehigh Valley exit and go south on PA 209 thru Lehighton into Jim Thorpe. Make a left at first stoplight in Jim Thorpe and head uphill through town for 4 miles. The park entrance is on left.*

The Park
Coal excavated from the mines on Summit Hill here departed on an ingenious journey to the markets in Philadelphia beginning in 1828. Gravity took unpowered wooden coal cars down a switchbacking rail into the town of Mauch Chunk (now Jim Thorpe). Barges in the Lehigh River then floated the coal through a series of brilliantly engineered locks and canals. Meanwhile, mules hauled the empty cars back up the mountain on a parallel track for the next load. Steam power eventually replaced the mules but the gravity railroad lasted until 1933 - its final years spent as one of America's first rollercoasters and a popular tourist destination for thrill seekers. The lake and 2,500-acre park were completed in 1972 to control floods and as a recreational facility and public drinking supply for Jim Thorpe.

The Walks
The marquee trail in the park is the *Switchback Trail* that has been developed as a corridor to the recreation facilities of the valley and the town of Jim Thorpe. The down track follows the gentle 2% grade while the back track is a heartier canine hike. The trail, that crosses itself to create an elongated figure-eight configuration, climbs to Mt. Pisgah and numerous views of the Lehigh River gorge. The full up-and-down canine hike will cover about 11 miles. For dogs not ready to bite off this ambitious hike, the *Shoreline Trail* stays in the park and slips between mixed hardwoods and open shoreline around the lake. The full circuit covers six miles, almost all of it across easy, level terrain. You can also explore the *Fireline Trail*, a 3.5-mile shale roadway that runs along the top of the Mauch Chunk Ridge. Again, this is an easy ramble for your dog.

> **Where The Paw Meets The Earth:** Natural and paved surfaces
> **Workout For Your Dog** - Yes, long hikes
> **Swimming** - Plenty of good swimming in Mauch Chunk Lake
> **Restrictions On Dogs** - Dogs can use the trails but can't go in the beach or swimming areas or stay overnight in the campground

Something Extra
If you take the *Switchback Trail* into the town of Jim Thorpe walk your dog past the Asa Packer Mansion, a grand Italianate Villa that was the home of philanthropist, railroad magnate, and founder of Lehigh University, Asa Packer. It is easily identified by its red-ribbed tin roof and central cupola. The home was built in 1861 over a cast iron frame at the cost of $14,000 dollars (the equivalent of $2.3 million dollars today) and renovated twenty years later with another $85,000. The most amazing story about this National Historic Landmark is that the mansion was boarded up from 1912 until 1956 and it was never vandalized and nothing was ever stolen from the house.

McKaig Nature Education Center

Phone - None
Website - None
Admission Fee - None
Directions - *Upper Merion, Montgomery County; bounded roughly by King of Prussia Road, Brower Road and Croton Road. Parking is available on Brower Road (one or two cars on the roadside) and at the Roberts School on Croton Road. From Route 202, take Warner Road south to the end. Make a left on Croton Road and the school is on the right.*

The Park

The Upper Merion Park and Historic Foundation was created in 1964 to preserve the area's rapidly diminishing open space. Small accruals of land gifts began accumulating and today the McKaig Nature Education Center pushes back the encroaching development with 89 wooded acres.

The Walks

A jewel among the region's small parks, McKaig features three wide and well-maintained trails that range in walking time from 15 minutes to 45 minutes. The *Cadet Trail* is a linear exploration running up the spine of the property. Two loop trails branch off the Cadet: the *Nancy Long Trail* and the short, but steep *Laurel Trail*. The loops are hillier than the *Cadet Trail* but the trails work around the hillside rather than straight up the slopes on these sporty walks.

> **Where The Paw Meets The Earth:** Paw-friendly dirt
> **Workout For Your Dog** - Yes, out of the stream valley
> **Swimming** - The Crow Creek is a tumbling, pleasing little brook but seldom deep enough for anything beyond doggie splashing
> **Restrictions On Dogs** - None

Something Extra

This is one of the best places to walk for arboreal education. Many of the trees along the *Nancy Long Trail* are marked for identification, including a rare American Chestnut. The greatest tree in the Colonial forest, the American Chestnut was struck down by a pandemic chestnut blight in the 1930s. Full-grown specimens of the tree have become nearly extinct, although some hardy shoots have survived. But as they mature, they too will fall victim to the fatal blight, as will this sapling.

Middle Creek Wildlife Management Area

Phone - (717) 733-1512
Website - http://www.pgc.state.pa.us/pgc/cwp/view.
asp?a=487&q=159288
Admission Fee - None
Directions - *Kleinfeltersville, on the Lancaster-Lebanon County border. The park Visitor Center is on Hopeland Road, south of Kleinfeltersville from Route 897 or north of Clay from Route 322.*

The Park
A large chunk of Furnace Hills woodland was purchased in the 1930s with money from hunting licenses and the preserve was eventually built to more than 5,000 acres of wildfowl habitat. Today hunting license money maintains all operations at Middle Creek. Although conceived with Canada geese in mind, more than 280 species of birds have been identified around the 400-acre shallow water lake created by the damming of Middle Creek.

The Walks
If you begin your tour at the Visitor Center your first canine hike at Middle Creek will be on the *Conservation Trail*, a 1.5-mile loop of easy walking. The grass and dirt trail is the most paw-friendly of the hikes in the preserve. More challenging is the *Millstone Trail*, that grinds 300 feet up into the Furnace Hills south of the lake at White Oak Picnic Area (the trailhead is across Millstone Road). The entire mile-plus affair is conducted under a lush canopy of hardwoods. The best canine hike at Middle Creek is a forging of trails into a triangular circuit south of the Visitor Center with parking along Hopeland Road near the impoundment dam. To get the toughest stretch out of the way first, take the yellow-blazed *Horse-Shoe Trail* fork to the right for a narrow, rocky climb up the hillside. Elbow room awaits at the top of the hill and the remainder of the two-hour trek uses old roads (a left on the *Elders Run Trail*) and an abandoned trolley line (a final left on the *Middle Creek Trail*). This final leg traces a tumbling Middle Creek, not deep enough for canine swimming though.

> **Where The Paw Meets The Earth:** Soft grass to rocky dirt
> **Workout For Your Dog** - Yes, especially in the Furnace Hills
> **Swimming** - Creeks and pond on the property
> **Restrictions On Dogs** - None

Something Extra
A short stroll on the paved *Willow Point Trail* through open ground leads to the most scenic viewpoint of the 400-acre lake. On the way, scan the surrounding fields grazed by geese and listen for songbirds. During migrations, swans and snow geese blanket the sky above the point. One of Pennsylvania's three-score eagle nests can be seen across the water here.

Money Rocks County Park

Phone - (717) 299-8215
Website - http://co.lancaster.pa.us/parks/cwp/view.asp?a=676&q=518297&parksNav=|7871|
Admission Fee - None
Directions - *New Holland, Lancaster County; from Route 23 East pick up Route 322 East. After four miles take a right onto Narvon Road. Climb for about a mile and look for the parking lot at the top of the rise on the right.*

The Park

If you are looking for long, solitary walks through the woods with your dog in Lancaster County you can head for the Furnace Hills, the largest continuous forest remaining in the county or the Welsh Mountains, with the second most. The latter is home to Money Rocks Park - so-named because it was long believed that Pequa Valley farmers hid cash in the outcroppings - with more than 300 acres of mature woodland.

The Walks

The trail system at Money Rocks travels on a spiderweb of old mining and logging roads. Most are paw-friendly dirt, others are rock-filled, but all are wide and airy under the mature black birch trees that dominate the ridge. There are two named trails: *Overlook* (white) and *Cockscomb* (red), named for another line of rock outcroppings further down the ridge from Money Rocks. The *Cockscomb* penetrates deeper into the woods on a long buttonhook that eventually drops down off the ridge before heading back up the hill. This is the hardiest climb you will encounter at Money Rocks.

> **Where The Paw Meets The Earth:** Some soft dirt, some stony paths
> **Workout For Your Dog** - Moderate climbs and longish trails
> **Swimming** - None; you will walk a long way before you stumble across a little stream
> **Restrictions On Dogs** - None

Something Extra

The exposed ridge and rock outcroppings at Money Rocks serve up impressive views of surrounding farmlands and distant towns with not a great deal of purchase on your canine hike.

Monocacy Hill

Phone - (800) 354-8383
Website - http://www.monocacyhill.org/
Admission Fee - None
Directions - *Douglassville, Berks County; Take 422 West
approximately 1 mile past Route 662 to right turn at Monocacy
Creek Road. Turn right and continue to first stop sign at Loyalsock
Drive. Follow to end and turn right on to Hill Road. Follow for
.7 mile to Y in road. Bear left at Y on to Geiger Road.
Proceed up hill to parking lot on left.*

The Park

Monocacy Hill Recreation Area is a 420-acre forest located in Amity
Township. This recreation area was purchased by Amity Township in
1967 for open space and recreation purposes. The park has a wide
variety of plant life. To date, 170 species of herbaceous plants have
been identified, along with 65 species of trees and shrubs, and 17
species of ferns and related plants.

The Walks

There are five miles of interesting trail time on Monocacy Hill with
the star being the white-blazed *Monocacy Hill Trail* that scales the
860-foot hilltop that dominates the surrounding landscape. Views
extend to the west from the summit. Providing a contrast to the hill
climb is the green-blazed *Creek Trail* that scampers through a wet,
low-lying area to loop around a small waterfall and pool. Various connecting trails circle around the hill on wide, wooded paths. Hunting
is allowed on Monocacy Hill so plan a Sunday trip with your dog in
huntng season.

> **Where The Paw Meets The Earth:** Dirt trails and rock-
> hopping at the summit of Monocacy Hill
> **Workout For Your Dog** - It is a steady but not overly
> arduous climb to the top
> **Swimming** - The creeks in the conservation area are
> narrow and shallow
> **Restrictions On Dogs** - None

Something Extra

The Reading Railroad ran across the southern tier of the property a
century ago, leaving an interesting array of structures behind.

Moon Lake Park

Phone - (570) 477-5467
Website - http://www.moonlakepark.com/
Admission Fee - None
Directions - *Hunlock Creek, Luzerne County; southwest of Wilkes Barre. The entrance road is off Route 29 (Lake Silkworth Road), accessed four miles south from Route 118 in Pike's Creek or north from Route 11 in West Nanticoke.*

The Park
Moon Lake is a natural 48-acre lake that was developed as a recreational oasis by Luzerne County in 1968. The 600 acres of farms and fields are the only facility of its type within the county.

The Walks
Most of the 20 miles of hiking trails are best suited for cross-country skiing. When the ground is snow-free the first choice for canine hikers will be the *Nature's Way Trail* that pushes away from the park office in a one-mile loop. The 29-station interpretive trail rolls gently through former farm fields that have been reclaimed by the forest. The path is narrow in most places and rocky under paw.

> **Where The Paw Meets The Earth:** Wooded dirt trails, often with rocky soil and grass
> **Workout For Your Dog** - The hills are rolling rather than demanding
> **Swimming** - Moon Lake suits the bill nicely
> **Restrictions On Dogs** - Dogss are not permitted in the swimming pool area or any restroom or shower area

Something Extra
On the *Nature's Way Trail* you can see a determined tree growing through a rock - a trenchant example of how the land is colonized by plants. Eventually the tree will cause the rock to split allowing lichens to grow freely and begin turning this rock into soil. Not anytime soon, however.

Mount Minsi

Phone - None
Website - None
Admission Fee - None
Directions - *East Stroudsburg, Monroe County; exit from I-80 south on PA 611 and turn right on Mountain Road in .8 mile. Steer left onto Lake Road at the approaching fork and park on the right.*

The Park
The Delaware River, the largest undammed and free-flowing river east of the Mississippi, makes an S-turn that has ground out the Delaware Water Gap at this point. The sentinels of the Gap are Mount Tammany in New Jersey and Mount Minsi in Pennsylvania.

The Walks
The *Appalachian Trail* enters - or exits - Pennsylvania at this point. You can tag the summit of Mount Minsi with your dog on a loop that includes the AT and an old fire road. Most climbers head up on the steeper, twisting *Appalachian Trail* and come down on the wider, less severe fire road. You will be stopping often to soak in the views across the Water Gap from exposed rocks on the cliffs (this is not a dangerous route for your dog, however).

> **Where The Paw Meets The Earth:** Rocky dirt trail and rocky dirt road
> **Workout For Your Dog** - Tough, rewarding climbing
> **Swimming** - Lake Lenape is ideally situated at the beginning of the hike making it an ideal place for your dog to cool off after the climb - very easy access to the water for your dog as well
> **Restrictions On Dogs** - None

Something Extra
The splendid views give out before you reach the actual summit of 1,463 feet. To get to the top of Mount Minsi continue another quarter-mile along the *Appalachian Trail* and take a little detour to the remains of an old fire tower. Look amidst the spruce trees for a marker in the rocks.

Mount Penn

Phone - (610) 375-6399
Website - http://pagodaskyline.org
Admission Fee - None
Directions - *Reading, Berks County; on the eastern edge of the city. Several roads wind through neighborhoods from Business Route 422. Hill Road climbs to the summit.*

The Park

Much of the southern area of the Schuylkill River valley is underlaid by porous limestone and dolomite that produces rich, fertile farm-land. But a few fingers of resistant, granatic bedrock that form steep hills and ridges - known as the Reading Prong - dot the area. Mount Penn is one of those. In 1748 two sons of William Penn laid out the city of Reading, creating a grid that ran right up to the base of the mountain. Resorts and hotels sprang up on Mount Penn in the 1800s, with gravity railroads built to serve them. In 1900 automotile pioneer Charles Duryea moved to Reading and tested some of America's first cars on the slopes of Mount Penn.

The Walks

If you are starting a canine hiking day atop Mount Penn, descend the concrete stairs at the pagoda and enter the maze of trails across Mount Penn. These trails will take you across the mountain or down into the city of Reading. If you cross Skyline Drive you can hike the mountain down to the town of Mt. Penn or east 2.6 miles to a small nature center by Antietam Lake. Expect these trails to be rocky under paw in many places as you travel on old fire roads and some well-worn footpaths. Depending on your taste, you can tackle some severe climbs on these slopes.

> **Where The Paw Meets The Earth:** Lots of stones, pavement
> **Workout For Your Dog** - Yes, especially if you go down the mountain
> **Swimming** - An occasional stream and Antietam Lake if you go that far
> **Restrictions On Dogs** - None

Something Extra

William Witman was tearing Mount Penn up with his quarrying and then quit when he realized what he was doing. Instead he built a luxury hotel - based on a postcard with a pagoda-styled building. By 1908 - and $50,000 later - his red brick and tile pagoda in the style of a cattle castle of the Shogun Dynasty of Japan loomed 886 feet above the city. He was never able to secure a liquor license or get a decent access road built and his hotel never opened. In 1910 he sold the 72-foot pagoda to Jonathan Mould, who in turn sold it to the City of Reading for a single dollar.

Mt. Pisgah State Park

Phone - (570) 297-2734
Website - http://www.dcnr.state.pa.us/stateparks/parks/mtpisgah.aspx
Admission Fee - None
Directions - *Forksville, Bradford County; on Wallace Road (SR 3019), two miles north of US 6.*

The Park
The land that became Mt. Pisgah State Park was first cleared for farmland in the early 1800s. Later a resort hotel with a 27-meter observation tower was built on this isolated hill. The Commonwealth of Pennsylvania obtained the land in 1969 with funds from Project 70, a state bond issue. Facilities were developed through Project 500, another state bond issue, and a grant from the Federal Land and Water Conservation Fund. Stephen Foster Dam, named for the beloved composer who spent time in school in nearby Towanda, was completed in 1977. Mt Pisgah State Park was dedicated in 1979.

The Walks
An easy leg stretcher in the park is the 2-mile circumnavigation of Stephen Foster Lake on the *Oh! Susanna Trail*. Intrepid canine hikers will want to tag the Mt. Pisgah summit on the linear *Ridge Trail* that climbs over 800 feet but take a mile to do it. There are plenty of open air views and second-growth forest on the journey. Grab a park map before setting out on the other trails since not many loop in this park.

> **Where The Paw Meets The Earth:** Rocky dirt roads and grass
> **Workout For Your Dog** - Some of the best, toughest hiking around
> **Swimming** - Fine swimming for your dog is on tap in the lake
> **Restrictions On Dogs** - None

Something Extra
Look for stone walls that are remnants of the farmland cleared by New England immigrants to the area. Stone walls were used to mark property lines and constrain farm animals. Stone walls were not erected without great planning and care - often a farmer's wall had to be inspected by local authorities after it was constructed. If it passed scrutiny a farmer could not be held responsible for damage to his crops by neighboring animals.

Nescopeck State Park

Phone - (570) 403-2006
Website - http://www.dcnr.state.pa.us/stateparks/parks/nesco-peck.aspx
Admission Fee - None
Directions - *Drums, Luzerne County; traveling west on I-80 take Exit 273 (White Haven, Freeland). Turn right onto PA 940. At the stop sign, go straight onto PA 437 for about 4.5 miles. Directly after power lines go left onto Honey Hole Road. Travel about 2 miles to enter the Lake Frances Day Use Area. It will be on your left side opposite Lake Frances Road.*

The Park

Bordered on the south by the steeply rising Mount Yeager and on the north by Nescopeck Mountain, Nescopeck State Park, one of Pennsylvania's newest parks, encompasses 3,550 acres. Nescopeck Creek meanders through the valley providing water for wetlands and rich forests. Nescopeck State Park has traditionally been managed for the American woodcock, which is one of many game species found in the thickets and woods along the creek.

The Walks

A series of short loops emanate from Honey Hole Road and lead to Nescopeck Creek through light woods and abandoned farmfields. Most of your dog's trotting will take place on old roads on gentle grades. Make sure you grab a trail map to chart your hiking day on about a dozen short, marked, interconnecting trails.

> **Where The Paw Meets The Earth:** Dirt, grass and many soft spots
>
> **Workout For Your Dog** - Easy going in most of the park but for those dogs looking to work cross the road for the *Mountain Loop* up Nescopeck Mountain
>
> **Swimming** - Beaver ponds are splendid for your water-loving dog and so is Lake Frances; even Nescopeck Creek is deep enough for swims in spots
>
> **Restrictions On Dogs** - None

Something Extra

In 1898 several area farmers organized the Maitland Fair and Driving Park Association. Annual fairs and horseraces attracted large crowds for a dozen years. The site of the former racecourse is located in the park camping area on the *Woodland Ponds Trail*.

Neshaminy State Park

Phone - (215) 639-4538
Website - http://www.dcnr.state.pa.us/stateparks/Parks/neshaminy.aspx
Admission Fee - None
Directions - *Bensalem, Bucks County; from the Route 132 (Street Road) Exit off I-95, go east to State Road and turn left. The park is at the intersection of Dunks Ferry Road, less than one mile away.*

The Park

Neshaminy State Park takes its name from the confluence of Neshaminy Creek with the Delaware River. Although the water flows another 116 miles to the Atlantic Ocean, the river is still affected by the tides here. Indian tribes congregated here to build fishing weirs, small fences in the water that fish swim over at high tide and become trapped at low tide. Dunken Williams operated a ferry crossing of the Delaware River at this point in 1679 and Dunks Ferry Road on the eastern boundary of the park has been used for more than 300 years. The land was deeded to the Commonwealth of Pennsylvania in 1956.

The Walks

Neshaminy State Park is the best park in the area to experience the Delaware River. There are four miles of formal hiking trails on the 330-acre property shaped like a fingernail poking into the river. The *River View Trail* traces the shoreline providing access to the tidal marsh and river and affording riveting views of the ship traffic in the Delaware and the Philadelphia skyline. The *River Trail Inner Loop* explores the interior of the park. The *River Walk* is a shaded dirt trail; the inner loop is more open and follows a gravel road. There is an ample grass shoulder that that will save paws. Also available is the *Logan Walk*, a paved, tree-lined path that was the original drive to the former Robert Logan Home, whose Sarobia estate was the foundation for the park.

> **Where The Paw Meets The Earth:** Mostly soft natural trails
> **Workout For Your Dog** - Not much elevation change here
> **Swimming** - There is some of the best canine swimming in the area at a quarter-mile of open access to the Delaware River
> **Restrictions On Dogs** - None

Something Extra

In the northeast area of the park, along the Neshaminy Creek, are several acres of sand dunes that would not be out of place at the Atlantic seashore. This giant sandbox for your dog is at the end of the *Logan Walk*. Nearby is the Pine Plantation where wide, grassy swaths of trails wind among tall, fragrant pines.

Newlin Mill Park

Phone - (610) 459-2359
Website - http://www.newlingristmill.org/
Admission Fee - None
Directions - *Glen Mills, Delaware County; seven miles southwest of Media, on Route 1 at the intersection with South Cheyney Road.*

The Park
In 1704, nathaniel Newlin built a stone grist mill and dam on the headquarters of the West Branch of Chester Creek. The modest mill continued to ground flour commercially until 1941. In 1957, E. Mortimer Newlin, 9th in descent from the Newlin patriarch, Nicholas, who was granted 500 acres of land here in 1685, bought the mill. he created the Nicholas Newlin Foundation to preserve this cornerstone of American colonial life. Today the park encompasses 150 acres.

The Walks
An unmarked, but easy to follow, trail leads through the grounds of the restored mill along the race. once across the dam a three-mile trail system, again unmarked, branches out through woods and fields, including a Christmas tree nursery.

> **Where The Paw Meets The Earth:** Dirt and grass
>
> **Workout For Your Dog** - Away from the stream the terrain gets modestly hilly
>
> **Swimming** - the Chester Creek is a pretty stream but only deep enough mostly for splashing; a preferred spot is behind the dam
>
> **Restrictions On Dogs** - None

Something Extra
A regular planting of unusual trees, shrubs and wildflowers is executed each year at Newlin Mill. Today you can see a grove of California redwoods and sequoias and representatives of the three true cedars in the world: *Cedurs atlantica, C. deodora and C. libanotica*. The native trees are impressive as well - they include a giant ash and giant oak that were here before Nicholas Newlin emigrated from Ireland in 1683.

Nockamixon State Park

Phone - (215) 529-7300
Website - http://www.dcnr.state.pa.us/stateparks/Parks/nocka-mixon.aspx
Admission Fee - None
Directions - *Quakertown, Bucks County; the main entrance to the park is located on Route 563 and is reached from the south on Route 413/412. To reach Haycock Mountain in State Game Lands #157 go west 1.1 miles on Route 563 from the junction with Route 412. Turn onto Top Rock Road and go .6 miles to the parking lot on the left.*

The Park

Nockamixon State Park was planned and developed by the U.S. Army Corps of Engineers with the damming of the Tohickon Creek. The park officially opened in 1973 and the resulting Lake Nockamixon has become the premier destination for boating in southeast Pennsylvania. Combined with the adjacent State Game Land #157, more than 7,000 acres - the largest open space in Bucks County - is available for public recreation.

The Walks

The Lenni-Lenape Indians called the land "nocha-miska-ing" - "at the place of soft soil." Little has changed in the 400 years since. These low, often water-level trails are indeed soft and, many times, downright squishy. There are more than 20 miles of the soft equestrian trails and a paved 2.8-mile bicycle trail skirts the shoreline as well. A 21-mile circumnavigation of Lake Nockamixon can be parsed together with bridle paths, trails and back roads. A unique experience awaits the athletic dog at Haycock Mountain in State Game Land #157. The mountain is essentially a ridge of diabase boulders and the trail to the top calls for almost continuous rock-hopping, a technique called bouldering. The basaltic rock provides incredible traction for boot and paw. A narrow, red-blazed and stone-strewn trail leads uphill from the parking lot to the boulder field. After that the trails are marked by white and blue blazes but the way to the top is frequently obfuscated by scores of fallen trees.

> **Where The Paw Meets The Earth:** Dirt, mud, asphalt and boulders
> **Workout For Your Dog** - Long canine hikes around the lake and a big exercise session on Haystack Mountain
> **Swimming** - Good in the lake when it comes on the trail
> **Restrictions On Dogs** - None

Something Extra

At 960 feet Haycock Mountain wants only ten feet for being the highest point in Bucks County. Views from the heavily wooded summit are obscured in the summer but when the leaves drop a commanding view of Lake Nockamixon is revealed.

Nolde Forest Environmental Education Center

Phone - (610) 796-3699
Website - http://www.dcnr.state.pa.us/STATEPARKS/parks/noldeforest.aspx
Admission Fee - None
Directions - *Reading, Berks County; The Nolde Forest is southwest of the city, on Route 625. There are two entrances, the southern one is the Main Entrance Road, closed on weekends. The northern lot is the Sawmill parking area, open sunrise to sunset every day.*

The Park
Jacob Nolde arrived in Philadelphia as a 21-year old from Germany in 1880 and soon found himself among the German-speaking communities of Berks County. He found work as a weaver and within a decade had purchased enough knitting machines to start his own hosiery manufacturing business. In another ten years he had taken over an entire Reading city block and was operating the second largest textile plant in America. Nolde now had the time and resources to pursue his dream: to create "the most beautiful pine forest in Pennsylvania." He began by purchasing land where he discovered a single white pine tree growing in an abandoned meadow. The lone pine would soon be joined by more than a half-million neighbors - white pine, yellow pine, Norway spruce, Douglas fir, and other coniferous varieties.

The Walks
There are some 10 miles of trails coursing through the forest, mostly on wide, former access roads built by the plantation's foresters. The well-spaced conifers indeed give the feeling of rambling through a pine farm in places. Expect long, steady ascents and descents when creating circuit hikes on the roughly ten miles of trail here. The focal point for the canine hiking along the *Watershed Trail* through the center of the property is Punches Run that flows energetically through the valley floor. Strict adherence to the trail system will roughly generate a figure-eight hike but chances are you will be tempted to break off your intended route to explore something interesting in the verdant forest.

> **Where The Paw Meets The Earth:** Dirt and gravelly asphalt
> **Workout For Your Dog** - All the trails climb
> **Swimming** - North Pond is the best
> **Restrictions On Dogs** - None

Something Extra
Dogs looking to get in some dock diving practice will appreciate North Pond at Nolde Forest. Secluded North Pond is tucked away from many of the trails, use the *Beech Trail* to reach the Pond Loop or drive to a small parking lot on Church Road.

Norristown Farm Park

Phone - (610) 270-0215
Website - http://www.montcopa.org/parks/
norristown%20farm%20park.htm
Admission Fee - None
Directions - *Norristown, Montgomery County; main entrance is
off Germantown Pike on Upper Farm Road (the first house on the
right along the entrance road is Shannon Mansion, built in 1764
and the oldest building on the property). There is also parking on
Whitehall Road.*

The Park
The area that is today Norristown Farm Park was part of a 7000-acre
tract of land belonging to William Penn, known as "William-stadt."
The ownership of the Norris family dates to October 10, 1704 when
Penn's son sold the land to Isaac Norris and William Trent for the
hefty sum of 850 pounds. On November 11, 1717, Trent sold his
share of the manor to Norris. After many subsequent lords, in 1876
the Pennsylvania legislature authorized the purchase of the manor for
the Norristown State Hospital. The hospital eventually spread across
981 acres, 831 of which became a farm supplying not only food but
a supposed conduit to patient recovery. Farm operations became too
costly and ceased in 1975 and the farm fell into disrepair. In 1992,
Montgomery County leased 690 acres to create the county's second
largest park.

The Walks
There are wide, multi-use trails totalling more than five miles at Norristown Farm Park. The trails roughly combine to form adjacent loops
in a figure-eight pattern, passing through natural areas and cultivated
fields of the revitalized farm where corn, soybeans and winter grains
grow. The walking is easy across these rolling hills but there are long
periods without shade for the heat-sensitive dog.

> **Where The Paw Meets The Earth:** All trails are
> paved in macadam
> **Workout For Your Dog** - Gentle slopes
> **Swimming** - Two branches of the Stony Creek knife
> through the property before joining at the baseball field
> into one stream; although it reaches a swimming-friendly
> depth of four feet in places, the water is only accessed
> by the trail a few times
> **Restrictions On Dogs** - None

Something Extra
While many of the Hospital Farm's buildings have disappeared, the
unique dairy barn remains. Built in 1914, it is shaped like a wheel
with four spokes. The fame of the hospital's dairy operation was
widespread. In 1961 alone, nine cows produced 1.1 million pounds
of milk - more than 300 pounds of milk per cow per day.

Nottingham County Park

Phone - (610) 932-9195
Website - http://dsf.chesco.org/ccparks/cwp/view.asp?a=1550&
q=616472&ccparksNav=|34716|
Admission Fee - None
Directions - *Nottingham, Chester County; take Route 1 South and exit on Route 272, crossing back over the highway to the entrance of Herr's Snack Foods on the right. Make a right when you can turn left to the Herr's Factory and another right (Park Road) to the parking lot on the left.*

The Park

Although this area had already been settled for nearly two centuries, it was not until 1828 that serpentinite was dicovered in what is now Nottingham Park. By 1880 the Wood Mine dug to extract the mineral was 800 feet deep and the largest in the world. Chrome, asbestos and quartz were also mined here. The oldest of Chester County's parks, Nottingham was dedicated in 1963.

The Walks

There are 8 trails in Nottingham Park, which can all be covered in a day's hiking. Most of the trails criss-cross and do not loop, often just running out at the boundaries of the 600-acre park. Look for the "Mystery Hole," an abandoned mine now filled with water. The trails switch from wide fire roads to narrow footpaths through the rolling hills across the park. These hills can be formidable at times.

> **Where The Paw Meets The Earth:** Dirt and stone - the serpentine can be tough on the paw
> **Workout For Your Dog** - Some good climbs in store
> **Swimming** - McPherson Lake and Little Pond are open-field swimming holes for a doggie dip
> **Restrictions On Dogs** - None

Something Extra

Nottingham Park is home to the Serpentine Barrens, a seven-mile ridge of igneous rock that is one of only three such serpentine formations in North America. The early settlers called the area of scrub pine and oak "barrens" because its low nutrient-level was unfriendly to cultivation. The distinctive green serpentine rock was a popular building stone and can be seen in many of Chester County's historic structures, including several at West Chester University. An interpretive nature trail describes the fast-draining Serpentine Barrens and visits abandoned quarries.

Oakbourne Park

Phone - None
Website - None
Admission Fee - None
Directions - *Westtown, Chester County; coming south on Route 202, make a left on Matlack Street, which runs into Oakbourne Road and South Concord Road. Make a right into the driveway and proceed past the mansion to the parking lot. Coming north on Route 202, make a right on Route 926 (Street Road) and a left on Concord Road. The park is on the left.*

The Park

John Hulme built the first granite shelter on this land, selecting the highest area on the property for his homesite. In 1882 a wealthy Philadelphia lawyer named James Smith purchased the old Hulme house and renamed it Oakbourne. Oakbourne was soon the center-piece of a 27-acre estate with fountains, miniature lakes and rustic bridges. Smith even had its own private railroad station and post office. Oakbourne was willed out of the Smith family to the Phila-delphia Protestant Episcopal City Mission in 1896 for the operation of a convalescent home for women over 21 years of age. The next 70 years saw thousands of female "guests" treated here before the costly operation overwhelmed its directors. Westtown Township saved Oakbourne from developers in 1974, eventually creating a 90-acre park.

The Walks

Three connecting trails (*Creek, Nature* and *Park*) form a loop of nearly three miles to visit all areas of the park on both sides of Concord Road. The trails are all wooded, including native specimens and the remains of the Smiths' exotic plantings around the mansion. There is an interesting mix of terrain and sights on the remains of the country estate now engulfed by residential development. There are some dips and rolls in some of the wooded areas, including one good climb on the *Creek Trail*.

> **Where The Paw Meets The Earth:** Natural trails
> **Workout For Your Dog** - Rolling hills
> **Swimming** - Part of the trail hopscotches past Chester Creek and one of Smith's miniature lakes, encircled by reeds, is a pleasant canine swimming stop
> **Restrictions On Dogs** - None

Something Extra

The most striking feature of the estate was a 1,000-gallon, twin-tank water tower built on the lawn away from the mansion. Built of stone and brick to resemble a fortress, the tower features dormer-style twin roofs. Smith installed the finest of telescopes at Oakbourne that offered views across the countryside to Chester and Philadelphia.

Peace Valley Park

Phone - (215) 348-6114
Website - http://dsf.chesco.org/ccparks/cwp/view.asp?a=1550&
q=616437&ccparksNav=|34716|
Admission Fee - None
Directions - *Doylestown, Bucks County; three miles
north of town off Route 313, between Ferry Road and New Galena
Road.*

The Park
Ancient earthquakes once rumbled along a fault line under the north
branch of the Neshaminy Creek creating mineral veins of zinc, gold,
copper, silver and uranium. But mostly lead. The rich veins of lead
ore - some 90% pure - were as close as five feet from the surface.
Beginning in the 1860s the first of 26 mine shafts were sunk and
over the next 70 years 2600 tons of ore were hauled from the in-
nards of the earth before the high cost of pumping out water closed
the mines forever. In the 1970s the Neshaminy Creek was dammed
and the main pit flooded. The resulting 356-acre lake was named
Galena, Latin for "lead ore." Today, Peace Valley Park surrounding
Lake Galena includes over 1500 acres, making it one of the largest
parks in south-eastern Pennsylvania.

The Walks
The main hike at Peace Valley is a paved *Hike & Bike Trail* that goes
almost two-thirds of the way around Lake Galena at the western
end. Dogs are not allowed on the Nature Center trails so to complete
a lake circle requires a walk of more than a mile along the narrow
two-lane, shoulderless New Galena Road. It is not recommended.
Short, wooded bridle trails offer hiking on the south shore. There
are no hills at Peace Valley.

> **Where The Paw Meets The Earth:** Mostly pavement and
> some natural surfaces
> **Workout For Your Dog** - All easy going
> **Swimming** - The grassy, landscaped banks of Lake Galena
> provide an especially inviting entry to a doggie dip, even
> for dogs that routinely shy away from the water
> **Restrictions On Dogs** - No dogs in the Nature Center

Something Extra
At the end of Creek Road on the south shore is a parking lot with
close access to a dog training area where you can let the dog off the
leash to fetch objects from the water.

Pennypack Park

Phone - None
Website - None
Admission Fee - None
Directions - *Philadelphia; stretching from the eastern border of Montgomery County almost to the Delaware River. Parking is generally available near the major north-south cross roads through the park.*

The Park
Pennypack Park gets its name from the Lenni-Lenape Indians who hunted and fished along the creek for hundreds of years. The name means "dead deep water." Pennypack Park has often been called the Cradle of American Ornithology due to work done here by John James Audubon and Alexander Wilson. The City of Philadelphia established the park in 1905 to insure protection of 1600 acres of wood- lands and wetlands.

The Walks
Pennypack Park is the younger, rougher brother to the Wissahickon Gorge. The adventurous canine hiker can search out miles of little-used side trails, many quite narrow, off the main 18-mile multi-use trail. The land around the Pennypack Creek is modestly hilly, although you can walk for a long time without noticing it.

> **Where The Paw Meets The Earth:** Watch for paw-slicing glass on some of the dirt trails; the multi-use trail is paved
> **Workout For Your Dog** - Moderate hill-climbing
> **Swimming** - The fall line of the Pennypack Creek is in the park south of Frankford Avenue where the last set of rapids play out and the water drops to the level of its final destination, the Delaware River; after the fall line, the tides change the swimming pools from shallow to deep and back again in a twice-repeated daily cycle.
> **Restrictions On Dogs** - None

Something Extra
The fall line on the Pennypack Creek was the natural choice for ford-ing the creek back to Indian days. William Penn was not so patient in waiting for the tide to take the water away each day and in 1683 he asked that "an order be given for building a bridge over the Penny-pack." Each male resident was taxed in either money or labor to build the bridge, that, when completed in 1697, became the first Three Arch Stone bridge in America. Designated a National Civil Engineering Landmark, the bridge over Frankford Avenue in Pennypack Park is the oldest stone bridge still carrying heavy traffic in America.

Pennypack Preserve

Phone - (215) 657-0830
Website - http://www.pennypacktrust.org/about.htm
Admission Fee - None
Directions - *Bryn Athyn, Montgomery County; the trailhead for the wilderness trails is at the corner of Terwood Road and Creek Road. From the intersection of Huntingdon Pike (Route 232) and Old Welsh Road (Route 63), go west on Old Welsh Road and make the first right across the bridge onto Terwood Road. Creek Road is one mile on the right. The trails can also be accessed from Mason's Mill Park on Mason's Mill Road.*

The Park
The privately owned Pennypack Ecological Restoration Trust has been assembling a natural area preserve since 1970. Using land purchases, donations and conservation easements, the preserve has grown to 683 acres.

The Walks
There are 7 miles of trails here; dogs are allowed only in the Wilderness Area. Three connecting trails, each with its own personality, create a linear trail along the Pennypack Creek for about 2 1/2 miles. The longest, the *Deep Creek Road Trail*, is a country lane walk with plenty of access to the meandering stream. The middle leg, the *Pennypack Creek Trail*, hugs a hillside and is characterized by tall trees, especially conifers. The Pennypack Parkway is an old gravel access road, draped in a shaded canopy of trees. The walking here is mostly level with imperceptible ups and downs along the way.

> **Where The Paw Meets The Earth:** Natural trails and gravel
> **Workout For Your Dog** - Long, easy walks
> **Swimming** - The Pennypack Creek is seldom more than two feet deep, save for the base of Huntingdon Road where there are deep pools
> for doggie paddling
> **Restrictions On Dogs** - None

Something Extra
A floodplain is a safety valve for the release of a raging creek's overflow. Along the *Paper Mill Trail*, just off the *Creek Road Trail*, is an exhibit on managing these protective wetlands that create a unique wildlife habitat. The stone double-arch bridge next to the floodplain exhibit was built in 1847.

Pocono Environmental Education Center

Phone - (570) 828-2319
Website - http://www.peec.org/
Admission Fee - None
Directions - *Dingmans Ferry, Pike County; from PA 209 in the Delaware Gap National Recreation Area, turn at the sign onto Briscoe Mountain Road and climb to the center parking lot on the right.*

The Park
This area was once home to a resort known as Honeymoon Haven. The property was acquired by the United States Army Corps of Engineers in anticipation of a projected damming of the Delaware River that would create a 37-mile long, 12,500-acre reservoir. The project fell through in 1972 and the skeleton of the resort was converted into the Pocono Environmental Education Center to provide education and cultural programs for the new national recreation area.

The Walks
The center offers five loops from its corps camp that lead to a variety of ecologically diverse attractions. The *Tumbling Waters Trail* stretches for three miles past two scenic ponds, through a pine-and-hemlock forest, up the ominously named Killer Hill to reach a switchbacking path to a series of powerful cataracts flowing down the mountain. The *Ridgeline Trail* is longest in the park at 4. 5miles and visits sharply-cut ravines, rock ledges and wetlands. The third main route here is the 1.25-mile *Fossil Trail* that leads to a series of rock ledges containing the remains of organisms from a prehistoric sea.

> **Where The Paw Meets The Earth:** Dirt paths - not as rocky as some other Pennsylvania mountain trails
> **Workout For Your Dog** - Plenty of hillclimbing for your dog with some steep spots
> **Swimming** - Pickerel Pond and Front Pond can be reached for a swim
> **Restrictions On Dogs** - None

Something Extra
Each of the trails comes with a detailed descriptive brochure that is rare for an outing with your dog. Among the attractions that might otherwise go overlooked is the "Ecology Cemetery" where headstones tell the tale of how long various materials take to decompose.

Promised Land State Park

Phone - (570) 676-3428
Website - http://www.dcnr.state.pa.us/stateparks/parks/prom-isedland.aspx
Admission Fee - None
Directions - Greentown, Pike County; 10 miles north of Canadensis, along PA 390.

The Park
There is a long tradition of irony in geographical place names - Greenland, for instance, is all ice. Promised Land was named by the Shakers, a religious sect who purchased land here in hopes of founding a Utopian agricultural community and found instead nothing but unplowable rocky soil. They quickly left. Early settlers of the area erected sawmills to process the large stands of conifer and hardwood trees. The land was repeatedly clear-cut. The Commonwealth of Pennsylvania purchased the land in 1902. Promised Land was the fourth Pennsylvania state park. The Commonwealth worked to protect and reclaim the area and the forest and wildlife began to return. The first park facilities were open to the public in 1905.

The Walks
Not much happened in the park until the Depression when Civilian Conservation Corps camps were established to reforest the land, carve roads and construct campgrounds. Today there are four campgrounds with 500 sites and it is a busy place in season. Several short trails are available in th park including a unique one-mile *Conservation Island Trail* on an island in Promised Land Lake and the *Little Falls Trail* that skips past severla waterfalls on the East Branch of Wallenpaupack Creek. For extended time on the trail with your dog, jump on the *Boundary Trail* for a trip arund Promised Land Lake, although the lake isn't a standout feature of this hike.

> **Where The Paw Meets The Earth:** Rocky soil and wet areas
> **Workout For Your Dog** - More in length than difficulty
> **Swimming** - Lakes aplenty in Promised Land
> **Restrictions On Dogs** - No dogs in the swimming areas

Something Extra
On Sunday evening, May 31, 1998, an F-2 tornado (winds of 113 -157 mph) passed through Promised Land State Park. It cut a northeasterly path through the park and crossed Lower Lake Road, PA 390 and North Shore Road near Sucker Brook. Over 500 people were trapped overnight in the park, but no one was seriously hurt. The park office has copies of *After the Wind Died Down*, a booklet about the tornado and its aftermath.

Ralph Stover State Park/Tohickon Valley Park

Phone - (610) 982-5560
Website - http://www.dcnr.state.pa.us/stateparks/parks/ralph-stover.aspx
Admission Fee - None
Directions - *Point Pleasant, Bucks County; on State Park Road and Stump Road. Tohickon Valley Park is two miles down Cafferty Road off Route 32.*

The Park
Ralph Stover State Park takes its name from the operator of a water-powered grain mill on the Tohickon Valley Creek in the late 1700s. Traces of the historic mill can still be seen above the dam. The Stover descendents donated the property to Pennsylvania in 1931 and recreational facilities in the 45-acre park were constructed during the 1930s by the Works Project Administration The High Rocks area was donated by Bucks County author James Michener.

The Walks
The *Red Dot Trail* sweeps in a wide arc for 5.5 miles connecting the two parks. Upon reaching the top of the High Rocks it is easy to feel like you have been parachuted into the heart of the Applachian mountains. Two hundred feet below you stretches a hillside tapestry of trees collared by a horsehoe turn in the Tohickon Creek. There is no similar view in the Delaware Valley. The trail itself rolls up and down across several ravine-slashing creeks. The dirt path is wide and easy on the paws, save for a steady diet of hopping on and across exposed tree roots. Three short walking trails course through Ralph Stover State Park and additional trails are maintained in Tohickon Valley Park across the creek for extended canine hiking.

> **Where The Paw Meets The Earth:** Natural surface
> **Workout For Your Dog** - The 200-foot elevation drop is handled gradually for the most part
> **Swimming** - The fast-flowing waters of the Tohickon can be treacherous when the water is high
> **Restrictions On Dogs** - None

Something Extra
The chance to watch experienced rock climbers tackling the 200-foot sheer rock face of the Tohickon Palisades. Climbers have identified more than three dozen routes up the slate-like rock.

Ricketts Glen State Park

Phone - (570) 477-5675
Website - http://www.dcnr.state.pa.us/stateparks/parks/rickett-sglen.aspx
Admission Fee - None
Directions - *Benton, Luzerne County; on PA 487. Also access to the* Falls Trail *on Route 118.*

The Park
One of the most uniquely scenic areas in the Northeast, Ricketts Glen was slated to become a national park in the 1930s but World War II shelved plans for this development. Instead, Ricketts Glen opened as a state park in 1944. Gradually the Commonwealth of Pennsylvania continued purchasing blocks of land from the descendents of Robert Bruce Ricketts until the park spread across more than 13,000 acres. Ricketts enlisted as a private in the United States Army in 1861 and after commanding a battery during the Civil War was discharged with the rank of Colonel. When the war ended, Colonel Ricketts began acquiring inaccessible virgin timber and he would eventually control over 80,000 acres of land. His Central Penn Lumber Company began harvesting the old growth forest, with some trees 900 years old, when the railroads arrived in 1890. By 1913 the timber was exhausted and the lumber town of Ricketts deserted.

The Walks
More than 20 miles of trails meander through the deep woods and mountain lakes at Ricketts Glen. The rocky *Cherry Run Trail* takes you away from the crowded Glens Natural Area into the eastern section of the park and the *Grand View Trail* is a 1.9-mile loop that reaches a fire tower with an almost complete 360-degree vista. Other less demanding trails mosey along near 245-acre Lake Jean.

>**Where The Paw Meets The Earth:** Dirt, mud, rocks, bridges - you name it along the *Falls Trail* - be careful
>**Workout For Your Dog** - One of the best
>**Swimming** - Plenty of pools and streams and ponds
>**Restrictions On Dogs** - None

Something Extra
The spectacular attraction of Ricketts Glen is the magical *Falls Trail*, a Y-shaped exploration of 23-named waterfalls. Two branches of the Kitchen Creek slice through the Ganoga Glen to the west and Glen Leigh to the east before uniting at Waters Meet. The stem of the trail flows through Ricketts Glen, among towering hemlocks and oaks, before tumbling over three cascades at Adams Falls at the trailhead. The two prongs of the trail connect via the 1.2-mile *Highland Trail*. The complete falls experience encompasses almost seven miles. If you take your dog on only one hike in the Mid-Atlantic region, this is it.

Ridley Creek State Park

Phone - (215) 234-8684
Website - http://www.dcnr.state.pa.us/stateparks/parks/ridley-creek.aspx
Admission Fee - None
Directions - *Media, Delaware County; on Route 3, 2.5 miles west of Newtown Square. The park may also be entered from Gradyville Road - east from Route 352 or west from Route 252.*

The Park
Settlement in this area dates back to the 1600s when villages grew around the mills sprinkled along the creeks and streams. Much of the park's 2,606 acres were consolidated in the Jefford family - their Hunting Hill mansion, built in 1914 around a 1789 stone farmhouse, now serves as the park office. The Commonwealth of Pennsylvania purchased the property in the 1960s - including 35 historic residences - and the park was dedicated in 1972.

The Walks
Ridley Creek features 12 miles of hiking on four main trails. The *White Trail* visits most of the areas of the park and the others intersect this lengthy loop at many points. A 5-mile multi-use loop is shared with bicyclists and joggers. Also, an unmarked trailhead just east of Ridley Creek on Gradyville Road offers one of the longest creekside walks in Delaware County. In addition, a 4.7-mile equestrian trail makes two large loops in the isolated western section of the park. These heavily wooded trails are narrow in many places and you and the dog will be prime targets for hitchhiking ticks. Most of the trails wind through rolling woodland and meadows. You'll be moving up and down often but only an occasional hardy climb is necessary.

>**Where The Paw Meets The Earth:** Dirt trails and macadam
>**Workout For Your Dog** - Moderate hill climbing on these trails
>**Swimming** - Ridley Creek, while extremely scenic, is a relatively minor feature of hiking at Ridley Creek State Park; it is deep enough for swimming when the trail touches upon it.
>**Restrictions On Dogs** - None

Something Extra
A handful of historic 18th century structures stand intact within park boundaries and are leased as highly coveted private residences. A group of these stone buildings include a miller's house, office and library, and several small millworkers' houses that have been designated as the "Ridley Creek Historic District" on the National Register of Historic Places.

Ringing Rocks Park

Phone - None
Website - http://www.buckscounty.org/government/depart-ments/ParksandRec/Parks/RingingRocks.aspx
Admission Fee - None
Directions - *Upper Black Eddy, Bucks County; two miles west of town on Ringing Rock Road.*

The Park
Stones do not usually ring, but when the boulders at this park are struck lightly with a hammer, they will vibrate and make a sound not unlike that of a bell. Why they do this is still a mystery to science. The rocks themselves are composed of diabase, the same type of rock that makes up most the earth's crust. Another part of the mystery is while all the rocks seem to be made of the same material (mostly iron and hard minerals) only one-third of them generate the ringing sound when hit. Rocks that ring are known as "live" rocks, and those that don't are referred to as "dead" rocks. In 1890, Dr. J.J. Ott collected a number of the rocks which rang at different pitches, then with the assistance of a brass band, played a number of musical selections on the rocks for the Buckwampum Historical Society. Some wags call Dr. Ott's performance the world's first "rock concert."

The Walks
This park features two outstanding attractions: in adition to the boulder field of volcanic rocks you can see the highest waterfall in Bucks County. Short, wide trails lead through the woods to the boulder field and, beyond, to the waterfall.

> **Where The Paw Meets The Earth:** Dirt all boulders
> **Workout For Your Dog** - The boulder-hopping can set a dog to panting
> **Swimming** - Below the waterfall the streams sometimes pools deep enough for a swim
> **Restrictions On Dogs** - None

Something Extra
Bring a hammer! Search out the ringing rocks in the boulder field and amaze your dog.

Riverbend Education Center

Phone - (610) 527-5234
Website - None
Admission Fee - None
Directions - *Gladwyne, Montgomery County; from the Blue Route (I-476) North, take Exit 6A for Conshohocken, Route 23 East. Make a left on Spring Mill Road, continue past the Philadelphia Country Club and bear left at the end of the road to the Education Center parking lot.*

The Park
The Riverbend story begins 300,000,000 years ago when a crack in the rock known as the Rosemont Fault turned what would become known as the Schuylkill River a full 90 degrees. The first settlers came to the area in the 1500s when the Lenni-Lenape Indians began planting vegetables in an area known as "Indian Fields." In 1904, Howard Wood, brother of steel magnate Alan Wood, created a 52-acre farm inside the river's elbow. Three generations later, in 1974, his descendents deed-ed half of the farm to serve as a wildlife refuge known as Riverbend Environmental Education Center.

The Walks
The feature trail at Riverbend, amidst two miles of hiking, is the *Aloha Trail* that circles the perimeter of the property. Unfortunately the walk is marred by the relentless pounding of traffic on the Schuylkill Expressway below. Look for Fiveleaf Akebia, an invasive plant that covers everything on the hillside above the roadway. The other trails are short connecting spurs of only several minutes duration. Avoid the *Jack-in-the-Pulpit* and *Poplar* trails- they can be overgrown. Another hike here is *Sid Thayer's Trail*, a linear trail on private property also plagued by traffic noise.

> **Where The Paw Meets The Earth:** Dirt all around
> **Workout For Your Dog** - Riverbend is situated on the knob of a hill so little flat walking to be had here
> **Swimming** - Riverbend sports the smallest pond in the tri-state area, alongside the *Bluebird Trail*; although scarcely ten feet across, smaller dogs can motor around and larger ones can drop in to cool off
> **Restrictions On Dogs** - None

Something Extra
The Visitor Center is a restoration of a 1923 Sears & Roebuck mail order barn. A century ago Sears sold anything and everything by mail - including kits for building houses and barns. The kit, which could cost as little as a few hundred dollars depending on style, would include rough lumber, framing timbers, plank flooring, shingles, hardware, sash and paint. Usually shipped by train from the west, the barn kit would be loaded onto a freight wagon and hauled to the building site for assembly by local carpenters.

Rocky Ridge County Park

Phone - (717) 840-7740
Website - http://ycwebserver.york-county.org/Parks/RockyRidge.htm
Admission Fee - None
Directions - *Hallam, York County; from Route 30, take Mt. Zion Road (Route 24) north for 1 mile. Turn right onto Deininger Road and follow into park. There are three parking areas - for the bulk of the trails make your first right towards the Oak Timbers Picnic Area and continue to a spacious lot in front of the power lines.*

The Park
The 750 acres of mature oak forest that would become Rocky Ridge Park was purchased in 1968, making it the granddaddy of all York County parks. The namesake rocks on the ridge are mostly Hellam Conglomerate, a sedimentary rock that contains rounded pebbles of quartz. The rock is one of the oldest sedimentary rocks in Pennsylvania, dating back an estimated 570 million years. Rocky Ridge is where you can find the area's largest exposure of this Hellam Conglomerate.

The Walks
There are nine short trails at Rocky Ridge that conspire to offer some 12 miles of canine hiking. If you don't have time to sample them all, start by passing under the crackling power lines to the trails in the east end of the park. These trails do not loop but they can easily be combined to create forge a variety of hiking circuits. When the trails drop off the ridge - especially on the north side on trails like #3 - the canine hiking gets downright HARD. But these steep ascents are easily forgiven on the wide tracks through the airy forest. You can comfortably maneuver two or three leashed dogs along the Rocky Ridge trail system. While indeed rocky, the maintained trails are not abusive under paw. It is also possible to create a hiking agenda that loops back to your centrally located car several times for a big day at Rocky Ridge park.

> **Where The Paw Meets The Earth:** Rocky paths - the name doesn't lie
> **Workout For Your Dog** - Oh, yes
> **Swimming** - None
> **Restrictions On Dogs** - None

Something Extra
Two observation decks are built on either side of Rocky Ridge. On the north side (*Trail #8*) you can soak in a panoramic view of Three Mile Island and on the south side you can look out over the York Valley (*Trail #1*). Mass flocks of migratory birds - hawks, raptors, songbirds - fly down the Susquehanna River and birding enthusiasts gather here to watch them come and go.

Rose Tree Park

Phone - None
Website - http://www.co.delaware.pa.us/depts/rosetree.html
Admission Fee - None
Directions - *Media, Delaware County; from Route 1 (Media By-pass), take Route 252 (Providence Road) to the park entrance on the right, just past Rose Tree Road.*

The Park

The Rose Tree Hunt Club, the oldest continuous fox-hunt club in America, was first organized here in 1859 by a group who met at the Rose Tree Tavern. The Club bought the inn, which maintained its own pack of hounds, in 1873. There was a trotting track on the grounds from the 1860s and in 1926 a new clubhouse and steeplechase track were added. On April 9, 1964 the Rose Tree Hunt Club staged its last meet here before moving to York County. Delaware County purchased the land for a 120-acre park but the Hunt Club returns once a year with its hounds for a ceremonial meet.

The Walks

The informal trails cross fields leading to a small wooded area in the middle of the park. This is more of a park for free-form canine hiking and romping with your dog.

> **Where The Paw Meets The Earth:** Paw-friendly soft dirt and grass
>
> **Workout For Your Dog** - Easy hills
>
> **Swimming** - The small branch of Crum Creek is for splashing only
>
> **Restrictions On Dogs** - None

Something Extra

No thoroughbred race horse ever captured the American imagination like Man o'War. When he died in 1947 at the age of 30 the large chestnut colt was embalmed and lay in state for two days. As many as 2,000 people attended his funeral and the burial service was broadcast nationally. Man o' War raced for only two years in 1919 and 1920 - and so completely crushed the opposition that in five races only one other horse dared enter. He beat one of those cheeky rivals by an estimated 100 lengths. His only loss in 21 races was to a colt named Upset and afterwards, whenever an unexpected team won a sports event, it was an "upset." His owner, local land baron and horseman Samuel Riddle, who purchased Man o'War for $5,000 as a yearling at the urging of his wife, brought the grea thorse to Rose Tree Hunt Club in October 1920 before retiring him to stud. Some 30,000 people, including tennis immortal Bill Tilden and boxing great Jack Dempsey, turned out to see Man o'War here.

Salt Springs State Park

Phone - None
Website - http://www.dcnr.state.pa.us/stateparks/parks/salt-springs.aspx
Admission Fee - None
Directions - *Franklin Forks, Susquehanna County; follow PA 29 north from Montrose for six miles to the town of Franklin Forks. Turn left onto Silver Creek Road and follow for one mile to the park entrance. From New York, take NY 7 to PA 29. At Franklin Forks, turn right onto Silver Creek Road and follow for one mile to the park. entrance.*

The Park
Salt Spring on the south side of Fall Brook is one of the salt springs for which the park is named. The first people to extract salt from the spring water were American Indians who traveled through the area during hunting expeditions. They attempted to keep the location of the spring secret from the settlers, but eventually and with a large enough sum of money, it was revealed. Numerous attempts were made by different entrepreneurs to develop the spring for commercial gain between 1795 and 1870. The brine obtained produced a high quality salt, but not enough could be coaxed out of the ground to yield a profit.

The Walks
Among the more than eight miles of trails at Salt Springs the star is the *Fall Brook Trail*, a difficult one-mile excursion through the hemlock gorge that will visit three waterfalls in short order. Footing can be tricky and the path climbs steeply at times. After the third waterfall, the trail flattens out and follows the brook past Buckley Road until it ends at the intersection with *Bunny Trail*. A variety of other short trails explore the park hillsides.

> **Where The Paw Meets The Earth:** Rocky trails, mud and slippery rocks
> **Workout For Your Dog** - Short trails and steep climbs will add up
> **Swimming** - Streams can pool deep enough for a swim
> **Restrictions On Dogs** - None

Something Extra
One of the great features of the park are the towering old growth hemlock trees, many estimated to be over 500 years old. The hemlock is the state tree of Pennsylvania. At the northeast entrance of the park is the historic homestead of the Wheaton family. Four buildings of the original homestead remain, as well as the foundation of the mill and woolen manufactory. The original home, built in the early 1840s by Nathan Philip Wheaton, is now the Wheaton House. This post and beam structure is timber framed with eastern hemlock. The hand-hewn beams are 40 feet long and the posts are two stories high.

Samuel S. Lewis State Park

Phone - None
Website - http://www.dcnr.state.pa.us/stateparks/parks/samu-elslewis.aspx
Admission Fee - None
Directions - *Wrightsville, York County; from US Route 30 take the Wrightsville exit onto Cool Creek Road, heading south. At Mt. Pisgah Road in 1.5 miles turn right and then left into the park in .5 miles.*

The Park

In 1954, following a distinguished career of service in local and state government, 79-year old Samuel S. Lewis donated 35 acres of his family farm to the Commonwealth of Pennsylvania. Lewis did not stop there. He convinced his neighbor, Walter Stine, to donate five acres on which he had been planting exotic species of trees for years. Some additional land was quickly purchased from the adjoining Almoney Farm and the park was opened to the public on Independence Day 1954. The Department of Conservation and Natural Resources annexed a final 14 acres in 1999 to bring Samuel S. Lewis State Park to its current size of 85 acres atop Mt. Pisgah.

The Walks

The canine hike at Samuel S. Lewis is the *Hill Top Trail*, a circuit loop of a little over a mile, partly through a small woodland and partly across open, mowed grass fields. The trail drops off the hilltop on the southern side into a mature pine plantation and injects a dose of hardiness for your dog into this pleasant stroll. At the top of 885-foot Mt. Pisgah, the end of a high ridge blocking Kreutz Creek Valley from East Prospect Valley, the trail slides through George E. Stine Arboretum. Although many trees fell victim to recent windstorms, several unique specimens still stand such as the European beech, much loved for its handsome trunk and copper-colored autumn leaves.

> **Where The Paw Meets The Earth:** Grass and dirt
> **Workout For Your Dog** - Level or imperseptible grades
> **Swimming** - None
> **Restrictions On Dogs** - None

Something Extra

The open fields on the east side of Mount Pisgah serve up a 20-mile sweeping view of the Susquehanna River. The area beneath you was under consideration as the site for the United States capital before the final selection on the Potomac trumped this safer inland site as a compromise with Virginian legislators.The first bridge across the river - one mile wide at this point - to replace the busy ferry operated by the Wright family was built in 1812 and was the longest covered bridge in the world at that time. The original Route 30 bridge (now Route 462) was finished in 1925 and is thought to be the world's longest multiple arch bridge.

Schuylkill Canal Park

Phone - None
Website - None
Admission Fee - None
Directions - *Mont Clare, Montgomery County; on Route 29 across the Schuylkill River from Phoenixville. Crossing the river on Bridge Street, make a left at the end of the bridge onto the entrance road for the upstream parking area. To reach the downstream parking lot, make the right at the light onto Port Providence Road and follow it through town and past the Container Corporation of America to the lot on the right.*

The Park
Pennsylvania's first canal system was cobbled together in 1815 using 120 locks to stretch 108 miles from the coal fields of Schuylkill County to Philadelphia. Railroads began chewing away at canal business in the 1860s and the last coal barges floated down the Schuylkill River in the 1920s. Today, the only sections of the canal in existence are at Man-ayunk and Lock 60, built by area name donor Thomas Oakes, at the Schuylkill Canal Park. In 1985 the Schuylkill Canal Association formed to keep the canal flowing and maintain the lock and towpath. In 1988, the area was added to the National Register of Historic Places.

The Walks
You can either enjoy the flattest walk in Montgomery County here or the steepest. The peaceful canal towpath covers 2 1/2 miles from the Lock House, built in 1836, to the eastern end of Port Providence. Across the canal are houses and town buildings looking much as they did throughout the canal era. Upstream from Lock 60 are the *Ravine Trail*, with three ascents to the 100-foot high rock bluffs overlooking the Schuylkill River, and the Valley View Trail, which deadends - for dog-walking - at the Upper Schuylkill Valley Park. No dogs are allowed in that park. There is also an 8-station self-guided nature walk from the Lock House to Route 29.
> **Where The Paw Meets The Earth:** Soft dirt and rock-strewn dirt
> **Workout For Your Dog** - Almost all flat save for the climbs to the bluffs
> **Swimming** - Fantastic swimming for your dog in the Schuylkill River or in the canal
> **Restrictions On Dogs** - None

Something Extra
After years of fundraising and handiwork volunteers have rebuilt Lock 60 and it is now in operating condition. You can see it work during Canal Days in June.

Scott Arboretum

Phone - (610) 328-8025
Website - http://www.scottarboretum.org/
Admission Fee - None
Directions - *Swarthmore, Delaware County; on Chester Road (Route 320) between I-95 and Baltimore Pike. Parking for the arboretum is just inside the entrance on College Road, on the left.*

The Park
The 300-acre Swarthmore campus is developed to be an arboretum, established in 1929 as a living memorial to Arthur Hoyt Scott, Class of 1895. The 3,000 different kinds of plants have been chosen as suggestions for the best trees, shrubs, perennials and annuals to use in home gardens in the Delaware Valley.

The Walks
Several area colleges welcome responsible dog owners - Swarthmore's Scott Arboretum serves the best canine hiking. The plant collections are integrated with the stone buildings of the college that dates to 1864. Leaving the cultivated plantings of the campus, a variety of hillside trails lead through the 200-acre Crum Woods down to Crum Creek.

> **Where The Paw Meets The Earth:** Dirt trails in the woods; macadam and grass around campus lawns and buildings
>
> **Workout For Your Dog** - Moderate hill climbing in the woods
>
> **Swimming** - Crum Creek is deep enough for dog paddling
>
> **Restrictions On Dogs** - Dogs are not only welcomed at Swarthmore, but there are water bowls chained to some of the drinking fountains; in the Crum Woods your dog need only be under voice control, not leashed

Something Extra
In the far southwestern area of campus, beyond the holly collection, is a meadow containing a Swarthmore version of Stonehenge. Like the original, its origins are mysterious. From the slate bench in the middle you can chance to see the SEPTA trolley rolling across a 50-foot trestle over Crum Creek.

Seven Tubs Nature Area

Phone - (570) 477-5467
Website - http://www.nature.org/wherewework/northamerica/
states/pennsylvania/preserves/art831.html
Admission Fee - None
Directions - *Wilkes Barre, Luzerne County; four miles southeast
of downtown on Route 115. The entrance is about 1.5 miles southeast of the I-81 interchange.*

The Park
The Tubs Nature Area is a 500-acre slice of wetlands and woods
whose prime lure is a series of large potholes gouged out of underly-
ing bedrock by Wheelbarrow Run. The potholes were a magnet for
local nature enthusiasts and others looking for a cool dip in a pothole
on a hot day for generations.The area was abused by litterers and
grafitti artists. In 1980 the county began a clean-up of the area and
the site was formally dedicated as a Nature Area by Luzerne County
in July of 1992.

The Walks
Two stacked loop trails explore this unique limestone stylings of
Wheelbarrow Run. The short *Tubs Trail* drops into the ravine but your
dog will do most of her leg stretching on the blue-blazed *Laurel Run
Trail* that hugs the quick flowing stream for almost a mile.

> **Where The Paw Meets The Earth:** Natural trails and
> bridges and a ladder
> **Workout For Your Dog** - Moderate climbing to the
> surrounding ridge
> **Swimming** - The streams do not support real canine
> swiming and any swimming in the potholes is prohibited
> **Restrictions On Dogs** - None

Something Extra
The tubs, of course. The largest is about 30 feet wide. The water in
the potholes appears to be deep but the real depth is still unknown because their bottoms are obscured by a layer of gravelly sediment.

Shank Park

Phone - None
Website - None
Admission Fee - None
Directions - *Hershey, Dauphin County; just east of the Route 422/Route 322 split, turn south on Bullfrog Valley Road on the western edge of the Hershey Medical Center of Pennsylvania State University. Go about two miles to the park entrance on the right.*

The Park
Shank Park, created in 1977, is the largest of the several Derry Township parks around Hershey. Although most of Shank Park's 90 acres are given over to ballfields, a 1.63-mile nature trail rings the property.

The Walks
The nature trail is a welcome find for your dog just minutes away from the crush of tourists. There are just enough woodlands to engulf the canine hiker in trees - many of which are marked to make this a good hike for tree identification. The route slips in and out of woods, through a pine plantation and up and down sporty hills. You can also access the 11-mile, paved *Jonathan Eshenour Memorial Trail* that connects Derry Township parks. The trail, that remembers a young victim of a bicycle accident in 1997, is paved and crosses many active roadways. In Bullfrog Valley Park, the first park north of Shank Park on the route, there is a scenic half-mile stretch against a wooded hillside that traces a duck pond and a lively stream. It is a worthy adjunct to a canine hike in Shank Park.

>**Where The Paw Meets The Earth:** Pavement, dirt and grass
>
>**Workout For Your Dog** - Shank Park is just hilly enough to make your dog work
>
>**Swimming** - A small stream and pond along the *Eschenour Trail*
>
>**Restrictions On Dogs** - None

Something Extra
In the 1850s this was the center of a bustling brownstone quarrying area. Eleven quarries operated to remove the prized building stone and a wagon road was built to transport the rough-cut brownstone to New York and Philadelphia and other major cities where it was used to build some of America's most elegant buildings. In 1892 the Brownstone-Middletown Railroad was built to link the quarries to the Reading Railroad. The quarries closed in the 1920s when brick became a less expensive building alternative and on July 10, 1939 the rail line closed after cleaning up leftover stone. The old roadbed is now part of the *Eshenour Trail*.

Shenk's Ferry Glen Wildflower Preserve

Phone - None
Website - None
Admission Fee - None
Directions - *Green Hill, Lancaster County; south of Lancaster on the Susquehanna River. From Route 324 take River Road north and make your second left onto River Hill Road. Turn right onto Green Hill Road and continue to the trailhead at the bottom of the hill. Alternatively, Green Hill Road can be accessed in the opposite direction from the village of Green Hill at River Road.*

The Park

The Shenk family operated a ferry across the Susquehanna River at this point in the 1800s. But they were not the first inhabitants here. When arch-eological digs uncovered an Indian village it was first believed to be a group of familiar Susquehannocks. But study of things like burial patterns indicated otherwise. These "lost people" were determined to be a prehistoric tribe from the 1300s who dis-appeared before European settlement. Now known as Shenks Ferry people, all that is known of them comes from bits and pieces of their culture found in the ground here. In more recent times the sheltered ravine was the site of mining operations and a dynamite factory. On June 9, 1906 the factory exploded, killing 11 men and levelling every building in the area. Today the fortunes of these 50 acres in the glen is in the hands of the PPL Corporation.

The Walks

Most people make their way to this remote region for the most im-pressive wildflower display in the region. More than 70 species burst into bloom in spring with another 60 biding their time until summer. The main *Wildflower Trail* heads straight out from the trailhead before winding up in a grotto. The path is wide and airy. Side trails scoot out of the ravine but the only way to create a circuit hike is to use the main dirt road.

> **Where The Paw Meets The Earth:** Dirt trails
> **Workout For Your Dog** - Easy hike with some strain on the ravine slopes
> **Swimming** - Grubb Run is just for splashing
> **Restrictions On Dogs** - None

Something Extra

Early Indians spent great time in preparing their pots, decorating them with lines, dots and distinctive tops to make them unique. In addition, different groups used different clays found in the soil near their villages, all of this led to a distinctive kind of pot for each group. The Shenks Ferry pottery is characterized by crushed granite or quartz with the cords aligned vertically to the vessel. Decoration would come from incised lines in geometric patterns around the rim. So pay attention if your dog starts digging with purpose.

Shuman Point Natural Area

Phone - None
Website - http://www.pplweb.com/lake+wallenpaupack/things+to+do/shuman+pt+natural.htm
Admission Fee - None
Directions - *Hawley, Wayne County; from Route 6 turn west on Route 590 one mile east of town. The parking area is two miles down on the left.*

The Park
Lake Wallenpaupack was created in 1926 by the Pennsylvania Power and Light Company as a source for hydroelectric power. The valley was flooded and the lake filled in for 13 miles to a depth of 60 feet. Lake Wallenpaupack is the largest impoundment of water anywhere in the Poconos - but it now serves as a rarely used auxiliary power source. Few residents mourned the loss of hardscrabble farms and small settlements like Wilsonville Village as they flocked to new shorelines created by Lake Wallenpaupack. Shuman Point, a 250-acre peninsular knob, is one of the last remaining undeveloped areas around the lake.

The Walks
This is a single-trail park - a 3-mile loop through the hardwoods that hug the shoreline for almost constant water views between the trees. The only real exertion comes immediately if you start the loop to your right as you cimb about 200 feet to the high point in the middle of the peninsula. The path is rocky along this climb and the toughest under paw on the circuit. Also be prepared for soggy trails from water seeps before reaching the lakeshore. The trail eventually drops down to the waterline where your dog will enjoy long, albeit rocky, stretches of access to some of the best swimming in the Poconos. After you climb easily away from the water you reach Shuman Point, accented with rows of old stone walls. You'll finish the loop on the wide remains of an old woods road that was once the main drag to Wilsonville Village.

>   **Where The Paw Meets The Earth:** Wooded dirt path
>   **Workout For Your Dog** - An elevation gain of about 200 feet
>   **Swimming** - Bring your dog's swim trunks for this hike
>   **Restrictions On Dogs** - None

Something Extra
Without question, the greatest tree in America prior to 1900 was the chestnut. Rot resistant with fine-grained wood, the chestnut tree supported both vibrant wildlife populations and entire rural economies. It was estimated that one in every four trees in the eastern forests was a chestnut tree - some as old as 600 years. But in 1904 an Asian fungus was discovered in the Bronx Zoo and the blight soon decimated the chestnut population. By 1950 millions of acres of woodlands were left with dead, standing trees. The chestnut blight remains 100% fatal - young chestnuts may reach 20 or 30 feet but are doomed to succumb to the disease. At Shuman Point look for sprouts of American chestnuts growing in old stumps.

Silver Lake Park

Phone - (215) 785-1177
Website - http://www.buckscounty.org/government/depart-
ments/ParksandRec/Parks/SilverLake.aspx
Admission Fee - None
Directions - *Bristol, Bucks County; on Bath Road off of Route 13.*

The Park
The centerpiece of Silver Lake Park is the Silver Lake Nature Center,
opened by the Bucks County Department of Parks and Recreation in
1960. Within its 235 protected acres are two rare habitats, a coastal
plain forest (Delhaas Woods) and an unglaciated bog, as well as two
animals and 11 plants on the Pennsylvania species of special concern
list. The Nature Center is flanked by two small lakes, the secluded
Magnolia Lake and the land-scaped Silver Lake.

The Walks
Ducking onto the quiet, scented trails of the Silver Lake Nature Center provides a complete escape from the hustle and bustle of surrounding Lower Bucks County. The well-groomed paths give way to
boardwalks over marshy ground and small streams as they lead into
the high swamp grass. A paved bicycle trail leads most of the way
around Silver Lake. Across Bath Road is a small opening in the trees
that leads to several miles of dirt trails in the 181 acres of wooded
wetlands in Delhaas Woods. All the walking at Silver Lake is across
level terrain.

> **Where The Paw Meets The Earth:** Boards, dirt, asphalt
> **Workout For Your Dog** - Easy, level terrain
> **Swimming** - There is access to Silver Lake for a
> doggie dip
> **Restrictions On Dogs** - None

Something Extra
It doesn't happen often but there is the chance to see the fun-loving
river otter in Silver Lake. Once nearly extinct from Pennsylvania, the
river otter population has been restored to each major drainage basin
of the state, thanks to funds raised from private donations and sales
of special Pennsylvania license plates. If spotted, the aquatic antics
of this playful weasel are not soon forgotten.

Speedwell Forge Park

Phone - (800) 354-8383
Website - http://www.co.lancaster.pa.us/parks/cwp/view.asp?a=
676&q=518304&parksNav=%7C9079%7C
Admission Fee - None
Directions - *Brickerville, Lancaster County; from the intersection of Routes 501 and 322 travel west on Route 322 for 200 yards and turn left onto Long Lane. Follow Long Lane to the end at a T-intersection in 1.5 miles. Turn left onto Speedwell Forge Road and after one-half mile cross a small bridge and turn right into the small park lot.*   .

The Park

James Old and David Caldwell built the Speedwell Forge in 1760. They selected 40 acres on Hammer Creek, 11 miles south of Lebanon for their nascent ironworks. The forge was kept busy producing munitions during the Revolution and at war's end Old sold the business to his son-in-law, a 38-year old Irish bookkeeper named Robert Coleman. Coleman used the Speedwell Forge as the keystone in a mining and foundry empire that would prosper to such an extent that he is widely regarded as Pennsylvania's first millionaire. The forge shut down just before the Civil War and nature gradually reclaimed the land. The county added 415 acres to its holdings in creating this undeveloped park.

The Walks

A quiet trail snakes through a variety of habitats in Speedwell Forge Park. You start on a paw-friendly grass and dirt path that traces the winding Hammer Creek wetlands before heading up into cultivated fields and a wildflower meadow. This mile-long loop returns to a stream and finishes down an old wooded, country lane. Of course, this canine hike is pleasant enough for you to turn around and do it again. Down the road from Speedwell Forge Park is Speedwell Forge Lake. No canine hiking, but a great place to stop for a doggie swim (boat launch at Zartman Mill Road).

> **Where The Paw Meets The Earth:** Paw-friendly soft dirt and grass
> **Workout For Your Dog** - Moderately rolling park
> **Swimming** - Hammer Creek is deep enough to act as a canine swimming hole
> **Restrictions On Dogs** - None

Something Extra

When Robert Coleman bought the Speedwell Forge it came with a three-story mansion built in 1760. The house stayed in his family until 1941 and is now being restored as a bed and breakfast. Included in the restoration of this historic property is a stone, three-hole outhouse. The "necessary" also features two doors and two windows.

Spring Valley County Park

Phone - (717) 840-7740
Website - http://ycwebserver.york-county.org/Parks/SpringValley.htm
Admission Fee - None
Directions - *New Freedom, York County; south of York. From I-83, take Exit 8, Glen Rock, and pick up Route 216 East. Before you accelerate turn right onto Potosi Road. Go 2 miles to an information board at Crest Road. Continue on Potosi to Line Road that runs along the north-south spine of the park.*

The Park
In 1972, when York County officials established Spring Valley County Park on 868 acres of old farm fields and a shaggy forest along the East Branch of Codorus Creek they wiped the name "Rehmeyer's Hollow" off local maps. Nelson Rehmeyer lived in this remote valley alone - even his wife resided outside the hollow - until a November night in 1928 when he was murdered by a man and two teenagers who believed the old man held a spell over them. The resulting trials for the "Hex Murders" brought southern York County worldwide attention - much of it negative as a backwards culture in a booming industrial age. For many local residents Spring Valley will never replace "Hex Hollow" - annual events related to the macabre events of 1928 remain popular fundraisers.

The Walks
Don't go to Spring Valley park without a mind to explore. Trails - there are six listed multi-use trails totalling about six miles - are marked sporadically or not at all. You are likely to pop out on a farm road or an open field or a horse ring. If you find yourself on a park road, however, you can easily continue your canine hike - you aren't likely to encounter much vehicular traffic in the park. The trails climb away from the East Branch of Codorus Creek up moderate slopes, usually on paw-friendly grass or dirt. Expect single-file passages in some places, leash-stretching going in others.

> **Where The Paw Meets The Earth:** Natural surface trails
> **Workout For Your Dog** - Moderate hill climbs
> **Swimming** - The East Branch of Codorus Creek is a narrow stream more suitable for canine splashing than swimming
> **Restrictions On Dogs** - Dogs are not allowed in the Fish For Fun Pond

Something Extra
Gold fever! It is believed that 1 in 6 York County streams contain gold - flakes about a quarter-inch in size that have eroded out of local quartz and settled in the sediment of streambeds. The Codorus Creek is one of the best for those seeking this placer gold. On the final Saturday of every July the park hosts a Gold Panning Seminar.

Springfield Trail

Phone - None
Website - None
Admission Fee - None
Directions - *Springfield, Delaware County; the easiest access is at Lownes Park and Smedley Park. The entrance for Smedley Park is on Baltimore Pike, just east of Exit 2 of the Blue Route. Park in the Paper Mill Road lot across the trolley tracks and pick up the Trail at the Comfort Station. Lownes Park is off Route 320 with street parking along Kennerly Road.*

The Park

The creation of trails in most parks seems fairly obvious - use established animal paths or fire roads. But the *Springfield Trail*, linking four parks in a 5-mile loop roughly corralled by Woodland Avenue, the Blue Route and the SEPTA Trolley line, required vision and imagination of Springfield Township and private property owners in 1969 to bring into existence.

The Walks

There are no shortcuts on the *Springfield Trail*; once you set off you sign on for the whole five miles. The strongest segment is from Jane Lownes Park to Smedley Park as the trail hugs the Crum Creek, often from a scenic ridge 100 feet above the water. Although it's noisy due to the adjacent Blue Route (the trail twice brings you directly beneath the superstructure) this is the walk to take if you decide to do an out-and-back. The hike along the trolley line from Smedley to Thompson Park is a wild and wooly excursion that brings you across train tracks, through dry creek beds, past ferns and wild roses and more. The quietest stretch on the *Springfield Trail* is the narrow trail along Whiskey Run.

> **Where The Paw Meets The Earth:** Mostly dirt, some sidewalk trotting along Woodland Road to close the loop
> **Workout For Your Dog** - A healthy workout; none of the climbs will bring your dog to his knees but they keep coming with dogged regularity
> **Swimming** - There are streams everywhere along the *Springfield Trail* but seldom is the water even a foot deep
> **Restrictions On Dogs** - None

Something Extra

The January birthstone: garnets. Mined for thousands of years, the ancients used the stone as bullets for the glowing red color was thought to increase the ferocity of the wound. Legend holds that garnets were carried by travellers to light up the night and protect from nightmares. Noah used a garnet lantern to navigate the Ark at night. Garnets come in every color and can even change hue in different light. And garnets were once mined along Crum Creek here so keep your eyes open on this walk.

Springington Manor Park

Phone - (610) 942-2450
Website - http://dsf.chesco.org/ccparks/cwp/view.asp?a=1550&
q=616437&ccparksNav=|34716|
Admission Fee - None
Directions - *Glenmoore, Chester County; take Route 282, Creek Road, out of Downingtown for five miles and make a left on Springton Road.The entrance to the park is up the hill on the left. of the main entrance.*

The Park
Springton Manor was originally an 8,313-acre parcel set aside by William Penn in 1701. The land has been farmed for almost three centuries and lives today as a demonstration farm. A small forge also operated here for much of the 18th century. Abraham McIlvaine built the main house in 1833. Springton Manor Farm is listed on the National Register of Historic Places for its importance in architecture, agriculture and conservation.

The Walks
The *Indian Run Trail* loops around the entire property - evenly divided between field and woods hiking. In July thesouthwestern edge of the field is bursting with the most accessible red raspberries in Chester County. There is also available a winding 1/3-mile *Penn Oak Interpretive Nature Trail*. The farmland sweeps down a long hillside providing gentle climbs and sparkling views; the lowlands surrounding Indian Run are flat.

> **Where The Paw Meets The Earth:** The *Indian Run Trail* is dirt and grass with some wood chips under foot; the *Nature Trail* is paved with macadam
> **Workout For Your Dog** - A nice hike up a rolling farm hill
> **Swimming** - The Farmer's Pond, at the edge of the *Nature Trail*, was built in 1896 as an additional water source for crops and livestock; the shallow-running Indian Run is good for splashing
> **Restrictions On Dogs** - None

Something Extra
Liberated from their sun-stealing neighbors of the crowded woods, the "King" and "Queen" White Oaks have spread out into a massive canopy of leaves. The "Queen" measures seventeen feet around at the thickest part of the trunk and the "King" is closer to twenty. The two trees are part of the "Penn's Woods" collection of 139 trees standing when William Penn arrived to survey his Pennsylvania colony. The arboreal oldsters reside at the last stop of the nature trail.

State Game Lands 43

Phone - None
Website - None
Admission Fee - None
Directions - *Saint Peters, Chester County; on Saint Peters Road, off Route 23 (Ridge Road). It is behind the buildings on the left, at the northern edge of town. In Pine Swamp there is a small, un-marked parking lot on Harmonyville Road, east of Route 345 (Pine Swamp Road).*

The Park
Three segments of these public lands, totalling 2,150 acres, lie in northwest Chester County. The most accessible - and scenic - of the three is at Saint Peters. Once known as the Falls of French Creek and a famous local tourist destination, Saint Peters was named for the town church when the post office moved away.

The Walks
The *Horse-Shoe Trail* cuts through the Saint Peters and Pine Swamp Tracts. The Saint Peters walk is heavily wooded; the Pine Swamp walk leads through a scruffy meadow on old access roads through light woods at the edge of fields. There are many other short inter-connecting trails at Saint Peters, crossing over small streams and meandering down an abandoned rail line.

> **Where The Paw Meets The Earth:** Natural surface trails with some very rocky stretches
> **Workout For Your Dog** - You'll find some hills at Saint Peters to set your dog to panting
> **Swimming** - French Creek rushes downhill through the property, pooling into an ideal swimming pond just south of the parking lot
> **Restrictions On Dogs** - None

Something Extra
Forty million years ago an igneous explosion occurred underground here and cooled very quickly leaving behind a particularly fine granite rock. Tourists and students of geology alike made the pilgrimmage to the Falls of French Creek to study the rock formations. Granite quarries mined the rock and granite from Saint Peters once received an award at the 1893 World's Columbian Exposition in Chicago as "a fine-grained polished cube, a good building and ornamental stone." The quarries closed in the 1960s and many pits can still be seen. Today the giant boulders in French Creek are ideal for your dog to scramble on - or just lie in the sun.

State Game Lands 110

Phone - None
Website - None
Admission Fee - None
Directions - *Shartlesville, Berks County; take Exit 23 (Old Exit 8) off I-78 at Shartlesville. Head north on Mountain Road, staying straight onto Forge Dam Road when Mountain veers right. Continue to the end of the road and the parking area at the gate, about 1.5 miles.*

The Park

Back in the early days of the 20th century a hardy group of Reading businessmen, many of Bavarian descent, amused themselves with outings on local mountains. The hikers tagged their band "The Fuszgangers," roughly translated as "men who made their way by foot." One of the Fuszgangers, Dr. Harry F. Rentschler, led a group into the Blue Mountains in search of a long-ago eagle's nest he had heard tale of above Shartlesville. The climbers enjoyed the hike so much they made regular treks thereafter to the Eagle's Nest, now located on Pennsylvania State Game Lands 110. New hikers to the mountaintop were even initiated by dangling them over the cliff to the spot of the one-time aerie.

The Walks

Your dog's adventure here begins past the gate and down a wooded, gravel road. Straight ahead in a little over one mile will be the *Appalachian Trail*, where the explorations will be quite rocky. If you are not chasing views, a better option for a canine hike on the State Game Lands 110 would be the light-blue *Sand Spring Trail*, the trailhead for which is just past the parking lot gate on the left. This trail also works its way to the Appalachian Trail but a 4.5-mile hiking loop can be crafted with the *Tom Lowe Memorial Trail*, located just past the namesake sandy spring, enclosed on three sides by a stone wall. Look for the sign and follow the orange blazes back down.

> **Where The Paw Meets The Earth:** These trails mix soft, paw-friendly dirt passages with plenty of rock-stepping
> **Workout For Your Dog** - You will envy your dog's four-wheel drive on the more tumultuous *Tom Lowe* track
> **Swimming** - Plenty of stream encounters to keep your dog refreshed
> **Restrictions On Dogs** - None

Something Extra

In 1988 the Eagle's Nest Shelter was added for thru-hikers on the Appalachian Trail, constructed off-site and flown in by a National Guard helicopter. Be careful with your dog at the Eagle's Nest. In addition to the precipitous cliff, rattlesnakes are known to frequent the rugged rocks.

State Game Lands 211

Phone - None
Website - None
Admission Fee - None
Directions - *Ellendale, Dauphin County; northeast of Harrisburg. The easiest access is to the western terminus of the Stony Valley Rail Trail. Take Route 322 north to the Dauphin/Stony Creek exit (Route 255). In short order, make a right at the Stony Creek sign onto Schuylkill Street; make a right onto Erie Street and go to the end of the road; turn left onto Stony Creek Road and follow to Ellendale Road in about five miles. Continue on Ellendale (unimproved) for two miles to the trailhead at the end of the road.*

The Park
The Pennsylvania State Game Lands 211 encompasses 25,000 acres in three counties and blankets four mountains. Beginning in the mid-1700s this region appeared on maps as "St. Anthony's Wildnerness." In the 1800s surface coal was discovered here and mining began in earnest. By the 1870s the Philadelphia & Reading Coal & Iron Company would become the largest corporation in the world. The mining operations faded away and nature began reclaiming the land. Today the State Game Lands 211 is the second largest completely roadless area in Pennsylvania.

The Walks
Almost anything your dog desires is open in the State Game Lands 211. The two most prominent access trails are 30 miles of the *Appalachian Trail* and the 19-mile *Stony Valley Rail Trail*. This nearly flat, wide trail uses the old rail bed of the Schuylkill and Susquehanna Railroad and makes for some of the easiest, most pleasant canine hiking around. The eastern trailhead for the rail-trail is on Gold Mine Road in Lebanon County.
> **Where The Paw Meets The Earth:** Dirt that is easy on the   paw
> **Workout For Your Dog** - More in distance than difficulty
> **Swimming** - There are streams and ponds and swamps but an outing here is mostly a trotting-only affair for your dog on the rail-trail
> **Restrictions On Dogs** - None

Something Extra
The Stony Valley is essentially a vast ghost town. The industrial activities here once supported as many as 2,000 people. As your dog pokes around you can chance upon the foundations of ancient dams and bridges, sawmills and forges, hotels and office buildings, railroad and mining relics and more.One of the most fascinating survivors of a time gone by is "The General" - a pioneering gas-powered shovel that stands rusting in the woods. It can be found just off a blue-blazed *Sand Spring Trail*, accessed from Route 325 along Clark Creek.

Stoever's Dam Park

Phone - None
Website - http://stoeversdam.8k.com/index.html
Admission Fee - None
Directions - *Lebanon City; take Route 422 into town and turn north onto 8th Avenue. After about 1.8 miles turn left onto Miller Street and continue until you see the Nature Barn in less than one mile.*

The Park

Stoever's Dam Park lies on the ancestral land of Martin Light who farmed around several springs in the late 1700s. His grandson sold the farm to John Stoever in 1821 and construction was promptly begun on a dam to provide water for the Union Canal. The venture was never a full success and the property including the dam passed through the Reading Railroad, the Lebanon Water Company and eventually Bethlehem Steel. In 1966 the land around the dam was leased by the City of Lebanon for recreational purposes and seven years later the city took ownership for one thousand and one dollars. In 1979 the dam was declared unsafe and recommended for permanent breaching. Instead local support saved the dam and the park has grown and thrived ever since.

The Walks

A walking path circumnavigates the lake, squeezing past farm fields, wetlands and residential housing. This is easy, level canine hiking with plenty of open air and sunshine. Another pleasant ramble with your dog in Stoever's Dam Park is through the widely spaced arboretum on a marked trail.

> **Where The Paw Meets The Earth:** Paw-friendly soft dirt and grass
>
> **Workout For Your Dog** - An easy canine hike
>
> **Swimming** - Absolutely in Stoever's Lake
>
> **Restrictions On Dogs** - None

Something Extra

A 125-year old barn has been converted into the "Nature Barn," with a greenhouse and displays on animals native to the park - including a working beehive with 10,000 bees. Nearby is a carefully planted arboretum.

Susquehannock State Park

Phone - (717) 432-5011
Website - http://www.dcnr.state.pa.us/stateparks/parks/susque-hannock.aspx
Admission Fee - None
Directions - *Drumore, Lancaster County; south of Lancaster on the Susquehanna River, about 4.5 miles off of PA 372. Turn south on Susquehannock Drive to Park Drive.*

The Park

The Susquehannock Indians were a small tribe whose only village was located a few miles north of the park. Often besieged by the much larger Iroquois Confederacy, they were eventually conquered and driven from the area in 1675. Many intermingled with the Iroquois but a tiny band returned to what is now present-day Conestoga, living under the protection of the Commonwealth of Pennsylvania. In 1763, during a period of settler-Indian conflict known as the Pontiac Wars, a vigilante group slaughtered most of the two dozen or so remaining Susquehannocks. Only two survived, working as servants on a Lancaster County farm. When they died, the Susquehannock tribe was buried with them on the farm.

The Walks

This is a canine hiker's park with more than five miles of named trails packed into 224 acres. The star walk at Susquehannock is the 1.2-mile *Rhododendron Trail* that rolls through dense growth of the namesake plants and past ruins of the homestead of Lieutenant Thomas Neel, a revolutionary war veteran. Look for a massive beech that has been growing for more than 400 years nearby. The rest of the park can be explored on a series of short trails that reach to all corners of the property. Almost all the canine hiking is among a rich variety of hardwoods; you will still be moving up and down but not as dramatically as along the *Rhododendron Trail*.

> **Where The Paw Meets The Earth:** Dirt trails, rocky on the slopes
> **Workout For Your Dog** - Expect this rollercoaster terrain to leave your dog panting in places - especially if you take advantage of the *Phites Eddy Trail* and take your dog down to Susquehanna River for a swim
> **Swimming** - The muddy banks of the Susquehanna
> **Restrictions On Dogs** - None

Something Extra

Susquehannock State Park is treasured for its river views, connected by a half-mile *Overlook Trail* between Hawk Point and Wissler's Run. Downstream from Hawk Point, 400 feet above he water is Mt. Johnson Island, site of the world's first bald eagle sanctuary. The offspring of the original nesting pair have flown the first nest and can be seen patrolling the islands closer to Hawk Point.

Tamamend Community Park

Phone - None
Website - None
Admission Fee - None
Directions - *Southampton, Bucks County; the entrance is on Second Street Pike (Route 232) between Bristol Road and Street Road (Route 132).*

The Park

In an elaborate treaty ceremony in his Philadelphia house in 1683, William Penn purchased all the land between Pennypack and Neshaminy Creeks. In turning over the lands, Chief Tamanend, a Lenape Sachem, declared the treaty of friendship would endure "as long as the grass is green and the rivers flow." Scarcely a half century later Penn's descendents had broken the treaty and driven the Lenape nation from Pennsylvania. This land was farmed for more than two centuries until the 1940s when William Long established Southampton Nurseries. In addition to the commercial stock, Long introduced exotic species of trees and shrubs as well. In 1975 Upper Southampton Township and the Centennial School District jointly purchased the 109-acre Tamanend Park for nearly one million dollars.

The Walks

For a small township park wedged between a rail line and a busy roadway, Tamanend sports a surprising variety of canine hikes. The *Red Arrowhead Trail* skirts the perimeter of the property for 2.3 miles and the *Blue Arrowhead* and *Yellow Arrowhead* trails are interior loops of about one mile in length. Two short, special trails are the stars at Tamanend, however. *The History Trail* interprets the heritage of the property and structures remaining from by-gone days. Highlights include the William Penn Treaty Elm, a fifth generation offspring of the great elm tree under which Penn negotiated with the Lenni Lenape, and a *Sequoia Giganteum*, a species of mountain redwood originally found only in China and California. The *Glenn Sokol Trail* is a quiet nature trail created in honor of a local naturalist.

> **Where The Paw Meets The Earth:** Wide dirt paths
> **Workout For Your Dog** - Easy canine hiking
> **Swimming** - Some dog paddling to be had in small Klinger Pond
> **Restrictions On Dogs** - None

Something Extra

The Glade is a special garden designed to spotlight a thick-trunked European Beech Tree, the Cedars of Lebanon and a giant Red Oak with thick, twisting wisteria vines climbing all the way to the crown. Set apart in the grass are Sweetbay Magnolia trees and two ancient Southern Magnolia trees.

Tannersville Cranberry Bog

Phone - None
Website - http://www.nature.org/wherewework/northamerica/
states/pennsylvania/preserves/art828.html
Admission Fee - None
Directions - *Tannersville, Monroe County; take PA 715 to PA 611
and make a left heading south. Turn left on Cherry Lane Road and
go 2.5 miles to Bog Road and make a right. In a half-mile there
is an unmarked pull-off on the left (look for an information kiosk
back from the road). Another quarter-mile down the road is a
barely discernible pull-off to the right for the* Fern Ridge Trail -
better to walk down Bog Road if you can.

The Park
The relict boreal bog was once a huge glacial lake. Since the ice receded 10,000-15,000 years ago, approximately 40 feet of peat has
accumulated on the floor of what was once a 715-acre lake. Today,
the bog stands out in contrast to the surrounding forests. The bog is
only open during regularly scheduled tours but two nearby woodland
trails are open for public use.

The Walks
The *North Wood Trail* is a stacked loop of almost a mile, with an extending option of a half-mile. This is an interpretive trail that sneaks
up a ridgeline and returns along the rise. The path is narrow with a
liberal sprinkling of inbedded rocks. The *Fern Ridge Trail* is unmarked
but you can make out the way by hopping rocks through a moist area
until the trail splits into a loop. This trail works easily up a hillside;
both trails are completely immeresed in upland forest.

> **Where The Paw Meets The Earth:** Natural surfaces with
> moist and rocky areas
> **Workout For Your Dog** - These are easy hikes for any
> dog on gentle
> grades along hillsides
> **Swimming** - None
> **Restrictions On Dogs** - None

Something Extra
You will invariably notice the abundance of mossy footfalls on the *Fern
Ridge Trail*. The vegetation here - sphagnum mosses, black spruce
trees, carniverous pitcher plants and tamaracks - are similar to that
found in the restricted Tannersville Cranberry Bog.

Taylor Arboretum

Phone - (610) 876-2649
Website - None
Admission Fee - None
Directions - *Chester, Delaware County; from I-95 take Exit 6 and follow Route 320 North. Just past 22nd Street, make a left on Chestnut Parkway and continue to the Arboretum entrance, making a left on Ridley Drive.*

The Park

The ownership of this property dates to William Penn who sold a thousand-acre land grant to John Sharpless in 1682. Sharpless descendents operated grist and cotton mills here for nearly two centuries. Taylor Memorial Arboretum was established in 1931 by a Chester lawyer, Joshua C. Taylor, in the memory of his wife, Anne Rulon Gray.

The Walks

The many trails through these 30 acres along Ridley Creek are short, interconnecting segments about evenly divided between woods and meadow. There are many highlights here, including plant-covered rock outcroppings, a bald cypress pond, and a groundwater spring. There is some slope on the   property down to the floodplain of the Ridley Creek but the walking is easy. The trail surfaces are soft dirt and grass and pine straw.

> **Where The Paw Meets The Earth:** Soft dirt and grass
> **Workout For Your Dog** - Gentle slopes across the property
> **Swimming** - The water behind the Sharpless Dam in the West Woods is excellent for canine swimming; in the East Woods the Ridley Creek offers a small stone beach and fast-flowing shallows for a doggie whirlpool
> **Restrictions On Dogs** - None

Something Extra

The Taylor Memorial Arboretum provides a 12-Tree Self-Guided Tour. The collection is especially strong in Far Eastern specimens and spotlights three Pennsylvania State Champion trees: the Needle Juniper, the Lacebark Elm and the Giant Dogwood. Also on the tour is a Dawn Redwood, an ancient tree known only through fossils until 1941 when a botany student tracked down living specimens in rural China. Some of the first seed to come to America resulted in this tree.

Theodore A. Parker III Natural Area

Phone - (717) 299-8215
Website - http://www.co.lancaster.pa.us/parks/cwp/view.asp?a=
676&q=518311&parksNav=|7871|
Admission Fee - None
Directions - *Quarryville, Lancaster County; in southeast Lancaster County, take Route 222 South through Quarryville for three miles and turn left on Blackburn Road after Solanco High School. Follow Blackburn Road for another three miles and make a sharp left back onto Wesley Road. The small parking lot is on the left, just past a small bridge.*

The Park

When ninety acres of unspoiled woodland was ticketed to become a Lancaster County park, it was named for Lancaster City native Theodore A. Parker III. Born in 1953, Parker quickly developed an affinity for birding. By the age of 13 he knew every bid by its Latin name and while still in high school he established a national record for most birds observed in North America in a single year. He would come to recognize 4000 different birds by call. Concentrating his life's work in the tropics, Parker became an internationally known ornithologist discovering and cataloging rare species of rain forest birds. Nearly 100 species were named for him before he died tragically in a plane crash in Ecuador in 1993.

The Walks

You will be leading your dog on a skinny interpretive trail that hugs the banks of Stewart Run through this lush ravine. To follow along you will need to make toeholds on exposed roots and scamper up and down wild rock formations. There isn't a distinct ending to your canine hike here once the information signs evaporate, it varies with your determination to forge ahead. Although essentially flat terrain, this is a spirited hike for your dog with the stream never more than a jump away and twists and turns up and around yellow poplars and black birches and massive boulders.

> **Where The Paw Meets The Earth:** Dirt with a little rock hopping
> **Workout For Your Dog** - A short climb here and there
> **Swimming** - The stream pools are seldom large enough for more than a few dog paddle strokes
> **Restrictions On Dogs** - None

Something Extra

The impressive rock formations and sheer walls in the ravine have been one of nature's longest ongoing projects. The metamorphic rocks date back 400 million years to the Cambrian-Ordovician Era, the Age of Marine Invertebrates. Pieces of quartzite can be seen shining in the waters of Stewart Run.

The Pinnacle

Phone - None
Website - None
Admission Fee - None
Directions - *Hamburg, Berks County; northeast of town. Take I-78 east into town or Route 61 north. Take Fourth Street east out of Hamburg for two miles and make a left on Reservoir Road. Cross Mountain Road to the end of the road and parking at the Hamburg Reservoir.*

The Park

The *Appalachian Trail* through Pennsylvania is not popular with many thru-hikers, derided as "the place where boots go to die" due to the rocky nature of the mountains. But one spot all agree is worth the purchase is the Pinnacle - a jumble of rock ledges offering a true panoramic view of the wooded Blue Mountain and the contrasting cultivated fields of the Cumberland Valley below.

The Walks

This is not a casual canine hike. Expect to devote a solid five hours to completing the 9-mile loop to the Pinnacle and back. The going is rough and rocky and athletic dogs only need apply. Tackling the loop counter-clockwise offers two routes to the Pinnacle: the rocky *Valley Rim Trail* (the path is not true to its name - there are no views from the trail) and a shortcut on a switch-backing access road to a mountaintop observatory (it is not a major time-saving shortcut). Your anticipation for the views at the Pinnacle will be whetted with a stop at Pulpit Rock across from the observatory. The mountain climbing ends at Pulpit Rock but not the treacherous footing for your dog as the trail to the Pinnacle is particularly rock-studded here. The return down the mountain is best taken down a fire road along the hemlock-draped Furnace Creek. This trail is a completely different experience from the climb up and gives the loop a feel of two canine hikes for the day.

> **Where The Paw Meets The Earth:** Much trotting on rocky patches with uneven pawfalls and considerable boulder-hopping in spots
> **Workout For Your Dog** - You may not find a better one
> **Swimming** - Furnace Creek is fast and fun but not for swimming
> **Restrictions On Dogs** - No dogs in the reservoir

Something Extra

Rocks are certainly a theme of a hike to the Pinnacle. From Pulpit Rock and the Pinnacle you get a commanding view of ariver of boulders 500 feet wide and a half-mile long known as the Blue Rocks. These erosion-resistant quartzite boulders are souvenirs of the last ice age when powerful glaciers left them behind.

Tobyhanna State Park

Phone - (570) 894-8336
Website - http://www.dcnr.state.pa.us/stateparks/parks/toby-hanna.aspx
Admission Fee - None
Directions - *Tobyhanna, Monroe County; the park entrance is 2.1 miles north of the community of Tobyhanna on PA 423. PA 423 intersects with I-380, 2.5 miles south of the park entrance. The park can also be reached from Interstate 84 via PA 507, PA 191 and PA 423, a total distance of 11.4 miles.*

The Park
The 5,440-acre park includes the 170-acre Tobyhanna Lake. Tobyhanna is derived from an American Indian word meaning "a stream whose banks are fringed with alder." In 1912, the federal government acquired land that would become the Tobyhanna Military Reservation that was used to train tank and ambulance corps during World War I. After the war, the property was used for artillery training. After World War II, the Commonwealth of Pennsylvania gained control of 26,000 acres of the military reservation, including the part that became the park. Tobyhanna opened to the public in 1949.

The Walks
The bulk of your canine hiking in the park will be on the *Lakeside Trail* that cirlces Tobyhanna Lake for 5.1 miles. The route only touches on the water on the east side of the shore but there are other water views including the Black Bear Swamp and Pole Bridge Run. This is a wide, easy exploration but if your dog demands more you can fill a day by heading down one of two linear connecting trails of about three miles each - the red-blazed *Frank Gantz Trail* that leads to Gouldsboro State Park or the *Yellow Trail* that crosses swampland to the park boundary at Route 196. Both are demanding treks that call for a good amount of rock-hopping.

> **Where The Paw Meets The Earth:** Asphalt, packed dirt, crushed stone
> **Workout For Your Dog** - Yes, in time on the trail; either of the spurs will test the most athletic dog
> **Swimming** - Absolutely, in Tobyhanna Lake
> **Restrictions On Dogs** - None, dogs are also allowed in the campground

Something Extra
Much of the park is the result of glaciation that scoured much of the soil from the ground, leaving an abundance of sphagnum moss bogs characterized by thin, moist, nutrient-poor soil. For sustenance plants turn to insects and several carniverous plants can be found here, including pitcher plants and the yellow bladderwort. In the underwater portion of the plant growing in bogs and Tobyhanna Lake, the bladderwort traps tiny aquatic animals in small sacks.

Tucquan Glen Nature Preserve

Phone - (717) 392-7891
Website - http://lancasterconservancy.org/
Admission Fee - None
Directions - *Mactic, Lancaster County; south of Lancaster on the Susquehanna River. It straddles River Road between Route 324 to the north and Route 372 to the south. Small parking lots are on both sides of the road but the lots in front of the trail are on the river side.*

The Park

Tucquan Glen, the crown jewel of the Lancaster County Conservancy, has long attracted visitors - both for its scenic wonders and natural resources. European settlement began early on and its tumbling waters first powered a sawmill in 1787. Millers remained active in the glen until the early 1900s when vacationers began arriving. The Conservancy purchased its first land in the glen in 1983 and has since built its holdings to 338 acres.

The Walks

This is an injection of the Poconos in the land of rolling farmland. Two trails envelop the Tucquan Creek. The southern leg supports most of the foot traffic as it hugs the banks all the way to the Susquehanna River and provides the best experience for enjoying the many waterfalls in the stream. Many folks just do the glen as out-and-back hike but canine hikers will want to loosen the grip on the leash by looping back on the north side. This less-   traveled route actually climbs to a rock promontory above the water for a completely different experience in the glen. The entire loop covers more than two miles. If you are in no hurry to leave Tucquan Glen, the long-distance *Conestoga Trail* (orange blazes) crosses the creek and travels north-south along the river.

> **Where The Paw Meets The Earth:** Dirt with some rocky spots
> **Workout For Your Dog** - Moderate work in the glen
> **Swimming** - For water-loving dogs make sure to keep going across the railroad tracks for a chance to swim in the Susquehanna River
> **Restrictions On Dogs** - None

Something Extra

It can be hard to imagine while trekking under the dark canopy of two score species of trees here but the forests of the Tucquan region were once energetically harvested for charcoal to fuel Lancaster's iron industry. Other important products from the Tucquan forests include tannin from the bark of the oak trees used by local tanneries, chestnut oak timbers that became railroad ties, locust trees for ship masts and tulip poplars valued in the furniture making industries and for building gliders.

Turkey Hill Trail

Phone - None
Website - http://lancasterconservancy.org/
Admission Fee - None
Directions - *Columbia, Lancaster County; from Washington Boro, at the junction of Water Street (Route 441) and Penn Street (Route 999), take River Road out of town. The northern trailhead is in a wooded patch about 1.5 miles down the road. There is limited parking here. A bigger lot is at the southern trailhead, past the Turkey Hill Dairy and behind the Highville fire station, still on River Road. To find the trailhead follow the fenceline on the right.*

The Park

Turkey Hill is a bulbous knob that juts into the Susquehanna River. A series of islands just north of the knob foster a rich fishing ground that has attracted interest since the days of the Susquehannock Indians. William Penn considered the area north of Turkey Hill for a "new Philadelphia" and Blue Rock Road was an early candidate as America's "Gateway to the West." The   rich farmland yielded great harvests of tobacco in the 1800s but is better know today for the Frey family dairy that began as a door-to-door milk delivery business during the Depression in the 1930s.The trail is under the stewardship of the Lancaster County Conservancy.

The Walks

The *Turkey Hill Trail* is a 3.3-mile string path that can be a challenge for canine hikers. The sensational views of the Susquehanna River that make this a popular hiker's destination are often found on exposed cliffs that will not favor an overly rambunctious dog. Active railroad tracks come into play on this canine hike. And without a car shuttle it can be a long hiking day for a dog to see the whole trail. Still, the actual hiking is not strenuous as you stay atop the ridgeline for most of the route. The hardwood forest makes for a pleasant passing and the overlooks are a great location for spying eagles, ospreys, vultures and hawks hunting in the waters below.

> **Where The Paw Meets The Earth:** Paw-friendly soft dirt and grass
> **Workout For Your Dog** - Spots of rough going
> **Swimming** - Wisslers Run and Manns Run are a water-loving dog's choices, rather than the Susquehanna River
> **Restrictions On Dogs** - None

Something Extra

Just a short hike from the northern trailhead as Wisslers Run is America's largest patch of pawpaw trees north of Washington DC. The pawpaw tree is a North American native found mostly in the south, although it can grow as far north as Ontario and west to Nebraska. It is known for its stubby banana-like fruit that is custard-like in texture.

Tuscarora State Park/Locust Lake State Park

Phone - (570) 467-2404
Website - http://www.dcnr.state.pa.us/stateParks/parks/tusca-rora.aspx
Directions - *Barnesville, Schuylkill County; two miles west of Tamaqua off of PA 309, south of Barnesville, which is on PA 54 between the Hometown Exit (131A) of I-81 and PA 309.*

The Park
The thick hemlock and chestnut forests that supported American Indians for ceturies were sacrificed to loggers to feed local tanneries in the 1800s. The forests were gone by the early 1900s, replaced by shrubby land prone to seasonal floods and forest fires. The denuded land was purchased by the Marshalonis Brothers as a fishing spot and picnic grove. When digging a lake, the brothers found a dam, boards and the hub of a waterwheel under seven feet of leaves, silt and debris. The remains of an old logging mill and dam were under silt from flooding and runoff caused by the removal of all of the trees for lumber during the logging era. The Commonwealth of Pennsylvania purchased the Marshalonis Brother's land in 1966. Locust Lake State Park, that is mostly a camping park, officially opened on June 10, 1972. Tuscarora Park is more for day use activities.

The Walks
The canine hiking at Tuscarora takes place on wide, old logging roads that move easily through the hillsides. A handful of designated paths through the regenerated hardwood forest are topped by the double-loop *Log Trail*; other short trails tour the developed picnic area on the wide, open shore of Tuscarora Lake. The longest park trail, the *Crow*, is a linear route connecting the lake and the park boundary. Canine hiking at Locust is for campers only until the off-season and much sportier on footpaths.

> **Where The Paw Meets The Earth:** Natural-surface roads and grass
>
> **Workout For Your Dog** - More at Locust; the hiking in Tuscaora requires easy hillclimbing
>
> **Swimming** - Super swimming for your dog in the lakes in the off-season
>
> **Restrictions On Dogs** - During the camping season, the only dogs permittted at Locust Lake State Park are those brought by campers; day use visitors can only bring pets to the park when the campground is closed

Something Extra
Tuscarora Lake is a great spot to fish, it offers the chance at the occasional monster walleye or musky. Outside the park season your dog will appreciate the beach area and easy access to the water.

Tyler State Park

Phone - (717) 840-7740
Website - http://www.dcnr.state.pa.us/stateParks/parks/tyler. aspx
Admission Fee - None
Directions - *Newtown, Bucks County; from Exit 27 follow Route 332 east to the park entrance at the intersection of Swamp Road and the four-lane bypass. From Exit 28 take Route 1 North to I-95 North to Exit 30 for Newtown-Yardley and follow the bypass west.*

The Park
The rolling lands along the Neshaminy Creek here have supported a vibrant farming community for over 300 years. Some of the stone dwellings peppered around the property date to the early 1700s. Funding from Pennsylvania conservation programs resulted in the opening of Tyler State Park in 1974. Today, more than 400 of the park's 1,711 acres are still under cultivation.

The Walks
Neshaminy Creek bisects Tyler State Park into two distinctly different halves. The eastern side is distinguished by a tightly bunched network of gravel hiking paths connecting the popular recreational areas located in this section of the park. The trails are shady and hilly. Across the creek, the trails stretch out for longer walks. There are more than ten miles of paved multi-purpose bicycle trails and almost as many miles of dirt-and-grass bridle paths. The trail system, one of the most elaborate in greater Philadelphia, can be customized into an endless array of short or long hikes. The terrain remains hilly, especially on the steep, self-guiding nature trail that loops its way around Parker Run as it feeds into Neshaminy Creek.

> **Where The Paw Meets The Earth:** Natural and asphalt surfaces
> **Workout For Your Dog** - Yes, plenty of trail time and hearty hills
> **Swimming** - The Neshaminy Creek is an excellent venue for canine aquatics with many access points from the trail above the dam
> **Restrictions On Dogs** - None

Something Extra
In the farthest northern section of Tyler State Park is the longest covered bridge in Bucks County. The 117-year old Schofield Ford Covered Bridge burned in 1991 but after five years of fundraising the 166-foot, two-span crossing was entirely rebuilt by volunteers on its original stone abutments using authentic period materials and methods.

Valley Forge National Historic Park

Phone - (610) 783-1000
Website - http://www.nps.gov/vafo/
Admission Fee - None
Directions - *Valley Forge, Chester County; the main park entrance is on Route 23 off Route 422.*

The Park
The most famous name in the American Revolution comes to us from a small iron forge built along Valley Creek in the 1740s. No battles were fought here, but during the winter of 1777-78, when Valley Forge grew to be the third largest city in America, hundreds of soldiers died from sickness and disease. America's attention was redirected to long-forgotten Valley Forge during a Centennial in 1878. Preservation efforts began with Wash-ington's Headquarters and evolved into the National Park.

The Walks
These are some of the most historic dog walks in America and some of the most beautiful in greater Philadelphia - panoramic vistas from rolling hills, long waterside hikes and climbs up wooded mountainsides. There are four marked trails, plus miles of unmarked hikes. The paved *Multi-Use Trail* loops the Colonial defensive lines and Grand Parade Ground and visits George Washington's headquarters. Sweeping field scenes are found all along the trail's six-mile length. The *Valley Creek Trail* is a flat, linear 1.2 mile walk along Valley Creek, past the Upper Forge site. Near the Valley Creek is the eastern terminus of the 133-mile *Horse-Shoe Trail* and demands a steep and strenuous climb up Mount Misery, the natural southern defender of Washington's encampment. Across the Schuylkill River is the 3-mile linear *Schuylkill River Trail* connecting the Pawling's Parking Area and the Betzwood Picnic Area. The flat dirt trail hugs the river the entire way. Nearby Walnut Hill provides miles more of unmarked hiking with your dog.

> **Where The Paw Meets The Earth:** Dirt and macadam
> **Workout For Your Dog** - Yes, long hikes and Mount Misery
> **Swimming** - Valley Creek is a delightful watering hole and the Schuylkill River is easily accessed for hard-core swimming canines
> **Restrictions On Dogs** - None

Something Extra
The *Multi-Use Trail* rolls past reconstructed huts and parade grounds that transport you back to the Revolution. The National Memorial Arch, a massive stone tribute dedicated in 1917, stands out along the route. The inscription reads: "Naked and starving as they are, we cannot enough admire the incomparable patience and fidelity of the soldiery. Washington at Valley Forge, February 16, 1778."

Warwick County Park

Phone - (610) 469-1916
Website - http://dsf.chesco.org/ccparks/cwp/view.
asp?A=1550&Q=616458
Admission Fee - None
Directions - *Knauertown, Chester County; on Route 23,
four miles west of Route 100. The main park entrance is located
on County Park Road and parking for the North Loop Trail is on Mt.
Pleasant Road, east of the main entrance.*

The Park
The woodlands in Warwick County Park's 455 acres provided much of
the timber for charcoal used in the American iron industry. The land
was an original grant to Samuel Nutt in 1718, who took to mining the
property. By 1738 the Warwick Furnace was established and it was
to be one of the most substantial in the American colonies. The first
Franklin Stove was cast here and the Warwick Cannon helped win the
Revolution. Charcoal hearths chiseled into the steep slopes can still
be seen flanking some trails. The park was dedicated in 1973.

The Walks
The premier walk in Warwick is the *Charcoal Trail Loop*, a narrow,
rocky, mile-long loop up and down the slopes of the French Creek
Valley. The *North Loop Trail*, designed like a long lasso, is a pleasant woods-and-field walk, much of it on the old bed of the Sowbelly
Railroad. Two of the *Horse-Shoe Trail's* 133 miles bisect the park and
there is a 1/2-mile *Adirondack Trail* where you can test your ability to identify the trees and shrubs commonly found in an Eastern
hardwood forest. The trail access from the Coventry Road parking
lot is overgrown and provides access only to the French Creek South
Branch, but not the rest of the park.

> **Where The Paw Meets The Earth:** Paw-friendly dirt
> and some rocks
> **Workout For Your Dog** - There are many long stretches
> of flat terrain but the *Charcoal Trail* will give your dog a
> cardiac workout
> **Swimming** - Very little water in the park
> **Restrictions On Dogs** - None

Something Extra
In 1850 Albert Fink, a German railroad engineer, designed and patented a bridge that used a latticework of rods instead of cables to
reinforce stiffness. This construction was cheap and sturdy, making
the Fink Truss one of the most commonly used railroad bridges in
the 1860s, especially favored by the powerful Baltimore & Ohio Railroad. Only one Fink Truss bridge remains in the United States - an
abandoned 108-foot span in Zoarsville, Ohio. A wooden reproduction
of a Fink Truss is in a field at Warwick County Park for you and your
dog to climb.

Welkinweir

Phone - (610) 469-4990
Website - http://www.greenvalleys.org/welkinweir.asp
Admission Fee - Yes
Directions - *Phoenixville, Chester County; from the intersection of Routes 23 and 100, take Route 100 south for 1.1 miles. Make a right on Prizer Road. Follow for .8 a mile to Welkinweir on the left. The Visitor Entrance is the second of three access points and is marked by a sign.*

The Park
Welkinweir ("where sky meets water") was a foundering farm during the Depression when the property was purchased by Everett and Grace Rodebaugh. The Rodebaughs reintroduced native trees and meadows and constructed a series of ponds in the valley beneath the farmhouse. In 1964, Everett Rode-baugh founded the Green Valleys Association to protect five watersheds draining 151 square miles of northern Chester County. In 1997 the Rodebaughs conveyed Welkinweir to the Green Valleys Association for use as a headquarters and educational center.

The Walks
A woodland trail loops around the 162-acre nature sanctuary, leading through wetlands, ponds, and meadows. The trail, which takes about an hour to complete, can be narrow and overgrown through the back of the property. For longer walks, the *Welkinweir Trail* features a short connector to the *Horse-Shoe Trail*, which skirts the property on two sides.

> **Where The Paw Meets The Earth:** Dirt mostly, some of the meadow trails are shaved stalks which are rough on your pet's paws
> **Workout For Your Dog** - This is hilly property, especially in the backstretch of the loop
> **Swimming** - Although the West Branch of Beaver Run is not deep enough for doggie dipping, it engorges into several ponds on the property
> **Restrictions On Dogs** - None

Something Extra
There are dramatic vistas from the garden areas around the property. As one visitor commented in the Welkinweir guest book: "It's a Grand Canyon of trees!"

Wildwood Lake Sanctuary

Phone - (717) 221-0292
Website - http://wildwoodlake.org/
Admission Fee - None
Directions - *Harrisburg, Dauphin County; in the northern part, just across I-81. From Route 322/22 North, take the Linglestown Road (Route 39) Exit and turn left. Make your first left at the light onto Industrial Road. There are three parking lots on your left heading down the road and another at Olewine Nature Center.*

The Park
For most of the 19th century this lake was known as Wetzel's Swamp and mostly ignored. In 1901 the City of Harrisburg established Wildwood Park as its part of the nationwide "City Beautiful" movement. Within a few years trails were built and pleasure boats were plying the gentle waters. Eventually a zoo and riding stables were included and Wildwood Park was a busy place indeed. But the zoo closed in the 1940s and interest in the park faded away. For decades the park changed from popular playground to popular dumping ground. The turnaround began in the 1980s in the form of detrmined volunteers and government grants. The National Audubon Society named Wildwood Lake one of its national Important Birding Areas and in the late 1990s food service magnate Ben Olewine donated $800,000 towards the creation of a state-of-the-art multi-million dollar nature center to complete the revitalization.

The Walks
The main canine hike here is a circle of a little more than three miles around the lake. The lake is shoehorned into a few hundred acres dominated by major roadways and an industrial park but once the barrage of vehicular noise and public address pages disappear into background noise, the magic of the sanctuary reveals itself. You start out on paw-friendly woodchips on the *Towpath Trail* before transitioning on pavement. The *Delta Boardwalk*, accessed across a drawbridge, meanders for a half-mile through an active marsh. The circuit is completed on a choice of the multi-use, paved *Wildwood Way Trail* or the traditional narrow dirt path on the *East Shore Trail*.

> **Where The Paw Meets The Earth:** Dirt, wood chips, boards and asphalt
> **Workout For Your Dog** - Mostly flat with a rise in the northeast corner
> **Swimming** - A little swimming in Wildwood Lake
> **Restrictions On Dogs** - None

Something Extra
Wildwood Lake is home to the endangered American lotus, a particularly showy member of the water lily family, found in only two places in Pennsylvania.

Wilkes-Barre Riverfront Parks

Phone - None
Website - None
Admission Fee - None
Directions - *Wilkes Barre, Luzerne County; Market Street, on either side of the Susquehanna River.*

The Park
The City of Wilkes-Barre owns and maintains 91 acres of open space and floodplain forest along the Susquehanna River in Wilkes-Barre, Kingston and Edwardsville. Initially set aside in 1773, these riverside parks provide exceptional access to the river and to the natural areas in the flood plain. The original Kirby Park (designed in 1921 by the Olmsted Brothers architecture firm) on the west bank of the river was bisected into two pieces by the 1936 levee project, creating, on one side, an urban recreational park and on the river side, the Kirby Park Natural Area. This park contains 65 acres of riparian forest exposing visitors to a wealth of animal, bird and plant life. Nesbitt Park, north of the Market Street Bridge, also offers access to the river.

The Walks
The Kirby Park Natural Area, resplendent with large silver maples and cottonwoods growing in the silt and sandy soil from the overflowing river, serves up a network of five marked trails. Nesbitt Park, north of the Market Street Bridge, also offers access to the river. The space between the levee and the river around Nesbitt Park offers mountain bikers up to eight miles of secluded trails. Dog owners can join the joggers and strollers enjoying the wide, lighted path atop the elevated dike that has only been breeched once - in 1972 during Tropical Storm Agnes.

> **Where The Paw Meets The Earth:** Asphalt, crushed gravel, soft dirt, grass
> **Workout For Your Dog** - Long, level canine hikes possible
> **Swimming** - In the "Muddy River," as the Susquehanna is translated into
> **Restrictions On Dogs** - None

Something Extra
The trail system is composed of four levees that have been engineered to contain the river. A series of walks and rambles have been laid out to emphasize the city's heritage: as a meeting place for early settlers, as an anthracite coal center and so on. Kiosks stationed around the park explain how the levees work and also display pictures of the region under extreme flood conditions.

William H. Kain County Park

Phone - (717) 840-7440
Website - http://ycwebserver.york-county.org/Parks/Kain.htm
Admission Fee - None
Directions - *York City; south of the city on the north edge of Jacobus. From I-83, take Exit 14, Leaders Heights Road west for one mile to Susquehanna Trail. Turn left and continue to the first of seven lots on the right at Lake Williams.*

The Park

William H. Kain founded the family law firm in 1842 in York, where he also served as Superintendent of Schools. One hundred and thirty-seven years later his grandson, William H. Kain Jr., president of the York Water Company, executed a 50-year lease agreement to use of the Water Company Reservoir Lands for a county park. The pioneering deal was the first United States county park developed in cooperation with a public utility. The William H. Kain County Park consists of 1,637 acres surrounding two lakes, Lake Williams (220 acres) and Lake Redman (290 acres).

The Walks

Kain County Park features 12 miles of multi-use trails - all used by horses and mountain bikes. There are seven numbered trails, most of which do not loop. It is difficult to patch together a circuit hike without taking your dog along a paved suburban road. If that is your idea of an invigorating canine hike you can actually circumnavigate the two lakes. Whatever trail you choose around Lake Williams and Lake Redman expect a healthy workout for your dog on the many hills in the park. Paths range from roomy fire roads to the occasional ribbon trail. You'll encounter stands of tall trees and stretches of wetlands and open hiking.

> **Where The Paw Meets The Earth:** Mostly dirt paths
> **Workout For Your Dog** - Many hills on long trails
> **Swimming** - The trails drop down to lakeside every now and then; Codurus Creek is deep enough for dog paddling in the park's extremities
> **Restrictions On Dogs** - None

Something Extra

With the help of 8,000 deck screws 350-foot walking deck juts into Lake Redman near the Iron Stone Hill Road parking lot. A variety of waterfowl can be viewed from the deck, especially during the spring and fall migrations.Look for Trail #5 to access the Bird Observation Deck, that required 8 months to obtain building permits.

Woodbourne Forest & Wildlife Preserve

Phone - None
Website - http://www.woodbourneforest.org/
Admission Fee - None
Directions - *Dimrock, Susquehanna County; on Route 29, one mile north of the blinking light in town or five miles south of Montrose.*

The Park

Henry Cope was a 19th century Philadelphia shipping merchant whose legacy is in fine summer homes that have surviced as nature preserves. His summer retreat outside Philadelphia in East Germantown is today the Awbury Arboretum and in the late 1800s the family began to summer in Dimrock.Eventually some Copes family members, prominent Quakers, stayed on the farm year-round. Francis R. Cope, Jr. grew up at Woodbourne, as did his daughter, the nature writer Theodora Stanwell-Fletcher, later known familiarly as Teddy Gray. In 1956, Francis, an avid naturalist and early supporter of the conservation of wild lands, donated the 600 acres that is now Woodbourne Forest and Wildlife Preserve to The Nature Conservancy.

The Walks

Of the three hiking loops in the preserve the star is the shortest - the *Yellow "Swamp Loop" Trail*. From the Visitor Shelter the natural surface trail trips down a hill through open fields to the swamp's edge and an observation tower overlooking the ghost trees left standing in the water. After some squishy hiking along the swamp you will enter the dark old-growth forest. Your option is to finish the loop - your dog has less than a mile of trail time - or jump across a stream onto the orange-blazed *Woodruff Hill Trail*. From here you can stitch together a loop around the swamp with the blue-blazed *Copes Ramble Trail*. For a big day of canine hiking you can take the entire 4.5-mile *Cope's Ramble* but don't forget to detour onto the Swamp Loop as well.

> **Where The Paw Meets The Earth:** Dirt paths
> **Workout For Your Dog** - Moderate hill-climbing
> **Swimming** - Come for the hiking
> **Restrictions On Dogs** - None

Something Extra

Woodbourne Forest is noted for containing the largest remaining stand of virgin, unlumbered forest in northeastern Pennsylvania. Some of the giants, mostly eastern hemlocks, around the 16-acre swamp are estimated to be between 200 and 400 years old.

Worlds End State Park

Phone - (570) 924-3287
Website - http://www.dcnr.state.pa.us/stateparks/parks/world-send.aspx
Admission Fee - None
Directions - *Forksville, Wyoming County; the park is along PA 154 and is easily reached from PA 42 from I-80 and south and PA 87 from Dushore and the north and east.*

The Park

Early maps called this place Worlds End, possibly due to the staggering views and difficulties in reaching the area. The unusual name may also be a reference to the swirling S-curve in Loyalsock Creek that blocked lumbered logs from flowing downstream, called "Whirls End." In 1929, the former Department of Forests and Waters began purchasing the logged-out land to create a state forest park. In 1932, $50 was allotted to create the park facilities, which purchased little more than four picnic tables. Four Civilian Conservation Corps (CCC) built many of the park facilities, like the swimming area and dam, cabins, hiking trails and roads.

The Walks

The over 20 miles of hiking trails of Worlds End State Park are mostly rocky with steep sections that climb the surrounding mountains. Some of the more awe-inspiring canine hiking is on the north side of the creek with dramatic views from routes such as the *High Rock Trail*. Across the way trips on the *Worlds End Trail* and *Double Run Trail* pentetrate deep into the vast woods. these adventures follow the paths of treacherous old horse trails that early settlers used to cross the Endless Mountains.

> **Where The Paw Meets The Earth:** Natural surface
> **Workout For Your Dog** - Some of the best, toughest hiking around
> **Swimming** - Down in Loyalsock Creek are canine swimming pools
> **Restrictions On Dogs** - No dogs allowed in the campground

Something Extra

In the eastern half of the park the *Canyon Vista Trail* is highlighted by a spectacular view of the Loyalsock Creek gorge at an elevation of 1750 feet. Many wildflowers grow beneath the canopy of maturing ash, sugar maple and black cherry trees. Be sure to explore the blocky maze of the Rock Garden adjacent to the vista. A second rock labyrinth is found in the easternmost section of the trail where it runs parallel to Cold Run Road.

NORTHERN VIRGINIA

Accotink Bay Wildlife Refuge

Phone - (703) 806-4007
Website - http://www.dgif.state.va.us/wildlife/vbwt/site.asp?trail=1&site=CMN05&loop=CMN
Admission Fee - None
Directions - *Fort Belvoir Military Base, Fairfax County; from I-95 take the Fort Belvoir/ Newington exit to the southern leg of the Fairfax County Parkway (Route 7100). Follow the parkway east approximately 3 miles until its end at Richmond Highway (Route 1). Turn left onto Route 1 and at the first light make a right into Tulley Gate. Follow to the refuge main entrance ahead on the right. Before that, the first parking lot you see is for the short handicap accessible trail; the second leads to the heart of the trail system. Access to the base can be limited without notice.*

The Park
The refuge was established in 1979 to protect sensitive wetlands and wildlife habitats associated with Accotink Bay and to provide opportunities for environmental education and low-intensity recreation. In 1988, Fort Belvoir established a second refuge, the Jackson Miles Abbott Wetland Refuge, to protect another sensitive wetland area. Abbott was an army engineer whose ornithological illustrations were chosen to appear on a duck stamp. Today, more than one-third of the installation's acreage has been preserved as a designated wildlife sanctuary encompassing over 1,300 acres.

The Walks
There are some fifteen short, intersecting trail segments on both sides of the Accotink Creek to explore with your dog here. The going can be a bit rough at times, especially along the creek where the narrow bands of pathway can be overgrown or muddy in wet tmes but overall this is easy going with some mild ups and downs. The highlight ramble in the refuge is the *Beaver Pond Trail* loop that slips past several small ponds filled with turtles and frogs. For a longer leg stretcher head down the *Great Blue Heron Trail* to a bird blind on the Accotink Bay. Across the suspension bridge are miles of dirt trails in the hardwood forest that was once used for target ranges. The Abbott Wetland Refuge has a one-mile asphalt trail with an observation deck overlooking the wetland area.

> **Where The Paw Meets The Earth:** Natural surface and asphalt
> **Workout For Your Dog** - Easy trotting
> **Swimming** - Accotink Creek is a great spot
> **Restrictions On Dogs** - None

Something Extra
The bridge across the Accotink Creek linking the trail system was built by D Company of the 11th Engineer Battalion.

Algonkian Regional Park

Phone - (703) 450-4655
Website - http://www.nvrpa.org/algonkian.html
Admission Fee - None
Directions - *Sterling, Loudoun County; from the Beltway (I-495), take Route 7 west 11 miles to Cascades Parkway north, and drive 3 miles to the park entrance.*

The Park
Located on the shores of the Potomac River, this busy recreation park serves up everything from golf to boating to miniature golf to waterparks.

The Walks
Algonkian Park features easy canine hiking across 800 acres of flat Potomac River floodplain. Most of the park is given over to recreational activities, principally a waterpark and a golf course, through which the paved park trail travels. In the western section of the park your dog can enter into light woods on a rooty, dirt nature trail for the better part of two miles. If you are a fan of whitetail deer, come to the park in the evenings with your dog. There are plenty of grassy fields for you to informally hike with your dog in the open air without crossing the golf course. Nearby you can stop at the boat ramp for extended play in the waters of the Potomac River.

> **Where The Paw Meets The Earth:** Dirt, grass and paved surfaces
> **Workout For Your Dog** - Your dog will be hard pressed to locate an uphill step here
> **Swimming** - Easy swimming in the Potomac River at the boat ramp
> **Restrictions On Dogs** - Dogs are not allowed in the recreational areas

Something Extra
This is one of the better places to indulge in birdwatching with the wide open fields and long views.

Ball's Bluff Regional Park

Phone - (703) 737-7800
Website - http://www.nvrpa.org/ballsbluff.html
Admission Fee - None
Directions - *Leesburg, Loudoun County; take Route 7 to Route 15 Bypass North, just east of Leesburg. From Route 15, turn right on Battlefield Parkway and left on Ball's Bluff Road to the parking lot at the end of the road.*

The Park
In the early days of the Civil War both armies centered around the Potomac River. General Charles P. Stone was directed to move the Confederates out of the Leesburg area and ordered a scouting party across the river from his camp in Maryland. Once across the Potomac haystacks were mistaken for enemy tents which lured the Union men deeper onto Ball's Bluff and attracted the attention of the Confederates. On the morning of October 21, 1861 the Southern soldiers engaged the enemy and drove the Union army back toward the bluff's edge. At 4:30 p.m. Colonel Edward Baker, a lifelong friend of President Abraham Lincoln, tried to rally the Northerners out of their trapped position. Baker leapt to the front of the line and was mortally wounded by four musket balls. Suddenly emboldened, the Confederates routed the Union soldiers and pushed them to the edge of the 80-foot bluff. Some scrambled down the cliff only to be picked off by Confederate bullets or drowned under the weight of their uniforms and ammunition. Five hundred and fifty-three Union troops, about 1/3 of their force, were captured.

The Walks
The centerpiece hike in the 223-acre park is a one-mile interpretive loop that can get steep and rugged in places after a benign start on soft wood chips. The *Old Cart Path* leads down the bluff to the edge of the Potomac River that gives you a feel of what the Union Army had to face to pull two howitzers and a cannon into position on the battlefield - and try to escape under withering enemy fire. There are other unmarked natural trails through the woods on the edge of the Potomac River.

> **Where The Paw Meets The Earth:** Dirt and wood chips
> **Workout For Your Dog** - Yes, into the ravines and out
> **Swimming** - The *Old Cart Path* will take your dog to the muddy banks of the Potomac for swim time in the river
> **Restrictions On Dogs** - None

Something Extra
The national cemetery at Ball's Bluff is one of the smallest in America, with only the remains of 54 Union soldiers buried in a semi-circle. The identity of only one fallen man is known.

Banshee Reeks Nature Preserve

Phone - (703) 669-0316
Website - http://www.co.loudoun.va.us/prcs/parks/banshee.htm
Admission Fee - None
Directions - *Leesburg, Loudoun County; take US Route 15 South for approximately 1/4-mile South of the Leesburg Bypass, turn left onto Route 621, Evergreen Mills Road. Proceed south along Evergreen Mills Road about five miles. Turn right onto The Woods Road (Route 771). Proceed down The Woods Road (a dirt road) for approximately one mile. Entrance to Banshee Reeks is on the left.*

The Park
Legend has it that an early landowner of these rolling hills was of Irish or Scottish descent. After a night of revelry in a nearby town he returned to his farm and heard what he thought were "banshees in the reeks" - translated from Gaelic as female spirits in the hills. When the 695-acre passive nature park was established the name of local lore was given to the preserve. The land was acquired by Loudoun County in 1995 and envisioned as a typical active recreation park of picnic sites and ballfields. But public agitation led to the establishment of the preserve, believed to be one of the few nature preserves of this scale operated by a county government in the country.

The Walks
Banshee Reeks was originally developed for use by organized groups but has been opened to the general public one weekend per month. Call ahead to determine if any restrictions are in effect. Canine hikers will want to make the special effort required to use these trails. Paw-friendly grass trails are cut through the stunning meadows and well-maintained trails traipse through riparian forests. Expect stream crossings and a good workout for you and your dog. Pay attention to avoid trails that are closed for maintenance or under construction so that public access will not be closed for maintenance or under construction so that public access will not be restricted.

> **Where The Paw Meets The Earth:** Dirt and grass
> **Workout For Your Dog** - Easy to moderate terrain
> **Swimming** - Check in at Goose Creek for canine aquatics
> **Restrictions On Dogs** - None that don't apply to people as well

Something Extra
Archeology is an ongoing concern at Banshee Reeks. The land has been occupied for thousands of years but not much history has been recorded. Initial efforts involved digging holes every 50 feet over the entire property in hopes of finding artifacts from the past. More obvious are the structures sprinkled throughout the preserve that include a manor house, an 1880s log cabin, a bank barn, long-abandoned silos and the ruins of a spring house.

Battlefields of Manassas

Phone - (703) 361-1339
Website - http://www.nps.gov/mana/
Admission Fee - Yes
Directions - *Manassas, Prince William County; travel west on I-66 to Exit 47B, Route 234 North (Sudley Road). Proceed through the first traffic light. The entrance to the Henry Hill Visitors Center is on the right, just past the Northern Virginia Community College.*

The Park
Twice in the first two years of the Civil War the Northern and Southern armies clashed five miles north of town near a creek called Bull Run, resulting in 30,000 casualties in an attempt to control that railroad junction. On July 21, 1861 the Civil War was expected to end. The fully-equipped Union Army under General Irvin McDowell was prepared to take the field for the first time at Bull Run. The complete submission of the rebels was such a certainty the Federal troops were accompanied by picnickers and sightseers. After ten hours of bloody fighting the Union Army was in retreat towards Washington and it was apparent this was not going to be a one-battle war. The armies returned to Bull Run a year later, seasoned and spirited. Robert E. Lee's Army of Northern Virginia was at the peak of its power and he outmaneuvered General John Pope's Union army in three days of struggle beginning August 28. With his masterful victory here Lee was able to carry the war to the North for the first time.

The Walks
The main canine hiking here is on two trails that interpret the two critical Civil War clashes over this ground. Each route covers more than five miles and offers a pleasing mix of open-field and woods hiking. Expect the fields - that retain much of its wartime character - to be muddy in times of wet weather. The *First Manassas Trail* takes in Bull Run and the Stone Bridge where the first shots were fired. It also features more open fields. The *Second Manassas Trail* across the western section of the park is the preferred route to take your dog on a busy day. If time is limited take the one-mile *Henry Hill Loop Trail* around the Visitor Center where the critical fighting in the first battle of the Civil War took place. The trail follows part of the Southern Line where General Thomas J. Jackson received his immortal nickname "Stonewall."

> **Where The Paw Meets The Earth:** Grass and dirt
> **Workout For Your Dog** - Long trots over rolling hills
> **Swimming** - Bull run can flow deep enough for dog swims
> **Restrictions On Dogs** - None

Something Extra
The battlefields are probably the best place in Northern Virginia to see whitetail deer. Come to the park late in the day to see the herds.

Bull Run-Occoquan Trail

Phone - None
Website - None
Admission Fee - None
Directions - *Access from several parks in Fairfax County.*

The Park

The word "Occoquan" is roughly translated from the Doag Indians of the Powhatan Confederacy who originally inhabited the stream valley, using it as a wilderness highway. With European settlement the indigenous peoples moved away and not much happened until the arrival of the Orange and Alexandria Railroad in 1848. When the Civil War erupted the first clash between the North and South took place on the south bank of Bull Run. The Bull Run/Occoquan River comprised the boundary of the "Alexandria Line" set up by the Confederates to protect against a Union move towards the capital in Richmond. The town of Clifton was the southernmost post for the Union. When the war ended Cifton enjoyed a brief flurry of prosperity as the home to the healing waters of Paradise Springs where several presidents reportedly came to take the cure. Clifton was the first town in Fairfax County to be electrified. After the county acquired over 5,000 acres of land along the rivers it created a series of parks cnnected by the *Bull Run-Occoquan Trail.*

The Walks

If you have a car shuttle this could be the best place to hike with your dog in northern Virginia. The 18-mile trail begins in the east in Fountainhead Regional Park and by the time you reach Bull Run Regional Park your dog will experience most of what the region has to offer. Hills and stream valleys predominate from Fountainhead to Bull Run Marina, a distance of about 6.5 miles. On the trail to Hemlock Regional Park stands of dark green Eastern hemlocks begin to mix into the forest with the tall beeches and oaks. When the trail reaches Bull Run it begins to level out and hug the shoreline. You'll emerge from the woods more often and the trail can even get muddy and downright impassable in wet weather. An access point where Route 28 crosses Bull Run slices the western segment of the trail into manageable hiking chunks (on the Fairfax side of the stream take the last driveway on the right before crossing the bridge).

> **Where The Paw Meets The Earth:** Natural surface
> **Workout For Your Dog** - Plenty of ups and downs but nothing brutal
> **Swimming** - yes, in Bull Run
> **Restrictions On Dogs** - None

Something Extra

Freshwater mussels like to live in shallow, swift-moving water as can be found in stretches of Bull Run.The United States has over 300 species of mussels, which is the most diverse anywhere in the world.

Bull Run Regional Park

Phone - (703) 631-0550
Website - http://www.nvrpa.org/bullrunpark.html
Admission Fee - Yes
Directions - *Centreville, Fairfax County; take I-66 to Exit 52 (Route 29) at Centreville, drive 2 miles south, turn left onto Bull Run Post Office Road and follow the signs to the park entrance.*

The Park
The first English settlers in the area called the peripatetic stream Bull Run, the term applied to creeks unaffected by tidal influence and therefore flowed in only one direction. The waterway provided easy transportation and sustenance to those who lived along it and it would have continued forever in anonymity like so many thousands of similar streams if it wasn't by chance a key defensive line between the North and South during the Civil War. Today the forest on the north shore of Bull Run is left undisturbed as a sanctuary protected by the Northern Virginia Regional Park Authority.

The Walks
The first thing your dog will find when he hangs his head out the window driving into Bull Run Regional Park is that he won't need his climbing gear. The next thing is the abundance of large, open fields. You could spend a sunny day just hiking with your dog around these wide open spaces in the 1,500-acre park and never venture onto the trails. The park is the northern terminus for the *Bull Run-Occoquan Trail* that runs for 18 miles along the water to Fountainhead Park. The segment here scrambles 1.72 miles to a parking lot on Route 28. This and other trails are wide and flat and make for easy canine hiking - and also muddy when wet.

> **Where The Paw Meets The Earth:** Natural surface trails and roads
> **Workout For Your Dog** - Flat and level land
> **Swimming** - The streams can occasionally flow deep enough to serve as more than a splashpool
> **Restrictions On Dogs** - None

Something Extra
The *Bluebell Walk* begins on the *Nature Trail* near the Visitor Center and makes its way to the confluence of Cub Run and Bull Run. This is a meandering 1.5-mile canine hike through the largest stand of bluebells on the East Coast. In springtime the display on the forest floor is unforgettable.

Burke Lake Park

Phone - (703) 323-6600
Website - http://www.fairfaxcounty.gov/parks/burkelake/
Admission Fee - Yes
Directions - *Fairfax Station, Fairfax County; from Route 66 take the Fairfax County Parkway, Exit 55A (7100 South towards Springfield). Continue on the Fairfax County Parkway for approximately five miles. Take a right onto Burke Lake Road. At the next light, turn left onto Ox Road (Route 123). The main entrance - past the boaters' lot - is on the right.*

The Park
Silas Burke, a wealthy plantation owner, was a high ranking Fairfax County official who was instrumental in bringing the Orange and Alexandria railroad to the area. A century later, however, there was not a similar celebration when a different mode of transportation wanted to serve the sparsely populated farming community. In the 1950s the federal government proposed building Dulles Airport in Burke, buying land and condemning property. The handful of local residents opposed the plan so vehemently that the government scuttled its plans and gave the land to the Fairfax County Park Authority who built the 889-acre park with its 218-acre, man-made lake as a centerpiece. A half-century later, instead of jet planes, visitors to Burke find instead a miniature railroad and the quiet hum of the occasional electric motorboat on the lake.

The Walks
There is but one trail at Burke Lake - a hard-packed dirt-and-crushed-stone affair that circumnavigates the lake. Once you set out you sign on for the entire 4.5 miles that hug the shoreline around the many fingers of the lake. The going is almost completely level and under trees just about the whole way around. Views of the lake are abundant and once you clear the active recreation area this lakeside canine hike can impart quite a sense of tranquility for such a developed area.

> **Where The Paw Meets The Earth:** Mostly natural surface with some crushed stone and asphalt
> **Workout For Your Dog** - Yes, for the full trip around the lake
> **Swimming** - Plenty of places to test the water for a doggie dip
> **Restrictions On Dogs** - None

Something Extra
Burke Lake has proven to be the best small lake fishing spot in northern Virginia for largemouth bass. The popular sportfish average three pounds with six-pounders being common. Anglers can also try their luck with muskies,walleye, white perch and black crappie. Rowboats can be rented in season.

C.M. Crockett Park

Phone - (540) 788-4867
Website - http://www.fauquiercounty.gov/government/departments/parksrec/index.cfm?action=crockett
Admission Fee - Yes
Directions - *Warrenton, Fauquier County; south of town on Route 643 (Meetze Road), just north of Route 28.*

The Park
Twelve German families migrated to this area in 1719 to mine ore on 1,805 acres on Licking Run. They were the first Europeans to establish a permanent settlement in what is now Fauquier County and created the first German reformed congregation in the Southern colonies. The town survived into the 20th century but was abandoned by World War II. No trace of the town remains today and the quarry from which they extracted ore has been filled in to create 109-acre Germantown Lake.

The Walks
There are two main hiking routes to enjoy with your dog on opposite ends of the park. Each offers a bit over a mile of easy going on maintained trails.The *Bluebird Cross Country Trail* takes in the open fields above the lake before dropping into the trees at the shoreline, crossing the dam and looping around the spillway. A mature woodland awaits across the picnic area on the *Four Seasons Nature Trail*, a series of three stacked loops. Your dog will find this ramble to be exceedingly paw-friendly and don't be surprised if he wants to go around again.

> **Where The Paw Meets The Earth:** Natural and paved surfaces
> **Workout For Your Dog** - Little hills around te lake
> **Swimming** - No swimming in the lake for dogs or people
> **Restrictions On Dogs** - None

Something Extra
The European sport of orienteering was introduced to America on the East Coast in the Valley Forge, Pennsylvania area. Crockett Park has developed permanent beginner and advanced courses for the practitioners of the art of map and compass. Try them and you can challenge your dog's nose in a wayfinding contest.

Claude Moore Park

Phone - (703) 444-1275
Website - http://www.co.loudoun.va.us/prcs/parks/claude.htm
Admission Fee - None
Directions - *Sterling, Loudoun County; from the Beltway (I-495), take Route 7 West and exit at Cascades Parkway South. Immediately get into left lane and stay on Cascades Parkway South for approximately ½ mile. You will go through two lights. After the second light, the first entrance to the park is on your left. Enter here for the nature area. If coming from the south the nature area is the second entrance on the right. Center is on the right, just past the Northern Virginia Community College.*

The Park

In 1941 Dr. Claude Moore purchased the property at auction from the family who had lived here for 170 years. In 1975 he donated the property to the National Wildlife Federation. In 1986 the NWF sold the property to developers and Moore, then in his 90s, was forced to initiate lawsuits to save the land that went all the way to the Virginia Supreme Court. He lost all his appeals but county residents passed a bond referendum to purchase the site and preserve one of the last remaining greenspaces in a vast area of houses and box stores. A year after the park opened in 1990, Moore, still living on the property, passed away at the age of 98.

The Walks

Claude Moore Park serves up a pastiche of a dozen short trails that add up to more than ten miles of canine hiking. Two trails - the white-blazed *Little Stoney Mountain Trail* and the blue-blazed *Scout Trail* - both follow essentially the same route to explore the entire park so you only have to choose one. A popular destination for first-time visitors is the scenic overlook at the north end of the park on Little Stoney Mountain (at 442 feet, the hill's name dates to a 1779 survey map). The scenic view is of the monolithic Sugarloaf Mountain in Maryland (another great place to take your dog hiking). Among the short trails around the Visitor's Center, the purple-blazed *Cedar Grove Trail* is a standout.

> **Where The Paw Meets The Earth:** Dirt and cobblestones
> **Workout For Your Dog** - Moderate haul to the top of Little Stoney
> **Swimming** - Dogs aren't permitted in the ponds
> **Restrictions On Dogs** - None

Something Extra

The last known undeveloped section of the historic Vestal's Gap Road runs across the park. This trail, first used by American Indians, was used as early as 1692 by the Rangers of the Potomac under David Strahan. It became the major route for travel between Alexandria and Winchester.

Conway-Robinson State Forest

Phone - None
Website - http://www.dgif.state.va.us/wildlife/vbwt/site.asp?trail
=3&site=PCU02&loop=PCU
Admission Fee - None
Directions - *Manassas, Prince William County; there are no signs
for the forest that is on the north side of the Lee Highway (Route
29) sandwiched between Manassas National Battlefield and I-66.
Look for a small picnic area.*

The Park
This swath of 444 acres of Prince William County open space provides
outdoor recreation opportunities and protects water quality conditions
in the Occoquan watershed. There are no facilities or amenities in
the park, save for a few scattered picnic tables.

The Walks
The trail system in the Conway-Robinson State Forest is a perimeter
loop embracing a series of stacked loops. Your canine hike begins as
a common woods walk but you shortly cross a pipeline cut and enter
an area known as The Pines - as lovely a stretch of path as you are
likely to find in the region.Most of the forest is on level ground - save
this outing for a dry day since the ground can get wet - although it
slopes a bit after the pipeline. The trail narrows again after the pine
trees as you move into a typical oak-hickory forest. The trail often
winds back on itself to give it the feel of a greater length than its
two miles.

> **Where The Paw Meets The Earth:** Natural dirt surfaces
> **Workout For Your Dog** - Easy going for your dog
> **Swimming** - None
> **Restrictions On Dogs** - None

Something Extra
The Manassas Gap Railroad was chartered in 1850 under the direction
of Edward Carrington Marshall, son of Chief Justice John Marshall.
The dream was to link the waterfront in Alexandria to Gainesville,
35 miles away. Construction began in 1854 but was slowed by de-
lays in acquiring land and the need to make substantial "cuts" and
"fills" to create a level grade. When the landscaping was finished and
rails were waiting in Alexandria the Panic of 1857 crippled America's
business environment and sent the Manassas Gap Railroad into deep
debt. No track was ever laid but a few years later Confederate troops
under Stonewall Jackson found the unfinished railroad cut handy in
establishing a defensive position during the 2nd Battle of Manassas.
Remnants of this cut slice across the Conway-Robinson State Forest
trail system.

Eastern Shore of Virginia National Wildlife Refuge

Phone - (757) 331-2760
Website - http://www.fws.gov/northeast/easternshore/
Admission Fee - None
Directions - *Cape Charles, Northampton County; on the east side of Route 13 directly north of the Chesapeake Bay Bridge-Tunnel.*

The Park
The Eastern Shore of Virginia National Wildlife Refuge, located at the southern tip of the Delmarva Peninsula, was established in 1984 for migratory and endangered species management and for wildlife oriented recreation. The 1153 acres of maritime forest, myrtle and bayberry thickets, grasslands, croplands, and fresh and brackish ponds provide important habitat for wildlife.

The Walks
Canine hiking in the refuge takes place on a pair of wide, grassy trails and lightly traveled park roads providing a pleasing mix of open air hiking and woodsy walking. The 1/2-mile *Interpretive Trail* loops through mixed hardwoods, past an old cemetery, and out to the saltmarsh overlook. A 1/2-mile *Butterfly Trail* winds through a field of flowers, brambles, grasses and shrubs.

> **Where The Paw Meets The Earth:** Sandy dirt roads and grass
> **Workout For Your Dog** - Flat and easy
> **Swimming** - None
> **Restrictions On Dogs** - None

Something Extra
A climb to the top of a WWII bunker affords a panoramic view of refuge marshes, barrier islands, bays, inlets, and the Atlantic Ocean.

Ellanor C. Lawrence Park

Phone - (703) 631-0013
Website - http://www.fairfaxcounty.gov/parks/ecl/
Admission Fee - None
Directions - *Chantilly, Fairfax County; take Beltway Exit 49 for I-66 West and go eleven miles to Exit 53B, Route 28 North (Sully Road). From Route 28, make an immediate right onto Walney Road. The visitor center is one mile up on the left.*

The Park

The first land patents in what is now western Fairfax County were issued in 1727. In that year, Francis Aubrey acquired the land now within the park south of Big Rocky Run. For the next 250 years the property known as Walney belonged to only three families who farmed tobacco, grew grain and raised livestock. Ellanor Campbell Lawrence, a native of South Carolina, moved to Washington, D.C. in 1916. She met and married David Lawrence, who would later found and publish U.S. News and World Report. The Lawrences used Walney as a country estate where Ellanor would landscape and garden. After her death in 1969, David Lawrence donated 640 acres of land in her memory to be preserved in a natural state.

The Walks

Lawrence Park is not a place where you'll strap a pack onto the back of your dog but there is great variety in its four miles of trails. From the Walney Pond lot you can take your dog through a field pond environment and across the street at Cabell's your dog can hike briefly on groomed meadow trails. The *Big Rocky Run Trail* begins its two-mile one-way jaunt through mature woodlands here. The star hike in Lawrence Park is the *North Loop* that begins in the back of the Walney Visitor Center. For about one mile this natural, paw-friendly path spreads across a mixed forest. In the stream cuts and ravines large hardwoods that were never cleared for cropland can be found while pines and cedars dominate in the flatlands as they reclaim the cultivated fields. Your dog certainly won't object to extending this genial canine hike by tacking on another half-mile down the *Wild Turkey Loop*.

> **Where The Paw Meets The Earth:** Soft dirt and grass
> **Workout For Your Dog** - Gentles slopes and some hills
> **Swimming** - Walney Pond is more for ducks
> **Restrictions On Dogs** - None

Something Extra

In 1875, while he was building an expansion on his house, James Machen enclosed a time capsule in a small wooden box. What he didn't realize was that his farm itself would become a time capsule for future generations. A short discovery trail leads through the remains of the dairy where butter and cheese were crafted, a smokehouse and an ice house.

Fountainhead Regional Park

Phone - (703) 250-9124
Website - http://www.nvrpa.org/fountainhead.html
Admission Fee - None
Directions - *Fairfax Station, Fairfax County; Take I-95 south of the Beltway, exit at Occoquan and travel north on Route 123 approximately 5 miles. Turn left onto Hampton Road and drive 3 miles to the entrance on the left.*

The Park

As far back as the 1950s, visionaries in Fairfax County began preserving watershed land along the northern banks of the Occoquan River. Eventually they acquired more than 5,000 acres, creating a green necklace of regional parks. Fountainhead, at the confluence of Bull Run and the Occoquan is the keystone of those efforts. With the population of the Occoquan watershed inching towards a half-million people dependent on the fresh water from the river, Fairfax County's actions seem downright prescient. Conversely, across the river the land was developed in Prince William County that now puts pressure on the region's drinking water supply.

The Walks

Fountainhead is a trail user's park. Equestrian trails cover the eastern section down to the reservoir, mountain bikers have their own eight miles of wooded paradise and those traveling under their own power have plenty to smile about as well. The white-blazed pedestrian trail is a snaking, two-mile excursion around wide ravines and through airy woods. The hard-packed dirt path can be rooty in places so keep your dog high-stepping. For real canine adventures you can set out on the 18-mile *Bull Run-Occoquan Trail*. Fountainhead is the southern terminus for the scenic, long-distance hike. If you just intend to sample the trail you'll find the Fountainhead leg to be a hilly exploration (sporty enough to require a switchback and wooden steps) of a finger of the Occoquan Reservoir. The trail is wide enough for a pack of dogs in most places.

> **Where The Paw Meets The Earth:** Well-maintained dirt
> **Workout For Your Dog** - Long canine hikes on moderate hills
> **Swimming** - Dogs aren't permitted in the Occoquan Reservoir
> **Restrictions On Dogs** - No dogs on the mountain bike trail

Something Extra

The Davis family cemetery, anchored by a majestic white oak, pops up in the woods just a few steps into the canine hike on both the white and blue trails. The graveyard was established in the 1860s. The ancestral Davis home was destroyed by fire during the Civil War, and a newer house was built to the east, but is now gone.

Franklin Park

Phone - (540) 338-7603
Website - http://www.co.loudoun.va.us/prcs/parks/franklin.htm
Admission Fee - None
Directions - *Purcellville, Loudoun County; take Route 7 west to-wards Winchester. Exit on the Route 7 Business ramp (approx. 20 miles west of Leesburg) towards Round Hill/Purcellville. Turn left at bottom of ramp on to business Route 7 at the bottom of the ramp. Drive .7 miles and turn right on Franklin Park Drive.*

The Park
Franklin Park is a regional park in the western portion of Loudoun County. Its 203 acres of rolling hills harbor majestic views of the Blue Ridge Mountains. Franklin Park opened July 4, 1998, offering a wide variety of outdoor activities, including canine hiking.

The Walks
Former dairy farms are the bedrock for this community park favored for its views of the Blue Ridge Mountains. Most of the park is given over to sports and recreation but two perimeter trails over three miles long circumnavigate the property. The *Inner Trail* is used mostly by equestrians so visiting canine hikers will want to set off on the *Outer Trail*. Most of the marked paths are wide open across the rolling hills but the trail dips into natural areas along the way.

> **Where The Paw Meets The Earth:** Natural and paved surfaces
> **Workout For Your Dog** - Gentle grades along the trail
> **Swimming** - Your dog can slip into the park pond when fishermen are not dropping a line
> **Restrictions On Dogs** - Dogs are not allowed in the sports complex, on the playing fields or in the fenced-in playground area

Something Extra
During the winter this is an ideal place to snowshoe or cross-country ski with your dog.

G. Richard Thompson Wildlife Refuge

Phone - None
Website - http://www.dgif.state.va.us/hunting/wma/thompson.html
Admission Fee - None
Directions - *Paris, Fauquier County; the park is located on the western border of the county off Route 688, north from I-66 or south from Route 50.*

The Park
The major portion of the management area's two parcels, totaling nearly 4,000 acres, are located in Northwestern Fauquier County. Beginning at its lower reaches, the property rises in a series of steep inclines and benches to the crest of the Blue Ridge. Elevations range from 700 to 2200 feet. Though predominantly a hardwood forest, there is some open land at the lower elevations and at the top of the Davenport Tract. Other physical features of the area include numerous rock outcroppings, and several major streams and ecologically unique spring seeps. Parking is provided in 11 designated parking lots; two on the eastern slopes along Route 688.

The Walks
Trails from both parking lots lead up to the *Appalachian Trail* although the most popular route is from the northern lot at Lake Thompson. This is not a mountain hike with stunning views, dramatic waterfalls or tumbling streams. You'll actually get none of those. But if you are looking for a long walk in the woods with your dog, Thompson Wildlife Refuge is your destination. The climb to the *Appalachian Trail* - that crosses the park for seven miles - is moderately strenuous and the full loop will cover about eight miles. Abandoned homesites and the occasional apple tree from long-ago orchards provide a bit of diversity.

> **Where The Paw Meets The Earth:** Dirt and rock
> **Workout For Your Dog** - That's the reason to come
> **Swimming** - The 10-acre Thompson Lake is a superb dog watering hole
> **Restrictions On Dogs** - None

Something Extra
The *Trillium rhomboideum* variety *grandiflorum* was given its name by French botanist Andre Michaux in 1803. The specific name, very appropriately means "large-flowered." Sometimes called Snow Trillium because it is the first trillium to bloom and therefore would be caught in a late snowfall, the white-flowered plants (the petals turn pink with age) prefer to inhabit slopes 1,000-3,500 feet in elevation. Of the 10 or so species of Trillium in the Blue Ridge, *grandiflorum* may be the most abundant. The largest colony in the country can be found in the G. Richard Thompson Wildlife Management Area, where an estimated 18 million plants thrive.

Great Falls Park

Phone - (703) 285-2965
Website - http://www.nps.gov/grfa/
Admission Fee - Yes
Directions - *Great Falls, Fairfax County; take Beltway Exit 44 for Route 193, Georgetown Pike, and head west. About three miles down the road, you will come to a traffic light at Old Dominion Drive where you will see a sign for the park. Make a right at the light. Old Dominion Drive will deadend at the entrance station, about one mile down the road.*

The Park

To George Washington the Great Falls of the Potomac were an obstacle that needed to be overcome to open the Ohio Valley to lucrative trade. The Patowmack Company was chartered in 1784 to construct a laborious series of five canals; it was considered the greatest engineering feat in early America. In the early 1900s John McLean and Steven Elkins acquired the lands surrounding Great Falls and built an amusement park. Flooding doomed the venture and after plans for a hydroelectric dam collapsed, the National Park Service acquired 800 acres of land to create Great Falls Park.

The Walks

The star canine hike at Great Falls is the *River Trail* that will take your dog to the edge of the 79-foot falls and the steep-walled Mather Gorge. The path travels through the remains of Matildaville, a thriving town from the long-ago canal age, as well as remnants of the Patowmack Canal. The blue-blazed trail twists through a rocky alpine-like environment not often seen in Northern Virginia. Another unique habitat in the park - also hiker-only - is the *Swamp Trail* that explores an ancient terrace of the Potomac River for about one mile. The bulk of the park's 15 miles of trails are on old carriage roads and roadbeds; these routes are wide and well-graded that make for an excellent canine hike.

> **Where The Paw Meets The Earth:** Dirt paths and gravelly roads
> **Workout For Your Dog** - Moderate hills and plenty of flat trotting
> **Swimming** - Don't let your dog try it
> **Restrictions On Dogs** - None

Something Extra

Near Overlook #2 is a High Water Mark Pole that marks the depths to which the Potomac far below can flood. The most recent marking is from January 21, 1996 when the river rose 85 feet in 48 hours. That mark is about eye-high to a beagle - it was only the fifth largest flood of the past 100 years. For the highest mark you'll have to look overhead to see where the waters ot the Great Potomac Flood of 1936 reached.

Hidden Oaks Nature Center

Phone - (703) 941-1065
Website - http://www.fairfaxcounty.gov/parks/hiddenoaks/
Admission Fee - None
Directions - *Annandale, Fairfax County; Take Beltway Exit 52B which is Little River Turnpike or Route 236 east to the first traffic light at Hummer Road. Turn left on Hummer Road and then left at the park entrance.*

The Park

This small 52-acre sanctuary is squeezed into the heart of Fairfax County, just inside the Beltway. The urban woodland forest features a vibrant diversity of plant and animal species thriving in a green oasis.

The Walks

The feature trail at Hidden Oaks is a 1/3-mile, wood-chip-covered interpretive *Old Oak Trail* around the nature center. The average oak, by the way, will drop about 5,000 acorns a year but less than 50 will sprout and half of those will die. For additional canine hiking you can take your dog into the Accotink Creek stream valley where the dirt trail crosses the water three times. There is modest elevation gain on this trail but nothing close to setting your dog to panting. The trails are wide and airy in the woods below the nature center.

> **Where The Paw Meets The Earth:** Soft dirt
> **Workout For Your Dog** - Dips and rolls around the stream but never taxing
> **Swimming** - The Accotink Creek is only deep enough for splashing
> **Restrictions On Dogs** - None

Something Extra

One of the most abundant plants growing at Hidden Oaks Nature Center is poison ivy. The tri-leaved plant grows on a hairy vine up a tree trunk or on vines on the forest floor and turns quite colorful in the fall. About half of the human population is allergic to poison ivy and if you are in the unlucky half even the bare, woody stems will trigger a reaction. Birds love to eat its waxy white berries. Dogs cannot get poison ivy but they can transmit it to you.

Huntley Meadows Park

Phone - (703) 768-2525
Website - http://www.fairfaxcounty.gov/parks/huntley/
Admission Fee - None
Directions - *Alexandria, Fairfax County; take Beltway Exit 1 (Richmond Highway, Route 1) and go south 3.5 miles. Make a right on Lockheed Boulevard to the park entrance in .5 miles on the left where the road makes a 90-degree right turn.*

The Park

Mario Casalegno, an Italian immigrant with a dubious past, saw the Hybla Valley as a place to create the world's largest airport with a 7200-foot runway and mooring fields for trans-Atlantic Zeppelin fleets. At the gates of the national capital, the airfield would also contain a shrine to George Washington. During 1929 he acquired over 1,500 acres of land from ten landowners but by 1935 all the land was in forecloseure and purchased by the federal government. In 1975, President Gerald Ford donated the land to the citizens of Fairfax County for exclusive use as a public park.

The Walks

The 1,424 acres of Huntley Meadows Park is one of the finest natural areas in the shadow of Washington D.C. - although not for dog owners. Dogs are allowed in the park and you can get an exceedingly pleasant, easy-going canine hike here but dogs are not allowed on the 1/2-mile boardwalk of the *Heron Trail* that leads into the cattail-studded freshwater marsh. The main dog-hiking route is on the *Cedar Trail/Deer Trail* leading away from the Visitor Center for about one mile. If you are enjoying the level grounds and shady woods consider the *Informal Trail* off the *Deer Trail*. This is a narrow band that is not maintained and best left alone when wet but is largely unused and a good place to wander off with your dog. Other options for canine hiking here include a path adjacent to the parking lot that leaves the park to the Huntley Manor House and the 1.2-mile linear *Hike-Bike Trail* that can be accessed from a parking lot on South Kings Highway.

> **Where The Paw Meets The Earth:** Natural dirt surfaces and crushed stone
> **Workout For Your Dog** - Flat and level
> **Swimming** - None
> **Restrictions On Dogs** - No boardwalks for your dog

Something Extra

When you reach the boardwalk, tie your dog up and step out to the observation tower. Here you'll see a rare northern Virginia freshwater marsh environment with beaver dams longer than a football field, muskrats and frogs, and over 200 species of birds.

John Marshall Birthplace Park

Phone - None
Website - http://www.dgif.state.va.us/wildlife/vbwt/site.asp?trail
=3&site=PCU06&loop=PCU
Admission Fee - None
Directions - *Oakpark, Fauquier County; southeast of Warren-*
ton. Take Route 643, Meetze Road, to its end at Route 28 (Catlett
Road). Make a right and then left on Germantown Road (Route
649). The park is on the left, just past the railroad tracks.

The Park
John Marshall was born in 1955, the oldest of fifteen children, in a log
cabin deep into the Virginia frontier that is now in southcentral Fauquier County. After serving in the Revolutionary War, Marshall began
practicing law in 1780. Marshall declined the appointment as Attorney
General under George Washington and also turned down a seat on the
Supreme Court. He finally accepted the position of Secretary of State
under John Adams and was nominated as the fourth Chief Justice of
the Supreme Court by Adams in 1800. He served for more than 34
years until his death, participating in more than 1000 decisions and
authored over 500 opinions. His legacy as the greatest shaper of
early constitutional law helped set America on its path through the
19th century. The small park remembers his beginnings.

The Walks
You can take your dog on a short country lane hike along a branch
of Licking Run. Listen to the cows and watch the corn sway in the
breeze. You'll pass through a wildflower meadow and reach the stone
memorial marking the location of Marshall's birthplace. You won't
learn much about John Marshall on this outing but it is more of a
place to reflect on where he was and where we are. A nice place to
bring your dog and let him run.

> **Where The Paw Meets The Earth:** Soft dirt
> **Workout For Your Dog** - Flat and easy going
> **Swimming** - None
> **Restrictions On Dogs** - None

Something Extra
If you visit in the fall you will have a chance to test your wits in the
Cows-n-Corn field maze located next to the park.

Jones Point Park

Phone - None
Website - http://www.ci.alexandria.va.us/recreation/parks/
jones_point_park.html
Admission Fee - None
Directions - *Alexandria, Arlington County; on the Potomac River off Washington Street under the Woodrow Wilson Bridge.*

The Park
In 1790, Congress requested President Washington to locate the Federal District. The survey placed the southern boundary of the new ten mile square District of Columbia Federal City at Jones Point where the marker was laid on the Potomac River shoreline. The land which George Washington had surveyed for the Federal City was within the capital boundaries for 45 years, from February 27, 1801 until September 7, 1846, when Alexandria was ceded back into Northern Virginia by Congress. By 1897, the commercial fisheries and fish processing plants located near Jones Point were the largest of any river on the East Coast, but pollution of the river increased, and the fishing industry declined to trivial importance by the end of World War I.

The Walks
There are large swaths of greenspace for your dog, short wooded trails and the Potomac River for a canine swimming pool.
>   **Where The Paw Meets The Earth:** Grass and paved surfaces
>   **Workout For Your Dog** - Flat ground
>   **Swimming** - Yes, in the Potomac River
>   **Restrictions On Dogs** - None

Something Extra
In 1855, the historic Jones Point Lighthouse was built close to the District of Columbia Federal City boundary marker. The Lighthouse guided ships past the area for 70 years from 1856 to 1926. This is the oldest inland waterway lighthouse in the United States. In 1926, the Department of Commerce built a 60 foot steel light tower on the river's edge, 100 yards from the Lighthouse. The steel tower was torn down in the late 1930's but the Lighthouse is still there surrounded by a picket fence.

Julie J. Metz Wetlands Mitigation Bank

Phone - None
Website - None
Admission Fee - None
Directions - *Woodbridge, Fairfax County; take Route 1 to Neab-*
sco Road. Turn left into the wetlands bank parking lot just past
Leesylvania Elementary School.

The Park

The Julie J. Metz. Wetlands Bank is the first wetlands bank in Northern Virginia approved by the U.S. Corps of Engineers. A mitigation bank is an area of constructed, restored or preserved wetlands that are important to filter run-off, prevent erosion, improve water quality and provide habitat for wildlife. Construction began in 1995 and the final grades were completed in 1997. The wetland preserve is named for Julie Metz, an environmental engineer with the Corps of Engineers who fell victim to breast cancer in 1995 at the age of 38. The 227-acre wetland preserve was donated to the Prince William County for ongoing care and maintenance.

The Walks

This is a rare chance in Northern Virginia for your dog to explore a wetlands environment. There are some two miles of level, easy-hiking paths cut into a mosaic around the various pods of the mostly dry marsh. Views are limited in the high marsh grasses that give way to shrubs and scrub forests. The main route is along a 12-station interpretive trail (go left out of the parking lot to pick it up in the designed order.

> **Where The Paw Meets The Earth:** The surface
> alternates between wood chips, grass and boardwalk - all
> paw-friendly
> **Workout For Your Dog** - Very easy going
> **Swimming** - None
> **Restrictions On Dogs** - None

Something Extra

Almost 200 species of birds have been recorded visiting the re-created wetland. One of the showiest is the snowy egret, recognized by its pure white plummage, black legs and yellow feet. In the latter part of the 19th century and into the early twentieth, snowy egret plumes were very popular on hats. The result was that these birds were hunted until they were nearly extinct. The snowy egret can be spotted from spring through fall, often at the edge of the water in a marsh. Their main foods are fish, crabs, amphibians, and insects.

Kiptopeke State Park

Phone - (757) 331-2267
Website - http://www.dcr.state.va.us/parks/kiptopek.htm
Admission Fee - Yes
Directions - *Cape Charles, Northampton County; on the eastern shore of Virginia, Kiptopeke is three miles from the northern terminus of the Chesapeake Bay Bridge Tunnel, on Route 13. Turn west on Route 704; the park entrance is within a half mile.*

The Park
The site was purchased by the Virginia Ferry Corporation for the northern terminus of the Virginia Beach to Eastern Shore Ferry. In 1949, when the terminus was moved from Cape Charles, the site was named Kiptopeke Beach in honor of the younger brother of a king of the Accawmack Indians who had befriended early settlers to the area. Kiptopeke means Big Water. In 1950 the terminus opened after the completion of a $2.75 million pier, promoted as the world's largest and most modern ferry pier.

The Walks
More than four miles of fun trails for your dog traverse this bayside park. The *Baywoods Trail* slips through an uplands hardwood forest on wide, old roads and connects with expansive, sandy beaches via an extensive network of wooden boardwalks through the dunes. The southern beach is perfect for a hike but observe signs designating the special habitat area that is closed to visitors. Bicycle trails are available along the park's entrance road and the Raptor, Songbird, Chickadee and Mockingbird trails.

> **Where The Paw Meets The Earth:** Soft dirt roads, sand, asphalt and boards
> **Workout For Your Dog** - Stairs take care of the bluffs
> **Swimming** - Fantastic swimming in the Chesapeake Bay for dogs
> **Restrictions On Dogs** - No dogs in the north beach swimming area; dogs are allowed in the campground but not in the yurts

Something Extra
Since 1963, Kiptopeke has been the site of bird population studies. Sponsored by the Coastal Virginia Wildlife Observatory, formerly known as KESTRSAL, and licensed by the U.S. Fish and Wildlife Service, volunteers capture, examine, weigh, band and release resident and migratory birds each year from mid-August through November. In the raptor research area, hawks, kestrels, osprey and other birds of prey are observed and banded from September through November. Kiptopeke's hawk observatory is among the top 15 nationwide.

Lake Fairfax Park

Phone - (703) 471-5415
Website - http://www.fairfaxcounty.gov/parks/lakefairfax/
Admission Fee - None
Directions - *Reston, Fairfax County; turn left on Baron Cameron Avenue from Leesburg Pike (Route 7) to the second left on Lake Fairfax Drive.*

The Park
One of three lakess operated by Fairfax County, the park is centered around recreation on the water including an aquatic playground.

The Walks
The lake and waterpark are stars here but a dogged canine hiker can find a reason to visit. A mostly natural trail leaves from behind the park office and climbs across the dam towards the campground as it ducks in an out of shaded woods. Exit through Loop C where you find a sign for the *Nature Trail*. Your dog will be stepping through some streams as you head towards the residential developments and onto part of the Reston Paths. You can also pick up the *Buttermilk Creek Nature Trail* that leaves the park for a trot down an old dairy farm road and cow path. This curvilinear trail runs for just short of a mile through meadows and forests.

> **Where The Paw Meets The Earth:** Dirt, grass and paved surfaces
> **Workout For Your Dog** - Some rolling hills but nothing strenuous
> **Swimming** - Swimming is prohibited in the lake
> **Restrictions On Dogs** - Dogs are allowed in the campground but not in recreational areas

Something Extra
Soapstone and serpentine were once mined here and you still may find bits of minerals along the route here.

Leesylvania State Park

Phone - (703) 730-8205
Website - http://www.state.va.us/dcr/parks/leesylva.htm
Admission Fee - None
Directions - *Woodbridge, Prince William County; from I-95, take Rippon Landing Exit 156; then go east on Route 784 to US 1. From US 1, follow Route 610 (Neabsco Road) east two miles.*

The Park

Henry Lee II, great-grandfather of Robert E. Lee, named this property Leesylvania, or "Lee's Woods." In the 1950s entrepreneur Carl Hill ingeniously took advantage of an ancient grant to Lord Baltimore in 1632 that gave rights to the Potomac River to Maryland. He built a pier out into the river and anchored a 200-foot cruise ship at its end for use as a floating nightclub and gambling spot - liquor and gambling both being illegal in Virginia at the time. Freestone Point opened as the "Pleasureland of the East" in 1957. But a gambling emporium in the shadow of Washington, DC was not going to rake in money unnoticed. Legislation was passed to doom Hill's slot parlor and he sold the land to the American-Hawaiian Steamship Company, owned by Daniel K. Ludwig. The reclusive Ludwig, tagged in his biography as the "Invisible Billionaire," was an admirer of the Lee legacy and donated the land to the Commonwealth for a state park. Leesylvania opened in 1992.

The Walks

There are three loops to enjoy with your dog in Leesylvania - the star being the *Lee's Woods Trail*. This canine hike packs history aplenty into its two sporty miles atop the bluffs overlooking the Potomac River. Look for the brick fireplace that is the only reminder of the hunting lodge, earthwork gun placements from a Civil War battery, foundations from the plantation home and a family cemetery all located along the old stony dirt roads used for this trail. *Powells Creek Trail* leads to long views across the water through woodlands away from the recreation areas of the park. For easy hiking with your dog take the *Potomac Trail* as it weaves through the former waterside amusement park that was part of the gambling gambit.

> **Where The Paw Meets The Earth:** Dirt and stony roads
> **Workout For Your Dog** - Moderate climbing to the bluffs on the Potomac
> **Swimming** - A sandy beach doggie heaven off-season
> **Restrictions On Dogs** - No dogs on the fishing pier

Something Extra

As you explore the bluffs and ravines around Free Stone Point you may not realize that they aren't all natural. A deep valley was excavated shortly after the Civil War to ease the grade for new railroad tracks. With the railroad long gone and the forest regenerated it looks like any other wide ravine.

Mason District Park

Phone - (703) 941-1730
Website - www.fairfaxcounty.gov/parks/omp.htm#23
Admission Fee - None
Directions - *Annandale, Fairfax County; take Exit 52B from the Beltway onto Route 236 East. two miles to a left on John Marr Drive. Turn right on Columbia Pike to park entrance on the right just before Sleepy Hollow Road.*

The Park

This land was first cultivated in 1650 as part of William Fitzhugh's mammoth Ravensworth Plantation. Ravensworth was the largest single parcel of land granted in Northern Virginia. This area began to be subdivided after 1797 and in 1808 - the same year the Columbia Pike opened - Aspen Hill Farm began. The soil started to give out before the Civil War and from 1870 to 1970 these hills supported a pony farm. The county acquired the land for a park in the 1970s but the park was slow to develop. In 1980 a local jogger trying to slog along the trails discovered that the staff lacked even a weed-whacker to maintain the park. Civic-minded volunteers organized the Friends of Mason District Park and staged the first park festival as a fundraiser in October 1980. Enough money was raised not only for a weed whacker but also a tractor. Today's 121-acre park is blend of recreational activities and a managed conservation area.

The Walks

The trail system leaves along Turkeycock Run on the shady *Forest Trail* that climbs into the back of the park on stony roads and dirt paths. A quick detour can be taken onto the quarter-mile *Meadow Trail* on wide grass paths. Both eventually reach the Meadowview Shelter for views. Maybe the best canine hike in Mason District Park is the trek to the dog park next to the Columbia Elementary School. It is about a half-mile on roomy, paw-friendly paths to reach the large, natural-surfaced fenced enclosure (capacity: 62 dogs).

> **Where The Paw Meets The Earth:** Some dirt, some grass, some asphalt
> **Workout For Your Dog** - Moderate hills across the park
> **Swimming** - Turkeycock Run is not suitable for a swim
> **Restrictions On Dogs** - None

Something Extra

Mason District Park hosts an extensive summer concert series in the Newton Edwards Amphitheatre. Check the schedule - there are evenings and Saturday morning performances for any musical taste. The events are free and your dog is invited.

Mason Neck National Wildlife Refuge

Phone - (703) 490-4979
Website - http://www.fws.gov/refuges/profiles/index.cfm?id=51610
Admission Fee - None
Directions - *Lorton, Fairfax County; from I-95 exit into Lorton on Route 642 East. Turn right on Route 1 (Richmond Highway) and left on Route 242 (Gunston Road). Continue on Route 600 past Gunston Plantation, making a right onto High Point Road at the sign for Mason Neck State Park/National Refuge and follow to park.*

The Park

George Mason, the brilliant mind behind the Virginia Bill of Rights, predecessor to the United States Bill of Rights, came to this wooded peninsula in 1775. He built a magnificent Georgian mansion he called Gunston Hall, which was his home until his death in 1792. Over the next 100 years the 8,000-acre peninsula was heavily logged until most of the mature pine and hardwoods were completely gone. By the 1960s residential development posed a threat to the regenerating forest and the local bald eagle population. In 1969 more than 6,000 acres were dedicated by the U.S. Fish & Wildlife Service as the first national wildlife refuge specifically established for the bald eagle.

The Walks

There are a few options for you and your dog to explore this quiet sanctuary with more than four miles of shoreline. The marquee hike in Mason Neck   NWR is the *Woodmarsh Trail* - flat, wide and leafy. This balloon-shaped trail takes you to the fringes of the Great Marsh and an observation tower to view the largest freshwater marsh in northern Virginia and the finest Great Blue heron rookery in the Mid-Atlantic region. A round trip will cover about three miles. If you want to spend extra time in these airy, hickory-and-oak woods you can set off with your dog down one of the refuge roads that are closed to the public or drive to the other side of the refuge and take the paved, 3/4-mile *Great Marsh Trail* down to another observation tower.

> **Where The Paw Meets The Earth:** Soft dirt and asphalt
> **Workout For Your Dog** - Easy trotting across level terrain
> **Swimming** - None
> **Restrictions On Dogs** - None

Something Extra

Mason Neck has been named one of the Top Ten sites in America for viewing bald eagles. The eagles arrive in October and spen the next two months courting and breeding where they are visible feeding in the marsh. By February they have re-built their nests and are ready to lay eggs. The eaglets hatch in April and spend the next several months gaining strength before the cycle begins anew.

Mason Neck State Park

Phone - (703) 339-2380
Website - http://www.dcr.state.va.us/parks//masonnec.htm
Admission Fee - Yes
Directions - *Lorton, Fairfax County; from I-95 exit on Route 642 East. Turn right on Route 1 (Richmond Highway) and left on Route 242 (Gunston Road). Continue on Route 600 past Gunston Plantation, making a right onto High Point Road at the sign for Mason Neck State Park/National Refuge and follow to park.*

The Park

In the 1960s, after it was determined that the widespread use of the pesticide DDT was decimating bald eagle populations by weakening their eggshells, a nesting pair was spotted on Mason Neck. The Mason Neck Conservation Committee was formed to protect the area. A plan for a state park was hatched and the Commonwealth began purchasing land on the peninsula in 1967. The group's mettle was tested immediately as they helped rebuff a steady parade of proposed development projects: a beltway, an airport, pipelines, a landfill. The long-dreamed-of state park finally opened for public use in 1985.

The Walks

There are a half-dozen canine hiking options in Mason Neck State Park, the stars being three loop trails of about one mile in length. All run easily through an attractive oak/holly forest on paw-friendly soft dirt and are pretty enough you will want to complete them all. You can actually use the *Wilson Spring Trail*, marked in yellow, to access them all with a bit of backtracking. The red-blazed *Bay View Trail* skips across two inlets from Belmont Bay and offers splendid open-water vistas and close-up looks at the marsh with its turtles and frogs. Mason Neck is a delight for your dog in any season but you may want to remember the wintertime for yourself when the leaves drop from the trees to allow easier sights of eagles diving for fish in the bay.

> **Where The Paw Meets The Earth:** Mostly dirt
> **Workout For Your Dog** - Mostly flat canine hiking here
> **Swimming** - It doesn't get any better for dogs than on the beach at the Belmont Bay off the *Bay View Trail*
> **Restrictions On Dogs** - None

Something Extra

If you take the 1.25-mile *Eagle Spur Trail* to the end you will reach an observation blind on Kane's Creek where you can sit with your dog and observe many of the more than 200 species of birds that visit Mason's Neck, including bald eagles throughout the year. Census counts of America's national symbol have ranged between 30 and 40 nesting pairs in recent years.

Mount Vernon

Phone - (703) 780-2000
Website - http://www.mountvernon.org/index.cfm/
Admission Fee - Yes
Directions - *Mount Vernon, Fairfax County; follow George Washington Parkway 8 miles south of Alexandria to the end of the Parkway.*

The Park

George Washington, an avid foxhunter, sought to breed a new type of dog to course the terrain around his estate at Mount Vernon. He crossed French hounds from his friend the Marquis de Lafayette, with his own smaller black-and-tan English hounds. Washington listed 30 new "American" foxhounds by name in his journal and hounds currently registered with the American Kennel Club are descended from those originals. The Father of Our Country often favored silly names for his beloved dogs: Drunkard, Tipler, Tipsy. The Mount Vernon estate was saved in 1853 by Ann Pamela Cunningham who spearheaded one of the oldest national historic preservation organizations in the country. Today Mount Vernon is the most visited home in America.

The Walks

George Washington wrote about his plantation on the Potomac River, "No estate in United America is more pleasantly situated than this." He controlled 8,000 acres here and today your dog can trot across much of the 500 acres that have been preserved. The *Forest Trail* is a short interpretive walk through a wooded area over a ravine and past an old cobble quarry that was used to create roadways, walkways and the main entrance. This little hike features one steep climb and a wide, groomed path for your dog.

> **Where The Paw Meets The Earth:** Grass and dirt paths
> **Workout For Your Dog** - Easy going on the estate
> **Swimming** - None
> **Restrictions On Dogs** - No dogs inside

Something Extra

Two days after the Battle of Germantown outside of Philadelphia on October 6, 1777 a dog was found wandering in the American Camp. Inspecting the dog's collar it was apparent the dog, whose name and breed is lost to history, belonged to British commander General William Howe, who remained at Germantown. Even with the loss of the Colonial capital of Philadelphia hanging over his head, General George Washington steadfastly adhered to the code of gentlemanly behavior in wartime by returning the dog with a handwritten note: "General Washington's compliments to General Howe. He does himself the pleasure to return him a dog, which accidentally fell into his hands, and by the inscription on the Collar appears to belong to General Howe."

Occoquan Regional Park

Phone - (703) 690-2121
Website - http://www.nvrpa.org/occoquan.html
Admission Fee - None
Directions - *Lorton, Fairfax County; exit off I-95 onto Route 123 North and follow 1.5 miles to the park entrance on right.*

The Park
In 1910 the federal government purchased land along the picturesque Occoquan River for a new prison. A product of the reform movement of the day, the new Occoquan Workhouse stressed that "a prisoner's hard physical work, learned skills and fresh air would transform him into a model citizen." So the small initial cadre of 60 inmates worked building and maintaining a 1,200-acre farm. The reform experiment ended shortly after suffragettes seeking the vote for women were detained here and reportedly mistreated. Bars and cells were built at Occoquan as the facility expanded to over 3,000 acres housing more than 7,000 inmates - far beyond its capacity. The outdated facility finally closed in 2001 sending 2,440 acres to Fairfax County, 400 of which were used for this spacious park along the river.

The Walks
Hiking is clearly not the recreation star at Occoquan - there are no trail maps and it takes a sharp eye to spot the trailheads but remain dogged in your determination to get your dog on the trail here and you wil be rewarded. You will find a Virginia state *Bird and Wildlife Trail* in the woods on the left just past the boat ramp, next to an elevated picnic shelter. It begins as a desultory affair, slogging uphill on a paw-unfriendly stony road and when the trail leaves the road it gets downright wild and wooly on a narrow, overgrown path. You'll even find the trail studded with long-ago discarded bricks. But stick with it. Soon the path opens up as it rolls aong ravines and into a stream valley. Another hiking option is the white-blazed *Ridge Trail* that climbs a bluff overlooking the Occoquan River. Look for a set of wooden stairs and work your way back towards the park entrance. The paved multi-use trail closes this loop.

> **Where The Paw Meets The Earth:** Dirt, pine straw, macadam, grass
> **Workout For Your Dog** - Moderate hills along the river
> **Swimming** - Use the boat at the Occoquan River for canine aquatics
> **Restrictions On Dogs** - None

Something Extra
In the center of the park is the last of nine beehive brick kilns that were used by prisoners to churn out many of the red bricks used in Northern Virginia buildings.

Pohick Bay Regional Park

Phone - (703) 339-6104
Website - http://www.nvrpa.org/pohickbay.html
Admission Fee - Yes
Directions - *Lorton, Fairfax County; take I-95 south of the Beltway, exit at Lorton. Turn left on Lorton Rd. At the 3rd traffic light, turn right onto Lorton Market Street. Follow Lorton Market Street to the first light which will be Rt. 1. Cross over Rt. 1, onto Gunston Rd. Continue 1.5 miles to golf course on the left; 3.5 miles to the main park on the left.*

The Park
The Indians called this land "Pohick," the Algonquin word for the "water place." Today, Pohick Bay is still the water place - a water-oriented park 25 miles south of the nation's capital.

The Walks
Most outings to Mason Neck with your dog will wind up in the state park or national wildlife refuge but you may want to make a stop in this expansive recreation and camping park along the Pohick Bay as well. There are about four miles of wide, level bridle trails your dog will share with the occasional horse. You'll be exploring a typical Eastern deciduous forest on flat, easy-trotting terrain. In places you'll touch on Pohick Bay for superior swimming for your dog. Dogs are also allowed in the campground.

> **Where The Paw Meets The Earth:** Soft dirt and sandy soil
> **Workout For Your Dog** - Level terrain throughout
> **Swimming** - Yes, in non-recreational parts of the Pohick Bay shoreline
> **Restrictions On Dogs** - None

Something Extra
Bluebird nesting boxes have been scattered around the park's 1,000 acres with sparse ground cover - you can recognize an artificial bluebird home because there is no perch.

Potomac Heritage Trail

Phone - None
Website - http://www.nps.gov/archive/gwmp/vapa/pht.htm
Admission Fee - None
Directions - *McLean, Arlington County; several trailheads off the George Washington Memorial Parkway between Theodore Roosevelt Island and the American Legion Bridge.*

The Park

The George Washington Memorial Parkway was developed in 1932 to commemorate the bicentennial of the first President's birth and to preserve the beauty of the Potomac River corridor. Tucked inside the Parkway between Theodore Roosevelt Island and the American Legion Bridge is the *Potomac Heritage Trail*, a segment of the *Potomac Heritage National Scenic Trail* that is a 425-mile corridor of trails between the Chesapeake Bay and Allegheny Highlands.

The Walks

This 10-mile linear riverwalk can be broken into manageable chunks with the numerous access points to the trail. Of course, the trail from parks such as Potomac Overlook Park, Gulf Branch Nature Center and Turkey Run Park to the PHT can be a hike in themselves. This canine hike can be a cracking good adventure for your dog. The floodplain path is often muddy and there will be several stream crossings that must be made, and after heavy rains will be impassable (the highest recorded level of the river reached 15 feet above the trail in 1936). You will encounter steep passages that will set you and your dog to panting. Most of the trail is under a steady parade of thick shade trees. It is easy to forget that you are just across the river from the nation's capital - although you will not escape the noise of traffic and airplanes heading for Reagan National Airport.

> **Where The Paw Meets The Earth:** Natural surface most of the way
> **Workout For Your Dog** - Yes, almost everywhere your dog jumps on
> **Swimming** - Carefully allow your dog in the Potomac River
> **Restrictions On Dogs** - None

Something Extra

Just beyond Windy Run, less than two miles from the start of the trail in the Theodore Roosevelt Island parking lot are the rusty hulks of 19th-century boilers used to quarry Potomac bluestone. This 500-million year old schist was a popular building stone for many buildings around Northwest Washington, including the Old Stone House in Georgetown, built in 1765. Several of the animal houses in the National Zoo use Potomac bluestone, the Panda House and the Elephant House are just two. Rockville, Maryland is named for its abundance of Potomac bluestone.

Potomac Overlook Regional Park

Phone - (703) 528-5406
Website - http://www.nvrpa.org/potomacoverlook.html
Admission Fee - None
Directions - *Arlington City; take I-66 to the Spout Run exit. Turn left on Lee Highway, right on Military Road and right on Marcey Road, which deadends at the park.*

The Park
Unlike similar neighboring parks Potomac Overlook is not the result of any fervent conservation movement. In 1942, a developer, in fact, purchased 35 acres to build a residential community but couldn't sell any homesites. The land was never developed and was eventually purchased by NVRPA in 1966 and the wedge of woodland adjacent to the George Washington Parkway was developed into a 67-acre park with assistance from the National Audubon Society.

The Walks
Canine hiking is unfailingly pleasant in this park dominated by woodland. Your dog will find well-maintained, airy paths that roll easily around the property. There are some two miles of marked and named trails in Potomac Overlook Regional Park but you are seldom more than ten minutes from the Nature Center at the center of the property. The trails are peppered with massive tulip poplars and oaks and the green-blazed *Heritage Trail* scoots through a heritage orchard from the early 1900s. Tucked into the woods are many reminders of human habitation - house foundations, a spring house, a cemetery. You can also visit various gardens with your dog. Park trails link to several nearby trails outside the park including the *Donaldson Run Trail* that works down the ridge to the *Potomac River Heritage Trail*. You can transition from a leisurely stroll to an ardent hike with your dog with this option.

> **Where The Paw Meets The Earth:** Natural surface trails and old roads
> **Workout For Your Dog** - Moderate climbing as you go
> **Swimming** - None
> **Restrictions On Dogs** - None

Something Extra
Near the entrance, behind the tennis courts that are actually a part of Marcey Road Park, is a pure stand of Tree of Heaven. This invasive exotic species, used as an ornamental in the Far East, grows in disturbed soils and this section of the park was previously used as a dump. The Tree of Heaven grows at a rapid rate, outcompeting native species and producing a toxin in its bark and leaves that inhibits growth of most other species. At this time, there is no known control for this plant.

Prince William Forest Park

Phone - (703) 221-7181
Website - http://www.nps.gov/prwi/
Admission Fee - None
Directions - *Dumfries, Prince William County; take I-95 south of Washington to exit 150 (Joplin Road/VA Route 619). Take Route 619 West to the park entrance road (approximately 1/4 mile).*

The Park

This was some of the earliest European-settled land in the country buttobacco farming drained the land of much of its nutrients and for centuries only a few farms survived around the creeks flowing into the Potomac River. During the Depression of the 1930s this was one of 46 locations of marginal farm land selected to be developed for recreation and work camps from the Civilian Conservation Corps were established to build roads and trails and bridges. Five rustic cabin camps built at this time are listed on the National Register of Historic Places.

The Walks

The canine hiking here is through the only preserved Eastern Piedmont forest in the National Park Service. You will be working up and down and around the many slopes in the Quantico Creek watershed - often with long views through the forest that features little understory in many areas. Many of the trails lead away from Scenic Drive to the South Branch and the North Branch of Quantico Creek. In addition to the wide, well-marked hiking trails you can take off on several old access roads that deliver a country-lane feel to the hiking. You can also use the paved - but walkable - Scenic Drive to close some of your customized loops.

> **Where The Paw Meets The Earth:** Dirt paths and roads
> **Workout For Your Dog** - Long, hilly canine hikes
> **Swimming** - Some small pools deep enough for a good canine swim
> **Restrictions On Dogs** - None

Something Extra

If you head off on the *North Valley Trail* and continue about one mile down the *Pyrite Mine Trail* along the North Branch of the Quantico Creek you will reach the remains of the Cabin Branch Pyrite Mine. The mine opened in 1889, pulling nugget-like rocks known as "fool's gold" for their appearance to the precious metal. In fact pyrite is loaded with sulfur (needed to make gunpowder) that kept the operation profitable into the 1920s, including an important stretch during World War I when as many as 300 men worked the mine. Many acres of historic underground workings, pilings and foundations have been reclaimed by the Park Service and are remembered today.

Red Rock Wilderness Regional Park

Phone - (703) 737-7800
Website - http://www.nvrpa.org/redrock.html
Admission Fee - None
Directions - *Leesburg, Loudoun County; Take Route 7 West and then the Route 15 Bypass North. Turn right on Edwards Ferry Road (Route 773) and drive 1.5 miles to the park entrance on the left.*

The Park
This longtime farm on the palisades of the Upper Potomac River was purchased as a parkland with the help of Mrs. Frances Speck, who donated half the value of the property. The farmland has regenerated into woodlands that completely cover the 67-acre park.

The Walks
When you set out into the woods behind the parking lot there is no way for your dog to guess at the workout that awaits her. The birch and oak trees here are almost completely devoid of any understory and there is plenty of elbow room for a whole pack of dogs if need be. After a few easy steps a little hook trail detours down to the Potomac River floodplain for more easy hiking with your dog. Once back atop the bluff the trail begins to dip and turn in and out of two ravines before you reach the namesake overlook after about one mile. It is another half-mile back to the parking lot but the forest has changed completely, congested with cedars and pin oaks. The trail is narrower but the terrain is flat again. Several connector trails are available for additional time with your dog in this quiet woodland.

> **Where The Paw Meets The Earth:** Dirt trails
> **Workout For Your Dog** - Some hearty climbs along the river
> **Swimming** - In the Potomac River
> **Restrictions On Dogs** - None

Something Extra
The ruins of the 19th century farm are still scattered around the parking lot - a granary, a carriage house and a barn. A brick ice house built after the Civil War was restored in 1982. Ice was cut from the Potomac River and stored under hay in the ice house and was good through the summer.

Riverbend Park

Phone - (703) 759-9018
Website - http://www.fairfaxcounty.gov/parks/riverbend/
Admission Fee - No
Directions - *Great Falls, Fairfax County; take Beltway Exit 44 onto Route 193 West (Georgetown Pike) to River Bend Road. Turn right and right again on Jeffery Road and follow for approximately one mile to the park entrance.*

The Park
Conn's Ferry was established above the Falls of the Potomac in 1785 at the site of the present Riverbend Park. In 1814 President James Madison and his wife Dolley, fleeing the British and the burning of Washington, travelled over the rolling road to Conn's Ferry and escaped into Maryland. In 1974 Fairfax County established Riverbend Park to preserve 409 acres of mixed hardwoods, a large meadow and a river floodplain. The park features over two miles of frontage on the Potomac River.

The Walks
More than 10 miles of natural-surfaced trail spread out from the Visitors Center and the Nature Center in Riverbend Park. The two centers are only about 1/2-mile apart so you can start your explorations at either place without skipping one. Just about any hike you want to do with your dog is on the menu here: a long multi-hour trek or a short, invigorating loop; a hike in the shade of a mature hardwood forest or an open-air ramble through old fields and emerging trees. The long-distance *Potomac Heritage Trail* traces - appropriately - the bend in the Potomac River as it travels through the floodplain in the park. The best bet for your dog here (no bikes or horses) is the green-blazed *Paw Paw Passage Trail* (that is the tree, not a dogs-only trail) that departs the back of the Nature Center and rolls down to the Potomac River, passing through a variety of habitats. This sporty loop covers just over one mile.

> **Where The Paw Meets The Earth:** Natural surface paths
> **Workout For Your Dog** - Short, non-demanding climbs
> **Swimming** - The Potomac is tame enough here to enjoy a dog swim
> **Restrictions On Dogs** - None

Something Extra
The mottled brown American Woodcock is a long-time favorite of birdwatchers who cherish its unique courtship display. In springtime, at dusk, males arrive at "singing grounds" and begin flying in upward spiraling circles before swooping back to earth where they herald their flights in song. Woodcocks require four habitats in close proximity: feeding cover, nesting cover, roosting areas and open ground for courtship. These picky birds find just such conditions along the *Meadow Trail* in Riverbend Park.

Scotts Run Nature Preserve

Phone - None
Website - None
Admission Fee - None
Directions - *McLean, Fairfax County; from the Beltway take Exit 44 onto Route 193 West (Georgetown Pike). The smaller of two parking lots is almost immediately on your right. The main lot is a bit further down on the right.*

The Park
Scotts Run Nature Preserve is one that survived. It's not easy to halt the march of progress and like so much of its neighboring land this 340-acre tract of woodland known as the Burling Tract was slated to support a 300-home subdivision in 1970. Local residents, most prominently Elizabeth Miles Cooke, an artist and historian who lived in a 200-year old house near Swink's Mill Road and Georgetown Pike opposite the current park, fought the planned development bitterly. In a region where the scorecard clearly favored the developers this one went into the win column for the conservationists. Betty Cooke died in May 1999 at the age of 91 and the bridge that spans Scotts Run not far from her home was named after her.

The Walks
Setting out from the parking lot, the trail system in Scotts Run Nature Preserve pushes towards the Potomac River, either to rocky bluffs above the water or down to the shoreline itself. The journey will take you past shady hemlocks and stately hardwoods on wide, dirt paths (with an occasional stony road thrown in). Most of this is easy going for your dog (Fairfax County has erected wooden stairs where the climbs start to look daunting) save for the trip to the water's edge that travels on a rocky road. A full loop of the preserve can be crafted to cover about a two-mile canine hike but many secondary trails can lengthen your stay.

> **Where The Paw Meets The Earth:** Dirt paths and stony roads
> **Workout For Your Dog** - Modest hills along the route
> **Swimming** - More like splashing in Scotts Run and the Potomac
> **Restrictions On Dogs** - None

Something Extra
As it cuts over sharp rock outcroppings the clear waters of Scotts Run paint a pretty picture indeed - but it is a false impression. What appear to be pristine waters begin in culverts under the Tyson Corner Mall and are susceptible to storm runoff, sewer line breaks and dumping. Still, after such an ignominious beginning the stream finishes gloriously in the closest waterfall to Washington D.C.

Sky Meadows State Park

Phone - (540) 592-3556
Website - http://www.dcr.state.va.us/parks//skymeado.htm
Admission Fee - Yes
Directions - *Paris, Fauquier County; from Route 50 turn left on Route 17 South to park entrance on right. From I-66, take Exit 23 on Route 17 North seven miles to the park entrance on left.*

The Park

It was 1731 when James Ball picked up 7.883 acres on the eastern slopes of the Blue Ridge Mountain from Lord Fairfax. Over the years through inheritance the land was divided and divided and divided. In 1966 a housing development was planned that called for further division into 50-acre lots. At this Point Paul Mellon stepped in and eventually donated 1,132 acres that became Sky Meadows State Park in 1983. Mellon was happy enough with the results to donate an additional 462 acres across Route 17 that had originally been purchased by George Washington from Lord Fairfax.

The Walks

The real star here are the meadows - there simply aren't many open-air hikes available across Northern Virginia. The trail system offers about ten miles of marked paths that can be molded into canine hiking loops, the most popular being the North Ridge-South Ridge circuit. The *South Ridge Trail* utilizes an old farm road while the *North Ridge Trail* picks its way up the mountain like a traditional hiking trail. You are probably best served by going up the South Ridge since it is not as steep and are longer coming down the North side. For those looking for a full day of hiking with your dog the *Appalachian Trail* is 1.7 miles away and there are loop options up there as well. If you just want to enjoy the meadows you can confine your explorations to the *Piedmont Overlook Trail* on the North Ridge. It is also possible to enjoy the park without hard climbing on the *Snowden Trail* interpretive nature walk and the *Shearman's Mill Trail*.

> **Where The Paw Meets The Earth:** Dirt, grass and some old road
> **Workout For Your Dog** - Oh yes, your dog will be climbing
> **Swimming** - There are seasonal streams on the mountain and a reedy three-acre pond off Route 17 to refresh your dog after a hearty hike
> **Restrictions On Dogs** - No dogs on the bridle trails

Something Extra

Once a month, on Saturday evenings beginning in April, Sky Meadows hosts astronomy events behind the Mount Bleak House. Isaac Settle built the house and gave it to his son Abner as a wedding gift in 1835. It now serves as the park visitor center.

Theodore Roosevelt Island

Phone - (703) 289-2500
Website - http://www.nps.gov/this/
Admission Fee - None
Directions - *McLean, Fairfax County; accessible by foot from a parking lot off the northbound lanes of the George Washington Memorial Parkway. Traveling southbound, take Theodore Roosevelt Bridge to Constitution Ave. Take a right on 23rd Street and cross Memorial Bridge. Once on the bridge, bear right to return to the Parkway.*

The Park

During his presidency, Theodore Roosevelt set aside over 234 million acres of public lands as national parks, forests, monuments and wildlife refuges. After his death in 1919, Roosevelt admirers sought a suitable memorial - and what better way to honor his legacy of conservation than by dedicating this wooded, 88-acre island in the Potomac River in his memory? In Colonial times the island was a summer resort for wealthy Virginians; the Mason family owned it for 125 years. In the early 1800's, John Mason built a brick mansion and cultivated extensive gardens but abandoned the property in 1832 when a causeway built across the river stagnated his water. A hundred years later the Theodore Roosevelt Memorial Association purchased the island. Congress approved funds in 1960 and the memorial was dedicated on October 27, 1967.

The Walks

Three curvilinear trails conspire to cover the marsh, swamp and forest of the island. The *Upland Trail* and *Wood Trail* are covered with imbedded yellow stones; the *Swamp Trail* utilizes a boardwalk. All are extremely wide and ideal when more than one dog is in tow. There is enough elevation change to keep your interest and the thick woods produce a shady haven just yards from the crush of Washington bustle. Of course the speeding auto traffic and overhead flights from Reagan National Airport are sure to get your dog's attention.

> **Where The Paw Meets The Earth:** Dirt and pebbly roads
> **Workout For Your Dog** - Easy grades
> **Swimming** - Your dog can slip into the Potomac River for a dip in places, at the footbridge where it reaches the island, for one
> **Restrictions On Dogs** - None

Something Extra

Nestled in the center of the island, the Theodore Roosevelt Memorial is dominated by A 17-foot bronze statue by Paul Manship. It overlooks a diorama of fountains and four 21-foot granite tablets, inscribed with the tenets of Roosevelt's thoughts on Nature, Youth, Manhood and the State.

Turkey Run Park

Phone - (703) 289-2500
Website - http://www.nps.gov/archive/gwmp/vapa/turkey.htm
Admission Fee - No
Directions - *McLean, Fairfax County; from Beltway Exit 14, follow the George Washington Memorial Parkway two miles to the Turkey Run Park exit on the right. Follow signs into the park. From Washington and Old Town Alexandria: take the GWMP north eight miles and exit right at the Turkey Run Park sign. Make the first right turn into the park. Turkey Run is accessible only from the parkway.*

The Park

Turkey Run provided fine hunting and fishing grounds for American Indians who lived here for thousands of years until the 1700s. The Reid family acquired control of most of this land around 1820, raising corn and wheat for the next 80 years. Their farmstead was on property that now houses the CIA Headquarters, adjacent to Turkey Run Park. A grist mill no longer visible operated just north of Turkey Run stream. Before acquired by the National Park Service a dairy farm operated here until the 1930s. Now it serves primarily as a picnic park.

The Walks

The *Turkey Hill Loop Trail* is as hilly a workout as you can give your dog in the Northern Virginia suburbs. Rock steps and switchbacks are used to get you down to the bottom of a rugged little gorge take takes Turkey Run to the Potomac River. At the bottom of the palisades you can hook into the *Potomac Heritage Trail* that runs ten miles from Theodore Roosevelt Island to the American Legion Bridge. The hike to the American Legion Bridge from this point is a little more than 1.5 miles. Turkey Run cuts just one of twelve ravines in the park and it features water year-round. Back atop the 200-foot bluffs the *Woods Trail* rolls among all three picnic areas. The trees on the rocky hillsides have recovered so successfully since the Civil war that the hardwood forest - studded with beech and oak and hickory - is considered one of the finest hardwood forests in Northern Virginia.

> **Where The Paw Meets The Earth:** Dirt, sometimes rocky
> **Workout For Your Dog** - He can can a short, sporty hike here
> **Swimming** - The island-pocked Potomac is available
> **Restrictions On Dogs** - None

Something Extra

Turkey Run is one of the cleanest streams in the development-stressed Northern Virginia region. By carefully turning over rocks in the water you can look for larvae of caddisfly, mayfly and stonefly. These insects are intolerant to pollution so if you spot some it is an indication that the water quality is good.

Wakefield Park/Cross County Trail

Phone - None
Website - None
Admission Fee - None
Directions - *Annandale, Fairfax County; from I-495 take Beltway Exit 54A (Braddock Road) west ¼ mile to entrance of Park on right. From Burke: East on Braddock Road to left at Queensberry Avenue.*

The Park
Private trail enthusiasts and government agencies have come together to weld greenspace wrested from zealous development and preserve a trail over 40 miles long connecting the entire county from one end to the other -- the *Cross County Trail*. The *Cross County Trail* runs through some of the county's most scenic areas, beginning at Great Falls National Park on the mighty Potomac River and extending south to the Occoquan River and Laurel Hill, formerly known as Lorton Prison. Wakefield Park is one of the more popular access points for trail users.

The Walks
Most of the trails in this hourglass-shaped, 292-acre park are in the northern end and get most of their use from cross-country runners and mountain bikes. These may be the most heavily-used mountain bike trails in Northern Virginia. If that isn't enough to dissuade you, it is a healthy canine hike just to reach the trail system with your dog. The *Upland Loop* that squeezes against the Beltway in the southern half of Wakefield is a better choice if you bring your dog to this park. You can use the *Creek Trail* that hugs Accotink Creek to form large canine hiking loops with the *Cross County*.

> **Where The Paw Meets The Earth:** Dirt, asphalt and stonedust
> **Workout For Your Dog** - Plenty of modest hills to test your dog
> **Swimming** - More splashing than dog paddling in the Accotink Creek
> **Restrictions On Dogs** - None

Something Extra
On Wednesday afternoons between May and October bring your dog to the Wakefield Farmers' Market to sample a wide variety of freshly picked, locally grown fruits, vegetables, baked goods, cut flowers, potted plants, cider, honey, eggs, dairy, and meat.

Weston Wildlife Refuge

Phone - None
Website - None
Admission Fee - None
Directions - *Warrenton, Fauquier County; southeast of town. Take Route 643 East (Meetze Road) to Route 616 (Casanova Road) to the crossroads of Casanova. Pick up Route 747, Weston Road, to the end of the road and Weston. Take a left to the refuge parking area when you spot Weston outbuildings.*

The Park
The rambling frame building that is now Weston began life as a log cabin around 1810 and is one of the oldest Colonial houses in Fauquier County.Charles Joseph Nourse from Georgetown purchased the property in 1859 and named it for his ancestral home Weston Hall in England. Following Nourse's death in 1906, his widow, Annie, operated a school and summer camp here. During World War II the Nourse daughters maintained Weston as a hospitality center for servicemen, serving some 11,000 meals by the end of the war. Weston and its important collection of outbuildings is now a farm museum owned by the Warrenton Antiquarian Society on 10 acres of the 271-acre refuge.

The Walks
The canine hiking across the Weston Wildlife Refuge takes place on two stacked loop trails divided by an old woods road that can be used to close the loops. The orange-blazed *Nourse Woods Trail* rambles through an eastern deciduous forest on rough, unmaintained paths but the going is easy enough for any dog. The *Turkey Run Trail* trips through dense thickets of cedar that have replaced the former farmland. Turkey Run itself has high banks and limited, overgrown access. Be aware that the refuge is open to hunting but it is chase only - no firearms allowed. Primitive camping is also allowed in the refuge.

> **Where The Paw Meets The Earth:** Wooded dirt paths and some grassy lanes
> **Workout For Your Dog** - Moderate hills across the park
> **Swimming** - Turkey Run is wide enough for some spirited splashing but not deep enough for a swim
> **Restrictions On Dogs** - None

Something Extra
Weston Wildlife Refuge is a popular rabbit and dog-training area. The Casanova Hunt, founded in 1909, leases land here for its "Terrier Trials."

Whitney State Forest

Phone - None
Website - http://www.dgif.state.va.us/wildlife/vbwt/site.asp?trail
=3&site=PCU04&loop=PCU
Admission Fee - None
Directions - *Warrenton, Fauquier County; south of town. From the James Madison Highway make a right onto Lovers Lane (Route 744). Continue to the T-intersection at the end. Make a left onto Lees Ridge Road (Route 684) to the forest parking lot on the right.*

The Park
The Commonwealth uses this 147-acre forest for timber production and research. Whitney State Forest is a designated wildlife sanctuary. There are no facilities or amenities on the property.

The Walks
This off-the-beaten-path woodland serves up almost six miles of trails for your dog to enjoy. An old fire road runs through most of the property but you will want to slip off onto the extensive network of narrow dirt paths. Come with a mind to explore because you won't get any wayfinding aids in Whitney State Forest. This is mostly hardwood but you'll likely stumble on a surprise or two in this airy forest, like a grove of loblolly pines. The terrain can get downright hilly depending on the route you choose and you can get your dog quite a workout here.

> **Where The Paw Meets The Earth:** Natural surface footpaths and roads, completely under wooded canopy
> **Workout For Your Dog** - Easy to moderate going
> **Swimming** - None
> **Restrictions On Dogs** - None

Something Extra
Without question, the greatest tree in America prior to 1900 was the chestnut. Rot resistant with fine-grained wood, the chestnut tree supported both vibrant wildlife populations and entire rural economies. It was estimated that one in every four trees in the eastern forests was a chestnut tree - some as old as 600 years. But in 1904 an Asian fungus was discovered in the Bronx Zoo and the blight soon decimated the chestnut population. By 1950 millions of acres of woodlands were left with dead, standing trees. The chestnut blight remains 100% fatal - young chestnuts may reach 20 or 30 feet but are doomed to succumb to the disease. American chesnut saplings have been planted in clearings in the Whitney State Forest.

Your Dog At The Beach

It is hard to imagine many places a dog is happier than at a beach. Whether running around on the sand, jumping in the water or just lying in the sun, every dog deserves a day at the beach. But all too often dog owners stopping at a sandy stretch of beach are met with signs designed to make hearts - human and canine alike - droop: NO DOGS ON BEACH. Below are rules for taking your dog on a day trip to a Mid-Atlantic beach.

DELAWARE

Delaware Bay (from north to south):

Kitts Hummock	Private
North Bowers	Dogs allowed anytime; a wide, long sand beach with plenty of pebbles
Big Stone Beach	Dogs allowed anytime; a remote and desolate beach with good waves and little parking

Slaughter Beach	Dogs allowed anytime with beach access at small lots between residences; a sheltered, flat beach with little wave action
Fowler Beach	Dogs allowed anytime and this is one of the best places in Delaware to bring a dog; no development and backed by dunes, this is the bay beach that most resembles an ocean beach, the sloping beach promotes excellent wave action and you can walk for hours with your dog
Prime Hook Beach	Private
Broadkill Beach	Dogs allowed anytime; good wave action for canine swimming and plenty of room to hike up and down

Atlantic Ocean (from north to south):

Delaware State Law prohibits dogs from all swimming and sunbathing beaches from May 1 to September 30. You may also find restrictions on beaches that have been designated as shorebird nesting areas. Otherwise:

Lewes/Cape Henlopen	From May 1 to September 30 no dogs are allowed on the beach between 8:00 am and 6:30 pm
Rehoboth Beach	Dogs are prohibited from the beach and boardwalk from April 1 to October 31
Dewey Beach	Dogs are not allowed on the beach between 9:30 am to 5:30 pm in season
Delaware Seashore	Dogs are allowed on the beach in designated areas year-round; not on swimming beaches or Rehoboth Bay at Tower Road from May 1 to September 30
Bethany Beach	No dogs on the beach or boardwalk from April 1 to October 1
Fenwick Island	No dogs permitted on the beach from May 1 to September 30

Assateague Island National Seashore	Dogs allowed on the beach but not on the trails
Assateague State Park	Dogs are not allowed in the park
Ocean City	Dogs are allowed on the beach and boardwalk from October 1 to April 30

NEW JERSEY

Asbury Park	Dogs are allowed on the beach in off-season
Atlantic City	Dogs are not permitted on the beaches or boardwalk anytime
Avalon	Dogs are not permitted on the beach, boardwalk or dunes between March 1 and September 30
Avon-By-The-Sea	Dogs allowed on beach from November 1 to April 1 but never on the boardwalk
Barnegat Light	Dogs are prohibited from May 1 to October 1
Beach Haven	No dogs allowed on the beach
Belmar	Dogs are not allowed on the beach year-round
Bradley Beach	Dogs are allowed from October 15 to April 15
Brigantine	Dogs are allowed on the beach from 14th Street north to the northernmost jetty
Cape May	Dogs are not allowed on the beach, boardwalk or outdoor shopping areas any time
Cape May Point	No dogs allowed on the beach
Gateway National Recreation Area - Sandy Hook	Dogs allowed on the beach from Labor Day to March 15

Island Beach State Park	Dogs are not allowed in recreational areas but have access to other beaches any time of the year
Lavallette	No dogs allowed on beach but can go on boardwalk after Labor Day
Mantoloking	Dogs allowed on the beach October 1 to May 15 anytime; otherwise dogs allowed from sunrise to 8 AM and 6 PM to sunset
North Wildwood	Dogs are not allowed on the beach from May 15 to September 15
Ocean City	Dogs are never allowed on the boardwalk but can be leashed on the beach from October 1 to April 30
Ocean Grove	Dogs are permitted on the beach and boardwalk from October 1 to May 1
Point Pleasant	Dogs are allowed anytime from September 15 until June 15; before 8:00 AM and after 6:00 PM in the summer
Sea Isle City	No dogs are permitted on the beach, beach approaches or promenade at any time
Ship Bottom	No dogs allowed on the beach until October 1
Spring Lake	Dogs are allowed on the beach in the off-season
Stone Harbor	No dogs allowed on the beach, boardwalk or dunes anytime between March 1 and September 30
Surf City	No dogs allowed on the beach
Wildwood	No dogs allowed on the beach
Wildwood Crest	No animals of any kind allowed on the beach

Doggin The Chesapeake Bay

The Chesapeake Bay is one of our great recreation destinations (*http://www.bay-gateways.net*). More than 1 in every 15 Americans live within a short drive of the nation's largest estuary and millions come each year for the sailing, the lighthouses, the Atlantic Blue Crabs... What about for your dog? Some of the best Maryland state parks on the Bay don't allow dogs (Calvert Cliffs, Sandy Point) but there are some fine beaches to take your dog to nonetheless in Virginia and Maryland. Here are the ten best -

1.   KIPTOPEKE STATE PARK (*Virginia, eastern shore*)
Features more than a half-mile of wide sandy beaches, backed by dunes. Off-shore nine concrete World War II surplus ships have been sunk as a breakwater, leaving gentle waves for your dog to play in. Also an easy 1.5-mile *Baywoods Trail* when you want to take a break from the water. Dogs are welcome in the campground.

2.   FIRST LANDING STATE PARK (*Virginia, south mouth of Bay*)
One of the finest state parks you'll find anywhere features an ocean-type beach at the mouth of the Chesapeake Bay. You can easily hike with your dog for over an hour on the beach with views of the Chesapeake Bay Bridge Tunnel and ocean-going vessels in view the entire time.

3.   TERRAPIN PARK (*Maryland, eastern shore at Bay Bridge*)
Terrapin Park has over 4,000 feet of beach frontage at the tip of Kent Island. Your dog will enjoy frisky waves and canine swimming in the north shadow of the Bay Bridge. The trail to the beach takes you across oyster chaff.

4.   DOWNS MEMORIAL PARK (*Maryland, western shore north of Annapolis*)
Looking for a dog-friendly park? At Downs Memorial Park there is a "pet parking" stall outside the information center. A dog drinking bowl is chained to a human water fountain. Best of all is Dog Beach, an isolated, scruffy 40-yard stretch of sand where you can let the dog off leash for canine aquatics in the Chesapeake Bay. The wave action is just right for dogs and there is enough sand for digging. Need we say more?

5.   FLAG PONDS NATURE PARK (*Maryland, western shore - Lusby*)
Thick woods and an isolated sandy beach backed by wild grasses are prime attractions but don't come too early - the park doesn't open until 9:00 a.m and is only open Memorial Day to Labor Day daily and weekends all year round.

6.   **MATAPEAKE PARK** (*Maryland, eastern shore, south of Bay Bridge*)

This small park on the Chesapeake Bay features a pleasant one-mile wood-chip trail through a pine forest but the reason to come here is a stretch of sandy beach where your dog is welcome off-leash. The beach is a bit too industrial for sunbathers which makes it the perfect place for dogs to romp. Matapeake Park is just south of the Bay Bridge with splendid views of the bay and bridge.

7.   **WYE ISLAND NATURAL RESOURCES MANAGEMENT AREA** (*Maryland, eastern shore*)

The *Ferry Landing Trail* was once the only access road to the island, lined with Osage Orange trees imported to serve as a natural fence. Osage orange trees originated in a small region of Texas, Oklahoma and Arkansas, which was home to the Osage Indians, who used its wood for bows. This mile-long path ends at a small, sandy beach.

8.   **POINT LOOKOUT STATE PARK** (*Maryland, southern tip of western shore*)

A Civil War prison to hold Confederate soldiers was built here at the mouth of the Potomac River and is the main attraction of the park but dogs aren't allowed here. Before crossing the causeway to the island, however, is a small, sandy dog beach with excellent wave action.

9.   **EASTERN NECK NATIONAL WILDLIFE REFUGE** (*Maryland, eastern shore, south of Rock Hall*)

Technically the secluded sandy beach at the end of the *Boxes Point Trail* is on the Chester River but your dog won't quibble when she tests these fun waves.

10.   **NORTH POINT STATE PARK** (*Maryland, western shore, east of Baltimore*)

Although only 20 acres in size, the Bay Shore Park was considered one of the finest amusement parks ever built along the Chesapeake Bay. Opened in 1906, the park featured an Edwardian-style dance hall, bowling alley and restaurant set in among gardens and curving pathways. There were rides such as a water toboggan and Sea Swing. Visitors would travel to the shore from Baltimore on a trolley line. Your dog can explore the remains and dive in the Chesapeake at a small wading beach at the Visitor Center.

Tips For Taking Your Dog
To The Beach

- The majority of dogs can swim and love it, but dogs entering the water for the first time should be tested; never throw a dog into the water. Start in shallow water and call your dog's name - or try to coax him in with a treat or toy. Always keep your dog within reach.

- Another way to introduce your dog to the water is with a dog that already swims and is friendly with your dog. Let your dog follow his friend.

- If your dog begins to doggie paddle with his front legs only, lift his hind legs and help him float. He should quickly catch on and will keep his back end up.

- Swimming is a great form of exercise, but don't let your dog overdo it. He will be using new muscles and may tire quickly.

- Be careful of strong tides that are hazardous for even the best swimmers.

- Cool ocean water is tempting to your dog. Do not allow him to drink too much sea water. Salt in the water will make him sick. Salt and other minerals found in the ocean can damage your dog's coat so regular bathing is essential.

- Check with a lifeguard for daily water conditions - dogs are easy targets for jellyfish and sea lice.

- Dogs can get sunburned, especially short-haired dogs and ones with pink skin and white hair. Limit your dog's exposure when the sun is strong and apply sunblock to his ears and nose 30 minutes before going outside.

- If your dog is out of shape, don't encourage him to run on the sand, which is strenuous exercise and a dog that is out of shape can easily pull a tendon or ligament.

Your Dog In Camp

DELAWARE

KENT COUNTY

Killens Pond State Park
Felton - Kent County
Off US 13, 13 miles south of Dover; the camp-ground entrance is on Paradise Alley Road.
open year-round
(302) 284-3412

NEW CASTLE COUNTY

Lums Pond State Park
Kirkwood
On Route 71, one mile north of Route 896.
open March 1 to December 1
(302) 368-6989

SUSSEX COUNTY

Big Oaks Family Campground
Rehoboth Beach
US 1 south into Rehoboth at Big Oak Lane.
open May 1 to October 1
(302) 645-6838

Cape Henlopen State Park
Lewes
East of town at end of Route 18, past Cape May/Lewes Ferry terminal.
open March 1 to December 1
(302) 645-2103

Delaware Seashore State Park
Dewey Beach
South on US 1 to Indian River Inlet.
open year-round
(302) 539-7202

Gulls Way Campground
Dagsboro
Off Route 26, east of US 113; turn right at the traffic light and left on Vines Creek Road.
open April 15 to October 1
(302) 732-6383

Holly Lake Campsites
Millsboro
On Route 24, six miles west of US 1.
open May 1 to October 1
(302) 945-3410

Homestead Camping
Harbeson
Off US 9, .3 mile west of junction with Route 404; go north on Prettyman Road.
open May 1 to October 1
(302) 684-4278

Houston G & R Recreation Area
Houston
On Gun & Rod Club Road, south of Route 14 via Deep Grass Lane.
open year-round
(302) 398-8108

Steamboat Landing RV Park
Lewes
On Steamboat Landing Road, one mile east of US 1.
open May 1 to October 1
(302) 645-6500

Tall Pines Campground
Lewes
From US 1 go east on US 9 (Seashore Hwy) and turn left onto Joseph's Road, then right onto Log Cabin Hill Road to entrance on left.
open year-round
(302) 684-0300

Trap Pond State Park
Laurel
South of Route 24, five miles east of US 13.
open March 1 to December 1
(302) 875-2392

Treasure Beach RV Park
Selbyville
On Route 54, 7.5 miles west of US 1.
open May 1 to mid-October
(302) 436-8001

ALLEGANY COUNTY

Fifteen Mile Creek Campground
Little Orleans
Orleans Road, six miles south of I-68; 22 miles west of Hagerstown.
open year-round
(301) 739-4200

Hidden Springs Campground
Flintstone
MD 611, four miles south of US 50.
open mid-April to mid-October
(301) 641-0880

Little Orleans Campground
Little Orleans
Exit 68 off I-68 (Orleans Rd); at the top of the ramp, turn left, cross the highway bridge and follow signs.
open year-round
(301) 478-2325

Mason Dixon Campground
Finzel
From I-68 take Exit 29 and go 3.4 miles north on MD 546.
open mid-May to mid-October
(814) 634-5982

Paw Paw Campground
Paw Paw
On Route 9, 28 miles west of Route 522 in Berkley Springs, West Virginia.
open year-round
(301) 739-4200

Rocky Gap State Park
Flintstone
On Pleasant Valley Road, 7 miles east of Cumberland at Exit 50 of I-68.
open May 25 - December 10
(888) 432-2267

Spring Gap Campground
Spring Gap
On MD 51, 8 miles south of Cumberland.
open year-round
(301) 739-4200

ANNE ARUNDEL COUNTY

Capitol KOA Campground
Millersville
I-95 to US 50 East to 3 North Exit Veterans Highway and follow signs.
open March 1 to mid-November
(410) 923-2771

Duncan s Family Campground
Lothian
From I-95 Exit 11A go 9 miles on Route 4 South (Pennsylvania Ave) to Route 408 East; turn left on Sands Road to campground.
open year-round
(410) 741-9558
Note: Breeds not allowed: Doberman, Rottweiler, Boxer, Mastiff, German Shepherd, Airedale, Chow, Pit Bull

BALTIMORE COUNTY

Morris Meadows Recreation Farm
Freeland
Take Exit 36 off I-83 and bear right on MD 439 to stop sign; go north onto York Road (Route 45) one mile to traffic light and turn left onto Freeland Road for 3 miles.
open year-round
(800) 643-7056

Patapsco Valley State Park
Hilton Area   NO DOGS!
Catonsville

CAROLINE COUNTY

Holiday Park
Greensboro
On MD 314, .3 mile east of MD 313, to Route 255A (Drapers Mill Road).
open April 1 to November 1
(410) 482-6797
Note: Breeds not allowed: Doberman, Rottweiler, Boxer, Mastiff, German Shepherd, Airedale, Chow, Pit Bull

Martinak State Park   NO DOGS!
Denton

CECIL COUNTY

Elk Neck State Park
Northeast
At end of MD 272, south of I-95.
open year-round
(888) 432-2267

CHARLES COUNTY

Cedarville State Forest
Brandywine
Off US 301 on Cedarville Road, south of US 50.
open late April to late October
(888) 432-2267

Smallwood State Park
Marbury
On MD 224, four mles west of Pisgah.
open April 1- October 31
(888) 432-2267
Note: four pet sites only

FREDERICK COUNTY

Antietam Creek Campground
Sharpsburg
Off MD 65 south on Canal Road, 3.5 miles south of Sharpsburg.
open year-round
(301) 739-4200

Camp Misty Mount   NO DOGS!
Thurmont

Crow s Nest Campground
Thurmont
On MD 77, just west of the junction with US 15.
open year-round
(301) 271-7632

Cunningham Falls State Park NO DOGS!
Thurmont

Gambrill State Park
Thurmont
On US 40, six miles west of Frederick.
open late April to late October
(888) 432-2267

Owens Creek Campground
Thurmont
On MD 77, three miles west of US 15.
open April 15 to third Sunday in November
(301) 663-9388

GARRETT COUNTY

Big Run State Park
Luke
16 miles from Exit 24 off I-68.
open year-round
(301) 895-5453

Deep Creek Lake State Park
Swanton
Take Exit 14A (Route 219 South Deep Creek Lake) off I-68 and continue on Route 219 South for 18 miles; turn left onto Glendale Road to the left after the bridge onto State Park Road.
open mid-April to mid-October
(301) 387-5563

Double G RV Park
McHenry
Exit 14-A off I-68 West to South 219 for 12 1/2 miles; at first traffic light, turn left ontoMosser Road to park on right.
open year-round
(301) 387-5481

Garrett State Forest
Oakland
Off US 219, five miles northwest.
open year-round
(301) 334-2038

New Germany State Park NO DOGS!
Grantsville

Potomac State Forest
Oakland
Off MD 135, between the towns of Oakland and Westernport.
open year-round
(301) 334-2038

Savage River State Forest
Grantsville
I-68 to Exit 22 and three miles south to New Germany Road to headquarters.
open year-round
(301) 895-5453

Swallow Falls State Park
Oakland
I-68 to Exit 14 and Route 219 South 19.5 miles to Mayhew Inn Road; turn right and go 4.5 miles to end of road. Turn left onto Oakland Sang Run Roadand make first right onto Swallow Falls Road to park.
open April 30 to mid-December
(888) 432-2267

HARFORD COUNTY

Bar Harbor RV Park & Marina
Abingdon
Exit 80 off I-95 to MD 543 South for 1.5 miles and west on US 40 for 1.7 miles to south on Long Bar Harbor Road to campground.
open year-round
(410) 679-0880
Note: Dogs under 35 pounds only

Susquehanna State Park
Havre de Grace
On Route 71, one milenorth of Route 896.
open March 1 to December 1
(410) 368-6989

Woodlands Camping Resort
Joppa
Exit 109 from I-95 and south on MD 279 to US 40 and MD 7; cross US 40 on MD 7 and turn left on Old Elk Neck Road.
open year-round
(410) 368-6989

HOWARD COUNTY

Patapsco Valley State Park Hollofield Area
Ellicott City
Exit 15B off I-695 onto US 40 and three miles west to Baltimore National Pike.
open May 1 to late October
(410) 461-5006

KENT COUNTY

Duck Neck Campground
Chestertown
From US 301 take MD 544 W to Double Creek Rd. to Double Creek Point Road.
open March through November
(410) 778-3070

MONTGOMERY COUNTY

Little Bennett Regional Park
Clarksburg
On MD 355, take Exit 109 off I-270.
open April 1 to November 1, weekends in March and November
(301) 972-9222

PRINCE GEORGE'S COUNTY

Cherry Hill Park
College Park
On MD 212 off Exit 29B of I-95.
open year-round
(301) 937-7116

Greenbelt Park
Greenbelt
On Route 193, Exit 23 off I-95.
open year-round
(800) 365-2267

QUEEN ANNE'S COUNTY

Tuckahoe State Park
Queen Anne
Off Eveland Road from MD 480, near the intersection of MD 480 and MD 404.
open late March to late October
(410) 820-1668

ST. MARY'S COUNTY

Camp Merryelande   NO DOGS!
St. George Island

Dennis Point Marina
Drayden
US 301 S to MD 5 South, right on 249, left on Drayden Road (244); right on Windmill Point Road to end of paving, left on dirt road.
open year-round
(301) 994-2288

Point Lookout State Park
Scotland
At the end of MD 5.
open late March to late October
(301) 872-5688

Take It Easy Campground
Callaway
On MD 249, .8 mile east of MD 5.
open year-round
(301) 994-0494

SOMERSET COUNTY

Janes Island State Park   NO DOGS!
Crisfield

Lake Somerset Campground
Westover
On US13, 20 miles south of Salisbury.
open year-round
(410) 957-1866

Princess Anne Campground
Princess Anne
Off Route 362, west of junction with US 13.
open April 1 to December 1
(410) 651-1520

WASHINGTON COUNTY

Antietam Hagerstown KOA
Williamsport
From the junction Of I-70 and I-81 go west on I-70 to Exit 24; go south on MD 63, west on Everly Road, south on Rock Hill Road and west on Kemp Mill Road.
open mid-March to December 1
(301) 223-7571

Fort Frederick State Park
NO DOGS!
Big Pool

Greenbrier State Park
NO DOGS!
Hagerstown

Happy Hills Campground
Hancock
Take I-70 Exit 1B into Hancock and turn right on Route 144 for 2.4 miles, then left on Willow Road for 2.8 miles to Seavolt Road and left to campground entrance.
open year-round
(301) 678-7760

Maple Tree Campground
Gapland
Take Exit 52 from I-70 onto US 340W and go 15 miles to Route 67 ; travel north towards Boonsboro (5 miles) and turn right on Gapland Road (1.5 miles); turn left onto Townsend Road; camp entrance is 3rd lane on right.
open year-round
(301)432-5585

McCoys Ferry Campground
Hagerstown
McCoys Ferry Road off MD 56 from I-70, 15 miles west of Hagerstown.
open year-round
(301) 739-4200

Yogi Bear s Jellystone Park
Hagerstown
Off MD 68, east of I-81 from Exit 1.
open year-round
(301) 223-7117

WICOMICO COUNTY

Roaring Point Waterfront Campground
Nanticoke
On MD 349, 21.3 miles southwest of US 50.
open April 1 to October 31
(410) 873-2553

Sandy Hill Family Camp
Quantico
On Naticoke River at Sandy Hill Road.
open March to mid-December
(410) 873-2471

Woodlawn Campground
Delmar
On US 13, .3 mile south of junction with Route 54.
open April 1 to November 1
(410) 896-2979

Assateague Island State Park Campground   NO DOGS!
Assateague Island

Assateague Island National Seashore Campground
Assateague Island
MD 376 to end of MD 611, 8 miles southeast of US 50.
open year-round
(410) 641-3030

Eagle s Nest Campground
Berlin
On MD 611, north of MD 376.
open April 1 to mid-September
(410) 213-0097

Fort Whaley Campground
Whaleyville
Intersection of MD 610 and US 50.
open mid-April to mid-October
(410) 641-9785

Frontier Town Campground
Ocean City
MD 611, four miles south of US 50.
open mid-April to mid-October
(410) 641-0880

Island Resort Family Campground
Newark
End of Croppers Island Road off US 113, south of US 50.
open mid-April to late October
(410) 641-9838
Note: No Pitbulls or Rottweilers

Pocomoke River State Park Milburn Landing
Snow Hill
Off MD 364, 7 miles northeast of US 113.
open late April to mid-October
(888) 432-2267

Pocomoke River State Park Shad Landing   NO Dogs!
Pocomoke City

ATLANTIC COUNTY

Atlantic Blueberry Hill RV Resort
Port Republic
On Route 575, 2.5 miles west of Route 9.
open February 1 to December 15
(609) 652-1644

Birch Grove Park Family Campground
Northfield
In town on Burton Avenue.
open first Saturday in April to
Columbus Day
(800) 354-6201

Buena Vista Camping Resort
Buena
On Route 40 at the intersection with Route 54.
open April 1 to October 31
(856) 697-5555

Colonial Meadows Campground
English Creek
On Route 559 off Route 9.
open May 10 to October 5
(609) 653-8449

Country Oaks Campground
Dorothy
On Route 557, 8 miles from Route 40.
open mid-April thru mid-October
(609) 476-2143

Evergreen Woods
Pomona
At intersection of Route 575 & Moss Mill Road, east of GSP Exit 4 southbound.
open year-round
(609) 652-1577

Holiday Haven Campground
Estell Manor
At 230 Route 50.
open April 1 to October 15
(609) 476-2963

Holly Acres RV Park
Egg Harbor City
On Frankfurt Avenue east of town and one mile north of Route 30.
open April 15 to October 31
(609) 965-2287

Pleasant Valley Family Campground
Estell Manor
On US 50, one mile south of Mays Landing and South River Road.
open April 15 to October 15
(609) 625-1238

Pomona Campground
Pomona
On Route 575, one mile south of Route 30.
open year-round
(609) 965-2123

Scenic River Campground
Tuckahoe
On Route 49, 2.5 miles west of US 50.
open April 15 to October 31
(609) 628-4566

Shady Pines Campground
Absecon
On 6th Avenue, 1.5 miles from Garden State Parkway South, Exit 40.
open March 1 to November 1
(609) 652-1516

BURLINGTON COUNTY

Arrowhead Campground
New Gretna
Route 70 to Route 72 and right on Route 56; 14 miles to Spur 679 and 6 miles to campground.
open year-round
(609) 296-8599

Bass River State Forest   NO DOGS!
New Gretna

Belhaven Lake RV Resort
Green Bank
On Route 542, 3 miles east of Batsto.
open April 15 to October 1
(609) 965-2827

Brendan Byrne State Forest
NO DOGS!
New Lisbon

Chips Folly Family Campground
New Gretna
Take US 9 South to Route 542 West for three miles and turn onto Route 653 to entrance.
opens year-round
(609) 296-4434

Indian Branch Park Campground
Hammonton
On Route 322, 3.5 miles east of Route 54.
open late April to late September
(609) 561-4719

Pilgrim Lake Campground
New Gretna
Midway between Atlantic City and Long Beach Island at the junction of Route 653/654 and Stage Road.
open April 1 to October 31
(609) 296-4725

Timberline Lake Camping Resort
New Gretna
From Route 563 South go 14 miles to Route 679 and 6 miles to campground.
open May 1 to October 15
(609) 296-7900

Turtle Run Campground
Wading River
Route 9 to Route 542 West, then 3 1/2 miles to Wading River drawbridge; after crossing the bridge, turn left onto Turtle Creek Road to campground.
open May 1 to October 15
(609) 965-5343

Wading Pines Camping Resort
NO DOGS!
Chatsworth

Wharton State Forest   NO DOGS!
Hammonton

Acorn Campground
Green Creek
On Route 47, 3.5 miles north of Garden State Parkway, Exit 4A.
open early May to September 30
(609) 886-7119

Adventure Bound Camping Resort
Cape May Court House
Take Exit 9 off the Garden State Parkway, Mayville/Shell Bay Avenue, and go west one mile to campground on right.
open mid-April to mid-October
(609) 465-4440

Avalon Campground
Clermont
On US 9, south from junction of Route 83; 1.5 miles northwest of Garden State Parkway, Exit 13 Southbound.
open mid-April to mid-October
(609) 624-0075

Beachcomber Camping Resort
Cape May
Take Parkway south to Exit 4A (Rt. 47 north) to third traffic light; turn left onto Railroad Avenue to entrance on the right.
open mid-April to October 31
(609) 886-6035
Note: One dog per site

Belleplain State Forest   NO DOGS!
New Gretna

Big Timber Lake Camping Resort
Cape May Court House
On Swainton-Goshen Road (C.R. 646) off US 9 from Parkway Ecit 13.
open late April to mid-October
(609) 465-4456

Cape Island Resort
Cape May
From Parkway South Exit 0 turn right onto US. 9 and go 1.5 miles north to entrance on right.
open May 1 to November 1
(609) 884-5777

Cold Spring Campgound
Cape May
Towards the ferry, south on Seashore Road, then 1.5 miles on CR641 West to New England Road.
open May 15 to Columbus Day
(609) 884-8717

Depot Travel Park
West Cape May
On Route 626, two miles east of Route 9.
open May 1 to September 30
(609) 884-2533

Driftwood Camping Resort
Clermont
On US 9, 3 miles south of Parkway.
open April 15 to October 15
(609) 624-1899

Frontier Campground   NO DOGS!
Ocean View

Green Holly Campground
No DOGS!
Cape May Court House

Holly Shores Campground
Cape May
On US 9 between Cape May and Wildwood.
open April 15 to October 31
(609) 886-1234

King Nummy Trail Campground
Cape May Court House
On Route 47 south of Route 55 and Exit 6 of the Parkway.
open April 24 to October 1
(609) 465-4242

Lake Laurie Campground
NO DOGS!
Cape May

Little Oaks Campground
South Seaville
West on US 9 from Exit 17 off the Parkway and south .5 mile to Academy Lane; right to Kings Highway and left 1,000 feet to campground.
open April 1 to October 31
(609) 624-1682

Ocean View Resort Campground
Ocean View
On route 9, north of Sea Isle Boulevard off Parkway South Exit 17.
open April 15 to October 1
(609) 624-1675

Pine Haven Campground Resort
Ocean View
One half mile south of the Sea Isle City Boulevard on State Highway #9.
open May to September
(609) 624-3437

Ponderosa Campground
NO DOGS!
Cape May Court House

River Beach Campground
NO DOGS!
Mays Landing

Sea Grove Camping Resort
Ocean View
On Route 9, one mile north of Parkway Exit 17.
open April 1 to November 1
(609) 624-3529

Seashore Campsites
Cape May
Off Route 626 South from Exit 4A of the Parkway; go 2.7 miles and turn right beyond Methodist Church.
open April 15 to November 1
(609) 884-4010

Tamerlane Campground
Ocean View
On Route 9, 1 mile south of Parkway Exit 17.
open May 15 to October 1
(609) 624-0767

Whippoorwill Campground
Marmora
On US 9, 1.5 miles south of Parkway Exit 25.
open April 1 to October 31
(609) 390-3458

Winding River Campground
Mays Landing
On CR 559, 2 miles south of Route 322.
open May 1 to October 31
(609) 625-3191

Yogi Bear s Jellystone Park
Mays Landing
From the Atlantic City Expressway Exit 17 take Route 50 south 6 miles to Route 669 (Eleventh Avenue) and 4 miles to park.
open year-round
(609) 476-2811

GLOUCESTER COUNTY

Hospitality Creek Campground
Williamstown
42 South to Williamstown, then Route 322 East.
open late April to mid-October
(856) 629-5140

Lake Kandle Campground
NO DOGS!
Sewell

Timberlane Campground
Clarksboro
*From I-295 Exit 18 take Route 667 South and turn right on to Friendship Road; go one block and turn right to campground.*open
open year-round
(856) 423-6677

HUDSON COUNTY

Liberty Harbor RV Park
Jersey City
Take the Turnpike to Exit 14 C and the 2nd exit ramp after the tollbooth (Jersey City/ Grand Street); at the bottom of the ramp make three lefts in a row to Grand Street. Go approximately 8 city blocks to Luis Munoz Marin Blvd and make a right to the end and the office on the right.
open year-round
(201) 386-7500

HUNTERDON COUNTY

Bull s Island Recreation Area
NO DOGS!
Stockton

Jugtown Mountain Campsites
West Portal
Exit 11 off I-78, then Route 173 west for 1.5 miles to top of mountain.
open year-round
(908) 735-5995

Mountain View Campground
Little York
From I-78 Exit 11 take Route 614 through Pattenburg to Little York and turn right at crossroad; go 1/4 mile and turn right onto Goritz Road and look for sign (6 miles from I-78).
open mid-April to mid-October
(908) 996-2953

Round Valley Recreation Area
NO DOGS!
Clinton

Spruce Run Recreation Area
NO DOGS!
Clinton

Voorhees State Park   NO DOGS!
Glen Gardner

MONMOUTH COUNTY

Allaire State Park   NO DOGS!
Farmingdale

Cheesequake State Park
NO DOGS!
Matawan

Pine Cone Resort
Freehold
Six miles south on Route 9, then 1.5 miles West on West Farms Road.
open year-round
(732) 462-2230

Turkey Swamp Park

Lincroft
From I-195 take Exit 22; turn onto Jackson Mills Road north to Georgia Road and turn left for 1.7 miles to entrance on left.
open March 15 to November 30
(732) 462-7286

MORRIS COUNTY

Fla Net RV Park

Flanders
Off Route 206 south of I-80 for .5 miles to Old Ledgewood Road.
open April 1 to October 1
(973) 347-4467

Mahlon Dickerson Reservation

Lake Hopatcong
Route 15, five miles north of I-80 and take Weldon Road Exit for approximately 4 miles.
open year-round
(973) 663-0200

OCEAN COUNTY

Atlantic City North Family Campground

Tuckerton
From the Parkway Exit 58 take Route 539 south and make the first right onto Poor Man's Parkway; go 5 miles to end at Stage Road and turn left. Go one mile to entrance is on the right.
open early April to late October
(609) 296-9163

Baker s Acres Campground

Parkertown
Parkway Exit 58 south on Route 539 for .2 mile to Thomas Avenue; turn left for .8 mile and go right onto Railroad Avenue for one block to campground.
open May 1 to November 1
(609) 296-2664

Brookville Campground

Barnegat
Parkway Exit 67, then go west on Route 554 for 3 1/2 miles, turn right at Brookville State sign. Stay on road to stop, go right at church, make right down dirt road to campground.
open May 1 to October 1
(609) 698-3134

Butterfly Camping Resort

Jackson
From Exit 21 of I-195 onto Route 527; proceed 2.3 miles and turn left onto Butterfly Road to campground.
open April 1 to October 31
(732) 928-2107

Cedar Creek Campground

Bayville
On Route 9, 7 miles south of Toms River.
open year-round
(732) 2691413

Indian Rock Campground

Jackson
From I-195 Exit 16B east on Route 537 to 3rd traffic light (1/4 mile); turn right on Route 571 south to traffic light (4 miles); turn right on to Route 528 W (1 3/4 miles) to Indian Rock on right.
open year-round
(732) 928-0034

Maple Lake Campground

Jackson
From I-195 Exit 21, Route 527, go right to junction of 527/528.
open April 15 to October 15
(732) 367-0177

Scrubbie Pines Campground

Barnegat
On Route 72, 4 miles west of Garden State Parkway off Exit 63.
open April 1 to October 31
(609) 698-3488

Sea Pirate Campground

West Creek
On Route 9, 11 miles north of Garden State Parkway Exit 50.
open late April to September 30
(609) 296-7400

Surf And Stream Campground
Toms River
On Route 571, 1.5 miles south of Route 70.
open year-round
(732) 349-8919

Tip Tam Camping Resort
Jackson
On Brewers Bridge Road, 1.8 miles off Route 526, east Of I-195, Exit 21.
open April 15 to September 30
(732) 363-4036

Toby s Hide Away Campground
Jackson
Brewers Bridge Road to Clearstream Road, 1.8 miles off Route 526, east Of I-195, Exit 21.
open May 1 to October 30
(732) 363-3662

SALEM COUNTY

Four Seasons Family Campground
Pilesgrove
1.5 miles south of US 40 on CR 581 at junction of Woodstown-Daretown roads.
open February 1 to December 31
(856) 769-3635

Holly Green Campground
Monroeville
From southbound Route 55 take Exit 45 onto Route 553 and go right approximately 1 mile to blinking light; turn left onto Monroeville Road and campground on right.
open year-round
(856) 694-1690

Old Cedar Campground
Monroeville
On Richwood Road (Route 609), 5.5 miles south of Route 322.
open March 15 to October 30
(856) 358-4881

Tall Pines Camp Resorts
Elmer
On Beal Road, off Route 635, 5 miles from junction of route 40 and Route 77.
open March 31 to October 31
(856) 451-7479

SUSSEX COUNTY

Beaver Hill Campground
Hardyston
Off Route 94 south of Route 23; make right at the first right onto Beaver Run Road and left at fork in 2 miles to campground.
open May 1 to November 15
(973) 827-0670

Cedar Ridge Campground
Montague
Off Route 296 to last exit onto route 521N and three miles on right.
open April 1 to November 1
(973) 293-3512

Columbia Valley Campground
Andover
I-80 to Exit 25 and north on Route 206 to third traffic light, turn right on Lackawanna Drive for .5 miles.
open April 15 to October 15
(973) 691-0596

Green Valley Beach Campground
Newton
Route 611 (Greendell Road) off Route 206 at Springdale.; take the first left onto Huntsville Road to campground.
open May 1 to October 15
(973) 383-4026

Harmony Ridge Farm and Campground
Branchville
Off Route 206 at mile marker 118; turn right at Ridge Road to end and turn left, 1 block to Mattison Reservoir Avenue and right to campground on Risdon Drive.
open year-round
(973) 948-4941

High Point StatePark   NO DOGS!
Sussex

Kymer s Camping Resort
Branchville
On kymer Road off Route 519, 4 miles north of town.
open April 1 through October 31
973-875-3167
Note: No aggressive breeds

445

Panther Lake Camping Resort

Andover
On Route 206, 4.6 miles north of I-80 Exit 25.
open April 1 through October 31
(973) 347-4440

Pleasant Acres Farm Campground

Sussex
At corner of Route 23 and DeWitt Road, 5 miles north of town.
open mid-May to mid-October
(800) 722-4166

Rockview Valley Campground

Montague
On Route 521 (Old Mine Road), 5 miles north of Route 206.
open May 1 to October 15
(973) 293-3383

Smartswood State Park NO DOGS!

Stillwater

Stokes State Forest   NO DOGS!

Branchville

Windy Acres Campground

Hampton Township
On Swartswood Road (CR 622) off Mill Street (CR 519), norht on Newton via Route 206.
open May 15 to October 15
(973) 897-8695

Camp Taylor Campground

Columbia
Off Route 94, north of I-80 Exit 4; go 3.5 miles, turn left on Benton Road, make a right at Frog Pond Road and your first left on Wishing Well to the end and turn left.
open mid-April to mid-October
(800) 545-9662

Delaware River Family Campground

Delaware
On Route 46, three miles east of I-80 Exit 4B.
open April1 through October 31
908-475-4517
Note: No Pitbulls, Doberman Pinchers, Chow-Chows, Rottweilers or Wolf-hybrids

Jenny Jump State Forest NO DOGS!

Hope

Stephens State Park   NO DOGS!

Hackettstown

Triple Brook Family Campground NO DOGS!

Blairstown

Worthington State Forest NO DOGS!

Columbia

BERKS COUNTY

Appalachian Campsites
Shartlesville
On service road behnd Dutch Hotel at Exit 23 off I-78.
open May to October
(610) 488-6319

Blue Falls Grove Campground
Reading
Off Route 61 on Wiley's Road, 7 miles north of the city
open April 1 to December 31
(610) 926-4017

Blue Rocks Campground
Lenhartsville
From I-78 take Exit 35 (Lenhartsville) to Route 143 North for 1 mile, turn left and follow signs.
open early April to early November
(610) 756-6366

French Creek State Park
Elverson
On Route 345 north of Route 23, west of Route 100.
open year-round
(610) 988-8000

Lazy K Campground
Bechtelsville
Off Route 100 north of junction with Route 73 go right at the first light and left onto County Line Road for 2.5 miles and left on Township Line Road to campground.
open year-round
(610) 367-8576

Mountain Springs Camping Resort
Shartlesville
One mile north of Exit 23 off I-78.
open April 1 to October 31
(610) 488-6859

Pennsylvania Dutch Campground
Bernville
On Northkill/Campsite Road north of Old Route 22, .1 mile south of I-78 Exit 23.
open mid-April 1 to mid-October
(610) 488-6268

Pine Hill Campground
Kutztown
On Old Route 22, off Route 737 north of I-78 Exit 40.
open mid-April 1 to mid-November
(610) 285-6776

Robin Hill Camping Resort
Lenhartsville
Off I-78 West take Exit 40 or off I-78 East, take Exit 35 and follow signs for 3 miles.
open year-round
(610) 756-6117

Sacony Park Campsites
Kutztown
Off US 222 at the Virginville Exit of I-78.
open year-round
(610) 683-3939

BRADFORD COUNTY

Pine Cradle Family Campground
Rome
From US 6 go north on PA 187 and follow signs to Shoemaker Road.
open mid-April to mid-December
(570) 247-2424

Riverside Acres Campground
Towanda
At US 6 in Wysox go south on PA 187 for .5 miles and then 1.5 miles, following signs.
open mid-May to mid-October
(570) 265-3235

Beaver Valley Family Campground

Ottsville
Route 611 to Tohickon Valley Road, 1/2 mile on Durham Road, east 3 miles on Geigel Hill Road to Beaver Run Road and left to Claybridge Road and follow signs.
open April to October
(610) 847-5643

Colonial Woods Family Camping Resort

Upper Black Eddy
Off Route 611, 1 ¼ miles north of intersection with Route 412, turn right on Marienstein Road and follow signs.
open mid-April to November 1
(610) 847-5808

Little Red Barn Campground

Quakertown
3 miles east of town on Route 313 to Route 563, 2.5 miles north to Old Bethlehem Road and .7 miles northwest to campground.
open year-round
(215) 536-3357

Quakerwoods Campground

Quakertown
From Turnpike Northeast Extension Exit 44 go one mile northeast on Route 663, two miles north on Allentown Road and one mile east on Rosedale Road.
open early April to October 31
(215) 536-1984

Tohickon Family Campground

Quakertown
From Route 313 off Route 663 go east 2.25 miles to Thatcher Road; turn left for 4 miles to Covered Bridge Road and right to campground.
open mid-April to November 1
(866) 536-2267

Blue Ridge Campground

Ashfield
Off Route 895 between Route 309 in Snyders and Route 248 at Bowmanstown.
open May 1 to November 1
(570) 386-2911

Don Laine Campground

Palmerton
On Route 209, nine miles north of the Pennsylvania Turnpike Exit 74.
open May 1 to November 1
(610) 381-3381
Note: dogs allowed in the campground EXCEPT rottweilers, pitbulls and doberman pinschers

Hickory Run State Park Campground

White Haven
On PA 534, five miles east of I-80, Exit 274.
open May 1 to October 31
(570) 443-0400

Jim Thorpe Camping Resort

Jim Thorpe
From the Pennsylvania Turnpike take Exit 74 and follow signs for Route 209S and Lehighton. Continue over the long hill into Jim Thorpe and turn left at the light onto Broadway. Continue 2.2 miles as the road becomes Lentz Trail to the campground up the hill.
open April 1 to November 1
(570) 325-2644

Lehigh Gorge Campground

White Haven
Take Pocono Exit off the Pennsylvania Turnpike. Turn right onto Route 940 West and go 3 miles to the campground on the right.
open year-round
(570) 443-9191

Mauch Chunk Lake Park   NO DOGS!

Jim Thorpe

CHESTER COUNTY

Beechwood Campground
Coatesville
Two miles from Route 30; exit Bypass at Veterans Hospital and follow signs.
open April 1 to October 31
(610) 384-1457

Berry Patch Campground
Honeybrook
Follow berry-shaped signs on Route 10, 7.5 miles south of Turnpike Exit at Morgantown.
open April 1 to October 31
(610) 273-3720

Birchview Farm Campground
Coatesville
Off Route 340 at Bonsall Road and right on Martans Corner Road.
open May 1 to October 15
(610) 384-0500

Brandywine Creek Campground
Lyndell
On Route 282, 5 miles north of Downington and Route 30.
open April to October
(610) 942-9950

Brandywine Meadows Campground
Honeybrook
Take Route 322 east of town 3 miles and south on Birdell Road, east on Icedale Road to campground on the left.
open April to October 30
(610) 273-9753

Hidden Acres Campground
Coatesville
Off Route 340, 2.5 miles east of Route 10; follow signs to Hidden Acres Road.
open April 15 to October 15
(610) 857-3990

Philadelphia/West Chester KOA
Unionville
Route 82 three miles north of US 1, then three miles east on Route 162.
open April 1 to October 31
(610) 486-0447

Warwick Woods Campground
St. Peters
On Tryhall Road off Route 23, 3.5 miles west of Route 100.
open late March to early November
(610) 286-9655

DAUPHIN COUNTY

Harrisburg East Campground
Harrisburg
Take Exit 247 off Turnpike and go right on Eisenhower Boulevard for one mile to Campground Road on the right.
open year-round
(717) 939-4331

Hershey Highmeadow Campground
Hummelstown
Take Route 322 west as it becomes Hersheypark Drive and Route 39 West; go through one traffic light to campground entrance on the left.
open year-round
(717) 534-8999

LACKAWANNA COUNTY

Lackawanna State Park
NO DOGS!
Dalton

Beacon Hill Campground

Intercourse
On Route 772, six miles west of Route 30 from Gap.
open April 1 to November 1
(717) 768-8775

Coalico Creek Campground

Coalico
On East Maple Grove Road 2 miles off Route 625; 5.8 miles north of Route 23.
open mid-April to mid-October
(717) 336-2014

Country Acres Campground

Gordonville
On Hill Road, left from Route 272 at Zinn's Diner.
open late March to late November
(717) 687-8014

Country Haven Campground

New Holland
On Route 897, 2 miles north of Route 340.
open mid-March to mid-November
(717) 354-7926

Dutch Cousin Campground

Denver
On Hill Road, left from Route 272 at Zinn's Diner.
open year-round
(717) 336-6911

Elizabethtown/Hershey KOA Kampground

Elizabethtown
West on High Street, then 2.5 miles west on Tunpike Road.
open late March to early November
(717) 367-7718

Flory s Cottages & Camping

Ronks
On North Ronks Road between Routes 30 and 340.
open year-round
(717) 687-6670

Gretna Oaks Camping

Manheim
From Route 72 go 1 mile and turn right onto Cider Press Road right on Pinch Road and left onto Camp Road to campground on left.
open April 15 to October 30
(717) 665-7120

Hershey Conewago Campground

Elizabethtown
Six miles south of Hershey on Route 743.
open April 1 to November 1
(717) 367-1179

Hickory Run Family Campground

Denver
On Greenville Road south of town via Route 272 and right on Leisey Road.
open April 1 to November 1
(717) 336-5564

Lake In Wood Campground

Narvon
Route 272 North to Route 897 South for 2 miles; take first left onto Lauschtown Road for 2.5 miles to Route 625 and follow signs.
open late March to early November
(717) 445-5525

Loose Caboose Campground

Kinzer
On Route 741, .5 miles east of Hoover Road south of Route 30.
open year-round
(717) 442-8429

Mill Bridge Village Camp Resort

Paradise
On Ronks Road, .5 miles south of Route 30.
open year-round
(717) 687-8181

Muddy Run Recreation Park

Holtwood
On Route 372, two miles north of Holtwood Dam.
open April 1 to November 1
(717) 284-5850

Oak Creek Campground
Bowmansville
Route 272 to Route 897 South and left onto Lauschtown Road to end and right onto Route 625 South; go to next intersection and turn left onto Maple Grove Road to campground on right.
open year-round
(717) 445-6161

Old Mill Stream Campground
Lancaster
Five miles east of city on Route 30.
open year-round
(717) 299-2314

Olde Forge Campground
Holtwood
From Route 272 South to Route 372 West to Hilldale Road North 3/4 mi to McKelvey Lane.
open April 1 to November 1
(717) 284-2591

Pequea Creek Campground
Pequea
On Fox Hollow Road off Route 324.
open year-round
(717) 284-4587

Pinch Pond Family Campground
Manheim
Off Turnpike Exit 266 go south on Route 72 for i mile and west on Cider Press Road; campground is 1 mile north on Pinch Road.
open year-round
(717) 665-7640

Roamers Retreat Campground
Kinzer
On Route 30, 1.5 miles west of junction with Route 41.
open April 1 to October 31
(717) 442-4287

Starlite Camping Resort
Stevens
From Ephrata, go 5 miles west on Route 322 to Village of Clay and turn right on North Clay Road; follow signs 3 miles to campground.
open May 1 to October 31
(717) 733-9655

Shady Grove Campground
Denver
On Route 897, one mile north of Route 272 at Exit 286 of Turnpike.
open year-round
(717) 484-4225

Sill s Family Campground
Adamstown
On Bowmansville Road, east of Route 272, 3.5 miles north of Turnpike Exit 286.
open year-round
(717) 484-4806

Spring Gulch Resort
New Holland
On Route 897, 4 miles south of Route 10.
open April1 to December 1
(717) 354-3100

Sun Valley Campground
Bowmansville
On East Maple Grove Road 2 miles off Route 625; 5.8 miles north of Route 23.
open April 1 to October 31
(717) 445-6262

Tucquan Park Family Campground
Holtwood
5 Miles west of Route 272 on Route 372 and turn north on River Road; go 2 miles to the campground.
open April 1 to October 31
(717) 284-2156

White Oak Campground
Strasburg
Follow Route 896 South through traffic light in town of Strasburg as it becomes South Decatur Street and May Post Office Road outside of the borough; continue 4 miles and turn left on White Oak Rd to campground.
open year-round
(717) 687-6207

Yogi Bear s Jellystone Park
Quarryville
On Blackburn Road off Route 222, south of town.
open April 1 to October 31
(717) 786-3458

Adventure Bound   Eagles Peak

Robesonia

Take Route 501 North to Route 419 North to Newmanstown; turn right at the town light onto Sheridan Road and go 1.5 miles, turn left onto Eagles Peak Road.

open year-round

(610) 589-4800

Laurel Lake Campsites

New Ringgold

On Route 895, just west of intersection with Route 309 in Snyders.

open April to October

(570) 386-5301

81 80 RV Park And Campground

Drums

Off Route 309, .5 miles north of I-80 at 718 North Old Turnpike Road.

open year-round

(570) 788-3382

Council Cup Campground

Wapwallopen

From I-80 take Exit 256 onto Route 93. Go north for 3.8 miles and turn right on Route 239 north for 5.3 miles to Ruckle Hill Road. Turn left to the campground in one mile.

open year-round

(570) 379-2566

Frances Slocum State Park   NO DOGS!

Dallas

Moyer s Grove Campground & Country RV

Hobbie

Take I-80 West to Exit 256 (Conyngham). Turn right to SR 93 North and follow signs for 7.3 miles to the campground.

open year-round

(570) 379-3375

Ricketts Glen State Park   NO DOGS!

Benton

Sandy Valley Campground

White Haven

Take Exit 273 off I-80 and go .5 miles west on PA 940 then south on Lehigh Gorge Road and 3.5 miles on Sandy Run Road to Valley Road.

open year-round

(570) 636-0770

Chestnut Lake Campground

Brodheadsville

Off Route 209, one mile north of junction with PA 715. Turn on Frable Road and follow signs to campground.

open May 1 to November 1

(570) 992-6179

Cranberry Run Campground

Analomink

Three miles north of Stroudsburg on Route 191.

open April 1 to November 1

(570) 421-1462

Delaware Water Gap KOA Kampground

East Stroudsburg

On Route 209, 6.4 miles north of I-80. turn east on Hollow Road and go one mile to the campground.

open year-round

(570) 223-8000

Four Seasons Campground

Scotrun

Take I-80 Exit 299 north on PA 715 to Route 611. Turn left and go one mile and follow signs to campground.

open mid-April to mid-october

(570) 629-2504

Foxwood Family Campground

East Stroudsburg

Off Route 209, 1.7 miles north of I-80, Exit 309. Turn right onto Buttermilk Falls Road. Follow for approximately 1 mile to crest of hill and turn left onto Mt. Nebo Road. The campground is two miles on the left.

open year-round

(570) 421-1424

Hemlock Campground & Cottages
Tobyhanna
From I-380 Exit 3 take Route 940 East to Route 611. Turn left and go 1.5 miles north to Hemlock Drive. The campground is 1/4 mile on the right.
open mid-May to mid-October
(570) 894-4388

Mount Pocono Campground
Mount Pocono
Take I-80W to I-380N. Take PA-940, Exit 3 toward Pocono and proceed 2.5 miles. At the intersection of PA-940, Rt. 611 & PA-196, bear left onto PA-196N. Proceed 7/10 of a mile to our sign and turn right onto Edgewood Road. Follow Edgewood Road, straight through 2 stop signs.
open May 1 to November 1
(570) 839-8950

Mountain Vista Campground
New Columbia
Off Business Route 209, north of I-80. Go west on Craigs Meadow Road, then (left) 500 feet on Taylor Drive.
open mid-April to November 1
(570) 568-5541

Otter Lake Camp Resort
Marshalls Creek
From I-80 take Exit 309 to Route 209 North into Marshalls Creek. Turn left onto Route 402 and travel 300 feet. Turn left at the firehouse for seven mles to the campground.
open year-round
(570) 223-0123

Pocono Raceway Campground
Long Pond
On Long Pond Road, one mile East of Pocono Raceway; five miles south of I-80, Exit 284.
open April 15 to October 31
(570) 646-2300

Pocono Vacation Park
Stoudsburg
From I-80 take Exit 305 to Business Route 209 South; go two miles and take a right on Shafer School House Road to the campground.
open year-round
(570) 424-2587

Silver Valley Campsites
Broadheadsville
On Route 209; in town turn left at Meadow Brook Diner onto Silver Valley Drive and follow signs for one mile to the campground.
open May 1 to November 1
(570) 992-4824

WT Family Camping
Blakeslee
On Route 115, five miles south of I-80, Exit 284.
open April 1 to November 1
(570) 646-6317

MONTGOMERY COUNTY

Boulder Woods Campground
Green Lane
Route 63 to Route 563 East for 4 miles and left on Whites Mill Roadd for 2.2 miles; right on Long Road that changes to Camp Skymount Road and campground on left.
open April 1 to October 31
(215) 257-7178

Boulder Woods Campground
Trumbauersville
Two miles southwest of Quakertown on Trumbauersville Road off Route 309.
open year-round
(215) 257-3445

NORTHAMPTON COUNTY

Camp Charles Campground
Bangor
On Blue Mountain Drive six miles from I-80.
open April 4 to October 31
(610) 588-0553

Driftstone On The Delaware
Mount Bethel
Four miles south of the Portland, PA-Columbia, NJ bridge across the Delaware River on River Road.
open mid-May 1 to mid-September
(570) 897-6859
Note: one dog per campsite

Evergreen Lake Campground
Bath
North on Route 512, 8.6 miles north of US 22; go west on Route 946 to Copella Road and north to Benders Drive.
open April 15 to October 15
(610) 837-6401

Hickory Lake Campground
Bangor
From Route 611, south Of I-80, go into Mt. Bethel and turn right at T.K.'s Bar & Grill to the stop sign. Turn left onto Million Dollar Highway and go 2 miles. Make a right on Laurel Hill Road to the campground on the left.
open May 1 to October 31
(570) 897-5811

PIKE COUNTY

Dingmans Campground
Dingmans Ferry
On Route 209, south of the traffic light.
open May 1 to November 1
(570) 828-1551
Note: maximum of two dogs per campsite without prior approval

Ironwood Point Recreation Area NO DOGS!
Greentown

Promised Land State Park
Canadensis
On PA 390, five miles south of I-84, Exit 26.
open year-round
(570) 676-3428

River Beach Campsites
Milford
On Route 209, three miles south of I-84, Exit 53.
open April to November
(570) 296-7421

SCHUYLKILL COUNTY

Echo Valley Campground
Tremont
On Route 125, north of I-81 Exit 104.
open year-round
(570) 695-3659

Locust Lake State Park Camp ground
Barnesville
Exit 131 A/B from I-81 and follow signs.
open year-round
(570) 467-2772

Pine Grove KOA
Pine Grove
On Route 443, 4 miles north of Route 72.
open year-round
(717) 865-4602

Red Ridge Lake Campground
Zion Grove
From I-81 Exit 40 take Route 924 South or from Exit 38 take Route 93 South and follow signs.
open May 1 to September 30
(570) 384-4760

Rosemount Camping Resort
Tamaqua
Off Route 209, five miles south of town
open April 15 to October 15
(570) 668-2580

SULLIVAN COUNTY

Pioneer Campground
Laporte
On US 220, two miles south of town.
open mid-April to mid-October
(570) 946-9971

Worlds End State Park   NO DOGS!
Forksville

East Lake Campground

New Milford

Off I-81 at Exit 223 (New Milford/Lakeside Exit). Go right onto Route 492 East. Go 3/8 mile, then turn left onto East Lake Road. Proceed three miles and the campground entrance is on the left.

open mid-April to mid-october
(570) 465-2267

Shore Forest Campground

Hop Bottom

Take I-81 to Exit 211 (Lenox). Go left on Route 106 past the blinking light and on to Loomis Lake Road. Follow this road for 4 1/2 miles and make a right on Forest Street to the campground at the bottom of the hill on the right.

open mid-April to November 1
(570) 289-4666

WAYNE COUNTY

Cherry Ridge Campsites

Honesdale

Off Route 296 south of Route 6. Turn left onto Owego Turnpike and go 5.5 miles. Turn right on Melody Road and follow signs to campground.

open May 1 to November 1
(570) 488-6654

Countryside Family Campground

Honesdale

On PA 670, 6.5 miles north of PA 191.

open year-round
(570) 253-0424

Keen Lake Camping & Cottage Resort

Waymart

From I-81 take Exit 187 onto East 6 Carbondale (Robert Casey Highway). Travel 18.2 miles to the light at the intersection of Routes 6 and 296 on the outskirts of the town of Waymart. Continue east on Route 6 for 1.7 miles. Turn right on to Little Keen Road. At bottom of hill, turn left on Keen Lake Road.

open May 1 to Columbus Day
(570) 488-6161

Note: two dogs maximum per site without prior approval

Ponderosa Pines Campground

Honesdale

West of town on Route 6 and take PA 170 north for 3.5 miles and follow signs to campground.

open May 1 to November 1
(610) 381-3381

Note: dogs allowed in the campground EXCEPT chows, rottweilers, pitbulls, doberman pinschers and wolf-hybrids

Three Pines Campground

Lakeville

Off Route 590, halfway between Hamlin & Hawley.

open May 1 to October 30
(570) 226-6286

Valleyview Farm Campground

Waymart

From Route 6 turn north On PA 296 and go seven miles to the stop sign and another mile to the campground on the left.

open May 1 to October 15
(570) 448-2268

Day s End Campground
Meshoppen
From the junction of US 6 and PA 267 go 8.8 miles north on PA 267 and then east on SR 3004, just west on Chase Road.
open May 1 to mid-October
(570) 965-2144

Endless Mountain Campground
Laceyville
From Route 6 in Laceyville: Westbound take 3rd exit. Eastbound take 1st exit. At 'T' make a left. At bottom of hill turn right on Lacey Street. Go approximately 1/2 mile and turn left onto Lacey Street River Road #1. Go over the railroad tracks and make the first right.
open May 1 to October 31
(570) 869-2580

Highland Campground
Dalton
From I-81 take exit 194, the Clarks Summit exit. Follow US 6 West/11 North for 1 1/2 miles. Turn left onto Winola Road and go 1 mile to Route 307 North. Follow Route 307 North for 5 miles, turn right onto Highland Drive. Follow Highland Drive for 6/10 mile, turn left. Follow to stop sign. Continue straight for 1.2 miles to the entrance on left.
open year-round
(570) 586-0145

Sunrise Lake Family Campground
Nicholson
Go to end of the Pennsylvania Turnpike (Exit 39, Clarks Summit) and take US 6 /Route 11 North. Stay on Route 11 to Route 92 and go south 2 1/2 miles to the campground on right.
open April 1 to November 1
(570) 472-2214

Tunkhannock Family Campground
Tunkahannock
On US 6, two miles east of town.
open mid-April to mid-October
(570) 836-4122

Codorus State Park
Hanover
On Route 216 east of town.
open mid-April to mid-October
(717) 637-2816

Gamler s Boatyard Campground
Airville
Off Route 425, 4.2 miles north of Route 74 and right onto Indian Steps Road.
open May 1 to November 1
(717) 862-3303

Gifford Pinchot State Park
NO DOGS!
Lewisberry

Indian Rock Campground
York
Take I-83 Exit 14 three miles west on Route 182 to campground.
open year-round
(717) 741-1764

Otter Creek Campground
Airville
On Route 425, 4.2 miles north of Route 74.
open year-round
(717) 852-3628

Bull Run Regional Park Campground

Centreville

Take I-66 to Exit 52 (Route 29) at Centreville, drive two miles south and turn left on Bull Run Post Office Road and follow signs.

open March 15 to November 30

(703) 631-0550

Burke Lake Park Campground

Fairfax Station

South of Fairfax; from I-66 take the Fairfax County Parkway, Exit 55A (7100 South towards Springfield). Go 5 miles and turn right on Burke Lake Road. Turn left on Ox Road (Route 123) to the park entrance on the left.

open mid-April to late October

(703) 323-6600

Lake Fairfax Park Campground

Reston

Leave the Beltway (I-495) on Exit 47A to Route 7 (Leesburg Pike) west to a left on Baron Cameron Avenue to the second left on Lake Fairfax Drive.

open year-round

(703) 471-5415

Pohick Bay Regional Park Campground

Lorton

On Mason Neck; take I-95 and exit at Lorton. Turn left on Lorton Road, right on Armistead Road, right on Route 1 and left on Gunston Road to park on left.

open year-round

(703) 339-6104

Greenville Farm Family Campground

Haymarket

From I-66 take Exit 40 and go four miles north on Route 15. Make a right on Route 234 and quickly left on Shelter Lane (Route 601).

open year-round

(703) 754-7944

Hillwood Camping Park

Gainesville

At 14222 Lee Highway (Route 29) in Gainesville; from I-66 take Exit 43A and the entrance is one mile on the right.

open year-round

(703) 754-6105

Prince William Forest Park Oak Ridge Campground

Dumfries

West of Dumfries; take I-95 south to exit 150-B (VA Route 619/Joplin Road). The park entrance is the second right.

open year-round

(703) 221-5843

Prince William Travel Trailer Village

Dumfries

From I-95 take Exit 152B for Manassas and go 2.5 miles to the campground on the left.

open year-round

(703) 221-2474

Index To 4-Paw Parks

Index To 4-Paw Parks

Index To 3-Paw Parks

Index To 3-Paw Parks

Index To 3-Paw Parks

Index To 3-Paw Parks

Printed in the United States
78117LV00001B/67-423